Politics and Letters

Interviews with New Left Review

Raymond Williams

With an Introduction
by Geoff Dyer

London • New York

This paperback edition, with a new introduction, first published by Verso 2015
First published by New Left Books 1979

1 3 5 7 9 10 8 6 4 2

Verso
UK: 6 Meard Street, London W1F 0EG
US: 20 Jay Street, Suite 1010, Brooklyn, NY 11201

www.versobooks.com

Verso is the imprint of New Left Books

ISBN-13: 978-1-78478-015-9 (PB)
eISBN-13: 978-1-78478-017-3 (US)
eISBN-13: 978-1-78478-016-6 (UK)

British Library Cataloguing in Publication Data
A catalogue record for this book is available from the British Library

The Library of Congress Cataloging-in-Publication Data
A catalog record for this book is available from the Library of Congress

Printed and bound in the UK by CPI Mackays

Contents

Introduction – *Geoff Dyer* vii

Foreword – NLR 7

Raymond Williams – Dates 11

I. Biography

1. Boyhood 21
2. Cambridge 39
3. War 55
4. Cambridge Again 61
5. *Politics and Letters* 65
6. Adult Education 78
7. The Fifties 84

II. Culture

1. *Culture and Society* 97
2. *The Long Revolution* 133
3. *Keywords* 175

III. Drama

1. *Drama from Ibsen to Eliot* 189
2. Brecht and Beyond 214

IV. Literature

1. *Reading and Criticism* 237
2. *The English Novel from Dickens to Lawrence* 243
3. The Welsh Trilogy; *The Volunteers* 271
4. *The Country and the City* 303
5. *Marxism and Literature* 324

V. Politics

1. Britain 1956–78 361
2. *Orwell* 384
3. The Russian Revolution 393
4. Two Roads to Change 406

Index 439

Introduction

'I come from Pandy ...' The first words spoken by Raymond Williams in this book may not have quite the rolling loquacity of the opening lines of Saul Bellow's *The Adventures of Augie March* – 'I am an American, Chicago born ...' – but in their brisk way they bespeak a similar confidence. Bellow's narrator immediately situates his experience in the heart of America; Williams announced one of his main concerns in the title of his first novel, *Border Country*. Borders – how they are constructed and recognized, how they impede and are crossed – are central to his thought. In contrast to March's unequivocal belief – 'I am an American' – Williams, whose work concentrated on the English literary and cultural tradition, came to identify himself as 'a Welsh European', emphasizing what lay either side of a presumed centre, both locally and within a larger international context.

'It happened that in a predominantly urban and industrial Britain I was born in a remote village, in a very old settled countryside, on the border between England and Wales.' This is the account Williams gives of his origins in *The Country and the City*,[1] the simple facts of the matter beginning to unfurl and expand in the recognizable style of his analytical writing: an authority that draws power from – rather than being hindered by – a suggested hesitancy; the unhurried accumulation of material and argument; a continual elaboration and deepening of meaning. Stylistically this is the opposite of the persuasive oratory of Aneurin Bevan ('not a style for serious argument' [p. 369]) that Williams had been hearing 'since about the age of two', or of the plain-speaking that he became suspicious of in Orwell: 'the plain man who bumps into experience in an unmediated way' (p. 385). While Williams was proudly conscious of the convolutions of his own method and mode – 'all my

[1] Oxford 1973, p. 2.

usual famous qualifying and complicating, my insistence on depths and ambiguities' – a former student, Terry Eagleton, remembers his lecturing style as that of 'somebody who was talking in a human voice'.[2] Eagleton was struck, also, by the way that although Williams's background might, by Cambridge standards, have been regarded as humble, it was also sufficiently 'privileged' to give him 'a sort of stability, a rootedness and self-assurance, and almost magisterial authority'.[3] It gave him the confidence, while still an undergraduate – albeit an undergraduate who had served in the war – to stand up and insist, after a talk in which L. C. Knights claimed that a corrupt and mechanical civilization could no longer understand neighbourliness, that he knew 'perfectly well, from Wales, what neighbour meant' (p. 67).

Confidence counts for little unless it is allied with determination. Combined with an Orwellian sense 'of the enormous injustice'[4] of the world, Williams had the resources to develop his early critical and theoretical project – one that stressed the importance of shared experience and common meanings – in comparative isolation. The single-mindedness of the endeavour was matched by its scale. In the process of becoming articulate in the language of a new and expansive kind of cultural history he also, in Raphael Samuel's words, 'constructed a conceptual vocabulary of his own'.[5] The vocabulary was more than conceptual; it was also the cerebral expression of a temperament shaped by a particular geography and history. In *Border Country* Harry Price, in discussion with Morgan Rosser, is 'waiting for terms he could feel'.[6] You could almost say he is waiting for the author to coin his most famous term, 'structure of feeling'. Going further back, to Wordsworth in 'Residence at Cambridge', Williams's thought, even at its most theoretical, 'is linked … with some feeling'. Where Williams came from was inextricably linked with what he came to say.

If Orwell's sense of the injustice of the world was fed by a disposition to dwell on its misery, then the 'privileged' background of the signalman's son over that of the old Etonian made the idea of defeat almost

[2] *Resources of Hope*, London 1989, p. 320; Terry Eagleton, *The Task of the Critic*, London 2009, p. 34.

[3] Ibid., p. 19.

[4] George Orwell, 'Writers and Leviathan', *All Art Is Propaganda*, New York 2009, p. 338.

[5] 'Making It Up', *London Review of Books*, 4 July 1996.

[6] Cardigan 1960, p. 172.

entirely alien. It also meant, according to his critics, that the political positions of his later years, with Thatcherism in full swing and the miners having suffered a catastrophic defeat, were nostalgic, even sentimental. Either way, the key thing is that his writing always carried an enormous freight of autobiography. He was explicit about this in a piece included in the posthumous collection *Resources of Hope*: 'I learned the reality of hegemony, I learned the saturating power of the structures of feeling of a given society, as much from my own mind and my own experience as from observing the lives of others. All through our lives, if we make the effort, we uncover layers of this kind of alien formation in ourselves, and deep in ourselves.'[7]

This double combination – complexity of thought and clarity of expression, with a depth and intensity of personal feeling – made Williams a commanding and inspirational figure for the generation of students who came of age in 1968 and looked to him for political and moral as well as intellectual guidance. In some cases former students shared platforms with him, or went on – like Eagleton – to become colleagues or friends. A representative of the next generation (ten in 1968), I set eyes on him precisely twice.

The first time was when he came to give a lecture at Oxford, where I was an undergraduate, in about 1978 or '79. Our tutor encouraged us to go, so we went. I had no idea who Williams was or what he was droning on about. Then, in the mid-1980s, I went to see him in conversation with Michael Ignatieff at the ICA. I'm guessing that the occasion was the publication of his novel *Loyalties* – though if it was, then how come I didn't get my copy signed? And even if it wasn't, why didn't I ask him to sign my copy of *Politics and Letters* (bought in Collets on the Tottenham Court Road, on 30 March 1983)? I can only assume I was too intimidated because by then the old bloke who'd waffled on at Oxford had entirely reshaped my sense of life and literature and the way they were related. The idea of 'lived experience' may have been part of the Leavisite vocabulary but whereas I had *read* the words in Leavis I *experienced* them in Williams. Before that, in a way that now seems hard to credit, I had no understanding of the social process I'd lived through even though it was, by then, a well-documented one: the working-class boy who keeps passing exams – exams that take him first

[7] *Resources of Hope*, p. 75.

to grammar school, then to an Oxbridge college – and discovers only in retrospect that there was more to all this than exams, or even education. It's entirely appropriate that *Culture and Society* – a new way of considering authors with whom I was already familiar – played a crucial part in this discovery. All the expected symptoms of the transformative reading experience were in evidence: the feeling of being addressed personally, of one's life making a sense that should have been apparent all along while being conscious, also, that the revelation was happening at just the right time. This was all the more acute because – and my gratitude on this score is boundless – it occurred independently, after university, not as part of some kind of assigned coursework. At the risk of placing more emphasis on the letters than the politics, I discovered and loved Williams in the way that, and at the same time as, friends were discovering and loving novelists such as Bellow.

And it happened in tandem with my discovery of another writer, John Berger. *The Country and the City* was published in 1973 and made into a film six years later by Mike Dibb. In 1971 in *Ways of Seeing* (also directed by Dibb) Berger had encapsulated one of Williams's arguments with a proto-Banksy bit of vandalism: nailing to the tree behind the landowners' heads in Gainsborough's portrait of Mr and Mrs Andrews a sign that reads 'Private Property Keep Out.'

I emphasize the kinship – what the author of *Culture and Society* might have called commonalities – between these two not because of their shared place in *my* autobiography but to pull Williams away from the slightly tweedy company he is assumed to keep. An undergraduate at Cambridge in the early 1990s, Zadie Smith recalls Williams being spoken of 'as the equal of Foucault or Barthes'.[8] There followed a long and gradual shrinking of a legacy and influence that had seemed assured. If, more than a quarter century after his death, Williams is to become a vital rather than remembered or spent force it is necessary to do two things that might appear contradictory: to concede that, with the exception of *Border Country*, the fiction to which he devoted so much energy and on which he placed so much importance was dull; and to free the rest of his work from the once-modish tundra of Cultural Studies, let alone the pack ice of Theory. Perhaps then he will be read with the same passion and adoration that still attends the discovery of Berger (whose

[8] In private correspondence.

absence in these pages is perhaps a sign of how Williams's horizons were – and his posthumous reputation is – more bounded and hedged by the departmental and institutional borders he claimed to resent). A perverse and ironic fate: Williams, the internationalist, is seen as the worthy relic of a vanished, pre-Thatcherite Britain, a socialist writer read by a diminishing audience of Marxists, academics and students to whom his work is prescribed as retroactive treatment for a sickness (late capitalism) that has infected the furthest reaches of the global body politic. It was the least surprising thing in the world to see, in the Occupy Camp at St Pauls a few years ago, a much-pierced protester reading Berger's *Hold Everything Dear*; it was equally unsurprising that no one was holding *The Country and the City.*

I mention that book partly because of its relevance to the issues raised by Occupy, partly because of the moment in this one when the *New Left Review* interlocutors quote a passage about the great country houses and the landscape that surrounds them (see pp. 345–6). I hadn't looked at this in years but when I started to reread it here I could not see the page for tears. I went back to my own edition of *The Country and the City* and saw the same passage, in the original as it were: heavily underscored, the margins marked by long pencil lines of admiring gratitude. In a late essay D. H. Lawrence looked back on 'Nottingham and the Mining Country', the part of the world where he 'came in to consciousness'.[9] The welling up of feeling that came from seeing again that passage from *The Country and the City* was due not simply to the power of its analysis. Certain books are held dear because they are also psychic landmarks revealing where and how they helped us come into consciousness. Inevitably, our perception of the world – and of other books – continues to be informed by such texts long after the precise details of their contents have been forgotten. Just before rereading *Politics and Letters* – that is, at maximum chronological distance from any previous reading of *The Country and the City* – I came across a long essay by Janet Malcolm about the Bloomsbury Group. After describing a meeting between Virginia and Vanessa Stephen with Clive Bell in 1908, Malcolm writes: 'In his hard-core aestheticism, Clive was behaving as few Victorian men behaved. Clive came from a rich family that had made its money from mines in Wales and had built a hideous and pretentious mansion in Wiltshire,

[9] D. H. Lawrence, *Selected Essays*, London 1950, p. 116.

decorated with fake-Gothic ornament and animal trophies. Numerous sardonic descriptions of the place have come down to us from Vanessa, who would visit there as a dutiful daughter-in-law and write to Virginia of the "combination of new art and deer's hoofs." '[10]

The passage itself is unremarkable; what was extraordinary was how thoroughly my reading of it was permeated by the earlier exposure to *The Country and the City*: how its implications were deepened and its meaning extended beyond the scene and circumstances intended. Who would have thought that Wales had played such a proximate role in the exquisite preoccupations of Bloomsbury, such a formative part in the decorative aesthetics of Charleston? Even when half-buried from view certain landmark texts – the foundations of our adult consciousness – retain the power to radically reroute or reconfigure things far beyond their expected reach.

Even the tough-minded NLR interrogators deem the passage from *The Country and the City* 'extraordinarily moving' (p. 346) – before resuming their cross-examination. Williams's is the only name to appear on the cover and title page but the part played by Perry Anderson, Anthony Barnett and Francis Mulhern can hardly be overstated. The book is a far more thoroughgoing collaboration than the subtitle *Interviews with New Left Review* modestly suggests. I can't help likening these intellectually bruising encounters to an experience shared by myself and two friends in Oxford shortly after we'd graduated. On the street outside a house party, we found ourselves being sucked in by the gravitational threat of a guy – Welsh, as it happens – who was spoiling for a fight. 'Come on, all three of you rush me!' he said at one point. That's how I think of these sessions, with the inquisitors forcing Williams – whose style of thought and expression rendered him impervious to being rushed – vigorously to defend himself, to reconsider previous positions and lines of argument. On one occasion he pulls rank rather wonderfully: 'You have got to remember that I read my own books too, and that in a competition for critical readers I shall at least be on the final list' (p. 106). He responds with the expected qualifications, revisions and elaborations but also with off-the-cuff comments quite different in tone to his normal expository style. His reasons for stopping taking the *Times* in the mid-fifties – 'I will simply not begin the day with those people in

[10] Janet Malcolm, *Forty-One False Starts*, New York 2013, p. 67.

the house' (p. 91) – seems sounder than ever in the Murdoch era. The verdict on *The Spoils of Poynton* – that 'people should be sent to read' it right after 'the first chapter of *Capital*' (p. 258) – both complements and cancels out Ezra Pound's famous complaint that it was a lot of 'damned fuss about furniture'. Not that Williams was an aphorist. After being accused of diagnosing Orwell as simply 'tired', he agrees that this might have seemed a 'sentimental' response and then proceeds to historicize that tiredness: 'what is interesting is that he had available to him a way of being tired, so to speak, which was unthinkable for a Deutscher or Trotsky. That was the notion, which was extraordinarily widespread in England, that British society could be transformed through the conduct of the war' (p. 386).

Williams's own experiences in that war have since been extensively documented in Dai Smith's biography, *Raymond Williams: A Warrior's Tale*, but for a long while *Politics and Letters* was the only source of information about this part of his life and how deeply it affected his subsequent thinking. Discussing the invasions of Hungary and Czechoslovakia, he talks about the idea of the tank, 'which I was both less frightened of and more immediately emotionally involved in than people who'd never been inside one' (p. 89). But the experience 'of having fought in tanks going into a city' also gave him a devastating awareness of 'what an army which is really not holding back can do to a city' (pp. 422, 90). It is another instance of Williams unconsciously echoing Orwell (by appeal to experience), who took issue with Auden's 'conscious acceptance of guilt in the necessary murder' on the grounds that the poet could only say such things because he had probably 'never even seen a murdered man's corpse'.[11]

More broadly, the undertow of the peculiar 'privilege' of Williams's upbringing is felt throughout the book's long discussions. In *Culture and Society* he reminded us that Lawrence's 'first social responses were those, not of a man observing the processes of industrialism, but of one caught in them, at an exposed point, and destined, in the normal course, to be enlisted in their regiments': a vivid instance of how Williams's critical writings double as vicarious autobiography.[12] Class struggle and the other components of Marxist theory were not just

[11] George Orwell, *The Complete Works of George Orwell: Facing Unpleasant Facts, 1937–1939*, London 2008, p. 244.

[12] New York 1958 (1983), p. 202.

concepts to Williams; they were in his blood, part of his inheritance, of who he was. This is not to say that he always had – or should be allowed – the last word. Looking back on a lecture in which he made a point about George Eliot and *Middlemarch,* Williams recalls that 'Terry Eagleton, who was sitting in the front row, sat bolt upright because he was so inside the argument – we talked all the time – that he could see immediately the shift of judgement that had just come out of the logic of the argument' (p. 244). The authentic drama of the moment is somewhat compromised, unfortunately, by the way that Eagleton, in his own book of interviews, *The Task of the Critic*, claims such a thing could not have happened. 'I'm wondering whether that's a phantom memory. I never sat in the front row; I lurked at the back.'[13]

It's a minor point, a mere detail. More substantially, Smith's biography provides a less comfortable, more complex picture of the young Raymond's relationship with his father than the one offered here. First-person testimony is notoriously unreliable, the conventions of the memoir encouraging – perhaps even requiring – a self-serving drift towards the fictive. Again, the sympathetic severity of the questioning is crucial in ensuring that *Politics and Letters* bears little resemblance to a memoir or intellectual autobiography. When he was shown proofs of the book Williams said, 'It feels like a quite new form.'[14] This, to put it in the style of his interlocutors, is well said – and not simply because of the book's formal originality. What is so unusual is that a volume that might be regarded as a postscript or addendum to the main body of the work turns out to be an integral part of it.

Geoff Dyer 2014

13 *The Task of the Critic*, p. 33.

14 From Francis Mulhern's preface to Raymond Williams, *What I Came to Say*, London 1990, unpaginated.

Foreword

Raymond Williams occupies a unique position among socialist writers in the English-speaking world today. No contemporary figure of the Left has so extensive an oeuvre to their credit. The range of this work, moreover, is probably unprecedented in either England or America, including political intervention, cultural theory, history of ideas, sociology, literary criticism, analysis of drama, semantic inquiry, novels, plays and documentary film scripts. Williams's audience is by any comparative measure a very large one: some 750,000 copies of his books have by now been sold in UK editions alone.[1] Few socialists in any of the advanced capitalist countries could claim so wide a readership, won and held by writings of so unfailing, and often taxing, an intellectual standard.

Yet until very recently sustained discussion of Williams's work has been relatively wanting. Despite its increasing authority and influence in the field of English studies, since the war perhaps the most sensitive single area in the formation of the national intelligentsia in Britain, there has so far been no attempt to meet it at full stretch on the Right. The immense variety of Williams's writing, crossing academic boundaries and confounding disciplinary expectations, has no doubt been one of the reasons for this hostile quiet. In part, something of the same intellectual difficulty has surely been felt on the Left. But in this case another, more significant factor has also been at work. In the past decade, for the first time since the war, active socialist culture in England has come to be predominantly Marxist – a change due at once to the fruition of the work of the outstanding group of native historians originally formed in the late thirties and forties, the exhaustion of Fabianism as a source of political and social

[1] *Culture and Society*, for example, has sold some 160,000 copies, and *Communications*, approximately 150,000. *The Long Revolution, Drama from Ibsen to Brecht, Orwell* and *Keywords* have all sold more than 50,000 copies since publication – the most recent among them (*Keywords*), in only two years.

argument, and the dissemination of international ideas and idioms among a new generation formed during or after the dramatic struggles of the late sixties. This Marxism stood at a respectful distance from the work of Williams. Two important essays were written, by Victor Kiernan on *Culture and Society* and Edward Thompson on *The Long Revolution*, when these books appeared – in 1958 and 1961 respectively.[2] But thereafter the divergence of Williams's more specialist concerns – with drama, literature or television – from those of professional historians seems to have hampered close or continuing discourse between the two. Among younger socialists there was for a long time still less direct engagement with his work, even if here the discordances were more of vocabulary and theoretical allegiance than of interest. However, it was from this generation that the first overall assessment came, with the appearance in 1976 of the first chapter of *Criticism and Ideology* by Terry Eagleton, a Marxist critic and former pupil of Williams.[3] Virtually simultaneously, Williams for his part for the first time addressed himself to major definitions and problems of historical materialism, with the publication of *Marxism and Literature* in 1977, and in doing so revealed something of the unrecorded history of his own relations with Marxism.

It was in this setting that *New Left Review* conceived the idea of a volume of interviews with Raymond Williams, exploring in depth and detail the whole substance and pattern of his work. NLR, as it took shape in the mid-sixties, had repeatedly expressed the view that no autonomous or mature Marxism could emerge in Britain without taking the full measure of Williams's contribution to socialist thought.[4] This programmatic position was accompanied by the publication of key political and theoretical essays by Williams in the Review. These were to include 'The British Left' (NLR 30), 'Literature and Sociology: in Memory of Lucien Goldmann' (NLR 67), 'Base and Superstructure in Marxist Cultural Theory' (NLR 82), 'Notes on British Marxism Since the War' (NLR 100)

[2] Victor Kiernan, 'Culture and Society', *The New Reasoner*, 9, Summer 1959; Edward Thompson, 'The Long Revolution', *New Left Review* 9 and 10, May–June and July–August 1961.

[3] *Criticism and Ideology*, NLB, 1976, pp. 21–42; first published as 'Criticism and Politics: the Work of Raymond Williams', in *New Left Review*, 95, January–February 1976. An earlier survey can be found in Michael Green, 'Raymond Williams and Cultural Studies', *Cultural Studies*, 6, Spring 1975.

[4] See, for example, Perry Anderson, 'Socialism and Pseudo-Empiricism', *New Left Review*, 35, January–February 1966, p. 32.

and 'Problems of Materialism' (NLR 109). Yet the Review proved no more able than other journals of the Left in these years to take adequate stock of Williams's growing achievement. In relation to modern traditions of socialist theory, its major effort lay elsewhere. In this period NLR pursued a systematic enterprise of introduction and evaluation of the main schools within continental Marxism – whether those of Lukács or Sartre, Gramsci or Althusser, Adorno or Della Volpe. The principles of this policy were two-fold: to set out clearly and coherently the organizing concepts and themes of each current within Western Marxism, and then to appraise them equitably yet firmly and critically, in a spirit at once of independence and of solidarity. This commitment has set the Review apart from two reactions to be found among older and younger generations to the broadening of Marxist culture in England: vehement anathemas on foreign doctrines as alien intrusions of theory into the national tradition, or hierophantic espousals of one school at the expense of all others, as the site of a privileged knowledge. The results of NLR's contrasting stance can be examined in the texts collected in *Western Marxism – A Critical Reader*.[5] The present volume is a natural and necessary extension of that work, turning to consider the pre-eminent intellectual representative of socialism in contemporary Britain, at a time when Williams's own writing has consciously rejoined a wider international Marxist debate. Immediately, it grew out of the engagement with Williams's oeuvre in an essay by Anthony Barnett, of the editorial committee of NLR, in 1976 ('Raymond Williams and Marxism: a Rejoinder to Terry Eagleton'), which sought to explore and appreciate the particular distinction of Williams's socialism.[6] To develop that engagement into a full and direct exchange, the project of a book of interviews was conceived.

The interview is historically an invention of modern journalism, scarcely a hundred years old. Designed for newspapers, it has only recently and sporadically been employed for books. As a form, it customarily suffers from the limitation of an artificial reticence: the interviewers who elicit the responses of the interviewed do not themselves speak to declare their own positions. Partly in consequence, interviews – perhaps especially in intellectual matters – are often also uncritical, since real critical inquiries presuppose the ability and willingness to argue

[5] NLB, 1977.
[6] *New Left Review*, 99, September–October 1976.

alternatives. Where possible, *New Left Review* has tried to develop another model of interview allowing for statement and argument on both sides.[7] This volume follows that practice. Its scale is, however, unusual. That is due at once to our judgment of the quality and importance of Williams's work – fully the equal and in some crucial respects the superior of its counterparts elsewhere in Europe – and to the unreserved willingness of Williams himself, which can have few precedents, to respond to the questions, criticisms and counter-arguments that were put to him. The interviews were conducted at Cambridge in June–November 1977, except for those on the novels, which took place in September 1978.

NLR

[7] Interviews with Jean-Paul Sartre and Lucio Colletti (NLR 58 and 86 respectively) are cases in point.

Raymond Williams – Dates

1921 Born Llwyn Derw, Pandy, Abergavenny, Gwent; only son of Henry Joseph Williams and Esther Gwendolene (Bird). Father railway signalman, Pandy (GWR). Father born 1896, third son of farm labourer, later roadman; mother born 1890, third daughter of farm bailiff.

1925 To Llanfihangel Crucorney (NP; Church of Wales) elementary school.

1926 Father involved in General Strike and secretary of Branch Labour Party.

1932 County scholarship to King Henry VIII Grammar School, Abergavenny.

1935 Declined confirmation in Church of Wales.
Worked for Labour Party candidate (Michael Foot) in General Election.

1936 School Certificate (Central Welsh Board); exemption from matriculation.

1937 Joined Left Book Club group, Abergavenny.
Aug: Welsh League of Nations Union scholarship to Youth Conference, Geneva.

1938 July: Higher School Certificate (English, French, Latin); State Scholarship.
Sept: Speaker at public meeting against Munich agreement, Abergavenny.

1939 Spring: worked full-time for Labour Party candidate (Frank Hancock, member of Peace Pledge Union), by-election.
October: entered Trinity College, Cambridge; joined Cambridge

University Socialist Club.
December: joined Student branch, Communist Party.

1940 Member of CUSC Writers' Group; wrote short stories *Mother Chapel* and *Red Earth*; articles on *Defence Against Air Raids* and *Literature and the Cult of Sensibility*; collaborated on pamphlet on Soviet invasion of Finland.
April–June: editor *Cambridge University Journal* (newspaper).
June: Preliminary Examination, English Tripos.
July: joined LDV (Home Guard), Pandy.

1941 Editor *Outlook*.
Chairman, Arts and Education section, People's Convention, Cambridge.
Co-founder Trinity College Union.
June: English Tripos, Part One.
July: called up to Royal Corps of Signals, Prestatyn; trained as wireless operator.
Wrote *Sack Labourer* (publ. *English Story*).

1942 January–June: Officer Cadet Training Unit, Church Stretton and Larkhill.
June: commissioned into Royal Artillery; posted to 21st Anti-Tank Regiment, Guards Armoured Division (Somerset).
June: married Joy Dalling.

1943 Lieutenant, Royal Artillery; Instructors' Course on Sherman tank.

1944 June: with regiment to Normandy.
July: daughter (Merryn) born.
September: advance unit, liberation of Brussels.
Nijmegen–Arnhem operation.

1945 Operations Ardennes, Hamburg, Kiel Canal.
April–October: editor army newspaper, *Twentyone* (pseudonym, Michael Pope).
October: Class B release to return to Cambridge; placed on Class Z Reserve List of Officers.

1946 June: English Tripos, Part Two. Senior Scholarship, Trinity.
September: appointed Staff Tutor, Oxford University Tutorial

Classes Committee (joint committee of Extra-Mural Delegacy and Workers' Educational Association). Classes in International Relations.
September: son (Ederyn) born; moved to Seaford, Sussex.

1947 Wrote *Brynllwyd* (first version of Border Country); *A Fine Room to be Ill in* (*English Story*, 1948); began *Drama from Ibsen to Eliot*. Tutorial Classes in Literature.

1947–8 Editor, with Wolf Mankowitz and Clifford Collins, of *The Critic* and *Politics and Letters (incorporating The Critic)*; articles include *A Dialogue on Actors*; *Saints, Revolutionaries, Carpetbaggers*; *The Soviet Literary Controversy*; *The Lower Fourth at St Harry's*; *The Exiles of James Joyce*; *Radio Drama*; *The State and Popular Culture*; *... And Traitors Sneer*; *How to be Delicate when Shedding Blood*.

1948 Completed *Drama from Ibsen to Eliot* (publ. 1952).
Wrote documentary film script for Paul Rotha on the English agricultural and industrial revolutions (film not made).
Wrote radio script (rejected), subsequently novel (unpublished): *Ridyear*, of the Yukon goldrush.
Politics and Letters closed, following financial difficulties and personal disagreements among editors.

1949 Wrote second version of *Brynllwyd*.
Wrote *Reading and Criticism* (publ. 1950).
Class in Theories of Culture.

1950 Began *The Idea of Culture* (subsequently *Culture and Society*).
Wrote *Adamson* (unpublished novel).
Worked for Labour Party in General Election.
Son (Madawc) born.

1951 Recalled to Army, as Class Z Reserve Officer, for service in Korean War. Refused recall. Registered as conscientious objector after Tribunal hearing, Fulham. Discharged from Army.
Wrote *Village on the Border* (revision of *Brynllwyd*).
Wrote *The Grasshoppers* (unpublished novel).

1952 March: moved to Hastings.

Rewrote *Village on the Border.*

1953 Published The Idea of Culture (*Essays in Criticism*, I, iii). Wrote *Drama in Performance* (publ. 1954) and, with Michael Orrom, *Preface to Film* (publ. 1954).

1953– Contributor to *Highway, Adult Education, Essays in Criticism.*

1954 *Village on the Border* rewritten as *Border Village.*
Wrote *Culture and Society*, Part I, chapters 2–6.

1955 Wrote *Culture and Society*, Part I, 1 and 7, and Part II, 1–4.
Worked full-time for Labour Party in General Election.

1956 Completed *Culture and Society* (publ. 1958).

1957 *Border Village* rewritten as *Border Country.*
Wrote *King Macbeth* (unpublished play).
Aldermaston march.
Universities and Left Review Club, London.

1958 *Culture is Ordinary* (in *Conviction*).
Rewrote *Border Country* (publ. 1960).
Began *Essays and Principles* (subsequently *The Long Revolution).*

1959 Completed *The Long Revolution* (publ. 1961).
Wrote *Koba.*
Joined editorial board, *New Left Review.*

1959– Contributor *New Left Review, Tribune, Sanity, Essays in Criticism, Critical Quarterly, Kenyon Review, Partisan Review, Guardian, New Statesman, Views.*

1960 Began *Second Generation.*
July: moved to Oxford as Resident Tutor, Extra-Mural Delegacy.
Speaker at NUT conference on Popular Culture; *Communications* commissioned from this by Penguin.
Witness at *Lady Chatterley* trial.

1961 Wrote *Communications* (publ. 1962).
Appointed Lecturer in English, Cambridge; elected Fellow of Jesus College; moved to Hardwick, Cambridge, September.

1961–6 Member of CND; member of Labour Party.

1962 Completed *Second Generation* (publ. 1964).

1963 Began *Modern Tragedy*.
Wrote *David Hume: Reasoning and Experience* (*The English Mind*, 1964).

1964 Completed *Modern Tragedy* (publ. 1966).
Full-time work for Labour candidate, Cambridgeshire.

1965 Began *The Fight for Manod* (novel).
Began *The Country and the City*.
Member of Cambridge Left Forum; Vietnam Solidarity Campaign.

1966 Wrote *A Letter from the Country* (play produced BBC 2).
Revised *Drama from Ibsen to Eliot* as *Drama from Ibsen to Brecht* (publ. 1968).
February: worked for Labour Party candidate, Cambridge.
July: resigned from Labour Party.
August: planning meeting leading to *May Day Manifesto*.

1967 Wrote *Public Inquiry* (play produced BBC 1).
May: First *May Day Manifesto* published.
Convenor, May Day Manifesto working group.
Revised *Communications* (new edition publ. 1968).

1968 Wrote first half of *The Country and the City*.
May: Penguin *May Day Manifesto* published.
Lectures in Scandinavia and Italy.

1968–72 Contributor to *The Listener* (television reviews).

1969 Wrote (from lecture notes 1961–68) *The English Novel from Dickens to Lawrence* (publ. 1970) and *Introduction* to *Pelican Book of English Prose, II*.
Chairman, National Convention of the Left.
Chairman, Convention Commission.
Writing *The Fight for Manod*.
Wrote *Radical and/or Respectable* (*The Press We Deserve*, 1970).

1970 Wrote *Orwell* (publ. 1971).

Writing *The Volunteers* (novel).
Convention Commission breaks up, May, following disagreements on policy during General Election.
Wrote *Ideas of Nature* (publ. *The Shaping Inquiry*, 1971).

1971 Writing *The Country and the City*.
Began *The Brothers* (novel).
Memorial lecture for Lucien Goldmann (publ. NLR, 1971).
Lecturing in Italy.

1972 Writing *The Volunteers*; *Marxism and Literature*.
Wrote *Social Darwinism in Literature and Social Thought* (publ. *The Limits of Human Nature*, 1973).

1973 Lecturing in USA and Canada.
Wrote *Television: Technology and Cultural Form* (publ. 1974).

1974 February: worked for Labour Party in General Election.
Writing *Marxism and Literature*; *Keywords*; *The Fight for Manod*.
Appointed Professor of Drama, Cambridge.

1975 Completed *Keywords* (publ. 1976)
Writing *Marxism and Literature*; *The Fight for Manod*.
Revised *Communications* (new edition, 1976).
Lecturing in Germany.

1976 Completed *Marxism and Literature* (publ. 1977).
Completed *The Volunteers*.
Wrote: *The Social Significance of 1926* (*Llafur*, 1977); *The Case of English Naturalism* (in *English Drama: Forms and Development*, 1977); essay in *My Cambridge* (1977).
Lecturing in Italy, Yugoslavia, Germany, France.

1977 Wrote *The Fiction of Reform* (TLS); *Science-Fiction and Utopias* (*Studies in SF*, 1978).

1978 Completed *The Fight for Manod*; *Problems of Materialism*, NLR 109; *The Welsh Industrial Novel* (Cardiff, 1979); *Means of Communication as Means of Production* (*Prilozi*, Zagreb).

References

Raymond Williams's works are cited from the following editions, with accompanying abbreviations (date of original publication in parentheses):

Reading and Criticism (1950) (RC) Frederick Muller, 1966
Drama from Ibsen to Eliot (1952) (DIE) Peregrine Books, 1964
*Preface to Film** (1954) (PF) Film Drama, 1954
Drama in Performance (1954) (DP) Frederick Muller, 1954
Culture and Society (1958) (CS) Pelican Books, 1976
Border Country (1960) (BC) Chatto and Windus, 1960
The Long Revolution (1961) (LR) Pelican Books, 1975
Communications (1962) (C) Pelican Books, 1973
Second Generation (1964) (SG) Chatto and Windus, 1964
Modern Tragedy (1966) (MT) Chatto and Windus, 1966
Drama from Ibsen to Brecht (1968) (DIB) Chatto and Windus, 1971
May Day Manifesto † (1968) (MDM) Penguin Books, 1968
Orwell (1971) (O) Fontana, 1975
The English Novel from Dickens to Lawrence (1971) (ENDL) Chatto and Windus, 1971
The Country and the City (1973) (CC) Chatto and Windus, 1973
Television: Technology and Cultural Form (1974) (TTCF) Fontana, 1974
Keywords (1976) (K) Fontana, 1976
Marxism and Literature (1977) (ML) OUP, 1977
The Volunteers (1978) (V) Eyre Methuen, 1978
The Fight for Manod (1979) (FM) Chatto and Windus, 1979

* With Michael Orrom. † Edited.

Note: citations from *Communications* are from the second, rather than the third, revised edition.

Publisher's Note

The interviews presented here were conducted by Perry Anderson, Anthony Barnett and Francis Mulhern, of the editorial committee of *New Left Review*.

I

Biography

1. Boyhood

What was the character of your family and its immediate community?

I come from Pandy, which is a predominantly farming village with a characteristic Welsh rural structure: the farms are small family units. My father began work when he was a boy as a farm labourer. But through this valley had come the railway, and at fifteen he got a job as a boy porter on the railway, in which he remained until he went into the army during the First World War. When he came back he became an assistant signalman and then a signalman. So I grew up within a very particular situation – a distinctly rural social pattern of small farms, interlocked with another kind of social structure to which the railway workers belonged. They were unionized wage-workers, with a perception of a much wider social system beyond the village to which they were linked. Yet at the same time they were tied to the immediate locality, with its particular family farms.

There was all the time a certain pressure from the East, as we would say – from England – because we were right on the border of a different kind of rural residential life, with larger country-houses and retired Anglo-Indian proprietors. But that remained very marginal and external.

How large was the community?

It is a classic example of a dispersed, rather than nucleated, settlement – the characteristic pattern not only for rural Wales but for much of Western Britain generally. The immediate parish was three miles one way and four miles the other. About three to four hundred people lived in it. So the farms were about a quarter of a mile apart, although there were small clumps like the house in which I grew up which was one of a group of six. The contrast is very sharp with the typical Eastern English rural settlement nucleated around the church. The village was served by one school which was under the control of the Church of Wales, a church, a

Baptist Chapel and a Presbyterian Chapel. It had four pubs.

From what you say it sounds as if it was in many ways a very untypical region, in any case unusual for the English countryside proper, in that what you are describing is really small-holder agriculture without any major exploiting group. It was certainly nothing like the triad system of landowner-farmer-agricultural labourer which was the dominant pattern in England.

That's right.

At the same time, while your father worked in a classical working-class occupation, it was nevertheless very abstracted from the normal environment of the modern urban proletariat.

I think this is the point. It took me a long time to realize that my situation was not typical. More than half the population of the village were small farmers. The farmers were not on the whole involved in exploitation in their immediate activities (except within the family, where there was indeed a good deal of exploitation: but within the family, not outside it). They were not characteristically employers of labour. The average size of a farm would be no more than 60–100 acres, about half of which would be rough grazing land on the hill-sides, and half pasture in the valley. Nevertheless, the farmers were so clearly the real solid stratum of this community that other people did feel themselves to be, as it were, less established in the place than they. The others would be the usual mix. There was the railway, which would account for 15–20 families, the jobbing builders, a few people beginning to travel to work in town, ordinary rural craftsmen.

These farmers may have seemed very solid, but actually small-holding can be relatively insecure economically: you get good and bad years.

Yes, it was the depression then and small farming is still chronically undercapitalized today. Also, as I said, the labour within the family is exploitative, there is no question about that. There is pressure to delay marriage. You get great injustices between brothers and sisters according to the chance of what age the parents die, what happens in the disposition of the inheritance and, of course, the children are working from a very early age. They do not see this as exploitation but it is very hard work. But the strange thing is that when such a family sold up, it suddenly seemed as if they must have been very substantial property holders. One can get a very peculiar double vision, seeing the amount of value realized then. For in such families there is virtually never any disposable capital, it is all sunk in buildings or animals: the availability of a few pounds in cash at any given time is often less than many people have on a really low wage. Of course, selling up is a disaster, because it means the family has ended in some way.

All the time the process of engrossing which had been going on throughout the 19th century was still advancing. It is sometimes difficult to believe even now that there are so many small farms. But if you go back a hundred years there were two or three times that many. Since then there has been almost continuous emigration from this kind of area, so that even the surviving small holdings are engrossments of two or three farms of an earlier time.

The community as a whole was shrinking between the wars?

The population was diminishing because at all times there was a group which had got no obvious work waiting for them. They were the landless families like my own. My grandfather, for instance, had been a farm labourer and then he had a row with his boss – this was about twenty miles away. He then became a roadman. But other people I know of in the same situation went off to the mines – there was a lot of movement into the mining valleys – or into the towns to work. In the 20th century there was a big migration to Birmingham, where many of my family had gone. So people were constantly moving out. There had always been a huge exodus of women, which actually preceded that of men. The girls moved out into domestic service; the biggest loss of rural population in Wales was first of all among women. Then the men began to leave for alternative jobs. That is why the railway was so important: the job of a railwayman was incredibly highly valued, because it was regarded as secure. It sounds ironic now, but in the twenties and thirties the one thing that was always said about the railway was that it was steady well-paid work.

What were relations like between the railwaymen and the farmers?

There seemed to be absolutely no social barrier at all between them.

Typically, my father's closest friend was a farmer. He was a lifelong friend whom he would help in the harvest, in whose field he would plant his rows of potatoes which were an important part of our food. If you moved towards a few of the larger farmers you would begin to be aware of some social distance, in the sense that you would notice when somebody had a car, which two or three were beginning to acquire. The schoolmaster would also have a car.

The interesting thing is that the political leaders in the village were the railwaymen. Of the three signalmen in my father's box, one became the clerk of the parish council, one the district councillor, while my father was on the parish council. They were much more active than anyone else in the village. All of the railwaymen voted Labour. Most of the farmers, by contrast, voted Liberal. Within the village, there would be local divisions of interest between the two – typically over expenditure. The railwaymen were a modernizing element who, for example, wanted to introduce piped water and other amenities. They read a lot. They also talked endlessly. This is where their other social dimension, quite outside this locality, was decisive. Characteristically, because signalmen had long times of inactivity between trains, they talked for hours to each other on the telephone – to boxes as far away as Swindon or Crewe. They weren't supposed to, of course, but they did it all the time. So they were getting news directly from industrial South Wales, for example. They were in touch with a much wider social network, and were bringing modern politics into the village. That meant raising the rates, which the farmers opposed, since they literally did not have much disposable money. If the farmers counter-organized, they would tend to win. But apart from these conflicts, the regular personal relations between the two groups were very close: it would be typical to go to the signal box and find one or two small farmers sitting in the box, especially on a wet day, talking to the railwaymen. All of which had consequences, I think, for my initial perception of the shape of society.

What was the role of religious denominations in the area?

The farmers were overwhelmingly nonconformist, Baptist more than Presbyterian (Calvinistic Methodist). In my case, my father's and my mother's family were mixed Church and Chapel. My father was very hostile to religion. When my grandmother came to live with us and was strongly Chapel, I was sent to Chapel; when I was older I went to Church. Chapel was very much more consciously Welsh. Later, I refused to be confirmed, but my decision caused no crisis in the family.

Did you know Welsh?

We were not Welsh speaking. Ours was an area that had been Anglicized in the 1840s – the classic moment usually described as when 'the mothers stopping teaching their children Welsh'. In fact, of course, there was an intense and conscious pressure through the schools to eliminate the language, which included punishment for children who spoke Welsh. The result was to leave a minority of families who were bilingual and a majority who spoke only English. However, a certain number of Welsh expressions survived and also affected the speaking of English. Characteristically, these were everyday greetings and swearing. But for the majority of the population Welsh was now an unknown language.

At the same time, Welsh poems and songs were learnt by heart for special occasions. For this was one of the areas where the Welsh cultural revival started in the early 19th century. This often happens in border districts, which produce a conscious nationalism. In the elementary school, Welsh songs and poems were taught to the children.

What was your attitude to learning these songs? Did you at any time feel that they were an embarrassing archaism?

I felt that very strongly when I was at grammar school. My reaction then was associated with a general revulsion against what I saw and still see as the extreme narrowness of Welsh nonconformism. Its attitude to drink, for example, was very difficult for an adolescent to accept. What I did not perceive at the time but I now understand is that the grammar schools were implanted in the towns of Wales for the purpose of Anglicization. They imposed a completely English orientation, which cut one off thoroughly from Welshness. You can imagine how this combined with my hostility to the norms of Welsh nonconformist community. The result was a rejection of my Welshness which I did not work through until well into my thirties, when I began to read the history and understand it.

You've spoken of Welsh language and religion. But what about national identity as such? Would the people in your village, your father and your grandparents, if asked what they were, say they were Welsh? Or would they not use such a category at all?

They were very puzzled by this. I heard them talking about it. I think the sense of a specific local identity was much stronger. There were good historical reasons for that. For Wales had never been a nation: it had always had a cultural rather than a national existence. It was precisely incorporated into 'Britain' before it developed a really separate national identity. So people would always ask what Wales actually was. This is how I in the end understood the question myself, because I found that virtually all Welshmen ask themselves what it is to be Welsh. The problematic element is characteristic. Of course on the border, it was more problematic than in North or West Wales, in the still Welsh-speaking communities. They are that much further away from England. There was a curious sense in which we could speak of both Welsh and English as foreigners, as 'not us'. That may seem strange, but historically it reflects the fact that this was a frontier zone which had been the location of fighting for centuries.

Did you consider yourself as British?

No, the term was not used much, except by people one distrusted. 'British' was hardly ever used without 'Empire' following and for that nobody had any use at all, including the small farmers.

Could you say something about your father's political views and activities?

He had been very conscious as a boy of his father's political change, from Liberal to Labour. It was provoked by the traumatic moment when his father was sacked and turned out of his home – the classic case of the tied cottage – to become a roadman. When you are the victim of a farmer who is a Liberal, your class interest declares itself: at that point he went over to Labour. So this was already my father's orientation. Then he was very unwillingly conscripted into the First World War. He came out of the army in the mood of so many soldiers, by this time totally radicalized. Coming back to the railway, it happened that his first job was right down in the mining valleys which were very politicized, with a fairly advanced Socialist culture. By the time he moved home to the border again, he had acquired its perspectives.

So you grew up in a Socialist family and from your very earliest you were aware of that as such.

Absolutely. I was five at the time of the General Strike which was very bitterly fought out on a small scale in the village. The stationmaster was victimized by demotion for his role in it because he was a conscious Socialist. There was a very big conflict inside the second signal box when two of the men struck and the other did not. The chapter in *Border Country* which describes the Strike is very close to the facts. Then in 1929 I remember a euphoric atmosphere in the home when Labour won the elections. My father was running the Labour Party branch in the village, and we greeted the results with jubilation,

So the politics came mainly through your father and your mother accepted them? Was she active?

It was the classic situation of a Labour Party woman. She makes the tea, she addresses the envelopes, she takes them round – she does not have very many political activities in her own right. But my mother had her own opinions. She actually felt much more hostile to the farmers than did my father, who was mixing with them all the time. She still makes very hostile remarks about farmers as a class, whom she conceives as the ultimate in exploiters! But then these were about the only social relations she ever directly experienced. Her mother had been a dairy maid on a larger farm, and she had worked on one as a girl, so there was a sense of farmers as employers.

What about your own reading, your intellectual development as a boy?

I read extraordinarily little except school books. That was still so after grammar school. I think it probably had to do with the availability of books. We had very few in the house, hardly any apart from the Bible, the Beekeeper's Manual (which was my father's craze), and the usual things for children like The Wonder Book of Why and What. So where did you get books? You got them at school. Therefore I was strongly directed by the curriculum, at least until sixteen or seventeen when I began to get access to the Left Book Club. But it took me twenty to thirty years, if it ever changed, to get used to the idea that books were something to be bought. Mind you, this is a habit I share with a majority of the British people.

What about your pattern of choice within the school curriculum? Your eventual specialization at grammar school level was literary and linguistic – English, French and Latin. The absence of history from your adolescent intellectual interests seems very striking.

The explanation lies in the culture I received, not in my character. What history we were taught in the elementary school was a poisonous brand of romantic and medieval Welsh chauvinism given us by the schoolmaster. The reading was dreadful – nothing but how such and such a medieval Welsh prince defeated the Saxons, and took from them great quantities of cattle and gold. I threw up on that. It wasn't only that it didn't connect. It was absolutely contradicted by how we now were. The irony was that when I entered the grammar school we started to do the history of the British Empire. We plunged somewhere straight into the middle of the 18th century, with the conquest of Canada and then went through India and South Africa and the whole imperial expansion. That kind of history did not interest me very much either. The curious result was that I later had to reconstruct for myself the main lines of the history, not just of England, but even of my own region. I did not feel any loss at that time. But I felt it enormously later, when I had to settle down and read the main body of British history – including, of course, the history of Wales. The highest marks I got at school certificate were languages and English and so that is what I did, when I went to the sixth form.

Was it quite a big step to go from the elementary school in the village to the grammar school in Abergavenny?

It happened that the village had its golden year when I sat for the scholarship – seven pupils won County scholarships. There was a group photograph taken because it was such an exceptional event: six girls and me. But the girls – several of them were farmers' daughters – would usually go only as far as the fifth form and would then leave. The other boys from the village also went to the fifth form, where they then often had difficulties in passing the matric. So by the time I got to the sixth form I was the only one from Pandy.

But there was no sense of isolation from the village. The grammar school was intellectually deracinating, as I can see now. But I was not conscious of it at the time, because in everything that was not schoolwork there was no sense of separation.

The grammar school was seen from within the village, and by your family, as a completely natural extension of your life?

Oh, totally. Indeed, I used to blame my father – although I do not now – for pushing me too hard. It happened that I passed top of the County exam, so he assumed that when I went to the grammar school, I was automatically going to be top of the form. When I came second at the end of the first year, it was inexplicable to him. I felt extremely resentful that he could think that coming second was bad. I think that I probably started to feel then that shameful academic competitiveness which I finally got rid of only at my last examination.

But there was absolutely no sense in which education was felt as something curious in the community. Years later I talked to Hoggart about his sense in childhood of being described as 'bright', with the implication of something odd. My experience was quite the opposite. There was absolutely nothing wrong with being bright, winning a scholarship or writing a book. I think that this has something to do with what was still a Welsh cultural tradition within an Anglicized border area. Historically, Welsh intellectuals have come in very much larger numbers from poor families than have English intellectuals, so the movement is not regarded as abnormal or eccentric. The typical Welsh intellectual is – as we say – only one generation away from shirt sleeves. There was, after all, no establishment in Wales to maintain a class-dependent intelligentsia. Class-dependent intellectuals by definition emigrated. It is important to remember that the Welsh University Colleges were built by popular subscription in the 1880s, which would have been a difficult project in England at the time.

Education was, of course, also regarded as one way out of frustrating employment. I remember once, when I protested to my father: 'What is it for, anyway?', he said: 'Well, for example, you can get a job as a booking clerk.' That would mean a pound or two up a week.

Was that your perspective at the time?

No. But I wasn't thinking of further education either. The idea of a university came as a surprise to me. Indeed, it was done over my head. When I sat for the Higher School Certificate, the 'A' level equivalent, which I took very early because I had got through the course quickly, the headmaster decided to approach my father about my going to Cambridge. My father said afterwards: 'We didn't tell you in case you'd be disappointed if they'd not taken you.' The headmaster wrote to Trinity asking them to accept me; and they took me, without the ordinary admission or any examination. I had never been to Cambridge before I arrived there as an undergraduate. It was just presented to me. By that time, however, I had a definite view of what I wanted to be, in which the university was not primary but which it did not contradict.

What was that?

I think I can honestly say that it was very much what I am now. Not what I am as a university professor – I have to keep reminding myself that I am *that* – but as a writer. By the time I was sixteen, I was writing plays which were performed in the village, together with my closest friend, who was the son of the Baptist minister. We produced them together in the village hall, and everybody came. I also wrote a novel which nobody is ever going to see, called *Mountain Sunset*. It was about the revolution in Britain – one of whose critical battles took place on the border – I am afraid there was some infection from that despised Welsh history! I sent it to Gollancz, of whom I knew at this time because of the Left Book Club. They sent it back, of course, but with a kind note that they wanted to see more. Within six months I couldn't bear to reread it.

What was the character of the plays you wrote?

We did two full length ones. The most ambitious took the form of a detective play which yet uncovers a social villain. I would now know that this was fairly characteristic of radical melodrama. We were by this time regarded very differently from somebody like my father, because we were campaigning around in politics. Nevertheless everybody came, the village hall was packed.

Did you have village references within these plays?

Yes, some, but we had to be careful. When I was at Cambridge, I wrote a short story called *Mother Chapel* which was a criticism of a narrow nonconformist community radically reproving sexual error and deviance, in which the minister's daughter herself becomes pregnant before marriage – hence the title. Somehow, I still don't know how, the magazine in which it appeared got back home and all hell broke loose. A son of the village had gone away to slander it . . . Actually, the fictional episode was a fairly typical one. I had become very contemptuous of the hypocrisies involved. The earlier plays we did were much more respectful of local constraints.

What was the political campaigning which made you so differently regarded from your father?

In the 1935 elections the local Labour candidate was Michael Foot, straight from Oxford, for whom my father organized a meeting. We thought this very boring. We decided to go out to the Tory candidate. The constituency was Monmouth: the solid east-of-the-county vote always makes it Conservative. We had prepared figures for what black labourers in South Africa earned and we got up and asked him how he could justify them. He completely put us down, with a lot of support from the audience, saying that this was not a matter of great importance in the current county campaign, as he was sure the electors would agree – making fools of us, in effect. But this sort of question was a different political language from anything that was familiar in the village.

What was the local branch of the Left Book Club like, and the general impact of the Club on your development?

The Club in Abergavenny, which had about fifteen to twenty members, was run by Labour Party activists. They used to organize discussions and meetings and invite speakers. We weren't subscribers; I used to borrow books from whoever subscribed, so I didn't see them all. But it was from the Club that I read about imperialism and colonialism. This was the time of the war in Abyssinia. We were also very conscious of the Chinese Revolution, since we read Edgar Snow's *Red Star over China*, and of course the Spanish Civil War. Among the visiting speakers, I remember being especially impressed by Konni Zilliacus, who at that time was still working for the League of Nations; he seemed the first wholly cosmopolitan man I had met.

Your father's politics grew in a very direct sense out of his immediate work experience and family situation. Yet from what you have been saying it seems that much of the pressure and focus of your teenage politics was international, rather than local or even national?

Yes, to a fault – our interest was almost too much the other way. The traditional politics of locality and parliament in the Labour movement was seen as part of a boring, narrow world with which we were right out of sympathy. To us international actions were much more involving and interesting. This was where the crucial issues were being decided. The Left Book Club essentially represented the insertion of those larger perspectives and conflicts into the labour movement. Older people went along with it but I think that their sense was of benevolent association rather than of international solidarity. We made the leap to international solidarity without having to go through the other experiences, of local and national struggles – although it always seemed to me, even then, that the great problem of the Labour movement was how the two interests spoke to each other. But the times were changing and the issues actually were much more internationalist then.

Did you join the Labour Party and think of yourself as a Labour man?

No, I didn't join the Labour Party. My father, who was the branch secretary, asked me to in 1936. But I actually rather disliked Michael Foot – something that is easier to say now. He was a new phenomenon, straight out of the Oxford Union, who did sound a bit odd in Pandy village hall. I said to my father: 'What has this to do with the Labour Party?' He thought my attitude was quite wrong and that Foot was a very clever young man. But I did not particularly want to join. In fact, the only time I have ever been a member of the Labour Party was from 1961 to 1966, when I actually had a card – a very peculiar period to do so, of course.

Otherwise I would work for Labour in the elections because there was no other choice. But I always had a very reserved attitude to the Labour Party.

Did you have arguments with your father about this? Did he think that you would in the course of time join the Labour Party?

Yes, to the extent that after the War, he wrote to me and said that the whole group of which he was part, I suppose the survivors of the Left Book Club, wanted to propose me as the local candidate to fight the 1945 election. I think that he was hurt that I was not interested. Not that I think if they had proposed me, I would have been nominated: the Labour Party by that time was being run by a quite different sort of people in the constituency.

The milieu of the Left Book Club was much closer to the CP than the Labour Party. The whole field of its political culture was the Popular Front. When you were at Abergavenny didn't this present a conflict or choice for you? What was your attitude towards the Communist Party?

The really extraordinary fact – it might have been just accidental to that region – is that there was no awareness of a British Communist Party. You only had to go thirty miles to find some of the most solid Communist bastions in the country, in the Rhondda. Yet I was not conscious of any Labour-Communist antagonism, as positions between which you had to choose. You must understand that this had never been an issue with my father. He did not think of Communists as another or different force within the Labour movement: it was a matter of course to him that there were Communists in the leadership of the railway unions. Then these were now the days of the Popular Front, which rejected the whole idea of a division: our attitude was very much 'no enemies on the left'.

What you say is still slightly astonishing. After all, your father must have been aware of the Zinoviev letter. The Bolshevik menace, the un-English nature of Communism, were relentless themes of bourgeois propaganda in the inter-war period. These matters were national political issues.

That is what the bosses said. You did not believe it. Equally, these questions were not the terms in which your own struggle was formulated. I think that this is true of many of my father's generation and perhaps even of the succeeding one of Labour Party militants who joined before the Cold War and the conscious splits and proscriptions which followed it. Of course in the big industrial centres, there were organized and conscious ideological battles. But for many Socialists, Communism was a branch of the labour movement, and certainly if the press and the government attacked it, then it must be generally all right. There was a combination of acceptance and distance towards it.

Reconstructing your vision of the world up to the time of the university, what would have been your most representative image of the ruling or exploiting class?

The first one to come to mind would actually have been a very antique figure – the rural magnate or landlord, whom we mocked. The immediate cultural image was that of a Tory squire.

Did they really exist within the compass of your experience?

You could not go and see them. You could see a park wall, not beyond it. After that, we would characteristically have thought of bankers. I remember long discussions with my father about the ownership of industry by banks. Then, of course, there were the railway-owners and the mine-owners. But the rather archaic agrarian stereotype was still dominant. I don't think that it was just because I lived in a rural area. This displacement away from the decisive class enemy of the last hundred and fifty years, the industrial employer, to older antagonists has been surprisingly persistent in the perception of the ruling class on the British left. In my case, I also had the natural adolescent reaction that the ruling class was not just wrong but out-of-date – the characteristic conviction of the young that the rulers are old, irrelevant and not of our world. I thought all Tories were stupid by definition. This was a very common rhetoric in the thirties. It carried certain real feelings. On the other hand, it disarmed people, including me and a lot of my friends, from understanding the intelligence and capacity of the ruling class, and its contemporary implantation.

In my case, distance from London probably did have some importance. I never saw any of the central metropolitan power definitions. Of course, I knew of what the troops had done in the mining valleys – we were constantly told of it. But that was second-hand. We were in no doubt at all about the character of the employers, but the ruling class still did not seem very formidable. The result was to build up a sense, which was very characteristic of wide sectors of the Labour movement at the time, that the working class was the competent class that did the work and so could run society. That was said so much after the General Strike. It was disabling ultimately. But as an adolescent I remember looking at these men even with a certain resentment – they seemed so absolutely confident. I have never seen such self-confident people since.

One might say, then, that in your boyhood there was an absence of the typical town–country relation, absence of direct confrontation between privileged exploiters and working people, and absence of antagonism between manual and mental labour. Your early experience appears to have been exempt from a whole series of typical conflicts and tensions which most people of your generation from working-class families would have felt at some point. Your own history seems to have escaped nearly all of them. Firstly, which is in a way the most remarkable fact, there is the absence of any deep division between town and country. If you were from a major urban concentration, you would have inevitably been largely alienated from the natural world. This is something which was not true of you. Secondly, you came from a working-class family with a strong class consciousness, yet in an area which lacked any centrally important sector of the ruling class. Factory workers would have a different experience in large towns or in the capital. There the capitalists, the rulers, embody an unmistakable power: they are not comic, they are oppressive and they instil fear. That seems to have been absent from your environment in a real way. Thirdly, there does not seem to have been any real tension between manual and mental labour – something that can be very important in many working-class areas. You never encountered distrust or resentment of intellectual pursuits, or a difficult ambiguity of feeling about education, for instance – not uncommon patterns in other working-class cultural regions. Then there seems to have been no problem about religion. Your father was actually opposed to religion, and when you refused to be confirmed, it caused no crisis in the family. It was not a disturbance in your childhood – whereas in many areas of English working-class life the transition would not have been such a smooth process at all. Finally and most importantly, you did not have to effect a break to enter politics, in the way that even in core working-class districts it is possible to be a union man or to vote Labour, but actually to be politically active is a change beyond that – which can lead to tension in a family if somebody does so. But this was not the case in your family. Then beyond that again, there was a kind of generic unity or amity between what could be called left Labour or Communist positions – no sense of hardened divisions or barriers, and consequently of conflicts or crises in passing from one to the other. One gets the cumulative impression that by the time you reached the university, all your energies as a person must have been to an exceptional degree whole and available to you – that is, unimpaired by the sort of intense early conflicts that mark so many biographies. The passage through boyhood would typically be a more divisive, sometimes depleting struggle – whatever its long-term consequences. Your trajectory seems unusually free of direct strain, up to Cambridge. Would you say that was true?

I think it is true. It is never easy to talk about one's own personality in that sense, but for what it is worth my own estimate is that I arrived at the university with about as full an availability of energy as anyone could reasonably have. Indeed my expression of energy was unproblematic to a fault. All the problems came later. At the time, it was very much a sense of hitting Cambridge, being extraordinarily unafraid of it. I got relatively afraid of it afterwards. I measure myself against it today, with a kind of calm hostility, but then the notion that there were deep blocking forces to contend with never occurred to me. There are only about three or four people who really knew me as I was then: they would give a totally different account of my personality from those who reckon they know me now – the fraught, balancing, tense creature of some people's caricature. Anyway I was absolutely unlike that then.

In your essay 'Culture is Ordinary', you remark that on getting to Cambridge you quite liked the Tudor courts and chapels: Cambridge in no way oppressed or daunted you, because you felt that your own culture and history predated it.

Was much older, yes. There is the joke that someone says his family came over with the Normans and we reply: 'Are you liking it here?' But that was playing the game . . .

A school-boy or girl coming from a working-class urban background to Oxford or Cambridge would have been unlikely to have had that historical self-confidence. It is partly a question of Welshness, but also, within it, the fact that you came from a much denser school situation. If you go to a grammar school and a lot of working-class people living around you are not going to grammar school, then the social cleavages which are later represented and intensified by

Oxford and Cambridge are much more difficult to handle in childhood, as your working-class friends no longer wear the same clothes, or do the same things.

That is right. Those classic contradictions were to some extent not there. But in a way they were saved up to take their maximum effect later. Why didn't my headmaster send me to a university in Wales? That would have been an orientation which would have suited my life much better. It is no use going back over it, but it would have. But this is what he was there for – to find boys like me and send them to Cambridge. I don't say this in any spirit of hostility to him; he thought he was doing the best thing for me. But it was partly because of the devices of the English implantation in Wales that blockages were not there for me in a way that they typically were in British culture as a whole.

On the other hand, once I was sent to Cambridge, I had a very strong sense, which was revived briefly again in '45, of having my own people behind me in the enterprise. So that the characteristic experience of isolation or rejection of the institution did not occur. It was not till later that I saw that this was not something to be negotiated only at the emotional level – in the end you have to negotiate it in real relations, which are much harder things. But at the time I felt mainly the confidence of having people behind me. Even my brashness in writing *Mother Chapel* reflected it. When there was a problem with my grant coming through after the War, that supportive area was still close enough – despite the row the story had caused – for the local pub to make a collection for me straight away. There was no question about it: this was something that had to be done. My father, typically, paid the money back. So there was no sense of being cut off.

You went to Geneva for a youth Conference organized by the League of Nations, just before Cambridge?

Yes, it was my first journey abroad: I gave the report on the current international situation – there is an account of it in one of the League memoirs written by a thirties' journalist. On the way back, we stopped in Paris and I crept out of the hotel and went straight to the Soviet pavilion at the international Exhibition. I remember it very clearly. There was a peculiarly contemptible British pavilion with a large cardboard cut-out of Chamberlain and a fishing rod. The Soviet one had a massive sculpture of a man and woman with a hammer and sickle on top of it. I kept saying: 'What is a sickle?' – I had used the damned thing and we called it a hook. It was there that I bought a copy of the *Communist Manifesto*, and read Marx for the first time.

2. Cambridge

What was the impact of Cambridge on you – it was the first really major break in your life up till then?

I was wholly unprepared for it. I knew nothing about it. The normal process of coming to Cambridge, after all, is at least that you go for a preliminary interview or examination. But the university was totally strange to me when I came off the train. The college was virtually incomprehensible, except in the image of a larger school. To my surprise I found that although I had come to Trinity to do English, there was nobody there who taught it and so I was immediately sent out. In a college of that size there was not much of an attempt at integration. At first I put my name down for everything that I was interested in – for example rugby, because it was a continuation from school. I first registered that there was a problem about the social composition of the Cambridge student body when I went to the Union, which I naturally wanted to join, and was told that I had to be sponsored. I needed a proposer and seconder. I didn't of course know anybody to ask. They said: 'Haven't you got friends from school?' Although a technicality, this suddenly introduced the curiosity of my position.

But then I discovered the Socialist Club – I went to a recruiting meeting at Trinity on one of the first nights of term – and with it an immediately alternative and viable social culture, as well as political activity. It had a club room, it served lunches, it had film shows, it was a way of finding friends – it was not like just joining a political society. I went there for meals or whenever I had any time of my own, in the way that other people would live around the college whether they liked it or not. I immediately fell into this world of lunches and film shows. The films were particularly important. My friend Orrom, with whom I later wrote *Preface to Film*, was the great organizer of them. We saw a very big range in the club room, as many as two or three a day sometimes. There was also a wall newspaper, which was really how you got into politics – if you produced something for that. I wrote an article arguing that it would only be possible to fight Hitler if we had a revolution in England. It was very naively expressed, and when I typed it only the red part of my ribbon worked. But it immediately drew a response. I was asked to meet people whom I subsequently noted were important in the club. But my initiative was a purely personal one. That was a good thing about the club. It was – as I learnt later – at all its essential points fairly tightly directed. But on the other hand all its immediate activities were very open. Meanwhile, of course, I had to dine in Hall and the class stamp of Trinity at that time was not difficult to spot. But it did not have to be negotiated as the only context at Cambridge. The Socialist Club was a home from home.

Was the milieu of the Socialist Club congenial essentially because of political comradeship, or was it also a different social mix? Were the relatively new or non-traditional social layers at Cambridge especially numerous in the Club or did it more or less reflect the social composition of the university as a whole?

I have tried to think about this. My sense is that it was not in that way socially distinct. I think I am right to say that I met only one other person from a working-class family at Cambridge, and he was a mature student in his thirties, but had himself been a manual worker as an adult. I don't remember any others – although there must, of course, have been some, because the percentage in the university has been constant, at a very low figure, since about the 1920s. But I did not meet any. The overwhelming majority of people I encountered at the Socialist Club were in terms of education and family very much the ordinary Cambridge mix. It's true that I once noticed when we were in a pub one day and everyone said: 'There is not an Englishman among us' – we were Scots, Irish, London Jewish, a few Welsh. But that was a sorting out within the Club, which itself – if I remember its officers – was not very socially differentiated.

What sort of political education did the Club give a new member?

The central points of reference were Engels's *Socialism – Scientific and Utopian* and *Anti-Dühring*. These were taken more or less as the defining texts, especially the former. Marx was much less discussed, although one was told to read *Capital*, and I bought a copy. I studied it during that year, but with the usual difficulties over the first chapter. It was not till much later that I knew Marx as much more than the author of *Capital.* I have some reason to think that this was a fairly normal introduction to Marxism.

How about Marx's political writings? Weren't you given The 18th Brumaire?

That was not pushed. By contrast, we definitely did have to read the *History of the CPSU (B), Short Course*, chapter by chapter.

Weren't you given any Lenin to read?

State and Revolution, yes.

The Club was very large in size: but it was effectively run by the CP?

Yes. I remember that the speaker for the Club at the Trinity meeting where I was recruited spoke in a clearly CP way. I was enjoying most of it and then – it was a detail – I had to get up and ask how to join the club. I said, characteristically: 'Is this the only organization on the left, because I want to be with the reddest of the reds?' The speaker replied: 'Don't say that.' I then felt a bit embarrassed. Of course, they accepted my membership: the situation was quite unlike the post-war fragmentation of the left into different clubs, when it became a very sharp question which section you joined. This was still a unified club of the whole university left; an attempt to split it only came much later that year.

You joined the Socialist Club in October and within a month or so you joined the Communist Party. What led you to do that? How did it happen?

I had been speaking in the Union; I advocated certain positions, and – as I understood the system later – I was moved up a list of contacts until one day I was asked to join by a man I still know in Cambridge today (he's not now political). When put the question, I made the extraordinarily crass reply: 'How much does it cost?' It did not seem to me a political step into something new, because the request was prompted by what I had already been independently arguing in Union debates. Of course, it soon became quite clear that it was. But I didn't perceive it like that at the time. I queried it as a financial commitment rather than a programmatic leap. The CP seemed to me one of the organizations in the spectrum. I was sufficiently aware of it to think that it was where I was politically. But there was no sense that I was 'giving up Labour politics and becoming a Communist'. There wasn't a real opposition between the two in my background, as I explained.

Didn't you have a sense when joining the Communist Party that this was a revolutionary party and the Labour Party was a reformist party? Wasn't that opposition clear in your mind at the time?

Well yes, because by this time the positions of the two parties on the War were so sharply divergent. So far as definitions are concerned, there was an emphasis on the scientific and revolutionary character of Marxism, in terms largely taken from Engels. But that was not the principal thing I noticed on entering the Communist Party. It was much more that one was now in a disciplined organization. That was the main stress. The discipline was a novelty to me, particularly as it was exercized in a way it took me a long time to understand. The Secretariat would ask me to explain why I had said something in a Union speech, or would tell me that I had been nominated for some position. It trapped some people, while for other people it worked: it was a mixture of both for me. I remembered my father used to say that a disciplined organization is necessary – I was never tempted by the notion that this sort of organization could work without discipline. At the same time, it was never clear to me how the Secretariat, which functioned in a very well rehearsed way and would put on quite extraordinarily important airs, was formed. I do not even remember an election to it when I was there.

What sort of work did you do for the Party?

You were put into a group according to the subject you were reading: there you would discuss the intellectual problems of the subject. Ours was called the Writers' Group, because we were in the English Faculty. In that capacity, we were often called on to do rush jobs in propaganda. An example of the sort of task one was given was the pamphlet Eric Hobsbawm and I were assigned to write on the Russo-Finnish War, which argued that it was really a resumption of the Finnish Civil War of 1918 which had been won by Mannerheim and the Whites. We were given the job as people who could write quickly, from historical materials supplied for us. You were often in there writing about topics you did not know very much about, as a professional with words. The pamphlets were issued from on top, unsigned.

Was there no sense of strain within the Club due to the anti-war positions of the CP – given that the Second World War had broken out two months before you went up to Cambridge?

There must have been, but it was not at all obvious in the very open and friendly activity of the Club. I later realized that a great deal of centralized direction and organization of a fairly traditional kind existed all the time. Yet I never heard the switch and switch-back over the War within the national leadership of the CP debated in the Club. The dominant opinion in the Club was very much that this was an imperialist war, and that in any case it was possible to defeat fascism only through a socialist revolution. Any fight in common with this ruling class would not be a war against fascism. The only people who opposed this – I am speaking from long memory and may have forgotten some positions – were those who took a straight Labour Party line: 'Join together for the patriotic war against fascism; it is divisive to talk of social revolution; there will be reforms in the future.' They were a minority.

What is surprising is that after all the shattering international events of 1939–40 – including the Nazi–Soviet Pact – the confident culture of the left thirties had in an important sense survived. If there had been an attenuation, I was not in a position to observe it because I had not seen it prior to the summer of 1939. All I can say is that it was very strong and confident when I encountered it – operating on many different levels, from film to new kinds of poetry to political affiliations proper. I know people now who I don't think had anything more than a pretty marginal political commitment but who at the time would have said they were Communists. The main cultural pattern of the thirties still held, at least until the spring of 1940. It was the phoney war period, and people were still cynically convinced that countries like England or France would never really fight fascism. None of us felt menaced then. There was an almost unbelievable atmosphere of continuity. We first felt a real threat in May 1940, for obvious reasons. Then people started to talk of what they would do if they were conscripted.

What were the other activities of the Writers' Group?

There was some talk, although in view of later events extraordinarily little, about the internal organization of the English Faculty and what student demands on it might be. But it came to very little because the whole mood of our student culture was – 'What can you expect from this sort of teaching establishment?' We did not on the whole confront them; we tended to ignore them.

On the other hand, we did regularly discuss problems of literature. The central work on which most debate revolved was Ralph Fox's *The Novel and the People*. We also read Alick West and *Left Review*, of course.

Not Christopher Caudwell?

No, I did not come across Caudwell at this stage, so far as I can remember.

What about Leavis?

Nor was I conscious of Leavis. I did write an article in the Club bulletin, on 'Literature and the Cult of Sensibility'. So one key term in Leavis's criticism had obviously filtered through to me. But from what I recollect we bracketed any critical school which talked about sensibility together with Bloomsbury, as being the same thing – which was historically quite inaccurate. The article argued that this was a bourgeois cult that was totally irrelevant to the needs of a popular literature. But as the confusion about Bloomsbury shows, it was not based on any actual knowledge of what was going on inside the English Faculty. That was characteristic of the self-containment of the student culture of the time.

Yet Scrutiny *had directly challenged the emerging Marxist culture of the thirties. It is not as though the two cultures were so self-contained that they did not meet.* Scrutiny *attacked Marxism and in particular literary Marxism very vociferously. Why was there so little response from Communists who were involved in one way or other with literature to these attacks?*

That was the great debate that did not occur in the thirties. The reason is that the Communist response was to shift the argument on to different ground. We maintained that what was wrong with literature was that it was out of touch with a large majority of the people: it was not written for them, and it was not written by them. So the problem was not how to judge literature or respond to a poem, it was how to write a different kind of novel or poem. Since literature was class-restrictive, it was the job of a Socialist to break through this restriction, by producing another kind of literature. Questions of literary criticism or literary history thus largely went by the board. We felt that these were academic arguments that were neither here nor there. It was what happened to literature in our own time that mattered. In its positive emphasis, the position was not entirely wrong – I still feel it has a lot of strength in it. But the negative refusal to engage with major theoretical and practical questions in the discipline of English studies itself was a crucial failure. It may have seemed a natural response to retort that the point was not how to read a poem, but how to write one that meant something in the socio-political crisis of the time. But when the productive mood which was our way of replying by not replying faded away after the War, and we had to engage in literary criticism or history proper, we found we were left with nothing. Meanwhile English studies had matured as a discipline, establishing itself by prolonged specialism and detailed work in field after field, to which Marxists could oppose only a precarious handful of works whose contribution to literary study was easily dismissed as reductionism.

If the Writers' Group was so concerned with problems of literary production, what kind of aesthetic trends were represented in it? What were your models of a new literature?

We were pretty critical of socialist realism – our interests were very much more in modernism. To take my own case, before I arrived at Cambridge I wanted to write like Shaw and Wells, whom I read at school. Then I changed very rapidly, with an incredible mixture of influences. But by the second year Joyce was without question the most important author for us. *Ulysses* and *Finnegans Wake* – which had just appeared in 1939 – were the texts we most admired, and we counterposed to socialist realism. Joyce was much more attractive than Lawrence, for example, who was generally thought – although I doubted it – to be virtually a fascist. But our modernism was not by any means defined in exclusively literary terms. We were also drawn to surrealism, especially in the cinema. We thought that Vigo was quite as interesting as Pudovkin or Eisenstein – whom we anyway interpreted unorthodoxly. Jazz was another form that was important to us. By my second student year, in 1941, we consciously represented a cultural stance in opposition to what we by then would call 'party attitudes' to literature – which we criticized as narrow and stuffy. Of course, we would probably have denied that we were against socialist realism. We would have claimed that much more complex and dynamic techniques were needed for it than those that were officially recommended.

Didn't these attitudes arouse some hostility within the Party at Cambridge?

Certainly. Our opponents called us the 'Aesthetes' – a label we naturally rejected. I can now sympathize with them somewhat more. Socially, an upper-class style was prevalent in Cambridge Communism at the time. A party, for example, would be very unlike a post-war student affair. There would be good wine, not cans of beer, and people would talk quietly – no dancing. If you married that with particular cultural interests there was undoubtedly a cross-over to a London upper-class literary life-style. At this time John Lehmann was still editing *New Writing*, and coming regularly down to Cambridge to meet the young left writers. He had a room in the Arts Passage where we would go when he came on his visits. The makings of a neo-Bloomsbury atmosphere were certainly there, and the criticism of them was absolutely justified.

Your own schedule of activities does not appear to fit very obviously with the image of this sort of aesthetic type. You were Chairman of the University Union, editor of the University Journal *and of* Outlook, *and a militant in the People's Convention that the Party organized. How did you come to all these positions?*

The *Cambridge University Journal* was the weekly student newspaper – the predecessor of *Varsity*. I had written one or two things for it and was then astonished to be told (by the Secretariat, of course) that I was going to be the next editor. That was in my third term. It was not much of a time to be an editor because it spanned the fall of France, the Union debate over which was banned by the proctors. I printed the speeches and there was naturally trouble. *Outlook* was quite different: it was very much the publication of the group called the Aesthetes within the Party. It printed short stories and poems, all by people who were consciously Socialist, yet not written in the spirit of Party work. The story *Red Earth* which I published in it was satirical of precisely the milieu it represented, but whose interests of course I shared. So far as the People's Convention was concerned, it is symptomatic that almost as a matter of course I was put in charge of arts and education – that was the field with which I was associated inside the Party.

The Union was another sort of experience altogether. For that was the arena where one encountered the mass of Tory students. They always turned out in very great numbers – numerically, of course, they were an overwhelming majority at the university. My whole memory of addressing the Union was speaking against these baying ranks of the traditional right. It wasn't at all like student assemblies in the sixties, when the groundswell was on the left. I was very used to speaking, of course, from Wales. There was a considerable physical excitement of performing against that kind of opposition. It was very satisfying. On one occasion I broke the rules and got suspended for insulting a senior member. It was a time when we very consciously felt that we should be in the Union – I was most surprised when students told me in the late sixties: 'You don't go to *that*, you by-pass it!'

There remains something puzzling about your account. You say that the great majority of students at Cambridge were on the right. Yet the Communist Party seems to have been able not just to organize a very large Socialist Club, but actually to dominate the traditional undergraduate institutions of the university as a whole – the student Union, the student newspaper and so on. How do you explain the paradox?

I think the real right hadn't mastered the whole system of nominations and elections at which the Party was adept. So we were surprisingly effective at an organizational level, and in certain key positions in undergraduate life. It was very curious. We were increasingly isolated politically, because of the Party's position on the war, but by effort and organization, and by effective campaigning on issues like wartime arts degrees and call-up deferments until the examinations, Party members still got elected to representative offices and could seem to speak for student opinion. Yet the Tory faction was very strong and loud at the university. The Conservative Party itself was always numerically larger than the Socialist Club. It included a lot of people who went for the dances, of course. Their militants, however, put up a tremendous opposition in the Union, shouting down the left in massed ranks. My particular enemy at Trinity, to give you an example, was a student called Donaldson – who later became the Lord Justice of the Tory Industrial Relations Court.

Compared with the high level of militancy, the great amount of cultural activity, and the organizational ascendancy of the left, within the institutions of the university, the political culture of the time seems to have been rather thin in terms of the number of books or actual substantive issues that were being argued or discussed.

That is a point. When the *Daily Worker* was banned in 1941, the Writers' Group naturally went to a room and produced an underground edition – there was no question about our duty. But when we turned up the second night to produce the illegal edition of the *Daily Worker*, we did not know what to put in. It was not merely that we were cut off from access to ordinary news sources – by this time we really did not know what to write. Quite apart from the ambiguity over the War, it was not a productive time in terms of people really thinking or in the quality of the political debate. This is what I would say mainly, looking back. There were really major issues to discuss and we did not discuss them.

In the list of Socialist literature you cited earlier, it was noticeable that you did not mention a single book on the October Revolution –

Surely I knew Reed's *Ten Days that Shook the World*?

– One would not expect you to have read that because it was a completely banned work by then. Don't forget that Stalin isn't mentioned in the book; Trotsky appears on virtually every other page. It was only re-issued in the post-'53 period.

That's probably right. Our main source of information was the *History of the CPSU (B)*.

Were you aware of Trotsky's writings at all?

No. That was a crucial lack. It wasn't till much later that I really learnt of the existence of a socialist opposition in Russia.

Did you believe the account of the Short Course *at the time? There are no half-tones about that. Not only Trotsky but Zinoviev, Bukharin, Kamenev, virtually the whole of Lenin's Central Committee, are presented as fascist agents, Japenese collaborators or German spies. Did you think this actually was the case?*

No. When we talked late at night, people were doubtful about all sorts of things. Probably our view was that in circumstances of external danger, certain simplifications had to be made – this is the sort of thing that was said. I suppose we took without much questioning the official version of the opposition just because no representatives of it materialized as a living tendency in our own orbit. What puzzled me more was the inter-relations of the parties in 1917. I could not at all understand the problem about the role of the peasantry. Who were the S-Rs, who were described as the 'false friends' of the peasants? I could not see who they represented. I was uncertain about the whole way the class alliance between the proletariat and the peasantry was presented.

Can we ask one summarizing question? You were at Cambridge at the historical end of a period of extraordinary effervescence on the student left, which you saw at a high point. How would you compare it with the student revolt which occurred at the end of the sixties, which you could observe closely here at Cambridge? What were the essential differences?

First, the student left in the thirties was organized on a very much broader front. It included people who in the sixties would have been film buffs or running literary magazines, but who even if they were socialists would not have been in the same general organization. That is to say, the left of the sixties was more explicitly political. I think it both gained and lost by that. It gained in that the quality of its political debate, as I heard and overheard it, was very much higher. It involved more real political arguments. But the cultural influence was less. Second, we were indifferent to the university establishment: we of course thought it was oppressive, but we decided we could disregard it. We were sure we could create a sub-culture independent from it. If a Communist student wanted to do work, he was expected to work within the existing terms of the course, because it was important to have people within the Party who were academically successful. The contrast with the sixties is very evident. Third, there was a big shift in social perspective – at the level of student behaviour and relations to the non-student community. Of course we did things in the town in the thirties, but there was an invisible barrier around the immediate college area, and our own conduct inside that – I was always uneasy about it – was a much more limited and class-based one. The deliberate alteration of style, from dress onwards, was very marked in the sixties. Finally, the difference that struck me most was that I assumed from my experience of the thirties that once you'd got an upsurge of activity again you would have the same kind of active association of people with all the range of viewpoints that we then had, in a common organization and set of projects. The intense divisiveness of the late sixties kept surprising me. I found myself thinking it must be the result of error, or individual wilfulness, not realizing that it was connected with the nature of the political movement itself. The advantage of the later movement was that the quality of its internal argument was very much higher. On the other hand, I think that the earlier movement, because it was so much better organized and more associative, and so much less self-preoccupied, was able to look outward in a way which made it, even apart from the question of numbers, a more integrated general presence.

Reverting to your own development, you have not spoken much so far of your formal academic work at Cambridge. What was your experience of English studies in 1939–40?

In the first year it was not particularly problematic. We were mainly doing the earlier periods of English literature, in a relatively formal way. I found it basically a continuation of school work. Precisely because it did not go much later than Pope, it did not raise any acute problems for me. My tutor was Lionel Elvin, who was on the left although not a Communist – he knew I was when I attacked Pope's verse for aristocratic frigidity, which he told me would not do. Otherwise we got on well enough, as I wrote the sort of essays one did about Shakespeare and the energy released by the emergence of the bourgeoisie. But in my second year I was transferred to Tillyard. Of course, as soon as I said anything like that to Tillyard, the atmosphere became very difficult. We started doing the novel and I promptly produced the Party orientation – that it was necessary to see any bourgeois novel of the past from the perspective of the kind of novel that must now be written, in the present. Tillyard told me this was not a tenable procedure; it was a fantasy. How could you judge something that had been written from the perspective of something that hadn't? Not only was I hostile to Jane Austen, and interpreted Dickens or Hardy in a very simplifying way as just progressive, but I would also talk about the romantic poets, insisting that they represented a project of human liberation which was going to be completed in the future. Then he would say it was nothing to do with literature if some process was going to be completed or not.

In my first year, the habits of school work had held. God knows how I found the time with all the other things I did, but I used to prepare my essays and do my reading very thoroughly. In the second year, however, we were given so much else to do that the whole situation became at once that much more demanding and disintegrating. My work got very scamped. In part this was the typical problem of a socialist student of literature, as I have since experienced it. In any situation with a supervisor you are going to be damned lucky if you know anywhere near as much as he does. If you get involved in a tough argument, if he wants to he is going to be able to put you down. Because he can always think of examples that you have not read – 'How do you square that account of Dickens with . . .?' – then up comes a title or author that you may not even have heard of. It is very easy for a teacher to use his superiority in that way. In my case, I was involved in constant political activity, and other kinds of writing – practical priorities that were in keeping with my theoretical principles. In that sense I was living in totally good faith. But in my academic studies I was not able to produce the properly prepared and referenced and coherent work that I knew I needed to defend my positions. I was engaged in having to satisfy somebody who was professionally teaching a subject that my ideas were tenable and reasonable, and I could not. I was continually found out in ignorance, found out in confusion. That hit every habit of my school training: there was a tremendous frustration at realizing that I did not know enough to win the arguments. You must remember that a hell of a lot of my self-image was devoted to the notion that I could handle academic work. It now became clear to me that actually I could not. In that situation the easiest way to respond – one saw it again through the sixties – was to say all that was pedantic crap: that, my God, there was a war going on. It was not a very intelligent thing to say because Tillyard merely replied: 'Why then are you against it?' The truth is that for the first time in my life, long after it should have been, I looked at myself with a radical doubt. I did not feel very pleased. Nobody could construe from reading my published works the sort of person I then was. I was very hostile and angry in immediate ways with Tillyard, and very rude to him. The aggression was all from my side. Tillyard was not an aggressive man, and he did absolutely nothing against me, which he could easily have done. I just met a total incomprehension and sense of put-down. There was no one in the faculty then who could have spoken to my problems. Leavis would probably have responded much more angrily to my notion of how novels should be judged, although he might have answered in terms nearer to the language of objection.

So it was a total mess of a situation. At the same time it did seem pretty irrelevant. Because you knew that you were going into the army in a few months and it seemed improbable that anything would eventuate from all this in any case. I have also got to say that it was a time of quite extraordinary personal and emotional disorder. The last term of that year was really pretty horrible in a way. I was continually reminded of myself in the casualties of the contradictions and struggles of the sixties. In May–June 1941 I was one like that. It was a very sharp difference from my mood before that. I did not have anything as definable as a breakdown, but the situation was more than I could handle.

The whole crisis had an important bearing on my attitude when I returned to academic work in 1945. People often ask me now why I didn't carry on then from the Marxist arguments of the thirties. The reason is that I felt they had led me into an impasse. I had become convinced that their answers did not meet the questions, and that I had got to be prepared to meet the professional objections. I was damned well going to do it properly this time.

What exactly were the reasons why you left the Communist Party in 1941?

There is something I don't fully understand here myself. I did not resign. It was much more that I lapsed then I left. When I went into the army I was no longer a member of the Communist Party. It must have been connected with the tensions of my second year in Cambridge, or otherwise as someone who had not resigned from the Party I would surely have been given contacts as a member moving elsewhere. Yet I never consciously decided to leave the party, or resigned from it. I was conscious in 1945 that I would not rejoin it.

It seems very surprising that you became distant from the Party at that particular time. For most people on the left would surely have felt a very urgent reconnection with it. You took your exams in June 1941 and were called up in July. But June was the month of the German invasion of Russia. The whole political character of the War was genuinely transformed. It became a quite different sort of historical conflict.

Right. But Party policy was precisely defined in terms of production and military effort after the invasion of Russia. So it was totally compatible with what I was doing, going into the army. I am not sure what level of Party organization existed in the army, if any – I never encountered one. At all events, I had no problems with the new line. I had already decided in the winter of 1940, before the invasion of France, that I would join up. Naturally I was very conscious of the changed political character of the War in the summer of 1941. But it seemed to come together with what I was intending to do anyway.

It still seems somewhat of a mystery. There was a large downturn in the membership and morale of the CPGB after the outbreak of hostilities in September 1939, because of its opposition to the War as conflict between German and Anglo-French imperialism. Then there was a dramatic recovery and upswing after the invasion of the USSR, and the Soviet entry into the War. The maximum recruitment in the Party's history was around Stalingrad. Your affiliation was quite firm to the Party throughout the nadir of its fortunes, yet when Russia took the overwhelming brunt of the fighting and defeated Nazi Germany, you ceased to be a Communist.

No, no. I would not have said that I ceased to be a Communist. I don't fully understand this myself. But when we invaded France in 1944, I very consciously carried a map of the whole of Europe together with my ordinary battle maps, and my whole sense of the fighting was that this was a common struggle with the Red Army. My absence from the Party in England involved absolutely no change in my political positions. What I did feel, I think, was that I had moved beyond the peculiar social milieu of Cambridge Communism – it was not my world.

Yes, but it was obviously not a microcosm of the whole of the British Communist Party – with its overwhelmingly working-class membership and proletarian leadership. There was a far wider organization outside the university enclave. Contemporaries of yours at Cambridge like Edward Thompson or Eric Hobsbawm were in the war and went on being Communists.

Well, comically enough, within a month of being commissioned in the army I was told by my colonel to organize a current affairs meeting for a sergeant from the education corps, called Hobsbawm. When we met we talked together in just the same way as when we were in the Party at Cambridge. I ran into him again in Normandy. We discussed the War and our political positions were still the same. In my case, it was never suggested to me that it was possible to maintain active Party membership in the army. It may have been to others but it was certainly never explained to me what the modalities of this were. Remember that I was in a fighting unit – we were continually on the move from camp to camp, always away from cities. The opportunity for any kind of political activity never arose. But I saw the whole course and character of the War, from the invasion of Russia to the fall of Berlin, in precisely the way a Party member did.

3. War

Could you say something about what impact the army had on you? First of all in terms of milieu and ranking – you quite rapidly became an officer in the Guards Armoured Division?

All undergraduates at that stage of the War were being directed into the signal corps, where there had to be very rapid training in a moderately difficult skill. So I went to the signals training camp, where half of us were students. But because there was not much active fighting at that point they switched me – I was given some choice – to artillery and anti-tank weapons. I ended up commissioned in a tank unit of an artillery regiment within the Guards Armoured Division, which was primarily formed of regiments of tanks and household cavalry. We were then a support unit to a lot of different regiments, commanded by the classic type of Guards officers. But in our self-propelled tank guns, you were not a traditional officer commanding thirty people, but one of a crew of five in a tank with three other tanks under your control. You all had technical jobs to do. So the immediate social relations were not so hierarchical. Relations with the Guards officers themselves were much more difficult.

How did your image of the English ruling class as fumbling and antiquated fare in the War?

There was a general sense in which one raged at the apparent incompetence of it all. Incredibly, when we went into Normandy in '44 we had only a very few heavy guns that could knock out the two main German tanks, whereas they had guns that could knock out ours. Within a failure as massive as that, you saw a number of very brave and dashing people. But it was a campaign for which nobody knew the tactics. There were commanders experienced in the mobility of desert warfare, where new armoured tactics had evolved, but the Bocage was a crazy landscape for tank battles. A few units, including ours, had a gun that would knock the enemy out if you got close enough, but then our armour was not thick enough to get that close. If you were moving through wooded lanes and fields you'd be quite as likely to find the enemy behind you or come on to them round the corner. In that country, there was no possibility of tank mobility or long-range manoeuvre, although it started out on the maps and battle plans that way. In practice, you would find that the farmhouse supposed to be held by your neighbouring unit, where you went across to get the milk from, was occupied by Germans. I don't think the intricate chaos of that Normandy fighting has ever been recorded. Everyone was mixed up, in front and behind each other, with all the time an appalling level of casualties. In one major offensive we were bombed by our own planes before we started. Virtually every day during the Normandy fighting we would see tanks like our own going up. That was the constant fear you lived with, confined within this little metal interior of the tank surrounded by hundreds of rounds of high explosive ammunition and a considerable quantity of diesel fuel. If you got hit it was instant. I don't think that the situation would ever wholly have resolved itself, if it had not been that by sheer preponderance, as the Allied invasion built up, the Americans got round the back and the Germans had to pull out.

In that kind of fighting, what could you feel? You did not even know at times whether you were firing at your own troops or at others. Those were some of the worst experiences. Then on other occasions even the enemy lacked identity. Once a big attack was launched: we went in and made very substantial progress – when we looked around we had taken hundreds of prisoners. But they were Ukrainians and a whole mixture of other nationalities – there was hardly a German among them. This was a German tactic: they would put these troops in front and you would make six miles' progress. Then the German units would be waiting for you much better armed. Some of these prisoners did not even know which country they were in. They really did not know who they were fighting. The only time I felt anything like the clear political meaning that could be subsequently assigned to the War was when we discovered that two SS Panzer divisions had been sent from Germany for a local counter-offensive. There was a pitched battle, which was the one episode where I was acutely politically conscious of the outcome. For the rest, I used to go back to my map of Europe and listen to the radio news that the Red Army had taken Kharkov or Minsk. The Russian front was a positive relief because it seemed comprehensible.

Did you lose any tanks under your own command?

I lost two in that particular battle against the SS. I was actually overruled. I was told that I must occupy a wood which had a small railway line going through it, which I said was ludicrous because in a wood you can't see any more. You can't hear anything in these damn tanks because you have got to wear your helmet with the radiophones, to keep communication. The noise of the engines is very high, so you are totally dependent on sight. When we were ordered into the wood I divided the unit into two pairs, my pair going to one end and the other to the other end of the wood – that was the only way to do it. They never came back. Since we were subsequently withdrawn and put somewhere else, I never knew what happened to them. We went on calling and calling on the wireless trying to establish contact and not getting it. There was an extraordinary temptation to get out and look, but the entire wood was being shelled and there was no chance of that. Meanwhile we had destroyed probably one, perhaps two, SS tanks.

What was the overall effect of the experience of the War on you?

It was appalling. I don't think anybody really ever gets over it. First there is the guilt: about moments of cowardice, but also about moments of pure aggression and brutality. Are those really opposites? It is easy enough to feel guilty about when you felt frightened but much worse is the guilt once you've started recovering your full human perspective, which is radically reduced by the whole experience of fighting. Then you realize some of the things that you've done – not what others have done: if some farm had sheltered German tanks and had not come to tell us, you'd say shoot the bastards up and with a few rounds you could easily burn the whole barn. Reactions like that were frequent during fighting, but once you've recovered a full perspective the whole thing seems unbelievably bloody. This was a time when I was reading Tolstoy and he was absolutely right about what fighting is like, how unlike the military history of battles it is. There was also a dreadful sense of loss. If you have seen a tank with people you know in it go up, you never forget it. The Normandy battlefield was after all for some weeks relatively static, so that there were dead men and animals all over it. It was frightful. After we broke out from Normandy there were some bad times, but never again the same peculiar oppression and confusion.

Throughout, there was the difficulty of sustaining a perspective. There was something pathetic about the way I would go back to my atlas map of Europe and say: 'This is what is happening'. Although that was the correct perspective, it was so distant from our experience. In France, it was good that I could speak reasonable colloquial French, so I had to do all the negotiations with the local people and they were very welcoming. It was good in the sense that politically you were reminded what the War was all about. But otherwise an army functions so much as a true machine – the whole point of the training, although you don't realize it, is precisely to be able to do all these actions without being immediately motivated. You do in a battle what you did in an exercise, with of course much more chaos. What you lose is the most significant dimension to humanity – it is a commonplace about war, but is an absolute truth. You do function on a fighting animal level. I do not think that you ever sort it out afterwards. The first time I was able to look at an army unit with any feeling other than extreme scepticism and revulsion was when I was later in Yugoslavia. When I looked at the Yugoslav army I felt oddly like I might have felt in '44, that these were people who were doing something that I understood.

What was your impression of the fall of Germany itself?

When we got into Germany, we liberated one of the smaller concentration camps which was then used to detain SS officers. That was satisfying – we had after all played some significant part in the political victory over fascism. But that satisfaction was soon cancelled. The SS officers would come up to me and say: 'Why did we ever get into this ridiculous war with each other, when it is so clear who the common enemy is?' By this time the Russians were in Berlin. I reported this back to my superiors, and was told: 'They could be right, old boy.' Many of them already thought that the Wehrmacht was a fine army, and that the War had probably been a mistake. An assimilation to the perspectives of what was to be the Cold War had started as early as March 1945.

You weren't shaken by the stories of outrages by Russian troops which were widely used to create those perspectives?

No. I can imagine somebody in Intelligence, for example, would have been more shocked by them. By that time, quite honestly, we had been brutalized – you cannot fight for nine months through strange country without acquiring a totally different attitude to human suffering. The front line unit does not feel, it cannot have humane responses. One wishes that this was so but it does not have them. We were tough when we took prisoners, I don't think excessively, but we were certainly not all gentlemen together after the tournament. We were very angry with the SS officers and there were plenty of people quite willing to shoot them. When we went to take over Hamburg I was shaken because I had been told it was military targets and docks that had been bombed, and you could see quite clearly that there had been saturation bombing of the city. That shocked me, however, mainly because I had been lied to. The conduct of Russian troops in East Germany did damage to the Soviet Union throughout Europe. But in my peculiar situation I was insulated from it at the time.

At the end of the War you became the editor of a regimental newspaper, where you presumably had to comment on world affairs. Was that a resumption of your political activity? What did you find yourself editing and writing?

I edited a fairly normal *Daily Mirror* style of army newspaper north of Hamburg, where there was an intact printing press. There was sport and regimental news and pin-ups, and a lot of comic news material. I wrote a weekly political commentary with the pseudonym of Michael Pope. There was a lot of trouble when I attacked a proposal for a joint British-German war memorial service in the town after the armistice. I said this was total hypocrisy. I also wrote an article on the reports of Russian atrocities, in which I argued that many of them were probably true but that they were clearly separable from the nature of world Communism. That provoked many hostile letters. I was not sure afterwards whether this was not a somewhat abstract distinction. But it was my position at the time.

What was the atmosphere like in the army then? In '45 it effectively voted against Churchill, its real commander. What was the meaning of the vote, in the ranks?

It was a vote for a job. This is how most people talked about it. They associated the Tories with unemployment and depression. People knew what had happened when the army went back after 1918. There were a few Liberals, but hardly any Tories in our regiment. Of course, across in the Guards regiments the officer corps would have been Tory. Carrington, the Conservative Lord, was one of them. I realized recently, hearing him talk on the radio, that we must have fought together in the same operation, trying to break through to Arnhem.

How were you released to return to England? Was it a military instruction to go back to Cambridge?

It was a specific release. They decided in the demobilization programme that students whose courses had been interrupted would get what was called Class B release, which meant that you went ahead of your turn in the queue. That happened when I was still expecting to be sent to Burma.

4. Cambridge Again

You've written that when you got back to Cambridge after the War, you found it completely changed. In what ways?

The student culture had altered. There was a lot more religion about. There was also now a specific literary culture around Leavis, which was poles removed from what we had known in '41. There was really no longer a conscious left presence. The first person I met again whom I knew was Eric Hobsbawm. We agreed that we were in a different world.

The Labour victory of 1945 is normally represented as the product of a tremendous wave of radicalization in British culture and politics. Yet the impression given by your own accounts is that you actually came back to a more right-wing Cambridge. Are you suggesting that this was reflected in a much more rightist culture or atmosphere generally, throughout the country?

No. The movement to the right was specific to English intellectuals. At the national-political level my own view is that what had happened was not so much a really major Labour advance, although there had been a significant one, as a major Conservative collapse. If you look at the voting figures, the '45 election saw neither the highest post-war nor the highest Labour vote ever. There was a much bigger Labour vote in '50 and '51. But in '45 there was a very low Tory vote. On the other hand, the mood of the intelligentsia went in just the opposite direction, away from the left and from the climate of the thirties.

From your writings, it appears that you felt that on returning to Cambridge you did not want to get involved in student politics again – after all by then you were a grown man, in a sense that you weren't in 1939–41. You've also said that you were very strongly motivated to repair the earlier errors you felt you had made at the university. What were your main intentions and aims now?

I took up academic work quite fanatically. I had come back quite late; it was in effect already November when I arrived. My more general priority was a certain notion of cultural politics.

You speak in your essay 'My Cambridge' of the strange intensity of the Tripos that you finally did. What were you actually working on and writing about within English studies?

Essentially two subjects. Because I was ex-service, I could take a route through the Tripos which was more satisfactory – writing a fifteen thousand word thesis. I did mine on Ibsen. Then I also did the special paper on George Eliot. Nearly all my time was given to those – the rest was just hurriedly done at the end.

My work on George Eliot was a way of resuming my unfinished arguments about the novel. In fact I did a comparison of Eliot and Lawrence in the paper. You can find the results nearly word for word in the chapter of prose analysis in *Reading and Criticism*, where I take two passages from Eliot and two passages from Lawrence and counter-compare them in a slightly anti-*Scrutiny* fashion, since I argue you cannot deduce the quality of a writer from the analysis of a selected passage since the four passages are mutually contradictory: if you run one pair, George Eliot appears a better writer, and if you run the other pair, Lawrence emerges as the better writer. I then tried, not very eloquently, to relate that to their respective situations. For me, this was real progress over the state of the argument in 1941. Putting all this down in the ludicrous conditions of an examination seemed very important at the time. Yet it did not resolve the real problems.

The paper on Ibsen took much more of my attention. By then Ibsen was a standard author in the tragedy paper. I got totally and (in academic terms) quite unreasonably preoccupied with him. It was a very long involvement. The interpretation of Ibsen which I developed during that year I still in part hold today. The chapter on Ibsen in *Drama From Ibsen to Brecht* is that work. The reason for the intense significance that Ibsen possessed for me then was that he was the author who spoke nearest to my sense of my own condition at the time. Hence the particular emphasis I gave to the motif of coming 'to a tight place where you stick fast. There is no going forward or backward'.[1] That was exactly my sensation. The

[1] From *When We Dead Awaken*: See DIE, p. 106; DIB, pp. 73–4.

theme of my analysis of Ibsen is that although everybody is defeated in his work, the defeat never cancels the validity of the impulse that moved him; yet that the defeat has occurred is also crucial. The specific blockage does not involve – this was my dispute with other interpretations – renunciation of the original impulse. I think this was how I saw the fate of the impulse of the late thirties – an impulse that was not just personal but general. It had been right, but it had been defeated; yet the defeat did not cancel it. Today I would add a dimension to that analysis of Ibsen: for his goal is always one of individual liberation: he angrily excludes the project of social liberation.

More or less as you argue in Modern Tragedy?

That's right. *Modern Tragedy* was a correction of my earlier position and a criticism of what I call liberal tragedy. But at an earlier stage Ibsen reflected my situation. That protected me from the rapid retreat from the thirties which so many former comrades from the Party were conducting: that our whole outlook had been wrong, that we were not aware of original sin. This is why it was very important to argue in the analysis of Ibsen that he is not a dramatist of original sin or disenchantment, which was the conventional interpretation. In his plays, the experience of defeat does not diminish the value of the fight. That was precisely the personal 'structure of feeling' within which I lived from '45 to '51 at the deepest level.

You felt that the hope of a kind of fusion of your personal work as a writer with the general activities of a political militant in the thirties had been frustrated – hence you were in a situation like that which is at the centre of Ibsen's work?

Yes. My project of 1939–40, as I defined it to myself and tried to live it, had been confident and unproblematic. It now seemed incredibly problematic. It was in that context that certain themes in Ibsen affected me very strongly: the insistence on vocation, the concern with death, the idea that in the process of composition towards a project you accumulate from an environment that is not of your will or choice traits which frustrate the vocation. These themes were all related to my own preoccupations. I think that it was from that time that a quite different personality emerged, very unlike my earlier self. I became much more qualifying and anxious and careful, always stressing complexities and difficulties – all the characteristics of which people were later to complain. They were the absolute reverse of what I was in 1940.

How did you conceive your future after you had taken your final examinations? Did you consider the conventional option of going on to do a thesis?

No. There were two reasons for that. The work for the Tripos had been obsessive. It is unreasonable to put that amount of emotion into academic work: it is not worth that degree of commitment. But it was also in my mind that I had to work anyway, because we now had a daughter, born while I was in Normandy, and in September 1946 a son. You could say I had to support them, but in real terms, after the various crises, it was much more that they supported me. Trinity offered me a senior scholarship at £200 a year for three years, but the adult education job I saw advertised at Oxford paid £300 a year. So a financial factor came into it.

But the main reason was that I could not see the point. I was quite clear now that I'd got a hell of a lot of writing to do and I really wanted to get on with it. I particularly wanted to write a novel. It may sound odd in relation to the sense of being deeply blocked that I was describing, but I was still attempting to maintain the productive cultural emphasis of the thirties. Then I and my friends Wolf Mankowitz and Clifford Collins were going to run a journal – we were convinced we were going to be able to build up a periodical and a press. One of the other things that I was going to do was to write a documentary script for Michael Orrom who was by then an assistant director with Rotha. So we were going to make a film. We were going to start a magazine. These seemed much more exciting projects than doing a thesis. The shape of the immediate years was that one would take WEA classes to support oneself through them.

5. Politics and Letters

Could we now focus on Politics and Letters? *What were its origins? How did the idea of the journal germinate during your second period at Cambridge?*

I met Mankowitz and Collins by accident soon after I arrived – they were doing English like myself. We spent a fair amount of time in discussions together, which were in fact preparatory for the journal afterwards. Our intention was to produce a review that would, approximately, unite radical left politics with Leavisite literary criticism. We were to be left of the Labour party, but at a distance from the CP. Our affiliation to *Scrutiny* was guarded, but it was nevertheless quite a strong one.

That formulation raises two sets of questions. Firstly, why hadn't you rejoined the Communist Party after the War? Didn't any of your former comrades – say, Eric Hobsbawm or Edward Thompson – try to persuade you to do so? How did you now define your relationship to the Party?

When I got back in 1945, the Party was telling people that this was a period of social unity and reconstruction. Its attitude towards strikes was a very doubtful one. So there didn't seem to be any immediate cause to join again. Edward was in a different year, and I never really knew him. I did have discussions with Eric, but by now my commitment was really to a new cultural politics. We felt that Communist literary intellectuals did not understand much that we did. We felt that we could be more open and critical on the controversies of the day than the CP. But politically we remained very radical. I remember that Mankowitz and I attacked Tom Driberg fiercely at a meeting in his Essex constituency for what we thought was his ambiguous position on the closed shop. He said it had certain practical advantages. We said it was an absolute and fundamental discipline, to which he replied angrily: 'Are you members of the Labour Party?' We simply turned that evasion aside. I know this is very difficult to explain, but there was a moment when we were convinced that we were the most radical element in the culture. We were sure of this. We knew we were to the left of the Labour Party, and we regarded the British Communist Party as irrelevant because of the intellectual errors it had made .This was a confidence without a lot of basis and it did not last.

The second question, then, that your account raises is the nature of your affiliation to Scrutiny. *What was it in Leavis that attracted you or seized your imagination? How would you describe the extent of his influence over you in these years?*

The immense attraction of Leavis lay in his cultural radicalism, quite clearly. That may seem a problematic description today, but not at the time. It was the range of Leavis's attacks on academicism, on Bloomsbury, on metropolitan literary culture, on the commercial press, on advertising, that first took me. You must also allow for the sheer tone of critical irritation, which was very congenial to our mood.

Secondly, within literary studies themselves there was the discovery of practical criticism. That was intoxicating, something I cannot describe too strongly. Especially if you were as discontented as I then was. I said intoxication, which is a simultaneous condition of elation, excitement and loss of measure and intelligence. Yes, it was all those things, but let me put it on record that it was incredibly exciting. I still find it exciting, and at times I have positively to restrain myself from it because actually I can do it reasonably well, I think: I've taught it to other people. Today when I am writing about a novel, it is a procedure that comes very easily to me, but I try to refrain from using it. It always tends to become too dominant a mode, precisely because it evades both structural problems and in the end all questions of belief and ideology. But at the time we thought it was possible to combine this with what we intended to be a clear Socialist cultural position. In a way the idea was ludicrous, since Leavis's cultural position was being spelt out as precisely not that. But I suppose that was why we started our own review, rather than queueing up to become contributors to *Scrutiny*.

Finally, there was Leavis's great stress on education. He would always emphasize that there was an enormous educational job to be done. Of course, he defined it in his own terms. But the emphasis itself seemed completely right to me. When I heard of the possibility at Oxford – adult teaching of literature for the Workers' Educational Association – and Thomas Hodgkin, a communist, was secretary of the university committee who interviewed me, it seemed unbelievably lucky as a job. It was not to turn out so, but it seemed absolutely right. A lot of my subsequent work came out of that particular choice of jobs.

What would have been your reservations about Leavis at that time? Were there significant divergences?

I should explain that virtually all I heard of Leavis myself was at second-hand, from Mankowitz and Collins, who were regularly taught by him. They probably gave what he was saying a gloss that was closer to our outlook. I recollect one incident, however, which anticipated what was eventually to be my key disagreement with him. Mankowitz and I went to hear L. C. Knights give a talk on the meaning of 'neighbour' in Shakespeare. Leavis was leaning against the wall at the back of the room. When Knights said that nobody now can understand Shakespeare's meaning of neighbour, for in a corrupt mechanical civilization there are no neighbours, I got up and said I thought this was only differentially true; there were obviously successive kinds of community, and I knew perfectly well, from Wales, what neighbour meant. Mankowitz – that was characteristic of our relationship, which was very close – then attacked me bitterly for sentimental nonsense. Leavis was nodding approvingly while he was doing so.

The other major divergence was one I was much more conscious of at the time. That was the position given by Leavis to Eliot's later poetry. The *Four Quartets* completely dominated reading and discussion in Cambridge at the time. I did not succeed in articulating my rejection of the way in which they were being treated. But I recall coming out of one of these discussions, not with enemies but with friends who considered themselves active socialists and yet were endorsing Eliot's work. There must have been some radical lack of confidence in me that I didn't have the argument fully through with them. Instead I said to myself – a ridiculous expression that must have been some echo of an Eliot rhythm – 'here also the class struggle occurs'. Looking across at the university church and doing nothing about it. But my perception was itself a perfectly correct one. There was a class struggle occurring around those poems and that criticism. Because if you were to move into the world not just of Leavis's criticism, which contained radical, positive, energetic elements, but into the universe of the *Four Quartets*, then you were finished. You were then in the totally conventional post-war posture of the inevitability of failure, the absurdity of effort, the necessity of resignation –

Leavis himself never underwrote that, of course –

No, but that was what made for the curiosity of his whole dealing with Eliot and the *Four Quartets*. In a sense I admire him for trying to drive the Eliot and the Lawrence horses together. But no one can do that. You ought properly to get off both, but if you can't you cannot ride both. In a way it is the interest of Leavis – the thing that prevents the reduction of Leavis to the formula that was Leavisism – that he did try to ride these evidently incompatible mounts. It is what makes him a more complex character than the term Leavisism allows.

Moving to Politics and Letters *itself, how was the journal actually set up?*

We took an office in Noel Street in Soho, where we had our editorial meetings. The two reviews – *The Critic* was the companion journal – and other smaller things were published by us from there. But at this time Collins was still in Cambridge, Mankowitz was out in Essex and I was down in Sussex. We had one advantage in that as an ex-serviceman I qualified for a special allocation of paper, which was still rationed. Given the scarcity of reading matter after the War, we were sure we could make the venture viable because of that – for example, Smith's took the first issue of *The Critic* and put it on railway bookstalls, where they sold about half their order. Editorially, Mankowitz did the hardest work. He and Collins were old friends – there was always a slightly asymmetrical relation in that they would come for a weekend and plan the magazine and write things together, while I would get to the office less often.

What sort of audience were you aiming for? Did you have a specific circulation in mind when you launched the journals?

We wanted to sell 1,500–2,000 copies. We got perhaps some 500 subscriptions before they came out. The readership we hoped would extend from people still in the Communist Party to those who were in the orbit of Leavis. But increasingly what for me became the decisive world was adult education. Virtually every WEA tutor was a Socialist of one colour or another. We were all doing adult education ourselves. So we saw the journals as linked to this very hopeful formation with a national network of connection to the working-class movement. If there was a group to which *Politics and Letters* referred, it was adult education tutors and their students.

What exactly were the relations between the Scrutiny *group itself and* Politics and Letters? *Quantitatively, the weight of the former is striking – nine contributors, ten including Mankowitz, in four issues. There was a synoptic apology for* Scrutiny *by Mason, with a follow-up by Q. D. Leavis. Did you have personal contacts with any of these people? Did you solicit or did they offer articles?*

I only knew one or two, and them not well. The articles were solicited by Mankowitz and Collins. Probably most of the actual contributions were organized by Collins, who was still in Cambridge. My relation to the Leavis circle was almost entirely through them. My connection with it was real, but a displaced one. We were all, however, very anxious to see what Leavis would say about *us*. Because after all he never said anything good about a contemporary phenomenon. Mankowitz got him to write in *Politics and Letters*. What he said, with great tact, was that we would succeed if we lived up to a series of objectives that amounted to a description of *Scrutiny*.

How did you select your other contributors? Did you aim for editorial unity and consistency as far as possible, or not?

No. We were determined to have an open review. For example, we adopted the principle – I don't know that we always followed it – of antagonistic reviews. We were against supportive reviewing, which we thought characteristic of the London magazines. So that even if we thought a criticism wrong, like Taplin's article on Joyce – which I thought was ludicrous – we would still publish it. We were fairly deliberately running an open magazine. Hence the appearance of incompatibilities and inconsistencies in the journal. Our notion of a political commentary was that we would solicit one in each issue from a different point of view. Mind you, the first person we asked was Henry Collins, who was a Communist. But our general practice was a reaction against both the Party press and *Scrutiny*, which was now becoming a very tight magazine – strangely reminiscent in its way of party journals, with its sense of a line and of degrees of initiation into an inner circle.

You could get any contributor you wanted?

People were surprisingly willing. Orwell, who was then riding high on the success of *Animal Farm*, although now getting really ill, gave us his 'Writer and Leviathan' essay. Then when Collins went to see him in hospital he actually handed over the manuscript of his essay on Gissing and said: 'You are very welcome to this.' By the time it should have appeared the magazine had folded (incidentally inducing a dreadful moment since for quite a long time that essay on Gissing, which Orwell was naturally very anxious to get back, was lost: it eventually turned up under a pile of somebody's old papers). Equally, we had no difficulty in publishing translations of Sartre, for example.

The journal was launched in a specific political conjuncture: the first years of the post-war Labour government. We've talked so far mainly about 'letters'. What was your attitude towards the 'politics' of the time? How did you assess the development of the Attlee administration? Earlier, speaking of the Labour vote in 1945, you said very coolly: it was just jobs. Did you yourself have very limited and pragmatic expectations of the Labour government from the outset?

No. I reacted with enthusiasm, with a sense that a real historical break had occurred. In some ways that lasted longer, even into the fifties, than the political judgments I was making warranted. The two turning-points for me in the period of *Politics and Letters* were, I think, the acceptance of the American loan in late '45 and then the fuel crisis of the winter of '46–7. I remember feeling it was a crucial decision whether or not the American loan was taken. When it was accepted and the post-war monetary order was set down, I felt that the whole prospect of democratization after the War, with the collapse of the right at the political level, was now compromised: something vital was being lost. When I argued that we should have refused the US loan, this was generally regarded – even on the left – as wild idealism. Even Marxist economists said that it was impossible to inflict on the working class and the demobilized army the kind of extreme austerity which that would have involved. I still don't know whether rejection was anything more than a utopian notion. But in my view the loan and then the Marshall Plan rendered a Labour adaptation to the American version of the world inevitable. The second watershed, I think was the great fuel crisis of the winter of '46–7. The government then had the option of either going very hard for a life of common sharing, amidst the shortages, or of turning against the working class and exhorting it to 'produce to save the nation'. When it took the latter path, it seemed to me that henceforward the remaining reforms of the Labour government would be no more than residues of its initial impetus. Much earlier than I could easily have believed, it was becoming an objectively quite reactionary government. Very soon they were sending troops in to break the dock strike.

I had some direct involvement in the effect of its policies, towards both the working class and towards its intellectuals. When the railways were nationalized, I would talk to my father about the consequences of this move. Within six months he, who had always wanted it, was bitterly against the bureaucratic character of the new structure. It seemed to him the substitution of one kind of directorial board for another. He said that the immediate work discipline actually became harsher. The way he put it: 'There used to be one inspector, now there are two.' For myself, I worked on a film script of a documentary history of the agricultural and industrial revolutions, for Paul Rotha. Then we went to a meeting at the Central Office of Information, which financed these films, and they immediately started putting wholly unacceptable conditions on it. Instead of this big, ambitious project they were quite interested in something that would be a short introduction to a film about post-war reconstruction. It was an extraordinary scene. When these conditions had been put, Rotha – who was still a very confident person, who felt himself experienced and powerful – got up and walked, as I thought, to get something from his jacket which was hanging on the door of the office. In fact he put on his jacket and walked out. We were left there. We realized after a while that this meant the end of the discussion. In fact, it proved the end of the project. Quite soon Harold Wilson was at the Board of Trade, a really ominous figure. Then, as later, he really could never see these problems as social and cultural, but as organizational and financial. If you look, you will see that I was already attacking him in *Politics and Letters.*

When someone starts a literary-political review which is an organized intervention in the cultural and political life of society, they must – expressly or tacitly – have a general map in their mind of the array of forces that confronts them. You have described very clearly what you thought the constituency of Politics and Letters *was – above all, people in adult education of your own age, in their early twenties. That was the new generation and you felt the force of it behind you. But what was in front of you? In particular, how did you perceive the bulk of the established intelligentsia, people who had already made a public name for themselves? You've traced your own attitude to the Labour government. But one critical zone of your intervention would surely have been the inter-relations between the political regime of the time and the main ranks of the English intelligentsia. What was your orientation towards the latter?*

I think the simplest way of defining this is to say our principal enemy was *Horizon*. That was the object of an ambiguous dislike, because it essentially represented the continuation of a pre-war literary culture simultaneously opposed by Marxists as bourgeois and by Leavis as a fashionable metropolitan phenomenon. Connolly symbolized a self-indulgent decadence for us, which made him an obvious target for attack. The peculiar tone of much thirties culture – descended from the Bloomsbury ethos – found its final expression in this magazine of the forties: above all, an extreme subjectivism, projecting personal difficulties of being a writer as central social problems. These people could profess sympathy for the Labour government, but it was in bad faith. For their whole emphasis was how difficult it was to be a cultivated man in a period of extreme poverty and dislocation. Whether or not they still said they voted Labour was much less significant than the fact that they were trying to say it was more important for us to live the cultivated life than for this country to persist in its own terms. If it was going to persist in its own terms, in its own best terms shall we say, the road was going to be very hard and involve a continuation of the supportive popular discipline and self-discipline of the War. Connolly's response was just the opposite – it was the begging-bowl. He wrote an editorial appealing to American friends to fund the British cultural enterprise. This was precisely the direction being taken by the Labour government with its US loan at the time. I attacked Connolly with ferocity in *Politics and Letters*.

His wish came true, of course. The successor to Horizon *was financed by American espionage* – Encounter.

Yes. That was the Cold War sequel in the fifties. Connolly's own affiliations were probably still with the left. So in his appeal for American money to go on being a writer, there was an element of continuity with what we saw as the false pact of the writer and the revolution in the thirties. I have argued this often enough since. There is a sense in which a significant number of left writers of the thirties were saying: we must have a revolution so that we can write our poems. When you read it in detail, that is really what Edward Upward's trilogy *The Spiral Ascent* is about. Not to speak of intellectuals like Auden who had found more convenient ways of being poets, by going to California. I had intense hostility to that sort of self-regarding literary culture.

In general, there is a combativeness in *Politics and Letters* which disappears from a lot of my later work. There are about four people that I really went for. They give a good indication of where we stood at the time. One was Connolly in *Horizon*, one was Noel Coward, one was Rebecca West for *The Meaning of Treason* (that was very angry), and the other was John Lewis for his contribution to the Zoschenko controversy in the *Modern Quarterly*. The latter polemic was very important. For while magazines on the right like *Horizon* were telling us how difficult it was to be a cultured person in the new environment, the rhetoric of Zhdanovism was appearing to outflank us in a caricatural way on the left. Zhdanov was precisely telling people to stop minding their little souls and to get on with the tough job of Communist construction, as a licence for the actual repression of writers in Russia. So it was very important for me to attack and repudiate that too.

What were your own alternative cultural perspectives?

I thought that the Labour government had a choice: either for reconstruction of the cultural field in capitalist terms, or for funding institutions of popular education and popular culture that could have withstood the political campaigns in the bourgeois press that were already gathering momentum. In fact, there was a rapid option for conventional capitalist priorities – the refusal to finance the documentary film movement was an example. I still believe that the failure to fund the working-class movement culturally when the channels of popular education and popular culture were there in the forties became a key factor in the very quick disintegration of Labour's position in the fifties. I don't think you can understand the projects of the New Left in the late fifties unless you realize that people like Edward Thompson and myself, for all our differences, were positing the re-creation of that kind of union. Perhaps by that date it was no longer available. But our perspective seemed to us a reasonable one, even though it would have been very hard to achieve. At any rate that was the context in which we saw *Politics and Letters.*

You've said that the contradiction between these two poles would sooner or later have been untenable, that the idea of their union was foredoomed. Was that why Politics and Letters *closed in 1948?*

Not really. There were serious practical difficulties. We had hardly any working capital and there was the usual problem of late bookshop payments. But in that last year there were also increasing personal strains between the editors. It's hard to talk about that, after thirty years, but as I remember we had no quarrels about editorial policy. The decisive and concluding disagreement was in fact on a business matter. But we were all changing, Mankowitz and I especially. Probably Collins held us together, and it's worth saying, as Mankowitz and I have published so much since, that Collins at that time was the clearest of us about the need for *Politics and Letters*, a need which we constantly explored since he now often stayed in my house after taking adult classes. Then he and I planned a joint book, *English for Adults*, but sadly, through a complicated sequence of difficulties and misunderstandings, it didn't work out. Finally I wrote the book alone, rather differently, as *Reading and Criticism.* The effects of that episode interacted with the problems of the journal, though Collins and I later resumed our friendship, which stayed close for a number of years. However, in 1948, when all this came together, there was a formal break, and they tried to continue the journal without me, with another editor. But the financial difficulties remained and 1948 was a very bad, breaking year, quite generally. There must, under all this, have been deeper problems, of project and alignment, but if so it's interesting that they surfaced in these ways, and not as explicit differences about policy.

You've described how you attacked the irresponsibility of the Horizon *sector of the literary intelligentsia, its disaffiliation from the real political and social processes of post-war Britain. You also said that you thought the Labour government was moving in a similar direction in a much more serious way, with its international monetary arrangements. Did you publish consistent materials criticizing what the Labour government was actually doing in that period, to help orient your readers in the very confused conflicts of the time?*

No. When I look the review over, that was not there. We did criticize some episodes, but there was no sustained coverage. That is why I say that the project was wrongly conceived. The correct perspective was to try to help to build a very strong popular cultural mobilization to take part in a battle inside the Labour movement. But we still shared one illusion with precisely the position we were attacking. We thought we could do so simply by literary argument, by cultural discourse. That was the influence of Leavis, but the idea was shared by many others.

Wouldn't the kind of formation you were conjuring up within the Labour movement, adult education teachers and students, presuppose a directly political magazine in which the accent was at least as much on the politics as the letters – whereas in practice the proportions in Politics and Letters, *with its very generally* Scrutiny*-recruited critics, were heavily in the direction of letters rather than politics?*

I think that was partly a reflection of the spectrum of our own contributors. They were recruited from people who were reading and teaching literature, history, political theory, philosophy. There was a crucial absence of economists, when economics ought to have been the main battlefield. But this relates to a mistake only fully realized much later. There was an assumption, which was quite unjustified, that we knew what a left economic and political programme would be. The idea that we had a political programme can be more easily excused, because we did oppose the imperialistic adventures of the Labour government, and we did have some notion of popular political mobilization rather than increasingly distant representative government. But economically we had no answers at all. The lack of perspective over the American loan showed that. There was a simple kind of Left opposition, mainly in terms derived from

Russian fears and hostilities. But there was a crucial and continuing failure to carry the analysis through to the real problems of Britain, which was, after all, a gravely weakened capitalist economy, now in a social-democratic perspective trying to put through welfare reforms but at a basic level able only to define production for 'the nation'; in fact an autonomy which had both been lost in the war and which the new monetary arrangements were visibly undermining. The result, I'm afraid, was no consistent and coherent Left programme at all.

Did you declare editorially in Politics and Letters *that this was a Socialist journal?*

No.

The obvious point is: why not? Wasn't it the condition of an effective intervention vis-à-vis the Labour government, or even the formulation of a coherent and plain critique of Horizon, *that you should have declared your colours?*

Yes, I think you are right. The way the project defined itself limited and probably defeated it. The journal was designed for the new generation in the adult education movement. But its form was to be a critical review – this was the legacy of *Scrutiny* – that would be more significantly open in its range than its competitors. We thought that was more important than declaring a particular allegiance. Verbal commitments to Socialism, which at this time were often highly ambivalent, we were in any case cautious about. But I think it is also true that if we had declared our allegiance the alliance between left politics and Leavisite criticism would never have got off the ground.

It does often happen in a movement that people start out thinking they are associated and then they find they are not, not fully associated. In the end look at the different ways it broke. Collins retained most of Leavis's and Eliot's arguments, but was increasingly centred on Freudian and related ideas. Mankowitz, on the other hand, broke right away from the minority culture positions. He was already in effect a professional writer; I used to think he could write virtually anything. Beginning with that talent, he took his own material into the most popular forms: by the end of the fifties a film and a musical. Who can say, who can ever say whether these differences were always there between these three people? There ought to have been enough people who had enough in common to make such a journal. But so many people were reconstructing their lives after the War, and were caught in various situations, who is to know? If the intellectuals in the Communist Party had been moving towards our kind of project, as one could say many of them did in '56, they would have given it much more solidity on the political/economic/historical side. We were all literary people. I have just read Edward Thompson's paper on Caudwell, in which he describes the inner Party arguments about Caudwell in the late forties. My most immediate response was: 'Why weren't you writing this at the time in *Politics and Letters*?' There must have been many others like Edward. But they, of course, had a completely different perspective – they still thought that it was necessary to fight inside the Communist movement. The sort of formation that was necessary nearly occurred in '46–7. But it didn't happen.

What were your reactions to the closure of the journal?

The collapse of the periodical was a personal crisis for me. So many other initiatives, like the film, had also been blocked or failed. The experience confirmed the pattern of feeling I had found in Ibsen. For a period I was in such a state of fatigue and withdrawal that I stopped reading papers or listening to the news. At that point, apart from going on with the actual adult education teaching, I felt I could only write myself out of this in a non-collaborative way. I pulled back to do my own work. For the next ten years I wrote in nearly complete isolation.

6. Adult Education

What was your immediate working environment in the WEA?

When I got my job in the Extra-Mural Delegacy at Oxford, which controlled a scattered region extending from Staffordshire in the North to Sussex in the South, I was appointed to East Sussex, and went to live in Seaford. The social character of my classes was extremely mixed. At one level there was the class that I ran in Hastings, essentially with the local Trades Council, which was called Public Expression and simply involved specific training in public writing and public speaking. There seemed little point in teaching the writing of essays; I taught the writing of reports, minutes, memoranda, and committee speaking and oral reports – skills relevant to their work. At the other extreme you would get a class of commuter housewives at Haywards Heath who wanted to read some literature. Perfectly serious in their interest, but an entirely different social composition. Then I had a fair number in which there was a mixture of the two elements, including of course the substantial number of wage earners one discovers, who at the third or fourth meeting produce their novel or autobiography, short stories or poems – an enormous amount of unknown writing of this sort goes on. It was a mixture I could live with.

How do you judge in retrospect the whole nature of adult education, as you experienced it in practice over a decade?

I remember G.D.H. Cole, who was a university representative, saying at the meetings of the Delegacy: 'I am damned well not interested in adult education, I am interested in workers' education.' That was the conflict. He was a minority voice and he lost. Of course, some would say the battle had been fought and lost long before this. I don't think so myself, but I can see the way of writing the history which would make it out to be so. The adult education movement split before the First World War, with the famous Ruskin strike, between a consciously socialist-affiliated workers' education which eventually produced the National Council of Labour Colleges, and the Workers' Educational Association which attached itself to the universities, and tried – I think with more success than the NCLC said was possible – to develop a working-class education which would draw on the university claim of exploring all positions rather than teaching from an affiliated position. Today, when I read of the Ruskin strike and the foundation of *Plebs*, I think that the opponents of this WEA conception were right. They said: 'Do you suffer from class-consciousness? Come to Oxford and be cured.' They sensed that the universities would eventually incorporate the movement and that what would be taught in the name of academic standards and better learning would not be a socialist education. On the other hand there is no doubt that specifically class-affiliated education does in certain important respects run the risk of becoming subservient to particular party lines in particular periods, and genuinely losing some of its educational characteristics. The NCLC in certain areas was a more important working-class movement. In South Wales it produced far more educated militants than the WEA ever did. The WEA on the other hand tried to represent the notion of a distinct affiliation to a class which yet had to be mediated by a kind of education that made no presumptions – in Tawney's phrase you follow the argument where it leads. The balance between those two principles was still being fought out in the adult education movement in the forties, when I joined it. There is no question which eventually won and the reason was in the end a very crude one. The universities could financially sustain their version of adult education and were unwilling to sustain the alternative definition. But this does not mean, as some histories suggest, that it all ended in 1911; that the WEA was always a mere liberal or reformist diversion. For every time a class came up with working-class membership, and there were still many such, what they wanted was the original WEA form of education; although they did not want – and I think they were right – dogmatic instruction, being taken through any *Short Course*; they wanted an open orientation. I think we were affected by that. So the experience of the WEA was always very ambivalent for me.

Presumably the WEA differed from area to area. What was the character of the Oxford Delegacy?

There was an important radicalizing presence in North Staffordshire, a strongly working-class area. Together with Kent it made possible a miners' summer school. In Oxford itself, Thomas Hodgkin ran the department, with a very strong and principled conception of how to develop a popular working-class education. He believed that essentially the people to do it were committed socialists. He fought hard to say that tutors had the right, when it was relevant, to declare their position in the class, but to ensure within the open structure of the class that this position was always totally challengeable, naturally subject to opposition and discussion. That approach was attacked very bitterly, of course. The whole Delegacy was seen as a Communist cell. There was a violent assault on its whole organization and on Hodgkin in particular. Moreover, quite soon tutors were going out to West Africa and the Sudan – Hodgkin was an Africanist – practising this sort of education. So the Delegacy was perceived not simply as an internal conspiracy but as subversive externally. There was an extreme crisis within the institution during the late forties and early fifties. It was a sharp local form of the Cold War.

How did the conflict develop? What was your own role in it?

Well, of course I agreed that it would have been wholly wrong in classes not to declare your own position; and equally that you made no assumption at the beginning of the class that you shared anything else than an interest in the subject. You can see very easily the dangers one way, of teaching declining into a propaganda exercise. But in fact increasingly through the fifties the dangers were the opposite. For like all the other welfare services, the WEA started to become heavily used by the middle classes as a form of leisure and education. There was nothing wrong in this, except that in socially mixed communities they induced a quite different cultural atmosphere from that of the working-class student. You had to positively encourage specific working people's classes, organized round trade unions and so on. This was done. But all the time there was constant pressure from the university: you must improve academic standards, you must get written work, there must be no crossing of subject boundaries. As an adult tutor one lived on a very long lead. Living 100–150 miles away from Oxford, you had a hell of a lot of practical autonomy. Still, my syllabuses were constantly criticized on these grounds: of course a class in

English literature, but what is this other – including the first class in which I started discussing the themes of *Culture and Society?* What sort of class is this? The main spokesman for university standards was S.G. Raybould, who wrote various books on the subject. The effect was to tend to eliminate people without secondary education, since they found difficulty in producing that sort of written work. We tutors had to certify that such work was being produced in order to satisfy the conditions of the class to be approved and funded by the university and the Ministry. We replied, of course, that we were trying to create new standards of a different kind of work. The controversies, if anybody wants to look them up, are all there in the Adult Education *Highway* of the period – to which I contributed.

Over the years there in the end occurred a pretty successful conversion of the WEA into something that could be indifferently called Further Education: any other emphasis was deflected, except in certain specialized areas of trade union education. That only became totally clear to me when I moved to Oxford in 1960 as what was called a resident tutor, which was a kind of senior post. Immediately a plan was unfolded – it was quite explicit – to create a residential college in Wellington Square, whose focus would be on refresher courses for young graduates who had gone into industrial management, and so on. This was suddenly no longer the mixed situation I had lived in for fourteen years. When they moved to institutionalize these dreadful refresher courses for managers, then of course adult education ceased to have enough meaning. It was at that point that I knew that I wanted to move on. Though it happened quite unexpectedly. I got a letter saying I had been appointed a Lecturer in Cambridge, though I hadn't applied for it. But I was ready to go.

There is one question raised by your account that relates the WEA to Politics and Letters. *You've said that you took the position within the WEA, that as a teacher you would state your own views as a socialist but not impose these or assume that they were shared by your students. You would not, however, affect an unreal neutrality or suppression of your convictions. But in a way that is precisely what you did not do in* Politics and Letters. *It would have been quite possible for you to declare that this was a socialist journal, but on the other hand that it would publish any strong or valid objections from other points of view. You did not do so. What was the balance of considerations which led you to that presumably very central and conscious choice in '46–7, which you later changed in the WEA?*

I would be happier if I could say that it was conscious in *Politics and Letters*. I am not sure that it was not the unconscious process of the emerging terms of the collaboration between left politics and 'Leavisite' criticism. I think that the bad influence of the *Scrutiny* connection on us was to accredit the whole idea of the disinterested intelligence. You can see the way in which one could move from this free-floating concept of disinterested intelligence to the very much more defensible position of an essentially open style of intellectual work which nevertheless includes the non-dominative declaration of one's own position. It was the blurring of those two concepts that was responsible for the particular weakness of the journal. It took me a long time to sort them out – to see that the disinterested intelligence is a fantasy which is different from the much more viable and correct position which sounds so much like it. Or can sound like it. But I don't want to confuse my own later choices with the actual developments of adult education. The WEA had certain positives as against any closed internal propagandizing education. Yet in the end you cannot be financed and academically controlled by those kinds of universities, and carry out a programme of education of the working class. The WEA itself had the same ambiguity as the programme of *Politics and Letters*. There is no denying that.

Can we ask a more practical question about your actual working routines? Presumably during those years you must have read and written during the day and taught mainly in the evenings. Did you find that more advantageous for a writer than the typical teaching situation which would involve contact hours during the day and trying to read and write in the evening?

I don't know. All I can say is that it is the only regime I have ever been able to operate. If I had to do other work in the morning at all regularly I would probably start drying up. Adult education was actually physically a very wearing job; I felt that particularly later. The travelling in the evening, particularly in post-war conditions, on late buses and trains was very tiring. But it did mean that every morning I could write and every afternoon I could read, before leaving most evenings to teach. From '48, when I pulled back from most collaborative work, this was a routine of extraordinary regularity. It was also a process of self-education: it was only from '48 that I got any extensive knowledge of English literature. The selective three year course at Cambridge, particularly the way in which I had done it, had not given me that. I remember I used to put 50 or 75 per cent new literature into my teaching every year, so that I eventually knew I had gone through enough. These special conditions of work were very advantageous to me. But they meant that when I came back to Cambridge I adopted the very same routine and I still do – I could not now work in any other way.

7. The Fifties

You've said that you withdrew from any intellectual collaboration during this long period. But you were a contributor, even an editor, of Essays in Criticism *in the fifties. Bateson, when he created the journal, went out of his way to declare that it would publish Marxist essays, including contributions from the other side of the Iron Curtain. It was not a Cold War journal. You wrote in an editorial comment after you joined it that such university reviews could be central – against Eliot, who had just depreciated them. How significant was your subsequent relationship with* Essays in Criticism?

Bateson personally was a socialist and a genuine one. That was important. His project was also an open review – you see how the same structure kept repeating itself. With total good will, he looked around for people from a younger generation to bring on to the board. The way it then proceeded was that we could select from the list of articles submitted those we wanted to read. It often happened that I would send back very negative comments, and these were then perhaps relayed to the author, who eventually made some changes, or quite as often the article disappeared – there were plenty of others. In the meantime, I would get a copy of the magazine through the post, and dislike most of what was in it. I would tell Bateson, and he would reply: 'Why didn't you ask to see those articles?' That was fair enough. We were geographically scattered, so the whole direction of the journal was effectively always in Bateson's hands – quite rightly since he did most of the work. So my editorial membership of *Essays in Criticism* was very formal. It never turned into a real collaboration.

To me, the importance of the journal was much simpler. It was the one place where I could publish literary essays. I could write on Eliot, Orwell or Hoggart. It was through my essay 'The Idea of Culture' in it that I eventually got *Culture and Society* published at all. This was an intensely productive period for me: I was writing far more than I could find an outlet for. I now regret – it is one of the biggest regrets I have – that in the fifties the institutional set-up made the publication of literary criticism easier than anything else. I could publish in *Essays in Criticism*, I could publish certain things in *Highway*, but there was nowhere that I could publish political articles, and equally of the three or four novels that I wrote during that period only one, which kept on being reworked, ever got published. There was a big difference between what I was writing and what got published. I later felt that even the kind of literary criticism I was doing then had been a radical diversion. I had been determined by my time – I had not in any sense determined it. This was the last epoch of the dominance of literary criticism in English culture.

In retrospect, what Essays in Criticism *seems to have represented was the institutional absorption after the War of the so-called 'critical revolution' of the inter-war period, and the professionalization of what had previously always been a more or less oppositional movement within the academy. That would suggest a definite tension or ambiguity in your own intellectual relations with the journal. The formal programme of* Essays in Criticism *was to combine a historical approach to literature with critical 'standards'. But when Bateson talked about trying to develop a methodology for studying 'texts' and 'contexts', what he was essentially thinking of was a way of marrying traditional literary scholarship or literary history with the new discipline of 'judgment'. Whereas your own work on criticism and history was to be of a very different kind – involving a radical reconstruction of the whole object of study. Did that opposition become conscious in your dealings with* Essays in Criticism?

Yes, I certainly felt such a tension. At that time I was already working on problems that were later to surface in *The Country and the City*. In the course of attacking some articles submitted to *Essays in Criticism* on pastoral poetry, it became painfully clear to me – many people would say it never became clear to me, that I have still got it wrong – that I did not know what the particular traditions of pastoral were, historically. I understood pastoral just as falsely sentimental accounts of rural life, attached to the court. Bateson knew the huge tradition of classical, late medieval and Renaissance pastoral very well; rural writings were one of his major interests. The corrections he offered me I could not deny. There were many things I did not know, did not fully understand – in particular in the big area of classical literature, where I had done Latin but not Greek. So his literary scholarship was continually finding me out in ignorance. Bateson, even more than Tillyard had done, used to say to me: 'You simply are wrong, you have misunderstood this, you have not read that, you have used these technical terms inaccurately.' I think this is a very difficult moment for anybody trying to develop a new intellectual project, because you have to be able professionally to take on people who have a different perspective, and in doing so you can acquire certain characteristics of precisely that profession. I felt at the time that association with a professional organ was necessary for me, and that I had to be able to produce work that was valid in its terms. In the end I had read the texts and knew what most of the authorities said about them, and could show that they were wrong. The result of that process of learning and opposing the various English studies procedures is *The Country and the City*, particularly perhaps the chapters on the country-house poems.

You have explained your attitude to the Labour government in England from '45 to '51. But the period, of course, also and above all saw the onset of the Cold War throughout the world. What was your judgment of the development of the international working-class movement from '47 to '53? How did you respond to the major conflicts of that epoch?

The two big events which happened just after the end of *Politics and Letters* were the crisis in Czechoslovakia and the blockade of Berlin. That was in '48. At that time I was in the depths of my withdrawal, no longer reading newspapers or listening to the news. So I literally did not know they had happened till afterwards. Then I had consciously to read about them, in a way that is absurd for post-war events. The Berlin crisis never gelled in my mind very much. In the case of Czechoslovakia I rejected the orthodox account in the West of the change-over, which reduced it simply to an armed coup – I never accepted that version. Still, people who came back from Czechoslovakia reported that it was a very tough and repressive regime.

By '49, I was following events again, with a very different set of reactions. The event which seemed to me far the most important was the victory of the Chinese Revolution. It was the one development of the forties to which I strongly and unambiguously responded. Indeed, I remember being surprised that while people on the left were mostly glad of it, they on the whole gave it less attention than the main conflicts in Europe. Whereas I saw the Chinese Revolution as a decisive historical event, which had altered the whole shape of world politics. It was just the one good thing that had happened since the end of the War.

What was your reaction to the outbreak of the Korean conflict – the high point of the Cold War, which had direct domestic repercussions in England?

This was a crucial episode for me personally. So far as the way the war started was concerned, I did not believe what all my friends in the Party told me – that the South had invaded the North. But equally I did not believe the representation of the American and Western intervention as a United Nations crusade against the North Korean aggressor. I was extremely angry about it. The socio-political character of the conflict inside Korea was fairly clear. At the same time, the American army was obviously there to complete the US strategic position around China. The war in that sense was an extension of the conflict over the Chinese Revolution.

It soon became pretty obvious that it was only a matter of time before I would be recalled for service in Korea, as a reserve officer. My technical capacities and age meant I would be very early on the list. So I had to decide in a very practical sense what to do. At first the only way to refuse recall – which I had decided to do – was to go and refuse an order and then spend at least a month in prison. I arranged with Hodgkin to take that as my annual leave. Then, just in time, there was a new provision making it possible to go directly to a tribunal. But still everyone stressed that I should not lead with the politics. In fact the argument that I gave to the tribunal was that I would not again commit myself to a military organization in which my right to make choices was pre-empted by army discipline. There was a strong existentialist sub-note to it, the idea of a total retention of autonomy. But I meant it: my army experience was very recent. The whole nature of a military organization is such that whereas you may have at the beginning political notions of what the army is being trained to fight for, still, within the necessary functioning of this kind of hierarchical command structure, whatever you believe at the moment of initiation thereafter has no real existence at all: within a war you do not know what is evolving. I argued that these were moral grounds for objection to serving again in Korea. The tribunal accepted them. I was exempted because – the comedy of the situation! – I was heard by three presumably fair-minded civilians who after all had not been in the War, whereas I had: so they could not use any of the ordinary tactics of why shouldn't you serve your country too? The chairman was actually Pickard-Cambridge, the classical historian whom I had not heard of then, but whose work on the Greek theatre I later used in *Drama and Performance*. It was perfectly clear why they hardly troubled with what I was saying: somebody who had served through four years of the army at war had, they felt, a right to say he was not going to have any more. They took a very pragmatic line.

Suppose, as a hypothesis, you had gone along and said: 'I have no intention of serving in this war because my sympathies lie entirely with the liberation army of the North. This is a civil war and I hope they win', what would have been their reaction? Presumably they would have bundled you out of the room very quickly?

In fact, I had more or less exactly that exchange in an astonishing conversation on the telephone with the commanding officer of the unit to which I had been recalled, who had received the notification. In effect it was just that. I said: 'I would be no damn use to you, I'd be on the other side.' He totally lost his temper. Afterwards, they kicked me out of the army because I had committed the disgraceful act of objecting to my recall. I was deprived of my commission.

From March 1953 onwards, after the death of Stalin, the world Communist movement was shaken by a series of dramatic upheavals, of which the Hungarian Revolt of 1956 had the greatest general impact in the West. How did you view these events?

The death of Stalin itself was not of great significance to me, since I was not a member of the CP. By this time I had anyway come to believe that the centre of political gravity was not in the Soviet Union. The key event for me was the East German rising of June 1953. I am still not sure what the character of the revolt in the DDR was – different accounts of it appear to this day. But the intervention of Russian troops shocked me very badly. Before that all the really brazen aggressions had been from the imperialist camp. Even today, when I talk to Edward Thompson or John Saville, I notice this difference: for them Hungary in '56 was the decisive event, while for me it was East Germany in '53. People say that the rising in

Berlin was politically more ambiguous than the revolt in Budapest. But curiously I was actually slower than many people coming out of the Party in '56 to accept that the Hungarian rising was an authentic revolution in which the counter-revolutionary elements were minor and inevitable. I had more reservations, in common with people who were defending the stock Stalinist line about Hungary, than you might expect. Eventually, of course, I came to exactly the same conclusion as someone like Edward.

The whole question of the relation between the military power of the Soviet Union and the political character of the People's Democracies had always been intensely problematic for me, since my time in Germany at the end of the War. My position then, which I see no effective reason to alter, was that within the confrontation of the armies in Europe into which the end of the War had turned, it was impossible to underwrite the two-camp theory which proposed a socialist affiliation to one camp – because then a defensible military reasoning was going to repress social developments and initiatives which were precisely what such an affiliation should be to. An extraordinary development of militarism was overweighing the whole of Europe, East as well as West. In that epoch of wholly technological war, I was very near in several of these years – it can't be described as a phase because it kept coming back – to reconsidering the whole pacifist response as being the correct position.

You wrote once in the fifties that you regarded yourself as a pacifist in international relations. Presumably you meant that didn't apply to domestic revolutions or civil wars?

That is not a definition I could now sustain, nor do I think it meant quite as much as at the time I hoped it would. But it was an attempt to express an important distinction. Throughout this period I was still trying to work out at a quite different level my whole war experience and this was involved in a deep way in my responses too. There were the completely unambiguous situations, like the attack of British tanks in Greece in '44, including units I might have been in when it happened; or the succession of colonial and post-colonial wars which soon followed. Then there was the intervention of Russian tanks in Berlin in '53, and later the invasion of Czechoslovakia in '68. Always there was the image of the tank, which I was both less frightened of and more immediately emotionally involved in than people who'd never been inside one. I was amazed that people were so frightened of tanks, yet equally they do have that capacity of really brutal imposition. The horrible thing about Czechoslovakia was that with part of my mind, a very small and dim part, I could see that this was how to conduct that kind of military operation. I was also well aware, and this has coloured many of my attitudes since, of what an army which is really not holding back can do to a city. This has affected my attitude to the whole experience of urban guerrillas ever since. There is a very complicated balance of political restraints in the conduct of an army in a city, as well as what is externally assumed to be the real balance of military forces. The left has thought very little about the range of situations in which the nature of force and the use of violence are actually defined.

You have sketched out very clearly your reactions to major events in post-war Communism. You stressed earlier that your awareness of Soviet history was very limited in 1939–41, never having been an important part of the culture of Cambridge Communism. Presumably you remedied this in the post-war period. If so, what books did you read and what new sources of knowledge did you gain?

I did not remedy my ignorance until I seized upon Deutscher – the *Stalin* and the Trotsky books. I read Deutscher carefully, but then accepted him wholly. His interpretation of the Russian Revolution and its development made entire sense to me. However, although I never worked this through, the epoch after '45 seemed so much more decisive than the very intricate controversial period before the War. Much of Deutscher's work was concerned with the earlier period in the USSR. I took it as the necessary realignment. But I did not know where it left one on the political spectrum in the present.

Another way of getting to your relationship towards Communism and Marxism would be to ask: what newspapers were you reading?

I read the *Daily Worker* from 1945 till I gave up all papers in '48. Then I started to read it again in '52–3. Thereafter I took it regularly till '68, when my picture appeared on the front page as the Chairman of the National Convention of the Left, and I decided it was the moment to stop. I still miss it. I do often, if I see it on sale, buy it even today, when I take no papers regularly.

What other papers or periodicals were you reading over this period?

In the forties the *News Chronicle*, which seemed the most left paper in the bourgeois press. I subscribed throughout to *Tribune*, even taking out another subscription for my father – although he was very critical of it. In the fifties, I would take the *New Statesman* in bursts and then cancel it.

Did you never read The Times *or any other major bourgeois daily at all?*

I began reading *The Times* in 1953–4 and actually wrote several letters to it. I had to give it up because I could not do any work: the bloody thing would arrive in the morning and I would have about three or four letters to write in reply to everything. The only one that ever got published was at the time of the railway strike in '55 when I wrote a very angry letter about their attack on the strikers, as a son of a railwayman. That's the only one that ever got into print. I soon thought, and I have done ever since, that I will simply not begin the day with those people in the house. I don't even read things I ought to read, like the *TLS* for instance.

How would you characterize, in sum, your relationship to the British Communist Party over these years?

At the beginning in '45–7, there was no political differentiation at all. What kept me at a distance from the Party was a certain, I think contempt would not be too strong a word – although it was not a word I would have used then – for the style of work of the Party. By this style of work I do not mean the isolable elements of my Cambridge experience, or their combination with a certain modishness, but the manipulation and centralism. For example, the CP's pronouncements on Yugoslavia, the only unambiguously self-directed military revolution in Eastern Europe – the hurried charges and then retractions. Then later there were the differences I've described. Although by the time Edward Thompson and I were talking in '58, it was not at all clear which had been the right way to spend the years between '46 and '56, fighting inside the Party or trying to develop a separate position. I would be prepared to say that his was the better choice, but I felt so distant from that style and after all we thought, probably wrongly, that we had a more open style available to us which would nevertheless continue the common project of the thirties. We got the openness but not the project.

Had Leavis not existed as a positive alternative pole in '45, what do you think you would have done? Because your option raises the question of literary criticism as a specialized discipline. For historians matters would have been rather different, because political lines in history are so much more clearly drawn. In fact many of the Communist historians of your generation must have felt very much as you did about the official style of the Party. The institutionalization of lying was becoming very obvious in the Cold War period, and some of them must have been aware of it. Yet they generally stayed in the Party.

Yes. The Communist Party had a house at Hastings and by the time I moved there, I would often talk and drink with them. By that time they were quite openly admitting this – to which my response was: 'How can you stay in such a party?' Each of us thought the other was wrong. They were not defending it to me and they were still regarding me as someone who ought to be back in the Party. But the Party had absolutely no implantation of a kind I could respect in any of the fields of work I was involved in. It was not just Leavis. *Scrutiny* was actually more significant than Leavis himself. It is wrong to equate the two, as people do today. Denys Thompson's works *Between the Lines* and *Voice of Civilization*, which were part of the *Scrutiny* educational project, were as important to us as Leavis's: we particularly took up that sort of newspaper and advertisement analysis in our classes. Then there was Knights's *Drama and Society in the Age of Jonson*, which is totally different from any of Leavis's enterprises: it is a sustained attempt to understand a particular period of literature in terms of a specific epoch in the emergence of capitalism. I read and reread it throughout that period. I was dissatisfied with it, but it seemed much nearer to my focus of interest than what Leavis himself was writing.

What was your view of the CPGB in the fifties, after the death of Stalin?

By this time I had come to the conclusion that to a surprising extent it was an almost mimetically reproduced element of the Labour movement in Britain, which happened in a quite separate part of its mind to have a Soviet affiliation. There was absolutely no ground for saying that it possessed any alternative vision of society or change or anything which was differentiable from the main Labour movement. I am not talking, of course, of Gaitskellism, nor just of the consciously organized Labour left but of the ordinary Labour activists, the people who really keep the local parties going. That was very clear if you read the *Daily Worker* regularly. You could always get news in it which you would not find anywhere else – reporting of strikes or various social defence organizations, tenants' associations or community concerns, in an immediate perspective you shared. Then side by side with all the details of this sort of life, you would find comment about Bulgarian actresses or East German gymnasts. But the first element is the more important one actually. For an intellectual it is an indispensable line of connection. Whenever I reconsidered joining the Communist Party there was always that element in it that appealed to me. But that very close reproduction of the Labour left was not only a strength, it was also a limit. After '53 I ceased believing that the Party in any sense had the economic or political answers to the problems of socialism in Britain, in the way I had assumed it possessed them in '45–7. Its interpretations diverged too much from reality. I don't mean just in the special case of the USSR, where it was constrained. It was on this country that they were wrong, deeply wrong. By the fifties the Party was presenting a version of developments within the society which just did not fit what was happening in England.

Can we end with one very simple question: in the period from '47 up to '56 you must have been asked by other people on the left where you were at, how you would describe yourself. They must have been puzzled on the whole. Were you a Labour Party member? You would say no, you were not. Were you a Tribunite? You would say no. Were you a Communist? No. How did you define your position in those years?

It's a funny thing, it was only a difficult question to answer to people who were in the Party. For there was no political short-hand for it: a real answer meant spelling something difficult out. What other people said was: 'You are a Communist, not a member of the Party, but still a Communist.' I did not know what to reply. Neither no nor yes was the right answer. They would even say: 'With Party members we know where we are, but you are worse – a maverick.' During the disputes of those years, that was how people cast me.

II

Culture

1. Culture and Society

Could you tell us about the origins of Culture and Society *as a project, and what your strategic intentions for the book were when it was published?*

The whole process of writing *Culture and Society* was one of almost constant redefinition and reformulation. The initial impetus goes back to '48, when the publication of Eliot's *Notes towards the Definition of Culture* confirmed something I had already noticed: the concentration of a kind of social thought around this term which hadn't before appeared particularly important. That was already very marked around Leavis and certain kinds of anthropolgist when I returned to Cambridge in '45–6. Eliot's book quickly acquired great influence. I first started to look at the idea of culture in an adult education class, and it is very significant that the writers I discussed then were Eliot, Leavis, Clive Bell and Matthew Arnold. They were all I knew. The realization that the notion actually extended down from the industrial revolution was the result of a process of rather haphazard and accidental discoveries in the period between that class in '49 and about 1951. By then I was clear that since the term had emerged in the course of the industrial revolution, it was a very key moment in the interpretation of that experience and indeed in all the social thought that had accompanied it. But as can be seen from 'The Idea of Culture' my awareness of the history of the concept was far from supported by knowledge of all the particular writers I eventually studied: as late as 1954 I was still what felt like physically shifting the relations of texts around and continually coming on new material. It was only towards the very end, for example, that I decided I must cover what I called the interregnum period from 1870 to 1914.

What was my primary motivation in writing the book? It was oppositional – to counter the appropriation of a long line of thinking about culture to what were by now decisively reactionary positions. There was a question for me whether I should write a critique of that ideology in a wholly negative way, which at one time I considered, or whether the right course was not to try to recover the true complexity of the tradition it had confiscated – so that the appropriation could be seen for what it was. In the end I settled for the second strategy. For it allowed me to refute the increasing contemporary use of the concept of culture against democracy, socialism, the working class or popular education, in terms of the tradition itself. The selective version of culture could be historically controverted by the writings of the thinkers who contributed to the formation and discussion of the idea. Secondly, the possibility had occurred to me – it was very much in the back and not in the front of my mind – that this might also be a way of centring a different kind of discussion both in social-political and in literary analysis. What happened, I think, was that the second part of the project, which I had always seen as subsidiary, belonging much more to the sequel of *The Long Revolution* I was planning, assumed because of the moment of its publication a more important function than I had originally intended. The book was not primarily designed to found a new position. It was an oppositional work.

It is now twenty years since Culture and Society *was published. Could we put to you a series of questions and objections which readers coming to it for the first time today might pose – remembering that the intellectual context has changed enormously? One should also say that the very striking tone of equanimity and authority which you achieved in* Culture and Society *can produce an optical error: one tends to forget that it is actually a young man's book. When you finished it, you were about thirty-five. It does not read as if that was your age when you wrote it. So obviously we are interested in your own reflections on it now, two decades later. Can we try to bring these together in an ordered discussion?*

That would be best, yes.

One of the first queries that people often express is: what were your principles of selection in focussing on the writers you discuss in the book? You don't set your criteria out very clearly – there appears to be a tacit assumption that these are the figures who have written significantly about culture and society, and nobody else has. But certain omissions seem very strange. Everyone might have their own short list, but two obvious examples would be T.H. Green and Hazlitt. Green, in particular, was a commanding influence in his time, who wrote about all your key terms – industry, democracy, art, culture – and whose work is certainly far more substantial than, say, that of Mallock – for whom you find space. Such absences would appear to risk certain real distortions in your account – because it is presented not as a study of isolated thinkers but of the interconnections between them, the cumulative development of a tradition. How did you arrive at the list of people whom you did decide to include in your book?

It is an illusion of many readers today that there was anything like a process of selection from a pre-established range of writers. In all kinds of writing one now finds constant reference to the 'culture and society tradition' as if it was something I was taught at Cambridge and then critically assessed. Actually, I was reasonably well educated in 1948, and my notion of writers who had used the idea of culture went no further back than Clive Bell or Matthew Arnold. The fact is that I could not go, as you can normally if you are attempting this kind of study, to any academic authorities which, even if you disagree with them, at least map out the area of the subject. There was no area. I had to discover for myself Carlyle's *Signs of the Times* essay, which was the single most exciting revelation for me because it contained all the terms of the argument forty years before they were supposed to have emerged. I stumbled on *The Constitution of Church and State* quite accidentally by simply following a reference. The whole process of locating the writers who were relevant to my enquiry was a pretty amateur job of reading from one book to another, looking this and that up, and finding always that I had to keep revising the formation with which I had originally started. But it is a curious effect of the style of the book that it reads like somebody selecting and redisposing something which is already a common property. Whereas what the book was really doing was making it one. Now the very fact that every schoolboy as it were knows of the existence of this line of thinkers from the 1780s onwards is ironically the success of the book, which then allowed you to turn and ask, well is it such a complete account? Of course it is not.

Let me put on the record first the chapters that were in the book and were then excluded because it had to be shortened for the publisher. These were Godwin, in part one, and the English Freudians and Herbert Read, in part three. I was very sorry to let Godwin go. I was so hostile to Read that I was less distressed about that; although I regret it now because it would have been relevant in the sixties, when the whole question of Freud became so important in discussions of art. So far as your queries go, there are two answers. Hazlitt was omitted for a very specific reason. I knew Hazlitt extremely well, because I had been an absolute devotee of his. I cycled as a schoolboy to Wem just to see where Hazlitt had lived. I later experienced an intense revulsion against him. It was a feeling that was radically unfair, but one that at the time I could not handle. The result was that I was unable to deal with Hazlitt at all. Green, on the other hand, was really an area of ignorance. Today I would also say that I neglected much writing in fictional or poetic form prior to the 1840s. Wordsworth is quite inadequately treated. You said a short list – it is in fact a very long list. *Culture and Society* is not a book I am greatly attached to now. But ironically it is the very success of the book that has created the conditions for its critique.

Another range of objections that contemporary readers are liable to make of the book concerns the role of politics in it. There are a number of levels at which we'd like to probe this. The first could be put as follows. The book is entitled Culture and Society, *and these two terms are the essential prisms through which all the individual figures in it are perceived – as instances, exemplary models in some cases, of social and cultural thinking. The book changes register notably in the conclusion, when you move to something like a political discourse proper. But in the main corpus of the work, where you are discussing the actual tradition itself, there does appear to be a virtually systematic depreciation of the actual political dimension of all the figures whom you are discussing. The great majority of all these writers, perhaps indeed the totality of them, had very explicit and definite and often central views on the politics of the day. Yet much of the composition of the book simply writes that out in a way which one wonders how conscious you were of at the time. One of the latent* leitmotivs *of the book often appears to be a direct counterposition of the social core of the thought of successive thinkers against a mere political surface which can be somehow detached and dismissed. Can we cite some examples?*

The first case occurs on the second page of the book, where you write: 'The confutation of Burke on the French revolution is now a one-finger exercise in politics and history.'[1] *That is an extremely contemptuous phrase, which implies that everybody and anybody can do this and there is no further interest in the matter. But in fact, there were very many respected historians and*

[1] CS, p. 24.

political theorists who so far from regarding it as a one-finger exercise to refute Burke's views were confidently expounding and defending them as received truths. The issue was not simply historically settled at the time you were writing. Then, when you come to discuss the thought of the Romantics, you have this to say: 'In every case, however, the political criticism is now less interesting than the wider social criticism.'[2] *That is stated about Wordsworth, Coleridge, Shelley, Byron, Blake and Keats. It is a blanket judgment. These are two typical examples from the nineteenth century. Two from the twentieth century could be taken from your discussions of Eliot and Leavis. Regretting passages in* Notes towards the Definition of Culture *in which Eliot attacks Laski or Attlee, you demur in these terms: 'The most important disadvantage which has followed from these faults in the book is that they have allowed it to be plausibly dismissed by those of us whose prejudices are different.'*[3] *Once again politics are reduced to minima, to mere food for prejudice, in a tone of pained politeness. Later, when you criticize Leavis for elitism, you motivate your judgment like this: 'It is not so much a matter of announcing some political allegiance. It is a matter, rather, in our whole social experience, of declaring that "this is worth more than that, this rather than that is the direction in which to go".'*[4] *In all these cases a clear contrast seems to be posited between truth which is necessarily social, and politics which is a brittle and ephemeral adjunct separable from it. None of the phrases so far cited are structural pivots of your argument, but the pattern is nevertheless a persistent one. Was this a conscious polemical stance on your part, or were these comments written without your being entirely aware of the direction they were taking?*

Not all of these examples are of the same kind. Of course it was wrong to say that it was simple to confute Burke – I was even very conscious of the modern repetition of his political ideas. The sentence about Eliot is not something I could write today, although quite honestly between Eliot and the people he was immediately attacking there was an almost too easy rhetoric at the level of prejudice. The case of the Romantics is quite different. It remains my firm conviction that their political thought is of radically less interest than their social thinking. I think the only writer of whom this is not true would be Shelley. Much more argument was needed to substantiate the point. I didn't go into it, partly because of the

[2] CS, p. 49.
[3] CS, p. 229.
[4] CS, p. 255.

contradictory character of politics after 1795, and partly because the political thought of the Romantics seemed relatively well-trodden ground. Discussion of it tended to concentrate attention on the shift from support of the French Revolution towards opposition to it, or the transition from young radicals to old conservatives; whereas it seemed to me that the Romantic attempts to grasp the momentous social changes of their time, which were eventually to determine all politics, were of far greater significance. The centrality of their sense of society was much more interesting than what they were saying about events as they went past. Just as – to take a comparable example – it was really much more important that Jane Austen depicted a very complex transition in the world of English landowning and landholding than that she did not write about the Napoleonic Wars. It is the same kind of judgment. It is not a general dismissal of politics.

Yet elsewhere you do seem to make just such a generalization. In your conclusion, you periodize the tradition of the book into three phases. The first phase runs from 1790 to 1870; it is in this epoch that 'the major analysis is undertaken and the major opinions and descriptions emerge'.[5] *It is then followed by a second phase of which you say: 'Then, from about 1870 to 1914, there is a breaking down into narrower fronts, marked by a particular specialism in attitudes to art, and in the general field, by a preoccupation with direct politics.'*[6] *That is an express equation of direct politics with lesser, narrow vision, isn't it?*

The judgment about the interregnum is certainly wrong – that it represented a breakdown into something narrower: on the contrary. Indeed it is internally contradicted by the account of Morris. But I think that what you are pin-pointing is a tendency which does in a way express pretty accurately the period in which the book was written. I started work on it in '48, at a time when my separation from the possibilities of political action and collaboration was virtually complete. There was a breakdown of any collective project that I could perceive, political, literary or cultural. Later, during the fifties, I did become engaged in some political activity, but by then I had reached a conclusion that I do not wholly disavow today,

[5] CS, p. 286.
[6] CS, p. 286.

although I sharply watch myself through it: that there is a kind of politics whose local tactical modes positively prevent people from seeing what is happening in society – as distinct from a politics which is based on an understanding of the main lines of force in society and a choice of sides in the conflict between them. Politics often functions, not as I think you are using the term, as a conscious struggle or strategy formed by history and by theory, but as a routine reproduction of controversies or competitive interests without relation to the basic deep movements of society. I tried to express this distinction in the chapter on Burke when I wrote of 'politics saturated with thought' – by contrast with the kind of politics I was myself experiencing: ironically at that very time I was writing on Burke I was coming in from canvassing or speaking in the General Election of '55. It was a crucial distinction in my mind, which was the basis of the isolable contemptuous references to politics in the book. At the same time, no doubt there was also simply the element of fatigue with the complexities of politics at the time, expressing itself as superiority – a tone I both analysed and was subject to.

There is a second level, however, at which the same criticism can be made. That is, no longer of a general depreciation of politics, but of an inadvertently conservative bias in your particular descriptions of the different figures in the book. Take two sets of contrasts: on the one hand Burke and the Romantics, and on the other hand Carlyle and Morris. Your discussion of Burke contains virtually no limiting phrases at all: it ends by saying that we should be grateful to Burke for what you call his 'magnificent affirmation'.[7] *In the case of Carlyle, you do criticize his later writings briefly, but you still conclude that his 'purposes' were 'positive and ennobling' and that overall 'reverence' was 'his essential quality'.*[8]

By contrast, at the end of a sympathetic chapter on the Romantics, you write 'the last pages of Shelley's Defence of Poetry *are painful to read', you repeat the epithet 'painful' a few sentences later, and then you remark: 'We are not likely, when we remember the lives of any of these men, to be betrayed into the irritability of prosecution, but it is as well, also, if we can avoid the irritability of defence.'*[9] *Likewise, when you discuss Morris you twice use a*

[7] CS, p. 39.
[8] CS, pp. 90, 98.
[9] CS, pp. 63–4.

phrase which elsewhere you apply to Cobbett. Commenting on a denunciation by Morris of Oxford culture as 'cynically contemptuous of knowledge', you say: 'This is very typical of Morris's method, which is often no more than a kind of generalized swearing'; or again, 'As with Cobbett, we come to accept the impatience and ritualized swearing as the price of vitality, which has its own greatness.'[10]

Surely there is a striking inequity in your treatment of these writers? Burke is lauded for his 'magnificent affirmation', without a single reference to the negations – of equality, of democracy – which made him famous in his own day: the constant theme of the need to instil 'the principles of natural subordination' in the people. After all, what was the purpose of his central text? It was to prevent an English revolution – as you say in your recent introduction to the Pelican volume of English Prose.[11] *Not to speak of Burke's active and fanatical prosecution of the military war against the French Revolution. In the case of Carlyle, it seems incomprehensible that you could speak so unhesitatingly of 'reverence' as his essential quality. For Carlyle was an unbridled racist and imperialist. His role in the Governor Eyre Controversy is a notorious instance. Even as early as the 1840s he was writing an essay on the 'Nigger Question'. No other writer in the book produced a prose as frightful as Carlyle on these occasions, which you do not mention. Whereas, then you rebuke Shelley for his strained but innocuous claims for the poet as legislator, you found it necessary to say, 'we will not be betrayed into the irritability of prosecution' by them – surely they are scarcely a fit subject for 'prosecution'. Then if we take Morris, whom you charge with 'generalized swearing', might one not simply say that he tended to call a spade a spade? he could denounce with great vigour, certainly, but his language never acquires the pitch of violence that Carlyle used – quite apart from the justice of its political objects.*

Well, obviously there is truth in what you say. I would not want to claim that the balance is right. I don't think it is. But there are differences between these passages. What I called 'generalized swearing' in Morris still seems to me just that. Swearing is after all a very good activity. It is its generalization into a rhetoric that goes wrong. 'I wish to ask if it is too late to appeal to the mercy of the "Dons" to spare the few specimens of ancient

[10] CS, pp. 156, 160.
[11] PBEP, p. 28.

town architecture which they had not time to destroy'[12] – anybody who has walked down a street in Oxford knows that such an exaggeration defeats its own ends. In the case of Carlyle, I do in fact make a very sharp cut-off in the late 1840s. I was quite clear that by then the decisive shift had occurred towards what I call the 'contemptuous absolutism'[13] of *Shooting Niagara*. If I were writing the book now, I don't think I would withdraw my judgment of Carlyle, although I would make it with different reference points.

Would you really maintain the conclusion that 'the faults, alike of the man and of his influence, remain obvious. But there is one common word of his which continues to express his essential quality: the word reverence'?[14]

No, I admit that although I condemned his later work, I didn't – and this was a fault – make it qualify my general judgment. But what is really much more interesting is the opportunity that I missed in that essay on Carlyle. Because it still seems to me that Carlyle in *Signs of the Times* touched a nerve which was crucial and which other more progressive currents of thought were evading, and continued to evade through the rest of the century. That is the extent to which protest against the industrial revolution in terms either of its sheer chaos and confusion, or in terms of the political conflicts which necessarily developed out of new social relations, had masked fundamental changes within the labour process itself. These changes in turn had consequences for people's conceptions of nature, and for the relations between human society and the non-human physical environment, which were concealed from view in subsequent traditions of a more progressive and acceptable kind. In that sense the collapse of Carlyle into some of the worst thinking of the century should actually have been treated as a pivotal development. The conditions under which it occurred needed to be explained – in something like the way I was to do in my book on Orwell, including a look at what elements there might have been in the earlier thought which prefigure the collapse. Why didn't I do so? I had had so much of this marshalling of who were the progressive thinkers and who were the reactionary thinkers in the nineteenth century when I was a student: I too wrote my essay on Carlyle as a fascist when I

[12] Citation from Morris: CS, p. 156.
[13] CS, p. 95.
[14] CS, p. 98.

was an undergraduate. Part of the submerged history of the book is that there were all sorts of position which came almost too easily to the pen, which were then precisely what I was drawing back from. I had discovered themes profoundly related to my sense of the social crisis of my time and the socialist way out of it, not in the approved list of progressive thinkers, but in these paradoxical figures. I then overemphasized the place of these values in writers whose eventual development led them in a quite different direction. The honest thing to do and the right thing to do would have been to argue the case of each thinker fully and explicitly through, and say what was wrong with them. In some cases I do that. The chapter on Lawrence fully engages with him in that way. It is not what I would now say about Lawrence, but I can't think of any of the figures that I would feel about in the same way now.

We should say that we start ourselves from the premise that this was a book that vitally needed to be written, and which has played an extremely important and liberating role for socialist thought in this country. What we are asking is whether twenty years later you would not yourself assent to the view that there are particular and significant imbalances in it?

You have got to remember that I read my own books too, and that in a competition for critical readers I shall at least be on the final list. *Culture and Society* seems to me a book which is negatively marked by elements of a disgusted withdrawal – let me use a term as strong as that – from all immediate forms of collaboration, combined – and this eventually made the difference – with an intense disappointment that they were not available: a disappointment that connects, directly, to the nature of the renewal of belief which is the conclusion: the renewal in those terms which is the book's innovation in its period. But on my way through this I could slip into tones which are in effect the self-defence of an intellectual who has retired from immediate politics and is now, hopefully, looking at deeper forces. I am prepared to say that because I was actually aware of it at the time and I notice it now when I read the book. On the other hand, I am also prepared to say that by drawing back I was able to reintroduce certain themes and issues which have seemed to me the crucial stuff of action to this day, but which were absent from what I knew then and often know now as politics. In other words every withdrawal, or emphasis, of that kind is bought at a considerable price, and the price is the one which you are noting. But as a result I could make what I still think was a contribution to a different kind of politics. Today, when I hear the proposition, delivered as it is in that familiar tone of doctrinaire slander, that the reintroduction of the tradition of *Culture and Society* was merely a recuperation of reformism, I would say, aggressively if you like, that the failings caused by the elements of distance and confusion are regrettable mainly because they allow some people on the left – some recent ascriptions of Ideology remind me of the worst of the thirties – to go on evading the real issues it was attempting to reintroduce – the redefinition of what politics should be, and the remobilization, at every level, of the forces necessary for it. But, of course, if I had been able to make all that clearer it would have been that much better a book.

The kind of queries we are putting to you are within the framework of the assumption that the book could have been improved, as any work can.

Well, I respect *Culture and Society*, but it is not a book I could conceive myself writing now. I don't much know the person who wrote it. I read this book as I might read a book by someone else. It is a work most distant from me.

Yet it still remains very close to socialist debate in England today. That is why it is so important to gain a present perspective on it. One could formulate this need in another way. There is a third level at which the problem of politics is posed in the book, which is the most serious. This concerns not so much the balance of your judgment of particular persons as the central structure of the work, the overall way it is organized – although the two are connected. In the first half of the book who are the two figures to whom the greatest honour is paid? Unquestionably, Burke and Carlyle. What were the major works which actually dominated the attention of the public of Burke and Carlyle? They were books on the French Revolution. In each case, although in a different perspective, the purpose of these works was to combat the example of 1789 – to show that it represented everything that must not happen in England. Now this should be enough to show why the politics of the period cannot be treated as a series of transient judgments of particular episodes that are separable from a deeper social thought, and why the consequences of doing so are more than just a question of overgenerous assessments of people on the conservative side of this tradition, or too restrictive judgments of people who were on the other side.

Something much more central is involved. By not paying any attention, in the whole chapter on Carlyle, to his book on the French Revolution and by omitting any account of his attack on the French Revolution when you write on Burke, what you were doing was enforcing a separation in your own subject which was actually quite artificial. The way in which you present your narrative from 1780 to 1950 is as if there was a single discourse about the relation between the industrial revolution and the shape of civilization and culture. But actually throughout that period, from the very founding moment onwards, there was another *revolution that had occurred, not the industrial revolution in England but the political revolution in France. These were closely related for contemporaries – they were never events that existed in two quite separate universes. The pattern of Romantic response to them is sufficiently famous. Indeed, this was true not just of the first French revolution of 1789, but also of the second revolution of 1848, which was a decisive event for Mill or Arnold. Even the Commune in 1871 was an important event within English politics: think of George Eliot's reaction to it. At the outset of your book you pick out five key terms for your account. Two of them, democracy and class, cannot be discussed realistically in this period without central reference to the French revolutions and to the English response to them at the different levels of the governing classes, the state and the army, the intelligentsia and popular attitudes. This is the real objection, if you like, to the way in which* Culture and Society *appears to exclude the middle term of politics.*

It is nice to be able to agree in a more unqualified way. I think this is right. I think that the mistake follows from the original strategy of the book, which is the recovery of a very specific tradition. The result was to project back the appearance of a coherent discourse, which prevented me from fully re-engaging successive thinkers with their history. In any case I was deficient in the historical knowledge which would have made this possible. If I had read *The Making of the English Working Class* when I was writing *Culture and Society*, it would have been a quite different book. But then it was part of the conditions of the time that Edward was writing his Morris and then the early work on the making of the working class while I was writing *Culture and Society*, yet we were not in contact with each other – so these crucial conjunctions were never made.

Today, for example, I would like to write about the extraordinary transposition of varieties of radicalism that occurred between 1790 and 1840 – which I never mentioned in the book. One reason why I ought not to have allowed my personal difficulties about Hazlitt to prevent me from writing about him is that by doing so I could have explored this extreme complexity, because it is so central in him. Another moment of intense illumination and regret for me occurred when I found that Matthew Arnold's *Culture and Anarchy* was written in direct response to the Hyde Park riots in the suffrage campaign of 1866, in which John Stuart Mill was centrally involved on the other side. When I saw that this was the context which politically defined what 'anarchy' and what 'culture' were for Arnold, I thought my God, if I had known that I could have begun the book with the political forces and issues of 1867, including the Governor Eyre Controversy which you mentioned: that's where I could have started.

The fact is that the origins of the book lie in ideas of either explicitly conservative or contradictory thinkers in the nineteenth century – but conservatives who, at the point of irruption of a qualitatively new social order put many of the right questions to it but of course came out with wrong answers – or people with whom I shared certain impulses, like Leavis, moving towards explicitly reactionary positions in the twentieth century. All these used as a central term of their development the concept of culture. In the process of seeking to recover that concept and reconstruct the discourse around it, I allowed some degree of abstraction from history, and so didn't carry through strongly enough what was one of the book's innovating points: that it is only by a return to the modulations of the term through history that you can even understand the term itself. This is what I would now say. I have even built it into a general method in *Keywords*. Yet the recovery of the discourse about the term was in itself so difficult that at the time it was about as far as I could go. I have never known a book which more completely seemed to close itself with the last page that was written. I had the strongest sense I have ever experienced that now it was done, I was in a quite new position and could move on. Then the irony is that it is still the most widely read of my books and that everybody tries to pull me back to it.

But people who read the book do link your own name as a social and political thinker with it. Critical discussion of the work, which does not have to push you back to it, remains eminently worthwhile.

No, I didn't mean that. It was rather the curious circumstance that the book appeared at a moment which was quite unforeseen and unpredictable at the time either of its conception or indeed its writing. It appeared right in the middle of a situation of rapid political mobility, in which new issues were being raised and a new generation was defining itself around them. As a result the book was given a kind of centrality which in a sense it deserved, since it had raised these issues and laid down a body of reading and thinking about them, but which in another sense was misplaced because by the time it was published the context was so different. New journals and clubs had already appeared and were changing the perspectives of discussion. Then out comes the book looking so solid and dignified and all that, when it was the product of a phase in which I was living an entirely different life. It is not surprising that the contradictions eventually surfaced later. For example, Eagleton, who has recently attacked *Culture and Society* wholesale, went on reproducing the arguments of the book right up to '68–9 in a way that irritated me much more than his subsequent extreme revulsion from it. If you look at the essay comparing Eliot, Leavis and myself in *From Culture to Revolution*,[15] you will see that he simply laid it out again ten years later. That was a new epoch, that needed a quite different book. *Culture and Society* perhaps served as a bridge from one to the next, but a bridge is something that people pass over. Still today many American readers say, oh yes, we agree with your position, we read *Culture and Society* and that sort of thing. And I say that is not my position. And they say well it's still a very radical book, and I say, well, first-stage radicalism. What it mainly did was to shift what people who read English, people who study the history of social thought, were writing and talking about. It permitted a reconnection with a very complex tradition of social thought and of literature which had been short-circuited by *Scrutiny* and indeed by a whole class formation.

That brings us to another question. One of the anomalies of the book is that it discusses figures in nineteenth- and twentieth-century English social thinking in very general abstraction from the effective social history of the individuals concerned and their relations with classes. This is not entirely so, because in the case of Lawrence you emphatically do restore that context, but otherwise your thinkers are sociologically very disembodied. At the time, Victor Kiernan noted this absence in a friendly review of the book in the New Reasoner, *and commented: 'We think habitually of our eminent writers as so many Stylites,*

[15] 'The Idea of a Common Culture', *From Culture to Revolution*, edited by Terry Eagleton and Brian Wicker, London, 1968, pp. 35–57.

each perched solitarily on his pillar. It is useful to think of them at times as figures wedged inconspicuously into the second row in snapshots in family albums. Southey, Coleridge, Wordsworth are then seen hemmed in among naval brothers, legal cousins, clerical uncles, including the real notables of the family who are on the way to the dignities of Judge, Bishop, or Master of a College.'[16] *In other words, Kiernan was drawing attention to the fact that there existed in Victorian England something like a professional middle class, which probably produced a majority of the intellectuals you were writing about. He went on to say that socialists should not be inhibited from perceiving that there were real material interests peculiar to this social stratum. Kiernan argues, for instance, that the attitude of most of the writers of the time to the state is noticeably more indulgent and positive than that of their cousins in business and in other fields, which can be related to the fact that the state was a major employer of intellectuals in nineteenth-century England. He also makes the point that while most of these thinkers had quite a lot to say about industrialism, they had very little to say about servants – although there were fewer factory workers in England throughout the nineteenth century than there were domestic servants. Did you deliberately set aside this sort of reflection? We ask because you wrote a chapter on the social history of the English writer in* The Long Revolution, *which was an unprecedentedly accurate and precise survey of just this problem – the family origins, the educational experience, the employment position of English intellectuals over some four centuries. That was a tremendous advance over traditional discussions on the left: here at last was something more than the customary empty generalities – it was a real material history. Yet in* Culture and Society *that is absent. Was this a choice on your part?*

No, it was unrealized. I think that there were two blocks that kept me back from this perspective at the time. One was the sense that anybody could reel these writers off as the representative figures of a certain social class. Not that the description was necessarily wrong, but I knew that if you started from that kind of abstract delineation you didn't even have to read them – you read from it. The other problem was the social presence of these writers in the milieux where they were read. It is a paradox that not only Shelley and Byron, but Southey of all people, enjoyed an extraordinary popularity in the working class of the thirties and forties: or

[16] Victor Kiernan, 'Culture and Society', *The New Reasoner*, No. 9, Summer 1959, p. 80.

that Ruskin should have been of such extreme importance for the late nineteenth-century labour movement. I did not know how to broach these questions. Also, you mustn't forget that I had been professionally drilled into a way of thinking which excluded them. Distinctly, academically one had been trained to study individual writers – this was, after all, what a lot of *Scrutiny* criticism shared with the orthodox establishment.

But, of course, then you can end up with Virginia Woolf, imagining that all the great writers are simultaneously present in the Reading Room of the British Museum working at their desks, and that you simply have to attend to what they are writing. In fact my work on *Culture and Society* acted as a stimulus, a self-provocation, to get completely away from that mode. The ironic thing is that by the time I was reading Kiernan's review, we had already just completed the actual research for the social history of the English writer. That was the work I had immediately gone on to. Eventually, this was to lead to an explosion of the very idea of the text and of the definition of literary studies through the text, which I was not at yet. But by God when I got to it what should happen but a new and supposedly Leftist movement to revive the isolation of the text? It took another ten years to fight that back, if indeed we yet have.

In retrospect, although in a very different key, the book might be said to have discernible affinities with a certain phase of Communist Party cultural policy in the late forties and early fifties – i.e. around the time it was defining a national road to socialism at the political level. At least one of the Party's cultural organs, Arena, *set out to define a national past for the Party – a cultural lineage which would somehow fund Communist politics. Were you conscious at the time of any affiliation between your own project in* Culture and Society *and the discussion in* Arena? *Or did you subsequently have occasion to reflect on it?*

The short answer is that I was not conscious of any similarity at the time. I think it is possible, however, to see the two as comparable and related historical responses – they have elements in common, although you can't push them too far. I was much more conscious of the right. I knew perfectly well who I was writing against: Eliot, Leavis and the whole of the cultural conservatism that had formed around them – the people who had pre-empted the culture and literature of this country. In that sense the book was informed by a very specific national consciousness. Yet it was 'national' in a very specific way, because I deliberately kept it English. At this time my distance from Wales was at its most complete. However, unconsciously my Welsh experience was nevertheless operating on the strategy of the book. For when I concluded it with a discussion of cooperative community and solidarity, what I was really writing about – as if they were more widely available – was Welsh social relations. I was drawing very heavily on my experience of Wales, and in one way correctly locating it as a certain characteristic of working-class institutions, but with not nearly enough regional shading and sense of historical distinctions and complications.

The national definition of Culture and Society *raises another question. Your earlier critical book* Drama from Ibsen to Eliot *is remarkable for its international scope and range: you treat the experience of the rise of the bourgeois theatre as a European phenomenon that must be discussed as such. There is no question of confining your enquiry to a specific language. Yet there is no comparable international dimension in* Culture and Society *at all. That seems very surprising, because the process of industrialization was after all equally and eminently European, even if started in England. Why did you limit your account to a national tradition alone?*

I think the reason was that I initially conceived the project as a rather short response to a particular English situation. It then grew bigger and bigger until it became a tremendous struggle to get it into a reasonable shape as a book. The task of composition defined it as a discourse within a single culture.

The problem here is that the exclusion of any international discussion from the book is not just a formal limit; it affects the substance of some of your arguments. One of the central claims of Culture and Society, *after all, is that 'the idea of culture is the major English tradition'.*[17] *What if it was less so than you assumed? In actual fact, the whole argument of* Culture and Society *was in a sense also the main theme of European sociology from its founding moment onwards – a system of thought you never mention. If you look at Göran Therborn's study,* Science, Class and Society, *what emerges from it is that the entire trajectory of the discipline, from Comte and Saint-Simon down to*

[17] CS, p. 271.

Weber or Durkheim, was governed by one common preoccupation: what was the answer to the twin social crises brought on by the industrial revolution that started in England, and the political revolution that started in France? For all the major sociologists of the nineteenth century, the two key problems were the advent of a market society and the threat of a mass democracy – exactly the issues which agitated English writers from Southey to Arnold. What is even more striking is that the responses were very similar: in one form or another the antidote of classical sociology to the disintegrating forces of industrialism and democracy was always a more organic culture – a coherent order of values capable of conferring a new meaning and unity in society. The idea of culture in this sense is in no way specifically English. Indeed the famous opposition between a deeper, organic 'culture' and a more superficial, mechanical 'civilization' was a German one. Ironically, if you take Thomas Mann's Reflections of an Unpolitical Man, *written during the First World War, you find that it is England and France who are identified with mere civilization and democracy, while Germany represents the true tradition of culture. Such was one of the official themes of the propaganda of the Second Reich.*

Then again, the conclusion of your book turns on the idea of community. This is not a central organizing theme in the English thinkers you discuss, although they may use the term. But it was, precisely, the direct object of a major theory within European sociological thought. Tönnies's opposition between 'community' and 'society' effectively contributed the concept as such in its wider currency. Therborn in fact synthesizes the findings of his study in the category of the 'ideological community', whose discovery he argues was the specific achievement of sociology as a discipline – that is, a community bound together by shared norms and values. The formal similarity with your call for a 'common culture' is arresting. Surely this long history had a bearing on the tradition you were trying to reconstruct, and the discourse you developed out of it?

The absence of reference to it was not some personal overlooking, but a general condition of thought in this country. It was not even very clear at the time how very deep and close was Coleridge's relationship – in its most accurate sense, which is not a degrading sense – to German idealism and romanticism. Or Mill's connection with French positivism. Doubtless some specialists knew of them, but it was not a perspective within which one was then accustomed to read and think. It is now very clearly so. That is a major change.

Viewing the sociological tradition in Europe when I now know more about it, I think I would say that the market and democracy are more prominent themes within it than in the English tradition with which I was concerned, whereas the English tradition was more specifically concerned with industry. It was the very rapid and brutal experience of industrialization in England which was most directly reflected in social thought here – by comparison the English contribution to thinking about democracy or the market was always either secondary and derived or was very quickly surpassed in seriousness and extension elsewhere. But the thinking about the process of industrial transformation that was done in the period between Blake and Wordsworth and Southey and the young Carlyle, although it is very early and confused, still seems to me absolutely crucial. Some of the questions then asked, more persistently by Cobbett than by anyone else, about the whole nature of the industrial project and its consequences for social relations, still have to be answered today. *The Country and the City* was written very much in response to them. Now this form of thought was not an element that a subsequent ampler tradition has sufficiently taken into account except in what are self-evidently reactionary ways. By contrast, the characteristic rhetoric of the Marxism I had known in the thirties was precisely that capitalism was at fault because it had failed to produce, because it was responsible for the depression: whereas the image of the Soviet Union was exalted in terms of industrial productivity to the point of parody. What awaited that rhetoric after the War was the new kind of productive explosion that capitalism had in store. It was then that the questions posed by Blake or Cobbett acquired their force for me. They had a sense of the materiality of production that was largely lost afterwards. We all knew about the labour process, but we knew very little about the actual techniques of the labour process – or its by-products, which of course were also products. In those mixed English reactions to the industrial revolution was a response which it seems to me any Marxism in this part of the century would have to include. Later socialists, speaking abstractly of production, were really not able to grasp as these people who actually saw the industrial transformation what it meant on the ground – the literal ground. It is very curious that the historical-materialist theory should in that respect know the history but not the material. This is not true of Marx where the physical process is quite vivid.

However, that raises a further consequence of your organization of the book in purely national terms. For where do these leave space for Marxism? Only, apparently, when you can discuss the few English Marxists of the thirties, and their views on the restricted topic of art. What is so peculiar about this procedure is that Marx himself, not to speak of Engels, lived in Victorian England and worked and wrote like no other was to do in his day or after it on the English industrial revolution. He wrote about the full range of the subjects in your work, including of course a general theory of society in the sense of a whole way of life, to use your terms. He also possessed something that sets him completely apart from all the figures you discuss, which was a sense of the dialectical interrelationship, the bond of historical complementarity between utilitarianism and romanticism – the discourse of the market and the discourse of culture. You probably know the sentence in the Grundrisse *where he actually says: 'The bourgeois viewpoint has never advanced beyond the antithesis between itself and the romantic viewpoint, and the latter will accompany it as its legitimate antithesis up to its blessed end' –*

I was quite excited when I found it. But it was very recent.

– So Marx was very aware,[18] *he could keenly appreciate many of the figures you discuss, as well as figures from the opposite side – that of political economy. He paid great attention to Carlyle as well as to Ricardo. Objectively he is inserted in the most direct possible way into the field of your enquiry, with the one proviso that none of these Victorian gentlemen were aware of him. Although even that is not true of Morris. But by constructing your tradition in strictly national terms you necessarily had to write Marx out of it. That omission is an artificial one. The book would have read very differently if it had included a chapter on Marx and the industrial revolution. You must have considered whether to do this or not?*

Yes, I thought about it – particularly when I was shaping the chapter on industrial novels, which was originally to have been an account of a whole range of responses to industrial development in the thirties and forties. I was struck by the fact that Engels and Mrs Gaskell were active together in Manchester at the same moment: it seemed impossible that they should not have been in contact through the Statistical Society. *The Condition of the English Working Class* is certainly the most eloquent social indictment

[18] Karl Marx, *Grundrisse*. Pelican/NLR edition, London 1973, p. 162.

of the forties, precisely because it is the most broadly conceived. But there was the difficulty for the organization of the book that although Marx and Engels did their work here, it was written in another language and did not get back to these other people, not simply because they were indifferent but because of the isolation of exiles in the country. When I came to discuss the English Marxists, I was primarily interested in what had become a very altered argument. I made my bow by saying Marx was a contemporary of Ruskin and George Eliot, but at that stage it is perfectly true that I only talk about the theory of art. I don't know what would have happened to the book if I had inserted Marx. Although I might not have done it very well, I at least had read him as much as I had read anyone else. Well, it is entirely right. It would have radically improved the book. I also think that if I had taken the various different directions that I now see as desirable I would still be writing it. . . .

There is another problem which is in a sense the obverse of the absence of an international dimension to Culture and Society. *That is the silence of the book on the theme and problem of the nation as such. There are a number of reasons why it is not irrelevant to ask you about this. One can be put rather simply. The keynote of the conclusion of the book is the idea of community. Now that concept has many different meanings. But one thing can be said with some confidence of it: in the twentieth century the term community has probably been more frequently used about the nation as a unit than any other body of men and women – more so than region or class or any international entity. The normal attachment or companion term, at least in official rhetoric today, is very obviously the nation.*

Culture and Society *does not, of course, contain any direct reflection on the problem of nationalism, but if we look at the figures you deal with, many of them did have something to say about the nation –* their *nation. Burke's book on the French Revolution was not just a conservative manifesto, it was also an attempt to mobilize patriotic sentiment against a foreign menace, which became part of an extremely successful campaign by the ruling class at the time. In Carlyle, you find an imperialism and racism whose sharp edge is turned towards the black and the subject peoples of the colonial empire. The examples could be multiplied. Between 1790 and 1920 the society you were writing about was not just the seat of the first major industrial revolution, it was also a society which was physically conquering, annexing and exploiting a fifth of the globe – creating the largest empire the world had ever seen. This historical process was centrally present to the consciousness of all those who lived through the period whom you discuss. It was not something which was secondary and external – it was absolutely constitutive of the whole nature of the English political and social order. That is something which for anybody looking at the English social experience from the outside, a Frenchman or an Italian or a German or a Russian – not to speak of a Jamaican, a Nigerian or an Indian – is* the *salient fact. If you ask them what they associate with 19th-century England, they do think of the industrial revolution of course, but even more they think of the Pax Britannica.*

Now in Culture and Society, *there is only one sentence which alludes in any way to that experience. Right at the end, in defending and illustrating the sense of community within the English working class, you say: 'On occasion this has been limited by nationalism and imperialism.' But the point is that nationalism and imperialism were in many ways the dominant, reigning definitions* of *community. From everything you have said about your practical activity and consciousness, from your boyhood onwards, it is clear that you were always intensely aware of the nature of British imperial hegemony and oppression abroad, and the emergent colonial struggles against it. Yet there is no echo of them within the book. Why was that?*

Let me make a minor point before we get to the essential one. There are in fact two places in the book which do refer to the imperial experience, although in a way they confirm your general emphasis – the discussion of Carlyle's criticism of emigration as a social solution, and the analysis of the magical function of departures to the empire in the fiction of the period. But otherwise there is nothing about it. I don't discuss Disraeli in that connection, nor Mill's association with the India Office, nor the appalling relation of the Fabians to imperialism. Even something that interests me very much now, the conscious entry of a really deep and prolonged representation and evocation and critique of the imperial experience in the novels of the nineties, isn't there. I think one of the reasons for this is that the particular experience which ought to have enabled me to think much more closely and critically about it was for various reasons at that time very much in abeyance: the Welsh experience. The way I used the term community actually rested on my memories of Wales, as I've said. But the Welsh experience was also precisely one of subjection to English expansion and assimilation historically. That is what ought to have most alerted me to the dangers of a persuasive type of definition of community, which is at once dominant and exclusive.

Historically there was a real ambiguity in English in the distribution and bearing of community as a term. All the early definitions of the 1830s and 1840s which bring in the root 'common' have a very strong sense of community as deliberately contrasted to theories based on individualism. In the 1870s and 1880s 'communist' still meant in England a believer in the founding of communities, in a utopian sense. All these meanings changed greatly in the 20th century. The term 'community' was very widely used in the thirties and forties in the working class and the labour movement, especially in Wales, where it has also, in the realities of nonconformity, a religious sense. But by the sixties I was constantly hearing of the interest of the community over and against that of a small group of strikers, for example. This caused me to reflect that it is unusable as a term that enables one to make distinctions: one is never certain exactly to which formation the notion is referring. It was when I suddenly realized that no one ever used 'community' in a hostile sense that I saw how dangerous it was.

Yes, in Germany Tönnies, who coined the concept, was a sympathizer with the pre-war SPD. After the War, it was the Nazis who systematically utilized the term Volksgemeinschaft *as a* leitmotiv *of their internal propaganda, particularly towards the working class, within the Third Reich. Few notions have proved so ideologically malleable.*

The reason, I think, is that it permits a constant elision with other notions – above all, nation and state. So far as nation is concerned, I remember that the moment when its function exploded for me was when I was reading a passage of Leavis in which he started speaking once again of 'essential Englishness'. By this time I was no longer willing to use English as a synonym for the peoples of the mainland. The adjective 'essential' gives the operation away. I then also understood the really ideological function of literature as such, which has nothing to do with any specifiable function of particular works. The whole notion of the rise of a national literature, the definition of a nation through its literature, the idea of literature as the moral essence or spirit of the nation – these are supports of a specific political and social ideology. All I can say is that I did not see that when I was writing *Culture and Society*.

The confusion over the state has been even more serious. For a long time there was a habit not only in me but generally on the left of equating socialist advances with the state, because of the blurring effect of the indeterminate use of terms like 'community' or 'public', as in 'public ownership'. The very idea of 'nationalization', as a key political term, rested on the assumption by the left that the nation was an unproblematic entity. In other words, we were quite insufficiently aware of the post-war capitalist state. The most welcome single introduction into Marxist thought of the last decade has been the decisive re-entry of the problem of the capitalist state. All these terms are no longer so easily elided. I would myself no longer use the word 'community' in the way I did in *Culture and Society*.

Passing to another topic, there is a question we would like to pose about the epistemology of the book, so to speak. It concerns your method of assessment of the individual thinkers in it. At a number of points in the book you seem to be contrasting or counterposing ideas and arguments with what you call 'response' or 'experience'. The first example can be found in your treatment of Burke, of whom you say: 'The correctness of these ideas is not at first in question; and their truth is not, at first, to be assessed by their usefulness in historical understanding or in political insight. Burke's writing is an articulated experience, and as such has a validity which can survive even the demolition of its general conclusions.'[19] *Here there seems to be an opposition between the truth of ideas as usually understood – the sort that help us to understand history or politics – and a deeper or more durable experience that does not necessarily correspond to any kind of ordinary discursive truth. The same theme appears to recur in your conclusion on Coleridge: 'A whole position like that of Coleridge cannot be offered for conviction; it is not, and could not be, a suasive element. The most that a man like Coleridge can offer is an instance, but, to the extent that one realizes Coleridge's position, one realizes also that an instance is indeed the most valuable thing that can be offered.'*[20] *Your verdict on Carlyle is very similar: 'What is important in a thinker like Carlyle is the quality of his direct response: the terms, the formulations, the morphology of ideas are properly a secondary matter'.*[21] *These passages can appear to be devaluing the ordinary criteria of rational judgment – the sense in which we determine whether certain ideas are true or whether they are false.*

[19] CS, pp. 24–5.
[20] CS, pp. 81–2.
[21] CS, p. 85.

Their direction is very puzzling: the same suggestion does not occur anywhere else in your writing. What is the explanation of them? When writing of Mill, you say: 'There is a point, of course, at which one doubts whether there is any significant difference between the questions "Is it true?" and "What is the meaning of it?"'[22] *But normally speaking these two questions are very distinct. We first ask of an idea 'What is its meaning?' and then we decide whether it is true or false. It is disconcerting to see you fusing the two. Wasn't there the danger of a slide into irrationalism?*

There is a very difficult and deep issue here. The passages you have quoted are clearly the result of my literary training – the whole way in which I had been taught to read a text. For these were the terms in which a poem was normally defined – rather than any other piece of writing. The first duty of the reader was to respond to the articulated experience or instance that the poem represented, which was much more important than the ideas or beliefs that could be found in it – the question whether these were true or what other bearings they had was entirely secondary. The hard-learnt procedure of literary judgment was a kind of suspension before experience. What I was doing in *Culture and Society* was taking that across to kinds of writing which presented very different problems: not just the relatively simpler matters of truth or falsity, although these were very important, but the more complex questions of the proportion or connection between ideas and arguments within a work – where this stands in relation to that.

It helps to understand why this happened if you cast your mind back to something I said previously, about antagonistic modes of thought. I had responded so quickly and negatively in all my earlier years to writers I disliked. *Culture and Society* was written in reaction against that. It is significant that the judgments you quoted all concern pretty naturally antipathetic figures from my point of view. I was making a conscious effort to understand what someone like Burke or Coleridge must have been as a mind. Indeed, there was a sense in which as I was writing about each of these people I felt that I was looking at things so entirely in their terms that I was almost becoming them. That was praised as a quality of the book, although it is not one I value now. At the time I felt both 'this is a very important experience, this is the right way to read them'; I also felt 'this is

[22] CS, pp. 69–70.

ridiculous, I really cannot do it'. But I found that I was sinking so much into the material that it was a positive effort to control my own writing back from the mode of writing I was reworking. I think this enabled me to get nearer to some of the ideas of these writers than I might have otherwise done. I did become aware that it was very difficult to do this with Eliot, about whom I almost immediately started to write much more angrily. But I did not see where the argument would end if I shifted from my general position. One was so consistently told that if one moved from that position one moved out of contact with literature altogether.

As a matter of fact, if you reject that mode of reading of a certain kind of literature, you have to repudiate a great deal else. Today I think you do have to reject it, but the revaluation involved is much bigger than one might think when one takes the first step. My criticisms of Richards, later in *Culture and Society*, do actually start to identify what was wrong with it: the paradox of the induced passivity of the intensely active reader. I now believe that the precise relationship between reader and text which has so centrally defined that discipline is unsustainable and destructive. The theoretical position of the passive-active reader has to be abandoned. Of course, any alternative approach must be a very serious construction, because otherwise one knows how in a less attentive and less open reading questions of truth or falsity, harm or good, are settled so summarily.

The stress on articulated experience is not necessarily inappropriate when judging a poem or an autobiography: why should it be renounced altogether? It is its counterposition to ideas in political or social argument that is perilous.

I would not use the same terms now even for what I would regard as the retainable positive sense, say in the case of an autobiography. But it is true that one of the great interests of a body of writing which survives a particular life is that at one level it really is the articulation of a life experience, something which is unobtainable in any other way outside one's own immediate contemporary period and even then only to a limited extent. There is a sense in which the composition of a specific individual at any point of time is irreducible to what may nevertheless be more important questions about him – the degree to which he represented something, whether he did more harm than good, whether he was right or was wrong. I probably valued this sense then more than I do now. I don't think it is a relationship that is sustainable with a piece of writing, but one could imagine such a relationship with an irreducible instance from a period of the past which was otherwise inaccessible to one: not when the parties had separated out and the full tendencies of opinions had settled, but when these were actually interacting and contradicting each other within an individual mind. I think I have always had a stronger sense of the inherent contradictions and confusions within the actual *process* of somebody's work than another kind of account which summarize its overall *product* and say that is what the person stood for.

The reconstruction of the whole tradition of Culture and Society, *despite and through all these different criticisms and objections, has been an enduring achievement. The establishment of that tradition remains unshakably present for any reader, any socialist today. That is the truth of the matter. At the same time, the book contains another level of interest, which is your judgment of the specific figures within the tradition. This is not a secondary matter, because much of the power of the work comes from the sense of extreme delicacy and precision in your treatment of successive thinkers, isolating the characteristic difficulties or impasses in each of them. You don't, of course, give a complete endorsement to anybody. That said, every reader will have their own list of demurrers to particular appraisals. Perhaps we could start by enquiring whether you still feel now as you did then about Burke?*

Not at all. For I now know the English radicals of the 1770s and 1780s, to whom Burke was responding, as well as to the French Revolution. That made me see Burke wholly differently. English radicalism made its own contribution to the tradition, with the insight – even if from a rather simplified rationalist point of view – that you could reform character by environment, that all kinds of error and injustice should be seen in a social perspective, and then also in its encounter with a more complex experience at the point where its formula broke down. That encounter is more interesting than Burke's. Godwin, whom I was obliged to omit, was one of the prime carriers of this formula, that by patient explanation and rational enquiry you could uncover the causes of vice and injustice and thereby enable their reform with a change of institutions. What Godwin and the others then had to live was the negation of their position by brute authoritarian power – the response, not of rational discourse as assumed by them, but of prosecution, imprisonment and transportation. *Caleb Williams*, or as I prefer to call it, *Things as They Are*, was written within the pressure of this experience. The exertion of maximum state power against that version of rationality enforced a reconsideration of the consequences of the formula. *Things as They Are* seeks at the outset to illustrate the original argument and then throughout the rest of the book is driven to challenge and to deny it. That kind of straining at the limits of a position without giving up the intention behind it is pre-eminently the kind of political thought I was evoking as other than the application of received doctrines – the reworking of a formula through experience, both in the personal sense and in the most immediate social sense of what was actually happening inside England. It is a much more impressive example than Burke.

What about Arnold?

I was thought at the time to be very bad and dissident about Arnold. In the discipline to which I belonged it was a shock that I made any major criticism of Arnold. But what I would say about him now! To see Arnold reacting to a very trivial disturbance caused by official stupidity in Hyde Park during the suffrage campaign of 1866, by constructing a theory of 'anarchy' which was thereafter regarded as a peak of so-called literary and cultural thought – I would have to be savage today, nothing less would do. While poor Mill was caught on the other side of the argument, trying to persuade the reform movement not to meet again in the park but to go to a hall where they would not be troubled. A very decent instinct, but of course the correct thing was to go back to the park.

There is another figure whom you seem to have changed your mind very drastically about. That is Lawrence. You remarked earlier that in the 19th-century period you were actually doing what amounted to historical research, in the sense of uncovering a lot of figures who were unknown to you and were thoroughly unknown to your readership. Hence you could not be expected to make a complete coverage of the field. That seems right: you were in effect writing a new sort of book, which was not literary criticism and was not a standard history of ideas. But you said that in the 20th century you knew the figures much better on the whole and your political judgment was more confident and less subject to revision. One takes it that you knew Lawrence's work very well by then. Yet your account of him is very much at variance with later comments you have made. Citing Lawrence's dictum that 'no man shall try to determine the being of any other man, or of any other woman', you qualify this as a 'declaration of faith in democracy' – albeit one that was 'something rather different from the democracy of, say, a Utilitarian'.[23] *You go on to claim that so far as the state was concerned, Lawrence 'is very close to the socialism of a man like Morris, and there can be little doubt that he and Morris would have felt alike about much that has subsequently passed for socialism'.*[24] *Finally, discussing Lawrence's notions of equality and inequality, with their emphasis on relationship and acceptance of otherness between persons, you state categorically: 'This seems to me to be the best thing that has been written about equality in our period.'*[25] *Whereas in* The Country and the City *you write of Lawrence: 'It is characteristic and significant that he aligned the ideas of human independence and renewal with an opposition to democracy, to education, to the labour movement.'*[26] *What made you change your view?*

The mistake Lawrence made was to start with a notion of beings who have not experienced a determination before they come to relate. At a theoretical level it is impossible to think meaningfully about relationships – which he after all was intensely trying to do all the time and at so many levels of imaginative re-creation succeeded in doing – from that premise. To pose the problems in that way is to repeat the classic abstraction of individuals in traditional bourgeois thought, with its subsequent and separate formulation of social relations. I ought to have known this, because it was what Ibsen had above all shown – even tragically: by the time you realise yourself you are already a determined self. Ibsen's determinations are extremely negative – his people are determined in the strongest and most destructive sense. But there is no question in his work of isolated individuals encountering each other and entering into a determination: an idea as artificial as constructing a trade system from two people on an island. The fact is that the determination of being is a social process which Lawrence deliberately would not understand in the tensions of his own escape. I got much harder about Lawrence over the years. The particular climax of it was when Joy and I jointly edited a collection of Lawrence's writings on education. When we really had to pull out all that he said on

[23] CS, p. 208.
[24] CS, p. 209.
[25] CS, p. 210.
[26] CC, p. 271.

the subject, we almost gave up the commission. By then I was so hostile that I did not want to take any part in circulating it. That was too extreme. But once you had separated out everything that is so interesting in Lawrence, which is that other kind of writing, his theories were so unmediated in the political, social and educational texts that they provoked a revulsion. I still do not think that it was fascism. In a sense it was the most generous kind of bourgeois liberalism at that date, but it couldn't ever constitute its own subject because it was starting at too late a stage in the process.

Don't Lawrence's views on men and women contradict any such description? Bourgeois liberalism at its best would surely be Mill – whose essay on women remains a moving and contemporary document today? Whatever Lawrence's other merits, his writings on the sexes are scarcely very advanced.

I was referring to the idea that no one should determine the being of any other – not to the whole spectrum of Lawrence's positions, because he was a deeply contradictory figure who often could not even perceive his immediate personal situation. He was once fulminating against divorce when somebody simply said to him: 'Lawrence, you are married to a divorced woman, you are talking to another and living in the house of another.' His reply was: 'Oh, my God, that just shows!' However unpleasant, it was a plausible and continuous response. He was totally abashed and surprised because he had not connected the two – his own most immediate situation, which was pretty central to him, and his opinionation. There are people who say: 'Well, we must rule out his opinionation.' But it was very influential. If there was one person everybody wanted to be after the war, to the point of caricature, it was Lawrence.

Within his novels, *Women in Love* represents the fictional mode of characterization which corresponds to that notion of being. You start with four people who are liberated from all determinations, and you then witness the most intense exploration of relationships, positive and negative, creative and destructive. It is a very powerful work, but for me it is a moment of absolute degeneration of the novel as a form. Because at that point a bourgeois novel emerges in a much stricter sense than what is called the bourgeois fiction of the 19th century, which after all still presents a mixture of views, and remains very much more concerned with the social processes of production, including the production of people and relationships. *Women in Love* happens to acquire striking force because it is ostensibly the continuation of *The Rainbow*, a novel precisely written from within the process of the historical production of different kinds of relationship and character. The contrast is very marked between the two books, where the characters are nominally the same people but in fact are not. The only Lawrence I now read is the very late Lawrence, the versions of *Lady Chatterley* and the autobiographical texts he wrote just before he died. It is the powerful uncertainties there that are impressive.

In your introduction to Marxism and Literature, *you allude to the need for a revaluation of Christopher Caudwell – a process to which Edward Thompson has recently contributed in* The Socialist Register. *You wrote then, in a famous phrase, that he was 'not even specific enough to be wrong'.*[27] *What do you think of Caudwell now?*

I rejected *Illusion and Reality* in such a peremptory way in *Culture and Society* because I took it in the terms in which it was presented. *Illusion and Reality* looked like a book that the left wanted – sufficient scope, a theoretical position and a sort of classification. You must remember that I was then a very sharp practical critic and it provoked that professional response in me. I think as an enterprise it was bound to fail, but also that it must have been written under intolerable conditions. Even if history may not extend this sort of charity to what people produce, I should have realized that his pressure was greater than mine.

I became conscious of Caudwell again when I was writing the first part of *The Long Revolution*, about the creative process. That was one of Caudwell's interests too, and it enabled me to understand his project better. I would say today that I think the interesting parts of Caudwell's work are the *Studies in a Dying Culture* and *Further Studies*, although they are very variable. The most important mistake which he makes in them is a failure to separate the generic notion of what is exploited and what is alienated within present society from simplified projections of future man. He made the most serious attempt to think about the latter. I think that he did not succeed, because in a way who could? In particular, his movement back to anthropological or psychoanalytic concepts like the genotype was

[27] CS, p. 268.

wrong. But I can now see what he was trying to do; I can read with him, where in *Culture and Society* I was simply reading against him.

The other figure one wonders if you would still write about in anything like the same way is Morris. Your account of Morris is a very positive one. But one very much feels that there is no break in the texture of your attitude or treatment of Morris within the organization of the book. This has the subtle effect of reassimilating or neutralizing Morris, who is sandwiched between Ruskin and Mallock as if you are just proceeding from one equivalent author to another. Whereas what Morris really represents is the first time that this whole tradition centrally connects with the organized working class and the cause of socialism. That should surely have altered your presentation of him. There were, of course, important arguments afterwards and he did not say the last word on a number of critical questions. But he does occupy a special position, which the book does not exhibit to the reader.

In terms of where he stands I entirely agree with the description you have just made. Morris represents the classic moment of the transvaluation of the tradition. There is a particular problem with him, however. He is rather an isolated figure, if not as wholly isolated as has often been made out. The organization of the book would have been quite different if there had been an alternative line of development following from him. But that did not happen. The confluence he achieved ought to have been much more productive than it was. It is very important to enquire why it was not. On the other hand, reading Edward Thompson's very spirited defence of Morris in the postscript to the new edition of his book on him, I don't find that I take a diametrically different view today of what Morris achieved in his writing as distinct from the crucial confluence that he represented – and the incentive he can still be to that kind of junction. I am trying to do some work at the moment on the introduction of historical break and discontinuity into fictional forms. This involves considering the status of utopian novels. So I will be looking again at Morris and Wells in those terms, as well as at subsequent attempts in science fiction. I would hope to be able to find, but I rather expect I shall not find, that I could revise my judgment of the quality of what follows the realization of discontinuity. Because what the representation of discontinuity typically produces is a notion of social simplicity which is untenable. The extent to which the idea of socialism is attached to that simplicity is counter-productive. It seems to me that the break towards socialism can only be towards an unimaginably greater complexity.

There is another dimension to Morris, however, besides News from Nowhere *or* The Dream of John Ball. *You yourself quote a passage that Edward Thompson was to recall frequently, when in an extraordinary flash of historical imagination Morris conjured up something that was to be very much like the becalmed England of the Tory 1950s – when the workers would be 'better treated, better organized, helping to govern themselves, but with no more pretence to equality with the rich, nor any more hope for it than they have now'. You commented: 'This insight into what has been perhaps the actual course of events since his death is a measure of Morris's quality as a political thinker.'*[28] *This must be one of the very few times in the book when you salute somebody for the quality of their political – as opposed to social or cultural – thinking. But you then immediately check the effect of it by going on: 'Yet it was no more than an application under new circumstances, of the kind of appraisal which the century's thinking about the meanings of culture had made available.'*[29] *With these abstract phrases – 'century' and 'culture' – Morris is reintegrated. Their suggestion is that anybody who had absorbed the tradition could have made those predictions. In fact, to do so, Morris had to cross a class divide.*

The second sentence is clearly not true. It was not an application to different circumstances. Yet I think Morris had benefited from Ruskin's distinction between an alteration of relations and an alteration of conditions. That meaning had been provided, but Morris's use of it was a political break – you are right there.

Speaking of Ruskin, there is one other interesting silence in Culture and Society. *That is the relative absence of any attention to religion. For if one looks through the figures in the book, one notices immediately how central religion was to be development of the tradition. If you had asked them what their main ideas were in their own time, probably a numerical majority – Burke, Southey, Coleridge, Kingsley, Arnold, Ruskin, Hulme, Eliot, Tawney – would have replied with a centrally religious definition. This was not just an religion was to the development of the tradition. If you had asked them what*

[28] CS, p. 161.
[29] CS, p. 161.

adventitious or extrinsic phenomenon. Christian themes, whether in Anglican, dissenting, evangelical, Catholic forms – the whole gamut of possibilities of Protestant and non-Protestant variance – furnished one of the main ideological repertoires from which an industrial capitalism could be and indeed was criticized. This is very evident in the continental tradition as well. In the case of sociology, as you probably know, there was an attempt by Comte, who felt Christianity was inadequate, to create a new religion for the same purpose. Did you think it would clutter the book too much to refer to religion?

I think that it was much more a case of tone-deafness. Your criticism is utterly just, for of course religion was a very key issue. I think I was unconsciously making the assumption, characteristic of a Marxist tradition which has been effectively criticized by Christopher Hill, that if religious terms occurred in a discourse they were a transposition of social terms. I didn't look at them in their own right. That, incidentally, explains the omission of a figure like Mark Rutherford from the book, who should have been there. A later phenomenon that I didn't emphasize enough was the crucial role that the idea of literary value played in substituting for religious and ethical values – a movement that is very conscious in Arnold, as one can see by comparing *Culture and Anarchy* with *Literature and Dogma*, and which has had extraordinary consequences in the 20th century. But the whole question of the varieties of social thought and their relations to religious experience would be quite another book. I could never have written it sympathetically in the way Basil Willey does, because it would not have engaged me enough.

The one public modification of perspective you have made to Culture and Society *till now occurs in your postcript to the 1970 reimpression. There you cite a premonitory use of the word 'culture' by Milton, in his moving final pamphlet of 1660, written as the Restoration was closing in, and you say that you have come to regard the social thinking of the Commonwealth as a major source of the later tradition. The Commonwealth also, of course, represented the revolutionary cycle in English history that much of Victorian thought was determined to repress from national memory. Part of the interest of Green, which sets him apart from most of the figures you discuss in* Culture and Society, *is that for him modern English history had to be understood essentially from the perspective of the revolution of 1640. At the time you wrote* Culture and Society *that was obviously not a view you held.*

Presumably you felt such a deep discontinuity between the debates of the 17th century and those of the late 18th and 19th centuries that the earlier experience of the English revolution seemed to belong to a different world altogether?

Yes. I think that my historical perception was concentrated on the shape of the Industrial Revolution in a way that made it difficult to see the real connections with the Civil War. A good example is the way I later realized, after writing the chapter in *The Long Revolution* called 'The Growth of the Popular Press', that I had omitted the whole emergence of Puritan pamphlets and newspapers during the Civil War, which I did then bring back into my account. I suspect that there are in fact very deep underground continuities from the period of defeat in the later 17th century to the re-emergence of radicalism in the 1770s and 1780s. This is what I hope people will be increasingly able to demonstrate. But there are great difficulties in establishing the connections, less in historical and political relations than in literature and cultural thought, where they seem mainly to take the form of certain kinds of religious imagery or visions with a very strong social content. The articulate upper-class culture, of course, imposed its own discontinuity with its false interpretations of the 17th century.

One obvious point of negative connection, of course, is that the most powerful single image of society, against which your whole tradition was in a sense contending, was a product of the Civil War epoch – Leviathan. The Philosophy of Manufactures *in the 19th century is a direct descendant of Hobbes's universe.*

Yes. I regret that I have not written – or perhaps not yet written – the lectures that I gave quite soon after I came to Cambridge on Hobbes and the Jacobean dramatists, who were physically contemporaries although they are usually located historically at such different points, and then Hobbes and Restoration theatre. The quality of work in the 17th century is such that I did not want to venture until I was very sure. But that postscript revision of perspective is the correct one, particularly as we restore social and political relations to our understanding of the tradition.

How did the reception of Culture and Society *strike you at the time? What were the effects of its success on the conditions of your practice as a writer?*

The publisher who accepted the manuscript, really on the basis of *Drama from Ibsen to Eliot*, which had won a modest academic esteem, told me that it was the sort of book he liked to have on his list, a very reputable work, but of course very few people would want to read it. He said: 'I've got another book called *The Uses of Literacy*, of which I would say the same.' So the amount of attention it got was quite unexpected. The book was read, it was argued about, it seemed in one sense to initiate and in another sense to confirm a tendency towards a new sort of debate. In particular, a younger generation of readers seemed to understand it very well. On the other hand, it was by no means universally welcomed – the quotations used to sell the book today don't give an idea of the amount of negative reactions it aroused. An example was the very hostile review by the literary editor of the *Guardian*, Anthony Hartley. That sector of right-wing liberal opinion was very alarmed by the book, which it saw as a new attempt at a reassociation of culture and social thinking which it thought had been seen off after the thirties.

The most immediate effect on me was to take some kinds of pressure off, and put other kinds of pressure on. It ended the frustration of writing so much unpublished material. After *Culture and Society* I could much more easily publish what I was doing. It also earned a little money, which made a substantial material difference to us, since by that time we had a sizeable family. It had been very difficult to go on writing work of which more than half was unpublished, in conditions when other kinds of writing which I could have done – commercial writing – would have relieved the situation. For the first time since the end of the War, we didn't have to live under the pressure of an extreme shortage of money. The pressure it put on was that of henceforward working in a much more public domain. Suddenly people were saying, why don't you write about this or that? It was easier to get what I was writing anyway into print, but there was now a great deal of invitation to write things I didn't want to do. That is easy enough to deal with, but the much more difficult case is the project which you would not mind doing – something perfectly interesting in itself, but not necessarily what you would have done next. The question of priorities became very difficult. It took some time to work that through.

2. The Long Revolution

Could we ask then about the connection between Culture and Society *and* The Long Revolution? *How was the second book conceived?*

Essays and Principles in the Theory of Culture was my first title for it. The 'principles' were to be an account of the primacy of cultural production – the sense of cultural process which I had been thinking about all through writing on other people in *Culture and Society*. That later became Part I of *The Long Revolution*. The 'essays' were topics I had taught, or was going to teach, in adult classes – the reading public, the social history of writers, the press and dramatic forms. Those made up what was to be Part II of *The Long Revolution*. So the original project was a book which had just got these theoretical chapters plus the chapters on the history of particular institutions and forms. It was in response to the quite new situation of '57–9, including to some extent the discussion of *Culture and Society* itself, that I conceived the idea of writing the third section – 'Britain in the Sixties'. I wanted to be able to develop the position briefly outlined in the conclusion of *Culture and Society*, by a general analysis of contemporary culture and society, a wide structure of feeling in the society as it intersected with institutional developments. The work was a much more developing project even than *Culture and Society*, which of course now seems the more unified book. It was a case of bringing together certain impulses and trying to hold them in some sort of shape. The final form was discovered in the course of the research.

While we are on this subject, are we right in recollecting that The Long Revolution *got a much more inimical reception from the established press?*

The degree of hostility was quite unforgettable. There was a full-scale attack of the most bitter kind in certain key organs. The *TLS* was particularly violent and *ad hominem*. But the reaction was very general. I don't think I felt when *The Long Revolution* came out that anybody had really understood it. *Culture and Society* soon acquired the reputation of being a decent and honourable sort of book, whereas this was a scandalous work. It was a standard complaint that I had been corrupted by sociology, that I had got into theory. The fact is that it was perceived as a much more dangerous book. Just at that time I came back to Cambridge. The spirit of the experience was like '39–41 once again: there was a sense of really hard and bitter conflict.

The political situation of course, had changed very rapidly between '58 and '61. The Long Revolution *appeared in 1961 during the peak of the extremely violent press campaign against CND in the Labour Party, while Gaitskell was vowing an all-out struggle to it. There was a sudden fear of the left which had not existed a few years earlier, within the national political arena.*

That obviously affected the reception of the book. It is an ironic footnote that the one welcoming review of the book was written by Crossman, of all people. He misunderstood it fairly completely – in fact I don't know how much of it he read. Not long after I took part in a public debate on the press – a major topic of the book – with Crossman, in which he was radically on the other side: he actually refused to believe it when told by somebody afterwards that I was the person who had written the book.

What were your feelings on reading the long essay on the book written by Edward Thompson which appeared in New Left Review *at the time? Was that the first extended critical notice you had received from the left?*

I think it probably was – in print at any rate. The whole nature of the culture at that time was such that fierce arguments and debates occurred all the time informally. One of the difficulties I had in focussing Edward's critique, as I told him, was that at the time I was under intense attack from the right: it really was extremely difficult to know in which direction to look. The onslaught from the right was so strong that I felt at certain critical moments an inability on the left to sustain theoretical differences and yet present a common front. I am not referring here to the main argument of Edward's article, but to certain asides and tones. It was a period in which the left in general had difficulty in restraining itself from frustrated point-scoring, as distinct from the expression of theoretical differences which have the object of mutual clarification so that one can move on. Edward said some necessary and correct things. One central theme of his essay was a counterposition of ideas of society (and then culture?) as 'a way of life' and 'a way of struggle'. That pointed at a very crucial problem, which as a matter of fact has still not disappeared from his own work and certainly has not disappeared from mine. But the ambience of the time was such that it was capable of slipping very rapidly into something which, certainly in that review, becomes a less substantial, a polemical point.

What I mean is this. If someone were to define culture as a whole way of life excluding struggle – that would clearly have to be met with the sharpest opposition and correction. On the other hand, it seemed to me that there was a blurring between two kinds of formulation which were in fact used almost interchangeably on the left – 'class conflict' and 'class struggle'. There is no question that class conflict is inevitable within the capitalist social order: there is an absolute and impassable conflict of interests around which the whole social order is built and which it necessarily in one form or another reproduces. The term 'class struggle' properly refers to the moment at which that structural conflict becomes a conscious and mutual contention, an overt engagement of forces. Any socialist account of culture must necessarily include conflict as a structural condition of it as a whole way of life. Without *that* it would be wrong. But if you define the whole historical process as struggle, then you have to elude or foreshorten all the periods in which conflict is mediated in other forms, in which there are provisional resolutions or temporary compositions of it. I was after all particularly conscious of this, because the fifties in England had precisely been a period – this was what the whole political argument was then about – of marked diminution of class struggle in a situation in which there was nevertheless class conflict. Unless one could make this distinction, one was in danger of falling into the rhetoric of 'a whole way of struggle', which was peculiarly unfitted to a time in which what was permanently there as conflict was expressed in terms precisely other than struggle. I sensed in Edward's writing a strong feeling for the heroic periods of struggle in history, which was very understandable yet as it formulated itself particularly unsuitable for dealing with the unheroic decade which we had just been living through. For the fifties, in spite of a revival of a significant younger left, was a very base period, which appeared to have neutralized and incorporated many of the very institutions of struggle to which appeal was being made.

But at the same time I could see a danger on my own side. For there are elements of any cultural process which tend to form bonds between classes that are not merely antagonistic relations. Almost by definition, some cultural institutions involve positive relations, whatever their strain, between classes. In these cases conflicts emerge as arguments over the extent of the institutions, the nature of their content or curricula, and so on. It was always possible, studying these elements in the cultural process, for one's sense of struggle to diminish, to the point where one could miss real clashes between social classes. One of the areas where in fact that happened was in my work on the history of the popular press in the 19th century: it was precisely Edward who helped me to see that the popular press up to the late 1840s was a press of struggle, which I had not adequately registered. But, of course, the popular press after the 1840s unfortunately ceased to be so, and it seemed to me that a rhetoric of 'way of struggle' as opposed to 'way of life' might prevent one from understanding that later development: what I would now define as incorporation.

If one was to seek the most fundamental premise of The Long Revolution, *one should probably start with your initial definition of the title itself. At the beginning of the book, you set out three processes – the democratic revolution, the industrial revolution and the cultural revolution – which together compose a single 'long revolution' for you. The problem that this poses for a traditional Marxist position can be seen very clearly if one then looks at what you say about the interrelations between the practices involved in these three processes. Towards the end of the first part, you say: 'The truth about a society, it would seem, is to be found in the actual relations, always exceptionally complicated, between the system of decision, the system of communication and learning, the system of maintenance and the system of generation and nurture. It is not a question of looking for some absolute formula, by which the structure of these relations can be invariably determined. The formula that matters is that which, first, makes the essential connections between what are never really separable systems, and second, shows the historical variability of each of these systems, and therefore of the real organizations within which they operate and are lived.'*[30] *The key emphasis here is on the impossibility of separating these systems. A second significant statement occurs in the course of your discussion*

[30] LR, p. 36.

of the standard question of the relationship between art and society, conventionally defined. You write: 'If the art is a part of the society, there is no solid whole, outside it, to which, by the form of our question, we concede priority. The art is there, as an activity, with the production, the trading, the politics, the raising of families. To study the relations adequately we must study them actively, seeing all the activities as particular and contemporary forms of human energy. . . . It is then not a question of relating the art to the society, but of studying all the activities and their interrelations, without any concession of priority to any one of them we may choose to abstract.'[31] *Here you associate the idea of abstracting systems with that of ascribing priority to any one of them, rejecting either procedure. The logical conclusion is drawn most clearly in the first pages of the work you wrote immediately afterwards,* Communications, *where you declare: 'We are used to descriptions of our whole common life in political and economic terms. The emphasis on communications asserts, as a matter of experience, that men and societies are not confined to relationships of power, property and production. Their relationships, in describing, learning, persuading and exchanging experiences are seen as equally fundamental.'*[32]

These passages appear in frontal contradiction with a central tenet of historical materialism: the primacy, or determination in the last instance, of the economic within any social totality. Your arguments for rejecting it seem to be twofold. First you maintain that the various activities of a society are so closely interwoven that they are never separable in reality. Second you argue that since they are in effect simultaneous in our experience, they must be equivalent in their significance, for the overall shape of society. Now, in the period of time from The Long Revolution *up to* Marxism and Literature *your thought has clearly undergone very important changes and developments in a whole number of respects – cultural, political and theoretical. In your most recent two books,* Keywords *and* Marxism and Literature, *you say that you are writing within a general position of historical materialism. What we would like to ask you is whether the formulations from* The Long Revolution *and* Communications *which we have just quoted still represent your position on the nature of a social totality today?*

Let me try to get at it this way. There are two major qualifications that I

[31] LR, pp. 61–2.
[32] C, p. 18.

would now make to those earlier definitions. First, it is readily apparent that in certain periods there may exist a disparity of a very marked kind between the different systems of a society – the relative importance of different kinds of production and social process can be very uneven. That necessarily limits the idea of the parity of structures. Second, it is obvious that there is also a temporal unevenness in the formation and evolution of these structures. I was always aware of this problem, as you can see from so many of my particular analyses, but I was not able to negotiate it theoretically at the time. My present vocabulary of dominant, residual and emergent patterns within any given culture is intended to indicate precisely the phenomenon of this historical discrepancy. So in these respects there has been a quite decisive change in my thinking.

On the other hand, the thesis of what you call the inseparability of structures – the inextricable interrelations between politics, art, economics, family organization – is one I maintain. The way I would put it today is that these are indissoluble elements of a continuous social-material process. But I can see that my appeal to experience, in those earlier definitions, to found this unity was problematic. What I said in effect was that we know this to be so about our own lives – hence we can take it as a theoretical assumption. The difficulty with that argument, however, is that in certain epochs it is precisely experience in its weakest form which appears to block any realization of the unity of this process, concealing the connections between the different structures – not to speak of the unnoticed relationships of domination and subordination, disparity and unevenness, residue and emergence, which lend their particular nature to these connections. Indeed, it could be said that my own time was just such an epoch, and that the project of my books was precisely to force back, against the conclusions of experience in its simplest allusive sense, a renewed awareness of the indissolubility of the whole social-material process. Now, it did not seem to me that one could reawaken this sense of overall connection by the strategies I had previously seen followed. Essentially, these sought to show how determinant in particular cases economical-political practice had been over the whole of the rest of actual living. They characteristically involved an extreme selectivity in this demonstration of particular consequences, and an exclusion of other kinds of activity which did not bear the stamp of any such direct relation. Above all, the extraction of one area of emphasis within the society, the abstraction of the capitalist mode of production as such, tended to lead by repetition to a substitution of terms of analysis for terms of substance. If one took the notion of an indissoluble social-material process seriously, one could not concede the analytic priority of a particular extraction from it. For that would enable you to run certain causal connections, but it would not allow you to run certain others; in particular, since most of these techniques have been worked out historically, when you came to the analysis of contemporary society it would be relatively numb – it would simply start from one sector and assimilate the others to it.

Paradoxically, I think that in these earlier books I myself tended to counterpose the notion of cultural process, which seemed to be so extraordinarily overlooked, to what I took to be a previously emphasized and adequately expounded economic or political process. The result was that I in turn abstracted my area of emphasis from the whole historical process. In the effort of establishing that cultural production was a primary activity, I think that at times I gave the impression – especially given the ambiguity of my use of 'experience' – that I was denying determinations altogether, although the empirical studies scarcely suggest that. It took me a long time to find the key move to the notion of cultural production as itself material, which was implicit in a lot of my empirical work but which would have been better understood if it had been made explicit. Because once cultural production is itself seen as social and material, then this indissolubility of the whole social process has a different theoretical ground. It is no longer based on experience, but on the common character of the respective processes of production. However, at the time my effort to reinstate what had been the radically neglected area of cultural practice was taken by others, both in support (which I did not want) and in opposition (which was very easy), as a claim for its primacy over the other processes. Then, of course, the organization of the book could be seen in that light, since it contained a prolonged history of various cultural institutions but no account of the other kinds of practice which created very different institutions, which were inseparable from them. In other words, my work was subject to some of the same criticisms, that it was an approach from a sectoral definition, that I had made of others.

That is a helpful clarification of certain of the problems posed by your initial formulations. But there remain a number of other objections that will have occurred to anyone of more classical Marxist formation. One could be put to you by quoting a remark by a Marxist you particularly respected, Lucien

Goldmann. Commenting on what Marx meant by the primacy of economic production in historical process, Goldmann once said that this was an idea that should not be very difficult for anybody to understand and accept, once you think of the fact that throughout history up to the present epoch, the overwhelming bulk of conscious human lives have been spent in producing their own means of subsistence; quantitatively this is the absolutely dominant single experience and practice of the majority of human beings till now.[33] *It is hard to resist the conclusion that this area of activity must possess a real causal primacy over all other social activities. We are not saying that this is necessarily a wholly satisfactory explanation or definition, but what would be your response to it?*

It would be one of warm agreement and then asking where it left us, specifically in mid-20th-century advanced capitalist societies. That was certainly the ground of the radical redirection of intellectual life which Marx achieved, and which indeed in the crisis of the industrial revolution was being groped towards even by others. But once one has accepted it, two questions have to be raised. The first is the extraordinary extent to which – looking at it as a matter of historical and anthropological record – people at the very limits of the possibility of maintaining their own lives were by some means or other always involved in other activities. It continually amazes me, for example, going round Britain, to see the frequency of churches when you think of the sheer material effort involved in the production of these buildings, many of them fine churches in stone which have survived from periods in which hardly anybody actually would have had a stone house. It is very difficult, even within an emphasis which is natural and overwhelming, to fit them into simple notions of causal primacy – unless one were to argue that the building of a house to God was an integral part of the mode of production itself, indeed that, as Godelier might argue, it was a controlling element of the relations of production.

The other question concerns the specificity of capitalism. In *The Long Revolution* I spoke of the economy as a system of 'maintenance' rather than 'production', which was much criticized on the left. But the reason I did so was that capitalism seemed to me qualitatively a new order in its constant creation of novel kinds of production and need, for internal reasons of its own economic development. There was a danger of generalizing that

[33] Lucien Goldmann, *Recherches Dialectiques*, Paris 1959, p. 67.

process backwards in time – hence I chose to use the more limited term of maintenance. Probably that did lead to an insufficient emphasis in the other direction. Today, however, I am interested in the increasing influence of the idea, which derives originally from Lukács, that the domination of the economic order of society is peculiar to the capitalist epoch. I find that difficult to accept in its simplest sense, but it would explain one's sense of a qualitative alteration of the meaning of production precisely as the capitalist mode of production itself matured. It is at any rate noticeable that in the 20th century the exponents of capitalism have been the most insistent theorists of the causal primacy of economic production. If you want to be told that our whole existence is governed by the economy, go to the city pages of the bourgeois press – that is really how they see life.

Could we take you up on these points? Let us take your example – the astonishing sum of labour and energy invested in the building of churches, let us say in 11th-century England, at a time when stone houses were unknown to the overwhelming majority of the population. It is certainly true that there has been no epoch in which any society has ever been coextensive merely with the practices of economic production: cultural and political activity have always accompanied them. But just to insist on this fact is to return to the problematic of simultaneity. For structures can be temporally simultaneous, but they need not thereby be causally equal. In Anglo-Norman England there were so many houses of God, so few houses of men that were in any way comparable. Can we imagine a society, however, without any houses of men at all – just with houses of God? The question is a reductio ad absurdum: *obviously you could not, because the population would have nowhere to live. Could you, on the other hand, imagine a society just with houses of men, without any houses of God? The answer is yes, perfectly well. In fact such a society historically existed at no great distance from England. Much of Scandinavia had not yet been Christianized: in Sweden in the 11th century there were no houses of God. So we know as a matter of historical fact that this variation is possible. It is true that historical materialism does not possess any worked-out theory, even for one epoch, let alone trans-epochally, of the exact connections between the economic and political and cultural or ideological orders. But to dwell at exclusive length on this point can be a way of burking and evading the central fact that we can in a perfectly reasonable and empirically verifiable way assert that the processes of physical production have till now exerted an ultimate power of constraint over all others – that they form a framework for all other practices which all other practices do not form for the economy in the same sense. Would you accept that?*

Yes, I would certainly accept it – if it is defined in terms of inherent historical variability. I would not accept it, if it is taken as the ground on which to build an explanation of late capitalist society, because by this time so many other kinds of economic activities are operative that have nothing to do with physical subsistence or maintenance. Let me go back to that example of the churches. It is perfectly clear that this was a mode of construction imposed from above. But the success of this mode poses the very difficult question of the precise interconnections between structures of political power, actual relations of production and patterns of cultural incorporation – for primary producers who were actually near starvation did a lot, often under protest but at times of their own will, of productive labour on buildings which had nothing whatever to do with satisfying the physical urgency of survival. There were people who were physically exposed at the very time when they were building shelter for an authority which was not human, which was not of them, even when you have allowed for the other social functions that churches served. In other words, I think that the social distribution of energy invested in physical survival and physical reproduction is very historically variable. If indeed these ever become the primary human intention or an absolute priority, the entire society would be revolutionized. Even when you have allowed for the major kinds of domination and subordination, the imposition of political orders, the use of military force to compel a diversion of energy from those primary tasks, it is the degree to which they were not wholly perceived as such that is worrying for a historical analysis.

Another way of looking at the problem might be to pose the question very sharply of historical change. In some ways this could be regarded as the Achilles heel of your formulations of this period. There is one passage in The Long Revolution *which deals specifically with this question. In it you write: 'If we find, as often, that a particular activity came radically to change the whole organization, we can still not say that it is to this activity that all the others must be related; we can only study the varying ways in which, within the changing organization, the particular activities and their interrelations were affected. Further, since the particular activities will be serving varying and sometimes conflicting ends, the sort of change we must look for will rarely be of a simple kind: elements of persistence, adjustment, unconscious assimilation, active resistance, alternative effort, will all normally be present, in particular activities and in the whole organization.'*[34] *In effect, you here reject the very idea that historical change can yield evidence of causal hierarchy. You prefer to emphasize the ambiguity and heterogeneity of change anyway, 'the elements of persistence and adjustment', which are such that all we can do is 'study the particular activities and their interrelations'. Now it is not at all clear why, if one activity does radically change the whole organization of society, and you concede that this is often the case, one cannot say that all other activities must be related to it. Of course, they should also be related to each other, and of course all the changes in a society at any given moment won't be reducible to the activity which changes its overall structure. But one can still surely say that if a particular activity radically changes the whole organization of society, it possesses a causal primacy – that is the normal meaning of the term. Why were you unwilling to accept this?*

Another very simple way of putting the point would be this: what is the starting point for the whole of your own work in this period? It is the industrial revolution. If we look at the industrial revolution the one obvious fact is that it completely transformed English society as a whole. You have shown the way in which its advent also transformed the actual experience out of which literature came to be written: it is one of the most obvious themes of Culture and Society *and is very strongly present in the second part of* The Long Revolution. *Now if we ask ourselves: is it conceivable that instead of the industrial revolution there could have been such an event as a poetic revolution, capable of transforming the society in a similar way at a similar speed and to a similar depth? – the answer is plainly and patently no. That very commonsensical query merely returns us to the point that the economy typically possesses a causal reach and power that poetry does not. You seem to have felt in this period that to concede that point was somehow to demean the status of art or other cultural practices. This is not an implication which in any way need follow. All you have to concede is that there is an asymmetry of efficacy in the historical process. Historical change is the crux of the whole problem because it is there that one can most closely and evidently discern the relative order or hierarchy of practices.*

[34] LR, p. 62.

I don't find myself disagreeing with this. Including the possibility, even the probability, of understanding what I was saying as contradicting it. Of course, the key change is seen in these two books as the industrial revolution, which was a revolution in economic production; in that sense it had causal primacy. However, the kind of 'relating' I was thinking of when writing the passage you've just quoted was the idea that, say, because there was an industrial revolution there must have been industrial poetry. Actually there were industrial novels, as I demonstrated. But what there was not was the kind of entity postulated by Caudwell – 'capitalist poetry'. Yet it would seem to be a perfectly reasonable deduction from a very simple version of economic determination, that since the decisive phenomenon was the advent of capitalism, there should be capitalist poetry. When I was writing *The Long Revolution* I was probably over-preoccupied by these one-dimensional sorts of explanation and relation. What you are asking me to say, and what I would be very willing to say, is that the industrial revolution was causally primary across the whole field of my study. I would even argue that it had a disproportionate effect on all the other activities which could not survive it, even when they were consciously opposed to it.

But what one then has to go on to say is that it is ultimately impossible to treat the industrial revolution as a process which had external effects in a literature subsequent to it. For the industrial revolution was among other things a revolution in the production of literacy and it is at this point that the argument turns full circle. The steam press was as much a part of the industrial revolution as the steam jenny or the steam locomotive. What it was producing was literacy; and with it a new kind of newspaper and novel. The traditional formulations that I was attacking would have seen the press as only the reflection at a much later stage of the economic order, which had produced the political order which had then produced the cultural order which had produced the press. Whereas the revolution itself, as a transformation of the mode of production, already included many changes which the ordinary definitions – and this is where the whole problem started – said were not economic. The task was not to see how the industrial revolution affected other sectors, but see that it was an industrial revolution in the production of culture as much as an industrial revolution in the production of clothing – which I suppose was its first achievement – or in the production of light, of power, of building materials. Once one begins to break economic production down into its specific processes, it is not so surprising that in a society at that stage of historical development what was also being produced was popular literacy, political order, public opinion or entertainment. This is immensely difficult to put, and I am not saying at all that it is put correctly in *The Long Revolution.* I can see that the effort to establish a new emphasis led me, I don't think to deny, but not sufficiently to state that historical causation must be seen primarily in terms of production and changes in modes of production. But this had been specialized to a narrow definition of the economic which actually underestimated the degree to which it was true. Although I did not have the right terms at the time, that was the direction of my analysis. The fundamental materialist claim was not less but more true than was traditionally thought. I would add that I now find much support for my kind of emphasis in the work of socialists in economic anthropology.

At the risk of seeming insistent, we want to press a further question. It is a very striking feature of all your work that you discuss culture itself in materialist terms in a way that many Marxists who were declaiming the primacy of the economic never did. They tended to accept a division of spheres between culture, a less tangible reality relatively uninscribed in material practices, and an economy devoted to the physical production and reproduction of machines and the means of consumption. Your writing, by contrast, from The Long Revolution *through to* Marxism and Literature *has always explored the precise material elements of any cultural system. However, there is a way of emphasizing the materiality of cultural practices that leads back to a circular social whole. There can be the suggestion that since they are material, they can be causally equated with material practices of a more conventionally economic sort. This would be an advance over idealist versions of a social whole, but would it adequately answer our problem? In your case, after all, it is surely no accident that it was textile manufacturing, with its vast potential demand for objects of elementary physical need, which triggered the industrial revolution – not newspaper printing. Doesn't your own phrase for the cotton industry, 'its first achievement', in fact concede the relevant structural priority?*

One could take another historical problem to crystallize the issue. The most classical example of the extreme difficulty of relating a cultural phenomenon, comprising a vast set of material practices, to economic processes is, of course, the history of Christianity. A complex of religious practices sprang up in a remote province in the first century of the Roman Empire, grew until it became the official doctrine of the late Roman State, persisted through the Dark Ages, exercised ideological supremacy in the Middle Ages, then went through multiple transformations showing vitality and efficacy right through the Renaissance, the Reformation, the Enlightenment and down to the period of the Industrial Revolution itself, one of whose great changes was of course in religious feeling. Historians have often pointed to the history of Christianity as a standing refutation of the Marxist idea of a superstructure which must conform to an economic infrastructure, emerging and disappearing with it. Would it be an adequate reply to insist on the fact that this religion has always constituted a massive complex of material practices, many of them – monasteries, cathedrals, schools, taxes – directly imbricated in economic life? The answer is surely not. The fundamental point about the history of Christianity is rather that this immensely powerful cultural and ideological system could persist across epochs and civilizations, covering the whole of Europe with its monuments in stone, glass, paint, manuscript or print – yet can we point to any major historical change in the structure of society ever brought about by any transformation in Christianity? It is extremely difficult to do so. It is evident that between the classical world and the Middle Ages the structures of society were altered from top to bottom and that this transformation can very obviously be related to changes in production processes, from slave to feudal economies. But no comparable changes occurred in the structure of Christianity, enormously important though its history has been for us. The price of its very persistence is the limit of its determining power. It is in that kind of comparison that the asymmetry of effect between economy and culture can be most clearly seen.

I agree. Even when you have taken seriously the attempts to run the Reformation as responsible for the rise of capitalism, you still cannot in my view accept that as a historical explanation. On the other hand, one should not understimate the degree of internal transformation within the apparent continuity of these immensely prolonged belief-systems. Every key crisis in the society as a whole provoked great conflict in the system, which responded with reinterpretation, redistribution of emphasis, in many cases even positive denial. These responses then tended to form new configurations of residual, dominant and emergent religious feeling. The result is typically a simultaneity of multiple different relations between the presumed belief-system and the actually operative social system.

There is another crucial problem that I still quite insufficiently understand, which poses a similar theoretical difficulty. It is very remarkable that if you look across the whole gamut of Marxism, the material-physical importance of the human reproductive process has been generally overlooked. Correct and necessary points have been made about the exploitation of women or the role of the family, but no major account of this whole area is available. Yet it is scarcely possible to doubt the absolute centrality of human reproduction and nurture and the unquestioned physicality of it. Seen as a historico-material process, it clearly has complex relations to the other forms of production. If you were to say to me, can a change in the nature of the family cause the sort of change in a society that a change in the production of energy, or of clothing, has generated? – the answer is no, it cannot. We would still agree there. But at the same time I think that the category of production is itself an expression of the capitalist specialization of production to commodities, which then poses to us precisely these problems about forms of production that are not commodities. In the very energy of our protest against the ubiquity of commodities, our first response was to say that these were not areas of production at all. But the consequence was then to make them secondary. I think we now have to go back and say they are forms of production, while still registering that certain kinds of production have radically displacing and altering effects on others that others do not have on them. Too much is conceded rather than too much is contained, it seems to me, if we merely insist – as we should – that the production of food, shelter, and clothing must be primary in social life and that the way that is done is going to determine the way everything else is done. The particular difficulty is to integrate that kind of truth with an analysis of advanced capitalist society, where commodity production has become so much more extensive, while central areas of human life have been excluded from the category of production altogether.

It is interesting that one of the major omissions of The Long Revolution *should be of just the area you have mentioned. You argue that there are four essential systems within any society: the system of maintenance (economic), the system of decision (political), the system of communication (cultural), and the system of generation and nurture (familial). At the same time, however, it is striking that you describe the 'long revolution' itself at the outset as composed of three processes – the democratic revolution, the industrial revolution and the cultural revolution. In your conclusion, it is this triad again that you use to analyse British society in the sixties. Your discussion of industry, as a system of maintenance, takes the form of a very powerful criticism of the socialism of consumption and of bureaucratic nationalization: it represents the first extended case made within the New Left for a socialism of production, focussed on work relations. Your account of the political system of decision is less far-reaching, but contains some of the earliest criticisms of English electoralism and proposals for parliamentary reform in that period. Your enquiry into the cultural system includes what was then a highly original programme of institutional innovation, which you later developed in* Communications. *But in this otherwise comprehensive survey, there is one great silent area. The fourth system which you distinguish in your analytic theory of the composition of any social order receives no programmatic treatment at all – the system of generation and nurture. How should one interpret this absence? Does it mean that you felt the problems of the family, above all the position of women within it, were not amenable to deliberate social change in the same way as the other three systems? Given the general sensitivity of your writing to those areas which did not form part of conventional political discourse at the time, it is very surprising that problems of women and the family do not make any kind of entry at all in your work of this period.*

I think that is absolutely fair. It was not, however, that I wasn't thinking about them. In a sense the reflections then forming in my mind were very closely related to the kind of analysis developed in the last part of *The Long Revolution*. If I had written them out, my approach would have been to look at the contradictory features of what is also a revolution in that area. The emergence of a militant and explicit movement of women's liberation from the late sixties onwards was wholly welcome and necessary and overdue. But it has seemed to me insufficiently based on an analysis of these contradictions. What I mean by this is as follows. On the one hand, it is clear that the system of generation and nurture has continued to retain certain distinct priorities in human energy and attention: here is an area where people really do struggle to reserve certain absolutes against a capitalist order, under whatever pressure, devoting themselves to the care of others in the most extreme economic difficulties. On the other hand, alongside the reality and importance of this experience, there is also the frequent evidence of the break-up of relations under the strain of poverty or unemployment, and of the very ugly reproduction inside certain families of the repression and cruelty and frustration of the work situation, of which women and children are the primary victims. Now the contradiction of contemporary social changes has been that the unfinished attempt to liberate women and children from the traditional controls of extreme deprivation and from the reproduction of brutality within the family has itself become complicated, as every human liberation is within the capitalist order, by imperatives which are a product of the system itself. I have in mind not only that ideological reduction of sex to consumption which is now so common. I mean also that the counter-position of liberation to the family was at a certain stage solicited by capitalism itself – which, in its need to recruit cheap female labour, was in effect saying, 'Come out of your homes and do light work for us at a lower wage than we can pay men.' So today there is at once the unanswerable claim of women to be able to go out and work in the world, and the consequence created by capitalism in its usual wanton short-sightedness, that the whole system of generation and nurture has become problematic in some quite new ways, yet really nothing is done about it.

The women's liberation movement has given the right theoretical answer, that generation and nurture should by its very nature be a shared process of men and women. But the practical extent of liberation that is ever likely to occur under capitalism is likely to be determined by the priorities of the market. In this sense the current capitalist order is more intrusive even than in certain phases of the past when there was more actual scarcity and poverty. For problems of generation and nurture are now falsely assigned to a communal care which is then not adequately provided, or even provided at all. Instead of women minding children at home, they should send them to nurseries, but we haven't any money for those at the moment: that is now the characteristic capitalist and liberal message. Together with it goes the notion that work – work for wages, not freely-chosen work – has a categorical priority over any other disposition of human energy. Against that, the women's liberation movement has been entirely right to raise the transitional demand of payment for housework, or – something I feel very strongly about – for mothers of young children, who are incredibly hard worked and who are really neglected today because there is no profit to the social order from them, and they attract no significant political attention from any party. These are the kinds of contradiction within the very real process of liberation that I would have tried to analyse. I wish I had done so in *The Long Revolution*, and I also wish I understood what prevented me from doing so, because it wasn't that I was not thinking about the question. I think that the likelihood is that I had such a comparatively unproblematic experience both in my own home and in my own family, which were very good ones, that I was not as intensely aware of disorder and crisis in the family as I was in other areas. But it was nevertheless an intellectual failing not to confront the problem, especially since I had identified it.

Your work contains a very effective critique of the base/superstructure model of an economistic form of Marxism. At the same time, you have always insisted that any theory of society must be an inclusive one, with a grasp on the social totality as a whole. One of your criticisms of the base/superstructure model is precisely that, by marginalizing a whole set of key practices, it disables any grasp of the overall social process. But there is another Marxist model of determination, whose pivot is the concept of contradiction – the idea that capitalist society is driven by laws of accumulation that generate recurrent economic crises, and whose dynamic creates social conflicts between classes that produce the potential for its political overthrow. One of the difficulties with the general argument of The Long Revolution *is that one gets little sense of the dynamic of the total set of class relationships. In particular what are the contradictions at work in the process of what you call the 'cultural revolution'? What is it a revolution against?*

The classical theory of contradictions within the capitalist economy still seems to me to stand, although it is also evident that the theory must be made much more complex. The post-war development of capitalism showed, to the surprise of those who had accepted the rhetoric of the thirties, that it could for a long time avoid depressions by a series of adaptations. These adaptations then in turn produced other kinds of crisis, which we can see today. The lesson is that the contradictions of the capitalist economy work themselves out at a much deeper and more structural level than the forms in which they were initially presented to us. I think that still we must be prepared for some surprises in that respect. I hope not.

In a more general sense, however, there is something fundamentally contradictory in the capitalist mode of production which is not only to do with its internal economic laws. What capitalism produces in commodity form excludes certain crucial kinds of production which are permanent human needs. This is true not only of its initial turbulent period when it brutally transformed patterns of human settlement and immediate relationship, rhythms of work and dispositions of time, but also of the way it settled down into a more stable order. All the essential human needs that could not be co-ordinated by commodity production – health, habitation, family, education, what it calls leisure – have been repressed or specialized by the development of capitalism. The deepening of the division of labour, and the radical reduction of the notions of humanity and sociality that these processes have involved, have produced profound contradictions – more impossible for capitalism to solve than those which are generated within the market. This is not to diminish its economic contradictions in the traditional sense, which I think it will never resolve. But the cultural revolution finds its source in the perennial resistance to the suppression of so many basic and necessary forms of production by capitalism. The cultural revolution is then against the whole version of culture and society which the capitalist mode of production has imposed.

You say at one point in the book: 'It has been the gravest error of socialism, in revolt against class societies, to limit itself so often to the terms of its opponents: to propose a political and economic order, rather than a human order. It is of course necessary to see the facts of power and property as obstacles to this order, but the alternative society it has proposed must be in wider terms, if it is to generate the full energies necessary for its creation.' Any revolutionary socialist must agree with that. Then you go on: 'Indeed, the political and economic changes might come, and the human order be very little changed, unless these connections are made.'[35] *Weren't you in danger of overstating the emphasis here in the other direction? The argument is surely too totalistic – even granting what is presumably the tacit reference to Stalinism in the USSR. Soviet society may not be socialist, but one could not say that its immense political and economic changes have left the human order of pre-revolutionary Russia unaltered.*

I think it was an overstatement. I was actually thinking not just of the experience of Stalinism, but also of Fabianism – which even more disastrously would not know what a human order was. The immediate example I gave was the whole problem of work. I was writing in the spirit of the passage from Morris we discussed earlier. In that sense, the point has still to be made, about liberal capitalism and about actually existing socialism.

[35] LR, p. 131.

Turning to your own research for The Long Revolution, *you wrote: 'We have reasonably adequate and continuing accounts of the rise of industry and the growth of democracy in Britain. But we have no adequate history of our expanding culture.'*[36] *The second clause is so to speak the programme for Part II of the book. The first, however, seems a strange assumption for 1961, when you were writing. Today one's mind would go immediately to, say,* The Making of the English Working Class *and* Industry and Empire *as 'adequate accounts': the great flowering of socialist and Marxist historiography is essentially a phenomenon that post-dates your book. What were you referring to then?*

I only realized how inadequate the literature I had read was when Edward Thompson's remarkable *The Making of the English Working Class* appeared. But at least some books existed, whereas with subjects that I was dealing with, like the history of the press or of standard English, there was nothing at all. Actually, however, I might as well say that it was with something approaching panic that I wrote those particular lines. For I could see where my argument for a general account of the whole social process was leading me, and I knew what I was going to be able to produce in response to it in Part II – the particular chapters of cultural history, with the important addition of a projected history of habitation, which would have brought in much more of the economic order. In other words, I was aware that in a sense what I would develop was in contradiction with what I had advocated. So in part those sentences were a device to exempt me from that commitment. But I also knew that I could not do anything at all if I had to undertake anything beyond my own field. After all, the new knowledge you've cited is the product of a whole generation of historical research which I could never have done. Even my cultural research taxed me with learning English history as I went along, for the autobiographical reasons that I have explained.

That raises a second question. For the paradox of The Long Revolution *is not just that you plead passionately in Part I for a sense of the whole social process, polemicizing – at times too sharply – against even analytic separation of single areas or activities of that process from each other, and that then in Part II you concentrate on the cultural domain alone. It also lies with your treatment of*

[36] LR, p. 141.

culture itself. For what you give the reader is seven chapters, all of them pioneering studies, on education, literacy, press, spoken language, writers, drama and the novel. But there is no totalization at all of these chapters. In fact there is very little connection even of a written form between one and the next. The interconnection between the different processes is left unexplored, so that the sum of the changes you call 'the history of our expanding culture' is never brought together. This is all the more striking in that you give a very brilliant demonstration, which every reader would remember, of a systematic analysis of the interrelationship of different areas and activities in a particular historical conjuncture elsewhere in the book, in your synchronic account of the structure of feeling of the 1840s. Another aspect of the relative isolation of the institutional chapters from each other, which accentuates the distance between them, is that they share no common starting-point in time. The chapters on the spoken language, education and the reading public go back to the Middles Ages; on the popular press and novel to the industrial revolution; the chapter on English writers starts with the very earliest periods of English prose; whereas that on dramatic forms is concerned only with the modern period. Was it a deliberate decision to write Part II in a discontinuous way, without any attempt at a final interrelation of them?

I don't know how conscious it was. I could see the connections across, but I did not know how I could totalize them. I still find this difficult. I have attempted in a recent essay to totalize just one part of this process at the level of working-class culture, by running together what was happening in the drama, in the press, and in education; but even that does not include the political-cultural organizations of the working class. All I can say is that even that presented major problems, especially because of the very complex relations between the working class and what would eventually be called lower-middle-class elements within the urban popular culture. At the time, I felt that the essay on the 1840s was about as much as I could hold together. The second part of the book consists of a series of forays into certain areas, little more than that, which are not consolidated. The most I could do was to put education very deliberately first. I also regret that a chapter on advertising was omitted – it was kept back for a collective volume on the subject, which then (because the economists couldn't agree) never appeared: that would at least have supplied one crucial thread of connection to the economy. However, what is encouraging today is that a good deal of the necessary work of connection is now being done, yielding cross-correlations which often make me look again at my own material, which I am glad to do.

Why did you decide to adopt the term culture, in full consciousness of its accumulated semantic range, to denote a whole way of life – in preference to the term society, which in the opening pages of your analysis of culture you agree can have the same meaning? Your choice of the term of culture seems to be one of the options that constitutes your own work as a distinctive oeuvre *within socialist thought.*

I suppose I felt that, for all its difficulties, culture more conveniently indicates a total human order than society as it had come to be used. I also think by this time I had become so used to thinking with this concept that it was just a matter of persistence as much as anything else. After all most of the work I was doing was in an area which people called 'culture', even in the narrower sense, so that the term had a certain obviousness. But you know the number of times I've wished that I had never heard of the damned word. I have become more aware of its difficulties, not less, as I have gone on.

All the same, there are surely a number of significant connotations of the term culture as a synonym for society, in the sense of a 'whole way of life'. One is that culture puts a great emphasis, in a way society does not, on the lived texture of the social order: it is closer by its associations of inwardness to subjective experience. Another is that it can suggest an assimilation of the social order to one particular area of it, tending towards a culturalist perspective. Finally, and most importantly, the term culture has a strong normative element which society does not. You can be a hundred per cent opposed to capitalist society, but you cannot be one hundred per cent opposed to bourgeois culture, as Marx himself testifies. The concept of culture contains inherently positive components, whether a shared medium such as a national language, or the inheritances of high art.

There is another connotation which was very important to me when I was writing the book: the sense of culture as a process. Historically, culture was cultivation of something – it was an activity; whereas society can seem very static. I often liked the term for this reason. Its modern derivation is actually from Vico, who used it with precisely this emphasis on process.

The term 'the long revolution' was meant to convey a similar sense of a movement through a very long period. At the same time, of course, the concept of culture has itself classically been converted into an unchanging, timeless body of values or ideas. So the difficulties of vocabulary are acute. Between us and the historical process the problems of language are really formidable. This is why I have much more sympathy than most of my generation for the neologisms or importations of idiom which have been characteristic of the generation immediately younger than my own. It is terribly easy to mock these, but they are prompted by the fact that the existing terms have acquired so much ideological freight. On the other hand, you can run the argument the other way: if you do not contest the appropriation of terms like culture, which was then being constantly opposed to democracy and education, you surrender too much.

What specific advantages did you see in the term culture for socialist theory? How did you pose its relationship to class?

There are two answers to that. The single most shocking thesis to established liberal opinion in *Culture and Society*, including people who liked the book in other ways, was that I did not define working-class culture as a few proletarian novels – which they were quite prepared to look at as a regional genre – but as the institutions of the labour movement. That was the gain of talking about culture as a whole way of life. It was an advance over the conventional notions of working-class culture on the left too, which had concentrated on the struggles by the working class to articulate a body of poetry and autobiography, and eventually other kinds of writing. In my view, it was extremely important to recover and honour these, but it was false to present them as an alternative culture, which was a common tendency. What Welsh proletarian writers managed to say about their extraordinary experience in industrial Wales, for example, is of the greatest interest; but it is not to diminish our respect for the effort it represented to say that it remained a subordinate culture. I think this was a more Marxist position than the one with which it was contending.

On the other side, I also rejected for the same reasons the conventional descriptions on the left of the major thought and writing in England from the 16th to the 20th centuries as bourgeois culture. For the fact is that a great deal of that culture was produced by people who were actually fighting the bourgeoisie, even where they failed, even where they were deeply contaminated by bourgeois forms. It was crucial to retain the sense of that struggle, because otherwise the whole body of that essential work was simply appropriated by the right. By the fifties the trick was being turned that if you thought George Eliot was a good novelist, you had to be against socialism. There was a directly political confiscation of the past that was intolerable. I cannot emphasize strongly enough how important it seemed to contest this appropriation, and the notion of culture which was held to ratify and interpret it.

In doing so, of course I ran some risks. I realized that when someone said to me in the late fifties: 'I know what you are really doing – you are writing a socialist history of culture, but whenever you see a socialist term coming up you omit it and put in another term.' I said: 'This may be the effect but it is not the intention.' Because of the need to engage with the dominant interpretation, my language was very different from that in which I would have written between '39 and '41. I am not surprised that in the next phase of the arguments people felt they had to move to a quite alternative terminology, because they thought that the existing vocabulary confused the emergence of a different position too much.

The concept of 'structure of feeling' is one of the most notable theoretical innovations of The Long Revolution *and is one which you have consistently used and developed in the long span of time from that book right up to the present, with* Marxism and Literature. *At the outset, you define the structure of feeling as follows in* The Long Revolution: *'The term I would suggest is* structure of feeling: *it is as firm and definite as "structure" suggests, yet it operates in the most delicate and least tangible parts of our activity. In one sense, this structure of feeling is the culture of a period: it is the particular living result of all the elements in the general organization.'*[37] *You then go on: 'I do not mean that the structure of feeling, any more than the social character, is possessed in the same way by the many individuals in the community. But I think it is a very deep and wide possession, in all actual communities. . . . One generation may train its successor, with reasonable success, in the social character or the general cultural pattern, but the new generation will have its own structure of feeling, which will not appear to have come "from" anywhere.'*[38] *The essential point of reference for the notion of structure of*

[37] LR, p. 64.
[38] LR, p. 65.

feeling here appears to be not so much a class, or a society, as a generation. Although it is never brought out explicitly, the same emphasis recurs in your treatment of the 1840s and again much later in Marxism and Literature. *The passage just quoted continues: 'The new generation responds in its own ways to the unique world it is inheriting, taking up many continuities, that can be traced, and reproducing many aspects of the organization, which can be separately described, yet feeling its whole life in certain ways differently, and shaping its creative response into a new structure of feeling.'*[39] *The whole problematic of generations is, of course, also very important in your novels and other work. The first critical query we would like to pose about your definition of a structure of feeling is this: any given historical period will always contain at least three adult generations who are active and producing meanings within a single time-span – that is, setting aside the problem of plurality of classes. How can one speak of 'the structure of feeling' of a period, as you do in your account of the 1840s, when at least three structures of feeling would appear to be definitionally present in so far as there would be at least three active generations?*

The general reason is the close connection in my account between the notion of the structure of feeling as accessible for analysis and what appears to be new cultural work. For rightly or wrongly, I think on the whole rightly, we do usually identify the point at which a cultural generation seems to form with what is often, in terms of the actual lives of the people who compose that group, just a decade of their activity. If one takes for example the 1930s, one can trace the emergence of a particular structure of feeling there, in a set of young writers with whom that decade is then retrospectively identified, although most of them in fact continued to write until the sixties, some even into the seventies. The way in which I have tended to apply the term in analysis is to the generation that is doing the new cultural work, which normally means a group which would have a median age of around thirty, when it is beginning to articulate its structure of feeling. It follows that one would then identify the structure of feeling of the middle-aged and the elderly with earlier decades. It was in that sense that I spoke of the structure of feeling of the 1840s. But I did not sufficiently clarify my procedure there.

[39] LR, p. 65.

The second question, then, is how the concept can be articulated to a plurality of classes. For in Victorian England, to pursue the example, there were at least three major social classes – landed aristocracy, industrial bourgeoisie and urban proletariat, not to speak of agricultural labourers, rural small-holders, as well as a heterogeneous petty-bourgeoisie. Paradoxically, you do directly refer to these classes when you discuss the notion of 'social character', but not when you analyse the 'structure of feeling'. The impression is left that a structure of feeling could be common to all classes in a society, once its only referent is generational. What was your view of this problem?

It has exercised me greatly. The concept was initially developed from the accessible evidence of actual articulations in texts and works that I could read. The result was that in societies in which class contributions to that kind of writing were highly differential, it was all too possible to overlook the existence of alternative structures. There is certainly not enough stress on these in *The Long Revolution*, where the notion is presented in essentially temporal and general terms. I would now want to use the concept much more differentially between classes. But it is also important to note that this diversity is itself historically variable. For example, during the 1660s and 1670s two contemporary structures of feeling of absolutely contrasted character existed even among the limited social class that was actively contributing to cultural work. There are other periods, however, in which one structure seems to be more widespread. The 1840s was just such an example. For although the structure of feeling I was analysing in those novels, written mainly by middle-class or lower-middle-class writers, was a class possession – if one pushes the analysis its many class elements are quite clear – it was to a surprising extent shared by the working-class writers who were beginning to contribute at that time. The problem in a case like this, of course, is that the evidence for the concept is only going to be articulate and available in fully expressed work. Yet it can be objected that the notion illegitimately infers from this range of evidence the existence of a structure which is much wider and is unexpressed. I feel the force of this criticism.

How exactly did you come to develop the concept?

The first time I used it was actually in *Preface to Film*. The passage reads: 'In the study of a period, we may be able to reconstruct, with more or less accuracy, the material life, the social organization, and, to a large extent, the dominant ideas. It is not necessary to discuss here which, if any, of these aspects is, in the whole complex, determining; an important institution like the drama will, in all probability, take its colour in varying degrees from them all. . . . To relate a work of art to any part of that observed totality may, in varying degrees, be useful, but it is a common experience, in analysis, to realize that when one has measured the work against the separable parts, there yet remains some element for which there is no external counterpart. This element, I believe, is what I have named the *structure of feeling* of a period and it is only realizable through experience of the work of art itself, as a whole.'[40] In other words, the key to the notion, both to all it can do and to all the difficulties it still leaves, is that it was developed as an analytic procedure for actual written works, with a very strong stress on their forms and conventions. It is a much more straightforward notion when it is confined to that. Yet the pressure of the general argument was continually leading me to say, and I think correctly, that such works were the articulate record of something which was a much more general possession. This was the area of interaction between the official consciousness of an epoch – codified in its doctrines and legislation – and the whole process of actually living its consequences. I could see that here might very often be one of the social sources of art. The example I then worked on was the contrast between the formal ideology of the early Victorian middle class and the fiction its writers produced. The point of the deliberately contradictory phrase, with which I have never been happy, is that it was a structure in the sense that you could perceive it operating in one work after another which weren't otherwise connected – people weren't learning it from each other; yet it was one of feeling much more than of thought – a pattern of impulses, restraints, tones, for which the best evidence was often the actual conventions of literary or dramatic writing. To this day I find that I keep coming back to this notion from the actual experience of literary analysis rather than from any theoretical satisfaction with the concept itself.

Keeping to literary documentation for the moment, then, there still seems to be some uncertainty in your chronological application of the term. You've explained very clearly that the structure of feeling of any given period relates

[40] PF, pp. 21–2.

primarily to the creative work done by the active younger generation. You've written in Marxism and Literature *that while 'the effective formations of most actual art relate to already manifest social formations, dominant or residual', 'it is primarily to an emergent formation that the structure of feeling,* as solution, *relates'. In other words, other artistic formation represents structures of feeling as precipitate rather than as solution. That seems quite consistent. But on the same page you also say: 'At times the emergence of a new structure of feeling is best related to a rise of a class: England 1700–1760.'*[41] *That is a long time: 1700 to 1760. It is the better part of a century. Some three generations would have been active in that period at the median age of thirty. Again, in your work on drama you very tellingly use the concept of structure of feeling to trace the liberal deadlock between individual and society: yet this structure spans the whole epoch from Ibsen to Brecht or beyond. Again, a multi-generational process seems to be at work. Did you mean that there were successive structures of feeling which were generationally distinct but cognate in other ways, each representing a modulation of the last?*

I have no simple answer, but perhaps some clarification. The epoch from 1700 to 1760 is a very complex one, because it includes two radically opposed structures of feeling that are related to the rise of the same class – Augustan classicism and bourgeois realism. I keep trying to work on this, because it's theoretically so important. Of course it can be partly clarified by distinguishing fractions of the class, within a key variable in university education. Moreover it is a time of conscious cultural composition of the new class; I mean to write about Johnson in this sense. Certainly within one generation there was a dominant classicism and an emergent realism, but it is one of the extraordinary facts about the period from 1760 on that a very vigorous realism is eventually contained and displaced, for a further generation and even beyond. One way of tracking that down would be in the limits of each earlier structure of feeling. The methodological problem is similar to that in other fields. You isolate, by analysis, a particular structure, but when it is truly dominant, influencing or even determining later periods, you move almost without noticing it from a seized moment of structural analysis to what is of course, all the time, also a historical movement and development. But then, while acknowledging that there are also other movements, there is great value in tracing, as you put it,

[41] ML, p. 134.

successive modulations in a structure of feeling, until you reach the point where there is a qualitative break – the 1790s in England for example – and then you postulate a period and try to analyse a newly emerging structure of feeling.

Another problem posed by your unit of analysis, so to speak, is how one delimits a particular generation in any given society. For it is a delicate methodological question where you actually draw the lines between age-groups. To take your criterion, at any one moment there are those with a median age of thirty: but what about those with a median age of twenty-five or forty? Where do they fit? This is a problem that occurs quite frequently in everyday speech. What solution would you adopt for it?

This is a very difficult question. There are periods like the 1840s, which reveal a generation of writers – in this case novelists – who were not merely physically of the same age, but who were fully contemporary with each other in the sense that they manifestly share certain perceptions, preoccupations and styles of work. Then there are other periods in which a range of coeval writers do not seem to compose a generation in that sense at all: different figures are there and are doing different kinds of work. A further complication can occur if biological contemporaries compose or publish their work at a major temporal distance from each other, yet with close internal connections. An example which illustrates this problem is the fact that Hobbes was in age a contemporary of Jacobean dramatists like Webster or Tourneur. But the Jacobean playwrights were young men who published their plays in their twenties. Hobbes, because of all sorts of vicissitudes but also the nature of his work, did not publish until his middle or old age. So one might ask how a play like *The White Devil* or *The Atheist's Tragedy* could be described as contemporary with *Leviathan*. But I think if you read *Leviathan* beside them, you get a mutual illumination on both. They share a very precise structure of feeling in common, including the absolutely basic premise, contradicting so much of the official consciousness of the time, of an initial condition of war of all against all. The Jacobean dramatists produced this structure very suddenly, as a set of formal conventions; the action of a drama becomes a virtually endless series of struggles between mutually destructive individuals, from which there is no release. This very sharply contrasts with plays that had been written only ten years before, in which maximum havoc may be let loose but there is always the concept of an authority which will resolve it, at whatever level of loss. Hobbes takes the assumptions of Webster or Tourneur as his starting-point, but he works through them to a kind of resolution with a new definition of authority. That is the later, historical effect.

So the problem of generations is certainly a very tricky one: perhaps we need another term distinct from the biological category. I have been particularly conscious of this myself, since I have not since 1945 worked contemporarily with my own generation and I think these asymmetries always happen. Should one speak in this sort of cultural analysis of a generation of work rather than a generation of birth? I'm trying to resolve this now, with some new methodology of cultural formations.

Your discussion of structures of feeling frequently employs a contrast between past and present, in The Long Revolution. *You write, for example: 'It is only in our own time and place that we can expect to know, in any substantial way, the general organization. We can learn a great deal of the life of other places and times, but certain elements, it seems to me, will always be irrevocable. Even those that can be recovered are recovered in abstraction, and this is of crucial importance. We learn each element as a precipitate, but in the living experience of the time every element was in solution, an inseparable part of a complex whole. The most difficult thing to get hold of, in studying any past period, is this felt sense of the quality of life at a particular place and time: a sense of the ways in which the particular activities combined into a way of thinking and living.'*[42] *You go on to speak of living witnesses being 'silent' once we approach the past. The general suggestion is that it is much more difficult to seize or interpret a structure of feeling in the past than in the present, where an experience of it is immediately available. Yet surely your argument, if anything, should work in the opposite direction. In the present, the immensity of unselected cultural activity before us should make it very difficult to grasp, from within, the nature of the contemporary structures of feeling – particularly given the uncertainty as to what direction much of this activity will take. Whereas the past is typically characterized by a certain crystallization of historical judgment as to what works or documents were most central to it: its materials are more fixed. The fluidity and indeterminacy of the present surely render it at least as, if not more, difficult to interpret than the past? At times you seem close to conceding this – once when you say that not all those who*

[42] LR, p. 63.

experience or bear the structure of feeling of any given period may have any awareness of it at all, which must mean that it is no simple matter to discern at any one point. In another passage, in your chapter on dramatic forms, you say: 'It is never easy, in one's own generation, to see whether the [present] situation is that of 1630 or 1735, with plenty of activity, but on no lasting basis, or 1530 or 1890, at the beginning of a major movement.'[43] *This seems a much more plausible position. But how can you reconcile it with your earlier assertion?*

I think that I quite simply confused the quality of *presence*, which distinguishes a structure of feeling from an explicit or codified doctrine, with the historical present – which is another matter altogether. What I would now wish to say is that while a structure of feeling always exists in the present tense, so to speak grammatically, I do not now think it more recoverable or more accessible in the temporal present than in the past. I did feel, when I re-read *The Long Revolution* ten or fifteen years later, that the part which had stood up best was the concluding analysis of the structure of feeling at the time it was written – because it grasped the facts of widespread dissent, yet, situating them within the structure of feeling, saw the dissent as a largely negative reaction, out of which a new constructive period was rather unlikely to come. Of course, there was plenty of evidence for this in the actual conventions and styles of the period. So one might by lucky chance locate a structure of feeling in the present, but theoretically I would not say that it is easier to do so. For the structure is precisely something which can only be grasped as such by going beyond the indiscriminate flux of experiences that are contemporary with one. On the other hand I think the reason that the confusion arose was that I did want to insist very sharply on the true presence of a structure of feeling, as distinct from the official or received thought of a time, which always succeeds it.

The phrase you have just used has a ring of Scrutiny *to it. To what extent did the notion of structure of feeling represent a way of retaining Leavis's emphasis on experience, but giving it an objective and historical form?*

Yes, 'experience' was a term I took over from *Scrutiny*. But you must remember that I was all the time working on historical changes in literary

[43] LR, p. 297

conventions and forms. Leavis's strength was in reproducing and interpreting what he called 'the living content of a work'. By contrast, the whole *Scrutiny* tradition was very weak in all consideration of formal questions, particularly when it was a question of deep formal structures which had undergone historical change. I was very conscious of this when writing on drama. On the other hand, most ordinary kinds of English Marxist analysis I knew passed so quickly from the literary products to what they represented that it jumped over the works themselves in finding their social affiliations. The notion of a structure of feeling was designed to focus a mode of historical and social relations which was yet quite internal to the work, rather than deducible from it or supplied by some external placing or classification.

You've stressed the literary origins of the notion of 'structure of feeling' – its aid to your critical work on texts. Isn't there, however, a danger in The Long Revolution *of a kind of silent elision from the texts of a period as privileged evidence of the structures of feeling to the structures of feeling as privileged evidence of the social structure or historical epoch as such? The concept then tends to become an epistemology for gaining a comprehension of a whole society. That movement, from text to structure of feeling to history, seems much less defensible.*

I now feel very strongly the need to define the limits of the term. There are cases where the structure of feeling which is tangible in a particular set of works is undoubtedly an articulation of an area of experience which lies beyond them. This is especially evident at those specific and historically definable moments when very new work produces a sudden shock of *recognition*. What must be happening on these occasions is that an experience which is really very wide suddenly finds a semantic figure which articulates it. Such an experience I would now call pre-emergent. On the other hand, a dominant set of forms or conventions – and in that sense structures of feeling – can represent a profound blockage for subordinated groups in a society, above all an oppressed class. In these cases, it is very dangerous to presume that an articulate structure of feeling is necessarily equivalent to inarticulate experience. For example, it seems probable that the English working class was struggling to express an experience in the 1790s and 1830s which in a sense, because of the subordination of the class, its lack of access to means of cultural production, but also the dominance of certain modes, conventions of expression, was never fully articulated. If you look at their actual affiliations, what is striking is a great grasping at other writings. Working people used Shelley; they used Byron, of all people; they responded very strongly to Mrs Gaskell. Should they or should they not have? These works could only have been approximations or substitutes for their own structure of feeling. Then there are historical experiences which never do find their semantic figures at all. I felt this very much in writing *The Country and City*. Even though there is much more literary expression than is usually allowed, there are still vast areas of silence. One cannot fill that silence with other people's structures of feeling.

That delimits the notion of social experience from articulated structure of feeling. But there is still the problem of the epistemological privilege of experience itself in your work. In The Long Revolution *you say a number of times that the key to any description is the particular experience that is its starting-point. This idea, that experience is epistemologically determinant, finds a very central formulation in your introduction, where you write: 'I do not confine myself to British society because of any lack of interest in what is happening elsewhere, but because the kind of evidence I am interested in is only really available where one lives.'[44] This assumption leads to consequences that are quite unwarranted historically. For example, when you discuss the 1840s, you list seven decisive influences on the structure of feeling of the decade. Not one of them has anything to do with foreign or overseas developments. Yet if you look at Elizabeth Gaskell's* Mary Barton, *a novel you discuss, you find a direct warning to her readers of the dangers of a repetition in England of the Parisian insurrections of 1848. In fact, English contemporaries were keenly aware of the seismic upheaval of 1848 in Europe – only a few years earlier Peel was actually fortifying his country house against the dangers of possible armed attack on it. Yet because 1848 was not a national experience in the direct sense, it is not even mentioned in your account.*

The list of main features of the 1840s I gave was actually meant to mark off the way in which its history was conventionally assumed to be reflected in literature. The purpose of the analysis of literature was then to try to show all the pressures which were overlooked by it. Thus *Mary Barton* was

[44] LR, p. 14.

composed within a structure of feeling which made it peculiarly apposite to the conjuncture of 1848, when the European explosion occurred – that was the point of her introductory note. For one of the determining characteristics of so much of the English writing of the late 1840s was an anxious oscillation between sympathy for the oppressed and fear of their violence. That tension is one of the deep processes of composition of *Mary Barton*. You can also find it in George Eliot, who wrote a letter responding warmly to the French revolution of 1848, and wishing a similar event would occur here – but then typically saying that it could not, since the English poor lacked the necessary ideas and intelligence. That combination of movement of sympathy and fear of violence is very important to the structure of feeling I was describing. I would certainly stress it more today.

Your reply still remains within the terms of the lived experience you were reconstructing, however. The point is that the composition of your book appears to join these limits, by appealing in its turn to the privilege of national experience. There is a connection between your initial statement of method and the particular lack of the stress you have just noted.

I concede this. But I should explain that the sentences you've quoted from my introduction were really referring much more to Part III of *The Long Revolution*, where I actually was surveying the contemporary situation in England, and even attempting in outline the total analysis, whose absence you've pointed out in Part II. The claim about evidence where one lives wasn't related as such to the 1840s. However, I am not using this to evade the theoretical point, which I think is correct. If the mode of analysis is viable, it must be applicable anywhere. Some elements of a structure of feeling are, of course, only traceable through a rather close analysis of language, which will always be a national one. But the most normal evidence for such a structure is conventions, which are often international. My own view, as a matter of fact, is that the most interesting use I have been able to make of it is, much more than the essay on the 1840s, my accounts of Ibsen and Brecht – of whose contexts of experience I knew very little.

That is a very helpful clarification. But the wider problem of the category of experience remains perplexing. It must be the only word you use recurrently that is not given an entry in Keywords. *In Leavis's writing it is a subjectivist notion of value – of 'life'. Despite the fact that you have transformed its* Scrutiny *usage, the term does continue to carry something of its intellectual heritage. For your most recent discussion of a structure of feeling defines it as the field of contradiction between a consciously held ideology and emergent experience. The idea of an emergent experience beyond ideology seems to presuppose a kind of pristine contact between the subject and the reality in which this subject is immersed. Doesn't that leave the door sufficiently ajar for a Leavisian notion of 'life' or 'experience' to return?*

No. That should be very clear. For after all the basic argument of the first chapter of *The Long Revolution* is precisely that there is no natural seeing and therefore there cannot be a direct and unmediated contact with reality. On the other hand, in much linguistic theory and a certain kind of semiotics, we are in danger of reaching the opposite point in which the epistemological wholly absorbs the ontological: it is only in the ways of knowing that we exist at all. To formalist friends, of whom I have many, who affect to doubt the very possibility of an 'external' referent, it is necessary to recall an absolutely founding presumption of materialism: namely that the natural world exists whether anyone signifies it or not. The fact is that we have been passing through a phase of rabid idealism on the left in the sixties and seventies. It is a positive relief to read Timpanaro's reminder that physical organisms exist in an undeniably material world whether or not they have ever been signified.

That said, I think the relation between signification and referent in one's own situation differs from that in any other. This is very difficult to formulate. But in the case of other situations, one learns only through recorded articulations; all that one has is necessarily, as it were, texts or documents. Certainly in one's own time one gathers far more than most people realize from just these versions of an endless documentation. By contrast in the whole process of consciousness – here I would put a lot of stress on phenomena for which there is no easy knowing because there is too easy a name, the too easy name is 'the unconscious' – all sorts of occurrences cut across the established or offered relations between a signification and a reference. The formalist position that there is no signified without a signifier amounts to saying that it is only in articulation that we live at all. Now maybe this is just a generalization from my own history, but I have found that areas which I would call structures of feeling as often as not initially form as a certain kind of disturbance or unease, a particular type of tension, for which when you stand back or recall them you can sometimes find a referent. To put it another way, the peculiar location of a structure of feeling is the endless comparison that must occur in the process of consciousness between the articulated and the lived. The lived is only another word, if you like, for experience: but we have to find a word for that level. For all that is not fully articulated, all that comes through as disturbance, tension, blockage, emotional trouble seems to me precisely a source of major changes in the relation between the signifier and the signified, whether in literary language or conventions. We have to postulate at least the possibility of comparison in this process and if it is a comparison, then with what? If one immediately fills the gap with one of these great blockbuster words like experience, it can have very unfortunate effects over the rest of the argument. For it can suggest that this is always a superior instance, or make a god out of an unexamined subjectivity. But since I believe that the process of comparison occurs often in not particularly articulate ways, yet is a source of much of the change that is eventually evident in our articulation, one has to seek a term for that which is not fully articulated or not fully comfortable in various silences, although it is usually not very silent. I just don't know what the term should be.

There is a remarkable similarity between the formulations you've just used and Sartre's account of what he calls – precisely – l'expérience vécue, *in his late work on Flaubert. One way of trying to clarify the problem might be to broaden its terms of reference. To take the example of another thinker in France, one could contrast your use of experience till now with that of Althusser, as a diametrical opposite. In Althusser's work, experience is simply a synonym for illusion. It is ideology in its pure state – the opposite of science, or truth. That is a position he has taken over, more or less unmodified, from Spinoza: it represents an extreme form of the philosophical tradition of European rationalism. In your work up to this point the impression is conveyed that experience on the contrary is the domain of direct truth. At times, as we've seen in* Culture and Society, *you have even counterposed conceptual or discursive thought against immediate experience, as superficial and unreliable – a sphere of false fixity and clarity, the world of 'doctrines'. This emphasis obviously has a long history: it can be traced back, in fact, to Locke. Philosophically, it represents the classical position of European empiricism. Now there are obvious objections to be made to either stance. For example, in the case of Althusser's work, the exclusive opposition of science/ideology effectively equates the idea of truth with science. Since immediate experience is the medium of ideological illusion, Althusser in effect argues that it is only by the production of concepts that we can apprehend reality at all. Manifestly, however, this is not the case: we can look out of the window and tell whether the sun is shining or not without any knowledge of meteorology. Our report is a matter of immediate experience, and registers a truth. This is an elementary point. But that kind of experience escapes the Althusserian system altogether. On the other hand, your tendency to treat experience as the deepest field of truth incurs the opposite liability. For it is quite evident that people may have very powerful experiences, and be completely convinced of their connection to reality, which from a different social or historical perspective we can perceive as saturated with illusion and structured somewhere quite else. A familiar example is the case of certain kinds of psychological disorder or malady where a person is completely gripped by an experience that is very vivid to them, but of whose sources they are entirely unaware and can misinterpret radically. Similarly, to take the previous example, an ability to tell the weather does not suffice to give knowledge of the movement of the earth round the sun: immediate experience is directly contradicted by astronomy as a science.*

This is why the suggestion in The Long Revolution *that one should attempt to interpret a whole social structure by the canon of actually living within it, if taken seriously, is centrally disabling. For even within one national society there are manifestly many processes which are inherently inaccessible to our immediate experience. We cannot possibly, for instance, hope to work out the laws of accumulation of capital or the tendency of the rate of profit from our personal experience of daily life. Yet these may be an absolutely essential determinant of the way in which the whole society is moving. That is not to speak of the national limitation implied in the criterion, which would effectively rule out international enquiry or comparison altogether. But, of course, the world has been such for a very long time now that without knowledge of the whole international environment into which it is integrated, one can understand very little of one's own society. That is surely one of the first lessons of socialism.*

In your latest definition of a structure of feeling as the area of tension between ideology or articulation and primary experience, there remains a danger that these earlier limits – which you've criticized – may still not be entirely overcome. For there is a suggestion that articulation or ideology covers or informs – often deforms – an experience which is always wider than it. In the binary opposition which you use, experience necessarily exceeds articulation, producing meanings which may or may not be recorded – that's the problem of silence or otherwise – but always containing more than ideology can remit. In your recent political discussion of the notion of hegemony, you make the very effective point that the hegemony of a ruling class can never extend over the whole range of a society's experience, since by definition it operates through exclusion and limitation.[45] *The problem remains, however, that there are all kinds of great historical processes that cannot be encompassed within either of the two terms in which you formulate a structure of feeling – ideology or immediate experience. Any systematic discourse on history or society must aim at a scientific knowledge that is underivable from any literary text. To return to your analysis of the 1840s: in that decade there occurred a cataclysmic event, far more dramatic than anything that happened in England, a very short geographical distance away, whose consequences were directly governed by the established order of the English state. That was, of course, the famine in Ireland – a disaster without comparison in Europe. Yet if we consult the two maps of either the official ideology of the period or the recorded subjective experience of its novels, neither of them extended to include this catastrophe right on their doorstep, causally connected to socio-political processes in England. That is surely a reminder that one cannot run together different sorts of enquiry in the way that you sometimes seem to do in* The Long Revolution. *It is not possible to work back from texts to structures of feeling to experiences to social structures. There is a deep disjuncture between the literary text from which an experience can be reconstructed and the total historical process at the time. There is not a continuity at all.*

I accept this almost entirely. But I think one can differentiate its historical applications. It is very striking that the classic technique devised in response to the impossibility of understanding contemporary society from experience, the statistical mode of analysis, had its precise origins within the period of which you are speaking. For without the combination of statistical theory, which in a sense was already mathematically present, and arrangements for collection of statistical data, symbolized by the foundation of the Manchester Statistical Society, the society that was emerging out of the industrial revolution was literally unknowable. I tried

[45] ML, p. 125.

to develop this contrast in *The Country and the City* between the knowable community, a term used with irony because what is known is shown to be incomplete, and the new sense of the darkly unknowable. There are many kinds of response to that. After the industrial revolution the possibility of understanding an experience in terms of the available articulation of concepts and language was qualitatively altered. There were many responses to that. New forms had to be devised to penetrate what was rightly perceived to be to a large extent obscure. Dickens is a wonderful example of this, because he is continually trying to find fictional forms for seeing what is not seeable – as in the passages in *Dombey and Son* where he envisages the roofs of houses being taken off, or a black cloud that is the physical shape of all the lives that are lived yet otherwise cannot be represented at all. With these figures he is seeking to render the basic reality of the society, which is certainly not empirically observable. One could interrun this with the development of the statistical techniques of social enquiry. The contrast between Mayhew and Booth is very interesting. Mayhew's work is composed of a constant interaction between premises, observations, questions. He takes his assumptions of how people are living back into the streets and talks to people to find out if they are true: if somebody tells him that they do not earn that much as a watercress seller, it modifies his view of the world. It is not eccentric to call this social observation continually tempered by experience. Booth's method is quite different. Before he speaks to anybody in the East End of London, he has totally mapped its structure by streets, in an incredibly impressive job of work, and then he takes his classifications to the East End to prove that radical propaganda about it was false. To his credit, or I suppose that of Beatrice Webb, when actual observations contradicted the rationality of the model, there was some disturbance to the survey.

From the industrial revolution onwards, qualitatively altering a permanent problem, there has developed a type of society which is less and less interpretable from experience – meaning by experience a lived contact with the available articulations, including their comparison. The result is that we have become increasingly conscious of the positive power of techniques of analysis, which at their maximum are capable of interpreting, let us say, the movements of an integrated world economy, and of the negative qualities of a naive observation which can never gain knowledge of realities like these. But at the same time, it is an ideological crisis of just this society, that this inevitable awareness has also led to a privileged dominance of the techniques of rational penetration and a corresponding undervaluation of areas where there is some everyday commerce between the available articulations and the general process that has been termed 'experience'. Experience becomes a forbidden word, whereas what we ought to say about it is that it is a limited word, for there are many kinds of knowledge it will never give us, in any of its ordinary senses. That is a necessary correction. But I find that just as I am moving in that direction, I see a kind of appalling parody of it beyond me – the claim that all experience is ideology, that the subject is wholly an ideological illusion, which is the last stage of formalism – and I even start to pull back a bit. But I think the correction is right and in a way I should always have known it, because after all I was pretty dependent on statistical procedures in Part II of *The Long Revolution* for findings that I could not possibly have obtained from experience.

That balance seems very acceptable. One of the areas which you could have mentioned, where the notion of experience clearly keeps its credentials, is the practice of class struggle. It is normal in the political language of socialism to speak of a working-class militant as 'experienced' – Lenin did so hundreds of times – which means something quite precise, that someone with the same or greater degree of formal knowledge of the society but without that experience could not organize actions with anything like the same degree of effectiveness. Of course, it is also true that fetishization of experience within an organization can become a form of conservatism: experience won today does not necessarily dictate the tactics or the strategy of tomorrow – partly because the enemy itself learns from experience. But a correct emphasis on experience as practice in struggle is essential for any form of revolutionary politics. One gets the impression from The Long Revolution *that you felt socialist theory was then claiming a knowledge of contemporary society which actually did not meet with the practical experience of struggle against it. Is that so?*

Well, much of Part III is a conscious comparison between the received models of English society at the time and what seemed to me was actually happening. I drew on various kinds of alternative evidence in my own response to the very fiercely fought and agitated debates between right and left within the labour movement through the fifties. But what I essentially felt about them was that, although I was very much nearer the one than the other, neither really answered to the social experience to which they were attempting to speak. That is what explains the no doubt exaggerated judgment that socialism had almost wholly lost any contemporary meaning. What I was trying to say was that it was above all necessary not to pretend that there was a strong, well-rooted socialist movement which was in a position to change the society and that the first duty was affiliation to it. It was a time, on the contrary, when the real need was to contrast very rapidly changing social relations with the prevailing formulations which were helpless before them. I think out of that came certain directions for a relevant cultural practice, although I would now put them much more strongly.

Perhaps we could conclude by asking you a question about this last part of The Long Revolution. *You said earlier that you conceived the essay on 'Britain in the 60s' as an attempt to capture the structure of feeling at the time. Now this brings us back to one of the problems with which we started. If that was the case, how did you relate your analysis to the class divisions within the society? There were at least two major classes in England in this period, not to speak of many intermediate strata with their own sensibility and history and memory. Wouldn't your tacit reference to a structure of feeling in the singular have tended to blur that reality?*

I was using the term, in the sense I suggested earlier, of the structure of feeling of the emergent productive class. What I was trying to do was at once to register the strength with which it was emerging, and thereby rendering certain prior meanings residual, and yet also the fact that it was becoming contained within a predominantly bourgeois structure, which had incorporated a large part of organized working-class thinking within it. For example, I thought it was necessary to explain the so-called phenomenon of 'classlessness': to show what it was that made sense in that emergent structure of feeling, and what was strictly an ideology which was blocking the very emergence of this structure. Very obviously certain habits of deference and postponement were being lost. On the other hand, not only in the received ideologies but in many working people's descriptions of their own lives, there was a displacement of class relations from their necessary centrality to a curious mixture of a certain undoubted real loosening and a particular style of consumption, which was itself merely a shift in the market and nothing whatever to do with fundamental relations between classes. That is why I distinguished between what I called the open 'class-apparent' differential and the fundamental and unaltered differential of the ownership of capital. The focus of my account was the structure of feeling of working-class people, rather than the political doctrines or arguments of the time.

3. Keywords

The sort of historical philology represented by Keywords *seems to be an entirely original venture, at least within the English-speaking world. You explain in your introduction to it that* Keywords *grew out of materials that you couldn't include in* Culture and Society. *But in the twenty years between the writing of the two books your ideas obviously altered and developed.* Keywords *takes the principle of looking at changes of historical meaning much further and more systematically than* Culture and Society. *Were you influenced by or interested in other kinds of linguistic study in the interim, which had a direct bearing on* Keywords?

I started with the discovery in the fifties that I could understand the contemporary meanings of terms like 'culture' much more clearly once I had explored the historical semantics behind them, which was a great surprise to me. It was not an entirely unfamiliar method, of course, because the English course at Cambridge had involved the discussion of certain words like 'nature' to establish their historical usages; but this was regarded very much as an ancillary to literary appreciation. When I realized the potential wider interest of this procedure, I wrote an appendix to *Culture and Society*, taking a range of the words at issue in the book. The publisher didn't want to include it, for reasons of length. In the intervening years I went on noting further examples of terms that had undergone important changes of meaning. I was also reading more theory of language. But although I now know of one or two other schools which would have been relevant to me – for example, the German scholars who work on certain medieval terms – at the time I couldn't find any other enquiry which moved either practically or theoretically in the same direction. So in that sense it felt very much as if I was working on my own. Indeed most of the linguistics I was reading, especially in the sixties, was structuralist in bent, sheering away from the very notion of historical developments in meaning. I suppose I got some impulses in reaction to that, in the sense that I felt strongly that a historical semantics was needed as well as structural analyses. When *Keywords* was published, I invited readers at the end of the preface to send material on other terms which interested them. Since then I've received detailed notes on about two hundred words. So in a way people were already doing this, but in the margins of other kinds of work. Some readers also wrote to say that they didn't realize that there was a possibility here of a specific discipline or subject that could be consciously pursued. I now think that is what it should be – I would like to see this enquiry much more systematically extended. It pleases me that people who might previously have included some incidental paragraphs or sections on historical changes in the meaning of a word are now starting out their research from the facts of these changes. The theoretical drift had been the other way.

If one compares Keywords *with* Culture and Society, *one absolutely central point comes home much more forcibly in the later book, because of the wider range of the terms discussed, which is not merely the possibility but even the frequency of a 180 degree reversal of the meaning of a term – the way words can come to stand for the exact opposite of their original sense. 'Individual' is an arresting case in point, but there are many others. How would you sum up the significance of this drastic mutability, whose demonstration forms the substance of the book? What lessons would you draw from it?*

At the theoretical level, it underlines the fact that language is a continuous social production in its most dynamic sense. In other words, not in the sense which is compatible with structuralism – that a central body of meaning is created and propagated, but in the sense that like any other social production it is the arena of all sorts of shifts and interests and relations of dominance. Certain crises around certain experiences will occur, which are registered in language in often surprising ways. The result is a notion of language as not merely the creation of arbitrary signs which are then reproduced within groups, which is the structuralist model, but of signs which take on the changeable and often reversed social relations of a given society, so that what enters into them is the contradictory and conflict-ridden social history of the people who speak the language, including all the variations between signs at any given time. This also involves the rejection of idealist accounts of language as a common possession – at its best, Leavis's notion of language as a continuous legacy through the ages that carries the finest insights of the community. For while Leavis was right to stress the cultural importance of language, his notion of continuity was quite false, since it rested on an abstraction from what were always extraordinary historical transformations and reversals, and then on proposing a single heritage of meanings which were held to sanction particular contemporary values. So the kind of work I started in *Keywords* is a corrective to either of those two accounts of the nature of language: that is its theoretical importance. At the same time, it also allows us to look at a whole body of social evidence which can be quite precisely studied and related to the rest of social history, but which has so far never been fully explored. For people who might otherwise have been predisposed to do so have generally assumed that language is merely the instrument or the record of the changes which have happened elsewhere; whereas it seems to me that certain shifts of meaning indicate very interesting periods of confusion and contradiction of outcome, latencies in decision, and other processes of a real social history, which can be located rather precisely in this other way, and put alongside more familiar kinds of evidence. What would be really interesting is then to pursue this research across languages and see whether there are, as there must be, certain shared semantic changes in certain kinds of social orders.

The intellectual effect of the kind of work initiated by Keywords *could be regarded as akin to that of the Marxist critique of political economy – the demonstration that ideas and categories which are deemed universal and timeless are in fact eminently changeable and timebound. Linguistic custom, however, has a yet more natural air to it than economic practice. Language tends to accrete myths of longevity and essentiality about it perhaps more than any other domain of human life – hence the focus of so much philosophical mysticism in the twentieth century on it. Your strategy in* Keywords *is to register the changes of meaning across a whole vocabulary very pointedly indeed, but not actually to retrace the social agency of these changes. Presumably it would be possible to go over the same philological ground from the opposite direction, looking carefully at the first usages of terms or pilot shifts in meaning, and then at the diffusion of those usages and shifts, tracing the forces which were the bearers of them – in other words, writing a socially explanatory history?*

Yes. Once one has plotted the extraordinary transformations of a word like 'interest', for example, the next step would be to see in which areas of society specific usages of it started, in which they were then reversed, and so on. The same would hold for 'science'. It would probably also be interesting for 'family', where the shifts of usage could be located relatively early. In some cases a very close and differentiated account would be necessary, showing in which group a change of meaning started to occur, and then how and whether it was generalized – either diffused through the general educational system or in some other way, or remaining a term within a specific class. All these possibilities have to be explored.

One very striking fact about the vocabulary which you selected for treatment in Keywords, *which you don't mention anywhere in the book, is its etymological composition. There are entries for 110 words. Of these, no less than 106 are of Latin origin: a mere 4 are Anglo-Saxon formations. These proportions are, of course, dramatically discrepant from the general balance of English word-stock, which is about 55 per cent Latin to 45 per cent Anglo-Saxon. The pattern in* Keywords *has, in fact, a direct relation to an eloquent passage in* The Long Revolution *where you discuss the effects of the division between French and Old English after the Norman Conquest, prior to the emergence of a common language again by the 14th century. You write: 'English passed, during the separation [between two languages], into the mouths of the uneducated and the powerless. Thus the greater part of the vocabulary of learning and power, together with the bulk of the vocabulary of a richer way of living, came from Norman sources. . . . It is probably still important, in English, that so much of the language of learning should have this special kind of class stamp.'*[46] *It seems a reasonable guess, in fact, that for a readership that does not come from a class background whose education familiarizes it with the Latinate reaches of contemporary English, there may be a greater distance from the kind of vocabulary which forms the subject matter of* Keywords *than would be the case in countries with a much more homogeneous semantic stock like Germany or France. The problem of democratic comprehension and appropriation of the whole resources of the language is probably particularly acute in England, because of its divided linguistic inheritance.*

It is certainly my impression when I listen to a French militant or trade

[46] LR, p. 240.

union leader being interviewed that they command a much greater vocabulary than their English social equivalents, which may eventually have an effect on the quality of what they say. I also doubt whether you could come up with a similar list in German. I think you are right that the problem is especially intense in England. I was constantly distressed during my years in adult education at the blocks people encountered when some perfectly necessary concept was used, and the easy way that could slip into anti-intellectualism, or the more unfortunate case of somebody who comes across a word but doesn't fully understand it, yet starts to use it, often in the labour movement. That was why, after I couldn't include the appendix in *Culture and Society*, I wanted to write a series in *Tribune* on words that caused difficulty – typically enough, they were not interested. I had a very strong sense, as in everything else, that working-class people needed to command all the tools with which social transactions are conducted. Today, I notice people using *Keywords* who would not be interested in any of my other books, because they bump into one of these words and want to look it up. I deliberately included some terms in it because I felt that people did not know their more interesting and complex social history, and so were often either unsure about employing them, or recoiling from one of their meanings which had been heavily put by ruling-class papers or publicists. I wanted to give them confidence in their ability to use these terms.

One of the most welcome features of the book is that it exposes the crudity and illiteracy of the current campaigns in the bourgeois media for the preservation of our language. There has always been a connection, of course, between such watchdog attitudes and conservative politics. Mencken in America and Kraus in Austria were rather distinguished instances of this kind of conservatism; the English exponents of it are a caricature of them – what would Kraus have thought of the regular journalistic columns in The Times *devoted to the protection of our speech? The efforts to propagate the idea that words have only one meaning, which is laid down forever, and any departure from which is ignorance, have reached a crescendo in the last few years. You must have had these in mind when writing* Keywords?

Not at the time. But I've seen them since; and of course it's necessary to attack the whole position of these Establishment journalists, who mistake linguistic change for degeneration, and all those who try to co-opt words like 'democracy' or 'representation' for political purposes. As late as 1880 one dictionary definition of democracy in England was 'a republican form of government'. These propagandists are demonstrably ignorant of the very legacy they are claiming to defend.

Can we ask about a few terms which you didn't include? One is the rather important word 'experience', which we mentioned earlier. Was that a conscious choice?

It was marginally there in my discussion of the English divergence between 'experience' and 'experiment' in the 18th century, but under the heading of 'science'. It should be included when *Keywords* is revised.

Another word which is very prominent in contemporary vocabulary, and which would certainly have an interesting history is 'race'. Its current usage must be very recent?

I did a lot of reading on the term, and I don't know why in the end it was omitted. It expanded from local kin-groups and species to more (and falsely) generic and political indications. Another very important related term is 'sex', which was also excluded. I think the common notion of 'sex' as the man/woman differentiation, and then the specialized physical meaning attached to it, are fairly recent. I suspect there's a lot of social history in that one.

Your entry on the word 'unconscious' is of particular interest in Keywords, *since it seems to be the first time that you hint at your attitude towards the central category of psychoanalysis. In it, you say that it is often not clear whether the hypothesis of the unconscious indicates, within a range of experiences which are ordinarily in transition from unconscious to conscious, cases of a failed transition, or whether it denotes two fixed states, conscious and unconscious, as reified abstractions. You then refer to Freudian theory, without naming it, as a school which 'resists the implication of a "normal" transition [from unconscious to conscious] and by contrast insists on a fully unconscious area from which transition is not possible except by special methods'.*[47] *Should we take it, therefore, that you believe that there is a*

[47] K, p. 273.

normal and continuous process of transition from unconscious to conscious, with certain exceptions in which there is a failure of transit – is that what you regard as the most plausible and acceptable scientific hypothesis at present?

Let me put it this way. I would certainly not look, until I had been finally convinced that all other directions were fruitless, towards a prior categorization of an unconscious accessible only by certain specialized techniques. To say that the transition from unconscious to conscious is normal, however, is to claim too much. I think that two very important considerations come into play here, where much of the importance of Freud can be properly granted, and yet research proceed in a useful way. First, in the very interesting area of the relation between manifest speech and what Vološinov called inner speech, there are processes of which we must all be aware that are prior to articulation, and in that quite strict and literal sense not fully conscious. These processes are very difficult to identify, but I think that some of them are matters of everyday experience. Examples would include the way in which writers typically discover what they want to say in the act of writing itself. This means that it is a perfectly reasonable hypothesis to talk of unconscious processes which can be articulated and become conscious. But I don't think this can necessarily be called normal – it is often specialized. What is, on the other hand, a quite normal process is the socio-cultural development of language, as the historical or even further evolutionary possibility of that transition.

But haven't you already built in a bias towards the idea of normality, because after all manifest speech is what we speak all the time, so if there is an inner speech behind it there must be a constant ongoing process of transition?

That is where the second point arises, which interests me very much. It is an area into which Marxists especially should move. There are certain forms of quite literal repression – of the kind more ordinarily described in political, social, economic, indeed often military terms – which are virtually institutionalized in language. I mean (and it's a very difficult area because there is a major theoretical dispute inside it) that there are certain periods of language which impose silent areas, so what is theoretically a normal process of transition cannot occur. This is of special interest for Marxists since there will always be deeply social and historical conditions for that silence. The reason why I say it is a difficult area is because there is the well known Sapir-Whorf hypothesis that certain cultures don't have the capacity, as evidenced by their language, to think certain concepts. For myself, I am on the whole convinced by the arguments of Rossi-Landi that this is an idealist thesis. What I would nevertheless contend is that historically there are certain language situations which are repressive. People talk of language as a means of expression, but it is also evidently a means of selection. In certain social-historical circumstances, there are things which could not be said, and therefore, in any connecting way, not thought. This may help to explain the very common cultural phenomenon of an extraordinarily shocking innovation of discourse – Freud himself is an example of this – which yet produces elements of *recognition*. The possibility of a pre-emergent as well as an emergent structure of feeling corresponds, in my terms, to this phenomenon.

The way you've spoken about the unconscious is always in terms of an inner zone of silence, of pure repression. Whereas in Freud the unconscious is always active in speech; it is not so much a blank area that is not operative, that is completely repressed out of existence, as something like the hidden side of everything which is manifest. For him the cases of real repression are those where the normal processes of communication of the unconscious to the conscious are blocked, and the result is a determinate symptom of disturbance which can be traced in the conscious – there is an abnormal displacement. When you speak of the unconscious, it is as if it were a reserved sector, a special enclave, which can be created by certain kinds of social prohibitions, whereas for Freud it is coextensive with the conscious. The effect of your account of unconscious processes is to reduce their quantitative significance enormously, by comparison with that of Freud for whom the unconscious is an active structure which is at work in everything we do. The idea of the unconscious as a central psychological structure is separable from the particular map Freud drew of it, which is often very crude. Would you assent to it as such?

Sure, that is a much more acceptable way of putting it. But if we are to see the unconscious as permanently active in the conscious, then I would want to distinguish between different situations which have been unduly assimilated. It is obvious that there is a great deal of unwitting content in conscious expressions – we say more than we know, we reveal more than we realize. That other word 'unwitting' is fortunately available because there is nothing necessarily unconscious in a categorical sense about these processes, since often – and this is after all the acceptable claim of psychoanalysis – understanding of them is possible for someone who does not have these particular lapses of awareness or failures of connection, who can correct the unwittingness of the speaker. That is a highly rational process which we are constantly performing to each other at the very simple everyday level of saying – 'you realize if you say that' . . . or, 'why did you put it like that . . .?' This is very ordinary parlance, in emotional as well as in intellectual relations. Given the associations that the unconscious has acquired I would want to distinguish the category of the unwitting – if only to lend more importance to what can be genuinely called the unconscious, which is the really active disturbance of conscious interchange, of manifest speech, by forces which are not susceptible to the essentially normal process of clarification, reasoning out, subsequent elucidation. But then I do want to be sure, just because this area is so great a challenge, in which directions to look for light on it. It would be an extraordinary accident if as soon as its importance was scientifically recognized, although it had been described in literature many times before, there immediately arrived a categorical explanation of it, virtually precluding further open exploration of what would by definition be the most difficult human enquiry that had ever been made, precisely because it would be enquiring into the reasons that block such an enquiry.

What is your view of attempts to conjoin psychoanalysis with Marxism?

Although there has never been any attempt to say that the area of life indicated by the unconscious was unimportant, within Marxism it has never been seen as problematic in the same way that every social and economic relationship is seen as problematic. That has led to repeated efforts to make up for the silence within historical materialism by appeals to psychoanalysis, in various forms. I do not want to reserve Marxism from what I think is a major challenge to it – the importance of fundamental human drives which are not an idealist human nature, but which are simply biological, material conditions. But I don't think that Freudian instinct theory, or the notion of geno-types by which Caudwell was briefly very taken, provide a possible basis for an explanation of this area that has been unexplored in historical-materialist terms. I have never felt that Freud and Marx could be combined in that way. There can be no useful compromise between a description of basic realities as ahistorical and universal and a description of them as diversely created or modified by a changing human history. Though the biological data may indeed be universal, our relevant actions are *biological and cultural*, and neither can be reduced to the other.

Presumably you would also be sceptical of the actual therapy as well as the theory of psychoanalysis?

I speak in ignorance. If anyone can help anyone, if anyone can cure anyone, I'm not going to criticize them. What are called the emotional or psychological disorders of contemporary civilization are of such an extraordinary scale and intensity – it is difficult to know whether they are comparatively greater than in earlier periods, precisely because the lives of the majority of men and women were not recorded – that no reasonable form of therapy can be ruled out. However sceptical we may be about the ideology of the therapeutic function in psychoanalysis, it is very important to draw the line at a sort of Illich rejection of medical treatment, which although well intentioned becomes in the end cruel in alliance with all the forces of contemporary civilization which are indifferent towards suffering. But it is surely true that psychoanalysis has no outstanding or unique therapeutic record, as against other modes of therapy whose ideological superstructures would not for a moment be treated as respectable. It must also be said that the principle that you can only be brought through a difficult emotional crisis by a professional is an extraordinarily characteristic notion of bourgeois-bureaucratic society. I think that many people are brought through quite profound disorders by the actual development of ordinary relationships – and I don't think this would be denied by most medical workers. Certain kinds of social change can also have a very deep effect on people's psychological state. There is a truth in certain situations that action is curative, and that certain kinds of relationship are curative. If certain kinds of professional are also curative – well and good, so long as they don't claim a categorical caste privilege.

I feel especially uneasy about psychoanalysis now because of the intensity with which sections of the women's movement, which seems to me so central and decisive, have turned to it. I am wholly reluctant to oppose them, but some of their formulations are self-evidently hasty. The rush for instant authorities to provide 'the scientific account' of what really happens inside them is a condition of abject dependence, which is a fact about the culture. On the other hand, the very rapidity of the changes from one authority to another is encouraging because it means that a very active process of search is going on. Ultimately, however, the movement will have to take stock and get back to the apparently duller procedures of what, where and how.

III
Drama

1. Drama from Ibsen to Eliot

What are the origins of your special concern with drama, which is now your professional field at the university?

I had always been particularly interested in drama from an early time and when I was an undergraduate, the part of my course which attracted my energy most was my work on Ibsen. Then when I left Cambridge I went ahead and pursued the subject rather consciously as an academic project – my ideas on Ibsen were taken over directly into my first book on drama. So there has been a kind of academic continuity throughout. It has always happened that within a university context drama is what I have been mainly asked to teach. My other work, by contrast, developed from the very beginning outside the framework of the university, first in adult education and then very much as personal projects, even where they overlapped with my academic work.

Did you attach a political or cultural significance to the fact that dramatic forms are appropriated publicly and collectively, whereas literary ones are appropriated by multiples of individuals in private conditions?

Yes, that seemed to me important. At the same time, I soon realized that one of the functions of the theatre as it is organized today is to re-annex drama as a mode in such a way as to cut if off from any collective function. So you can find a familiar hostility to the theatre in such texts as 'A Dialogue on Actors' in *Politics and Letters* or even the introduction to *Drama from Ibsen to Eliot*, which stresses a certain opposition between drama and theatre. By that time I had good reason to see that over eighty years of European history the drama had to break from the theatre at every significant moment, in order to make any dramatic progress. There always seemed to be a conflict between the potential of drama as a new or collective mode and the particular formations of the theatre which blocked or reduced it.

Was Drama from Ibsen to Eliot *in effect the first book that you wrote?*

I think it was. The text was written in '47–8. There was then a two-year interval before I could find any publisher for it. When it was finally accepted, I added the section on *The Cocktail Party*, which had then just appeared.

One sign of your substantial distance from Leavis and his influence, even at the outset, was your attention to drama – an area that Leavis had essentially neglected. Hence the elements of apparent Leavisism to be found in Reading and Criticism *should perhaps not be overestimated, because* Drama from Ibsen to Eliot *– which preceded it – in one way pointed in a completely different direction. All the same, looking at the book, one is struck by the extent to which you seem to have conceived it programmatically as a direct extension of practical criticism. You write in the introduction: 'My criticism is, or is intended to be, literary criticism. It is literary criticism, also, which in its major part is of the kind based on demonstrated judgments from texts rather than on historical survey or generalized impressions; of the kind, that is to say, which is known in English as practical criticism. Practical criticism began in the work of Eliot, Richards, Leavis, Empson and Murry, mainly in relation to poetry. It has since been developed, by an important group of critics, in relation to the novel. In the drama, apart from the work of Eliot on Elizabethan dramatists and of other critics on Shakespeare, the usefulness of practical criticism remains to be tested. This book, in addition to its main objects, is intended, therefore, as a working experiment in the application of practical criticism methods to modern dramatic literature.'* [1]

That's right. But it is necessary to make a distinction here between practical criticism and Leavis. Leavis was certainly the most powerful exponent of practical criticism: therefore in retrospect he is often assumed to be its originator or director. But if you look at the actual history, the mode of practical criticism was established within Cambridge English during the twenties by Richards. It was he, after all, who coined the term. Thereafter it was an established procedure in the Faculty as a whole. So for example during the years in which Leavis was largely excluded from the English Faculty, practical criticism remained, as it has to this day, a

[1] DIE, p. 14.

compulsory paper at every stage of the course. Thus the notion that the adoption of a practical-critical procedure was simply an allegiance to Leavis is only partly true. One was following a mode of analysis of literary texts which by this time, at a level below the disagreements between Leavis and the rest of the Cambridge English Faculty, was well extended. We all practised it, whether we were interested in Leavis or in favour of him or not. It is a crucial mistake to equate the practical-critical procedure with the Leavis approach to literature, which was a very specialized application of it.

In a chapter entitled 'The Major Drama' from Preface to Film, *written in about the same period, you write: 'It is coming to be accepted, and perhaps particularly in England, that the definition of an art is to be looked for by reference to actual works, rather than in any abstract generalization over the art as a whole.'*[2] *One might argue that on one construction this is an unexceptionable sentiment. But isn't the suggestive intonation of 'perhaps particularly in England' striking a patriotically anti-theoretical note – together with the counter-position of 'abstract generalization' to 'actual works', when surely any adequate definition would involve elements of both? This emphasis seems quite specifically derived from Leavis, because after all Richards did venture generalizations on art, very unacceptable ones, but none the less propositions of a sort impossible to square with your formula.*

What Richards theorizes are problems of reading and meaning. That is one level of theory which I think is important and which in a sense was excluded from the subsequent development of practical criticism to its great cost. For this particular kind of reading became unproblematic as the description of it as practical, which actually begged all the questions, lost that theoretical dimension which Richards had sought to give it. On the other hand neither Richards nor anyone else but Bradbrook in Cambridge had done any generic analysis. When you work on drama you are inevitably brought up against problems of form in the most direct way. Yet if you look at Cambridge work on the novel or on poetry, what I would now define as basic problems of stance and mode were never really posed at all. This is the key to that whole epoch of which Leavis is merely one of the representatives: theorization when it appears is always a theorization of

[2] PF, p. 3.

reading – it is not a theorization of composition. So far as *Drama from Ibsen to Eliot* is concerned, my introduction can be seen as a combination of three tendencies. First, the adoption of the analytic mode of practical criticism in its most technical sense, which originally comes from Richards; secondly, the stress on community and sensibility which – unlike the first – does derive from Leavis; thirdly, the attempt to develop a generic theory of naturalism as a form. For that last aim, I could find no help at all in the Cambridge tradition. In fact, I later realized that the very issue of any definition of naturalism threatened the typical Leavisian mode of judgment, with its unproblematic reference to 'life' as the criterion of the text. At the time, those three tendencies resulted in confusion.

The nature of your debt to the various strands in the Cambridge English school at this stage still needs some exploration. Practical criticism was never simply a 'technique'. In Richards's case it was the instrument of a liberal theory of communications which presupposed that contradictions between the reader and the text were misunderstandings which could be eliminated. In Leavis's case it was allied to an ideology of the concrete which secured the validity of close reading. Now it is still not clear in what sense you used the term and accepted the directive of close reading. For on the one hand Culture and Society *contains a very succinct and forthright attack on Richards's individualist assumptions; while on the other hand your very early interest in theory was obviously quite out of step with* Scrutiny *positions. Yet in the prologue to* Drama and Performance *you say of art in general: 'Its study . . . may feed on scholarship, but its subsance is immediate personal response, and its methods are, and must be, the seizing and articulation of this response: that is to say, the practice of criticism.'[3] Such a formulation suggests that over and above your sense of the importance and recuperability of the procedures of close reading, a substantive inheritance from Richards and Leavis was still active in your work at this stage.*

Undoubtedly. One reason was the demonstration accomplished by Richards's *Practical Criticism* that the cultural consensus around certain earlier social notions of cultivation or taste could be quite brutally refuted by presenting people with texts without any cultural signals like the author's name, or any other cues to 'the right response'. If you asked people

[3] DP, p. 9.

about the authors who had written these pieces, they knew what to say within the terms of the consensus. When they actually had to read and describe their writings, the result was radically different – in some cases nearly the reverse. So the effect of Richards's practical criticism was anti-ideological in a very crucial sense: it exposed the disparity between the cultural pretensions of a class and its actual capacities. That was naturally an attractive element in the technique of close reading. However, this technique also underwent an ideological capture, by its very definition as practice in opposition to theory. In Richards's case, of course, it is true that *Practical Criticism* was written directly in association with *Principles of Literary Criticism*. But thereby practice was related essentially to the activity of reading, rather than to the process of composition. The result was the subsequent definition of the work as a *text*, an ideological capture which has persisted relatively intact from English Practical Criticism to American New Criticism right down to Literary Structuralism today.

So far as I was concerned at the time, I was trying to apply practical criticism in a new field. The technique had been developed for analysis of the short poem, where a close reading was theoretically and practically possible. It had then been very rashly extended to fiction by the extraction of passages for analysis which were held, yet never demonstrated, to be representative of the whole work. In drama it had really hardly been used at all, except in certain local analyses of imagery or rhythms in Shakespeare. Reading extensively through the literature on modern drama, it seemed to me that the element of close verbal analysis was crucially lacking. I still think so, but I would not call the remedy 'practical criticism' today: it is really a specific technique of very close analysis of verbal organization that has to be preserved. The purpose which it should serve is also quite different from that of practical criticism. Without being consciously aware of this at the time, I used the technique in an unorthodox way in my book on drama. Why do people close-analyse within the main practical-critical tradition? In order to clarify their response as evaluation. The verbal analysis of the Ibsen and Strindberg plays I undertook is scarcely concerned with response at all. Its aim is elucidation of the composition and of the continuity of theme within their works. This is the employment of what may look like the same technique for radically distinct purposes.

Turning to what you've called the second strand in your introduction to

Drama from Ibsen to Eliot, *the cultural themes taken from Leavis, what is startling about them today is their categorical, unqualified fidelity to Leavis's meta-historical conceptions. You write: 'For many reasons – and perhaps primarily under the pressure of that complex of forces which we call industrialism – contemporary* spoken *English is very rarely capable of exact expression of anything in any degree complex.'*[4] *Then you go on: 'The artist's sensibility – his capacity for experience, his ways of thinking, feeling, and conjunction – will often be finer and more developed than that of the mean of his audience. But if his sensibility is at least of the same kind, communication is possible. Where his sensibility is of the same kind, his language and the language of his audience will be closely and organically related; the common language will be the expression of the common sensibility. There is no such common sensibility today. The pressure of a mechanical environment has dictated mechanical ways of thought, feeling and conjunction, which artists, and a few of like temper, reject only by conscious resistance and great labour. That is why all serious literature in our own period tends to become a minority literature' – you do then add an important saving clause – 'although the minority is capable of extension and in my view has no social correlative.'*[5] *But you conclude: 'It is not the lack of common beliefs in society which restricts [the artist's] communication. It is rather the lack of certain qualities of living, certain capacities for experience. Thus drama at the present time, if it is to be serious in the full traditional sense, is inevitably minority drama.'*[6] *The set of propositions here is quite unlike anything else in your work. It seems to be a pure distillation of Leavis. What is your view now of the role of these themes in your book?*

There is no argument over your description. That paragraph is, indeed, a virtual reproduction of Leavis. The reason why I say a reproduction is that to an extraordinary extent the rest of the analysis in the book has no connection with it. Nothing follows from it. Of course, it is a historical fact that from the 1890s, for quite different reasons, the significant drama was always a minority breakaway from the majority commercial theatres. I think probably the only discussion where these terms actually impinge on the analysis is the contrast between Synge and O'Casey, which I would

[4] DIE, p. 30.
[5] DIE, p. 31.
[6] DIE, p. 32.

now rewrite, even though it is given more of the sense of a specific social transition from rural to urban speech. So although I accept the direct influence of Leavis on that part of my introduction, I would reject the general label of 'Left-Leavisism' which several people have given to my work at this date. What is wrong about the notion of Left-Leavisism is that it conjures up some sort of developed position which is a variant of the whole complex of ideas associated with Leavis. The reality in my view is that *Drama from Ibsen to Eliot* represents the absorption and reproduction of a whole series of influences which are incompatible. At that level the work simply does not cohere, whereas what is suggested by the term Left-Leavisism is a coherent position which has moved somewhat along the political spectrum. This is a false diagnosis because it leads to the projection of the whole complex onto the entire work. In fact, it was the elements of incoherence which were to prove decisive, such as the interest in forms which one was very carefully told was a misdirection of interest and energy – not to speak of the attention to drama itself, which involved a direct quarrel with Leavis over Yeats's plays, for example. The combination of contradictory directions made the position of the book an inherently unstable one. I suppose its full instabilities were not really resolved until the sixties.

There is another aspect of Drama from Ibsen to Eliot, *suggesting an affiliation between your method and Cambridge English, which leaves one uneasy. That is the willed intention to abstract the dramatic work of the authors whom you discuss from the effective cultural, national or any other social history of their time. You quite expressly attack and reject any kind of contextualization of their writing. With some rhetorical skill you cite a comment on Ibsen that he was not a man but a pen, and write: 'This unfortunate condition is not, of course, without its advantages. It serves at least to protect an artist from his biographers.'*[7] *In the case of Strindberg, you tell your readers: 'The biography can readily be used to gloss, but not to explain or judge, the literature. It is time to say, after fifteen wild Decembers, that criticism requires a different discipline. The present essay will be concerned solely with Strindberg as dramatist, and limitation of space is not pleaded as an apology.'*[8] *But why should sole concern with Strindberg as an artist be*

[7] DIE, p. 111; DIB, p. 75.
[8] DIE, p. 111; DIB, p. 75.

exclusive of any attempt to understand what his ideas, his life, the society within which he emerged actually were? At the time you do seem to have felt strongly that all this was quite external to drama and could be ignored. In the same chapter you in effect dismiss any concern with Strindberg's political or social attitudes. Yet Strindberg, a highly intelligent man in his own way, wrote at length and with passion on politics, class, sex, society, religion, outside his dramatic work, and these elements were in no way absent from his drama. You occasionally touch on them yourself. Yet by making a wilful abstraction in principle of one from the other, you surely end up by saying less than needs to be said about the substance of the drama itself?

Yes. The sentences you've quoted are samples of what might be called the Cambridge rhetoric. Get to the text and never mind anything else. Of course the same rhetoric also invited you to look at life and judge the text by that. But the essential message was: stick to the text; and the tone was one of confident self-righteousness. On the other hand, look at it the other way. What was this whole emphasis a response to? My comments on Strindberg were provoked by reading truly appalling 'biographies of the artist', which tell you which of his wives or girlfriends is which character, which episode is transcribed into which scene, and reduce every work to a neurosis of the author. Even if a social biography in a generalized sense were included, these studies merely discussed the components of an experience which were held to explain the work, but could never demonstrate the true composition of it. I think that my particularly violent rejection of that mode proved in a way to be helpful later, because it cleared the ground for seeing the problem in a completely different way, for exploring the real conditions of dramatic practice. There, today, I would go all the way: to the theatres, to the available forms, to the whole systems of thought within which particular forms and institutions were developed – but never to the kind of literary biography I was specifically attacking then. When I wrote about Strindberg again in *Modern Tragedy*, I related his work to a precise phase of social and ideological crisis, not to any number of wild Decembers. At the time, the junk that Cambridge criticism was throwing out prevented me from seeing its arrogant abstraction of the text, which of course proves unsupportable once you really get into any serious analysis of a work. One consequence was that I did, for example, refuse to explore the alternative endings of *Journey to the Frontier*, on the grounds that this could be explained in terms of Auden and Isherwood's political development and I was not concerned with that. This sort of distancing was in line with my standpoint. But one has got to remember the background to it.

The problem, however, is not just one of formal abstention: it affects some of your substantive judgments. One example is your cavalier treatment of the specifically social dimension of Ibsen's plays. You write dismissively of A Doll's House, *for instance:* 'A Doll's House *is now, as it has always been, a social rather than a literary phenomenon. Its excitement lay in its relation to feminism and, although Ibsen rejects the ascription of support for feminism, in practical terms this hardly seems to matter.'*[9] *Your assessment of the play ends: 'Ibsen's rejection of the conventional moral ending was only a limited cure for this deficiency' – the deficiency being his acceptance of romantic stage conventions – 'a partial negative within an essential acceptance. Any full cure would have involved the restoration of total dramatic substance.'*[10] *Now, one would not want to quarrel with the view that* A Doll's House *is a slighter work in certain respects than other plays by Ibsen, including some of the later works you discuss. But the tone in which you speak of it seems quite unnecessarily belittling. What you are actually saying is that Ibsen's acceptance of a stage convention was in a way more important than his rejection of a moral and social convention. This is a delicate matter to arbitrate – certainly not one for overpoliticized or anachronistically programmatic judgment. But was the impact of the play on Ibsen's audiences in his own time mere ideological illusion or complacency on their part? Surely the fact is that* A Doll's House *dramatized a statement about the situation of women in bourgeois society that is not without its force and was felt to be such by women at the time, and indeed later. In the context of a very long essay on Ibsen, you seem to give surprisingly little weight to this achievement. Isn't there consequently an imbalance – possibly a hidden conservatism – in your final judgment of Ibsen in the book?*

The point is that the overwhelming majority of Ibsen's plays do not involve even the temporary escape that is available in *A Doll's House* or perhaps *An Enemy of the People*. Again you have to understand what I was writing against – Shaw's *The Quintessence of Ibsenism*. Shaw had effected an ideological assimilation of Ibsen to something very different – a version

[9] DIE, pp. 75–6; DIB, p. 47–8.
[10] DIE, p. 78; DIB, p. 49.

of individualist liberation. To do that, he had precisely highlighted *A Doll's House* and *An Enemy of the People*, of course not *Ghosts*, and had radically misinterpreted – really quite wilfully – the rest of his work in order to avoid what Shaw would have to avoid, Ibsen's notion of barriers that you cannot get past. For Ibsen's drama is essentially not at all one of individualist liberation, it is what I later called liberal tragedy – a much more significant form. Now, because feminism is a crucial movement, every contribution to it (and Ibsen's disavowal was merely tactical), however unique, however untypical, is important. That I would now want to say and in that sense to correct. But equally it is necessary to see that the cases where liberation ambiguously succeeds, as an individual extricates herself from her situation – although after Nora slams the door, what happens? Ibsen explored various possible versions, including rewriting the play to bring her back – must be set against what is actually the much greater weight of Ibsen's work where there is a radical lack of belief in the liberal project of liberation. There is never a cancellation of its impulses, but there is a uniquely powerful perception of what blocks it: physical inheritance, social inheritance, every sort of circumstance. For Ibsen it is society in the full sense which thwarts any such emancipation. I still think it is much more important to emphasize Ibsen's extremely powerful creation of the forms of this blockage of the project of liberation, which he never renounces, than to look at the one or two cases where he suspends them and allows an ambiguous escape, because those are easier to assimilate to progressive thought.

That is entirely acceptable. But it is slightly different from what you suggested at the time. For instance, you mentioned Ghosts. *You go right on after your comments on* A Doll's House *to say the following:* 'Ghosts *is a play of the same essential kind as* A Doll's House, *but it is of a very different temper. Its issues are more serious'.*[11] *One must ask you in what sense are its issues more serious? For after all* Ghosts *exemplifies the most reductive and vitiated form of naturalism – the notion of a biological fatalism. Physiology is used as a paradigm of society. Anybody in Ibsen's time knew the difference: a hereditary disease is not the same thing as a social constraint. To confuse the two is dramatically false: that could be demonstrated from the play itself, which has powerful pieces of rhetoric, but many structural weaknesses. The idea that the*

[11] DIE, p. 78; DIB, p. 50.

issues of Ghosts *are more serious than those of* A Doll's House *does seem to be a concession to conservative ideology. You can say the play is more serious, but why the issues?*

They are clearly not. What I should have said is, not that the issues were more serious, but that the whole mode of composition is more serious. It includes more. *Ghosts* has a much more complicated set of relationships than *A Doll's House*, where Ibsen's dependence on previous conventions of miraculous resolution through good fortune limits the level at which he can handle experience at all. What I would say is that my precise formulations were wrong, but I think that the direction of the judgment is still right. Ibsen is the dramatist of blockages of liberation, which he still holds to as a project, rather than a dramatist of liberation as he had been presented. To take the problem of the position of women, if you go on from *A Doll's House* to *Lady from the Sea* or *Hedda Gabler* you can see that Nora's exit is a very temporary resolution within a particular form, and Ibsen does not maintain that kind of possibility; he sees an unstoppable impulse to liberation which then becomes of necessity a form of self-destruction. But I don't want to disagree with your original point, which is fair enough.

In the revised version of the book you restructured the second part into a section entitled 'The Irish Dramatists' – following the 'Generation of Masters' comprising Ibsen, Strindberg and Chekhov. You comment on it in your introduction: 'I turn then, in my second part, to one remarkable national tradition: that of the Irish dramatists, from Yeats in the 1890s through Synge and Joyce to O'Casey in the 1940s. This tradition, as it happens, includes most of the major modern dramatic forms, but in a particular national and historical situation, which requires emphasis.'[12] *Actually a reader of those Irish chapters does not find a great deal of emphasis on the historical or national situation in them. You do rebuke O'Casey effectively for the latent relationship to Irish people and Irish history discernible in his work, but on the whole even in this revision there is a persistent abstraction of the real national history – something incidentally not irrelevant to Ibsen's work either. Did you find it impracticable to reshape the form of the book when you came to rewrite it into* Drama from Ibsen to Brecht?

[12] DIB, p. 21.

Yes – the book had to remain essentially an analysis of dramatic forms. In grouping the Irish dramatists, I wanted to give a historical emphasis without actually writing the history – which I felt had been done elsewhere, whereas what had not been done was to show the very complex and variable forms of what is often just simply put as a single Irish dramatic tradition. I can now see that an interesting essay could be written analysing precisely the phases of the national movement in terms of the evolution of dramatic forms. Yeats's early drama constructs an image of the nation that is very characteristic of the beginnings of a national revival, heavily based in a legendary past. The encounter between the legend and contemporary social reality is very problematic: this form is soon the object of severe attack within the nationalist movement as anti-Irish and anti-popular. O'Casey's version of the civil war gives a new edge of realism against the legend, but at the same time over-emphasizes its chaos and confusion to the point of cancelling crucial social and historical elements in the project of national liberation itself. Then there is the very conscious rejection of Ireland altogether, within a continuing preoccupation, in the whole trajectory of Joyce. Certainly some elements of this same movement can be found in Ibsen, whose early work is inspired by Norwegian national feeling against Sweden – classically involving the whole problem of language which was of course the pivot of early cultural-political nationalism. I have been trying to work recently on the case of Wales, where there is precisely the same evolution from a Welsh cultural revival, harking back to a Celtic past continuous from Roman times, older than any English historical tradition and so exempt from the corrupting influences of modernism as a movement, to the development of a critique of this legendary affiliation in a new kind of nationalist writing, which had suffered the severe crisis of industrialism that wiped out so much use of the Welsh language.

That is the sort of essay that one could have written about Irish drama. But my book had been written as an account of dramatic forms. By the time I came to revise it, I had already developed the kind of social-ideological – rather than historical – analysis which thereafter seemed to me necessary to understand the conflict of these forms, in *Modern Tragedy*. I found it very difficult to revise the book anyway, because I had to include a good deal of new drama which I had not known when I wrote the original work. I had to change certain things and exclude others, and yet it still in some sense had to be the same book, conceived in the same framework.

Your work on the novel is a sustained defence and illustration of realism. You insist that there is a necessary unity between individuals and society; success in their representation in fiction depends on the ability to hold the two in a complex and delicate balance, in which the qualities of the one are rendered visible in the activities of the other. You attack at once the sociological and the psychological novel, in which the two poles of what should be a dialectical tension are broken apart in the typical abstractions of modernism in its opposite forms. Now one might say that the central paradox of your work on drama is that it seems to take a direction contrary to the whole impetus of your writing on the novel. For Drama from Ibsen to Eliot *is theoretically a sustained critique of naturalism as a form. One might think initially that this was a logical conjunction, taking naturalism to mean the kind of perversion or reification of realism that Lukács intends by the term. But if one looks at your book more closely this particular antithesis is not in fact operative in it. Indeed, if one takes the famous definitions of naturalism and realism given by Strindberg which you quote, it is very clear that what Strindberg conceived as naturalism was remarkably similar to what Lukács was to call realism, while what Strindberg calls realism is equivalent to what Lukács terms naturalism.*[13] *It is interesting in this connection that where particular plays come near to novelistic forms you on the whole attack them. For example, in your discussion of* Rosmersholm, *you charge Ibsen with trying to do something which the dramatist cannot achieve – to reproduce the psychological development of a character on the stage. That, you argue, is a procedure of the novel that is inappropriate to drama. Does this mean that you think the peculiar realist synthesis is inherently impossible in the theatre – in other words dramatic forms cannot represent that mutual interrelation and implication of the social and the personal which you hold to be the great achievement of the realist novel?*

At the same time, the obverse of your polemic against naturalism is a keen interest, even at times an exaltation, of verse-drama as the modern antidote to naturalism. This programmatic emphasis takes one form that seems particularly strange – your high appreciation of the merits of Eliot's drama, suggested by the first title of the book. It is perfectly true that you reserve your main admiration for Murder in the Cathedral, *and that you become*

[13] DIE, pp. 116–7; DIB, pp. 79–80.

progressively more disappointed or disabused with Eliot's subsequent writing; but you still find some words for plays which most people would now regard as merely meretricious, like The Cocktail Party. *At all events, whatever else any of Eliot's plays might be, they are not in any way remotely concerned with the unity of substance between personality and society. Yet you end your chapter on Eliot: 'The Theatre of Character and the Theatre of Ideas have, after all, lived in a willing and intimate union for seventy or eighty years; if we need a phrase for the kind of drama which Eliot is attempting to recreate we might speak of the* theatre of experience. *Eliot cannot be said to have solved all the problems which arose from the decay of romantic drama and from the limitations of the naturalist drama which replaced it. But he has perhaps brought us to a point at which such a solution can be envisaged. This is a very considerable achievement, whatever the immediate future of the drama may be; and in its nature it is beyond the mode of praise.'*[14] *Even if we set aside the questionable character of this judgment, can your verdicts on naturalism and verse-drama in this early work be reconciled with your later writing on realism?*

Let me say at the outset that it was impossible for me to write adequately about dramatic forms until I fully understand the nature of the historical movement of naturalism and realism, which I did not at the time. I have in fact moved back in the last seven or eight years to a defence of certain kinds of naturalist drama which is much closer to the position you correctly describe in my writing on the novel. There remains, however, an important distinction to be made between the modes of drama and the novel. What one finds again and again in plays which in the technical sense are naturalist, that is to say intent on reproducing real life on the stage, is that certain things that can relatively easily be achieved in the novel can be accommodated in drama only awkwardly or weakly, if at all. There happens to be a famous demonstration of this in the existence in Lawrence's work of a short story and a naturalist play which share so much material that you can properly call one the fictional and the other the dramatic version. I compared the two as early as '45–6. What Lawrence could do within the fictional mode and within the dramatic mode was radically different, because in the former he could include the more general social experience which was crucial to understanding the

[14] DIE, p. 270.

particular family experience with which he was concerned. In other cases the problem would be the integration of historical movement into the two forms. The whole basis of my developed analysis of the transition from naturalism into expressionism is that much of expressionism was an effort to reform the play itself to capture a wider social and historical experience than the naturalist limitation to the single playing space permitted. Yet the full inclusion of historical or social experience remains profoundly difficult within the dramatic form even after the liberation achieved by social expressionism, which could at least insert – it characteristically was an insertion – the sense of a much wider movement of society and history within which particular actions were displayed.

Now it happens that these technical problems are much less acute for the novelist. In a novel a character can arrive with a social history which is directly presented, often before he begins to speak. Indeed the typical method of the 19th-century realist novel was to introduce him with a lengthy description – including a much fuller definition of physical appearance and manner of speaking than the script of a play, whose stage directions are little more than a set of cues, can ever achieve. Even before the character arrives, a whole setting will be described, typically evoking the particular society or economy within which the action will occur. None of this is easily possible on the stage. So that, although I am very much more sympathetic to the naturalist project in drama now, about which I will say more, it remains more problematic than the realist project in the novel. Actually, some of the same difficulties have now reappeared within the novel, because of the drastic reduction in the physical scale of the novel that has occurred under the specific pressures of the economics of publishing, which have as a matter of fact cancelled many of the traditional advantages of the novel as a form, although it is not the only reason why this has happened.

Now, to return to your wider question, when I was writing *Drama from Ibsen to Eliot*, like everyone else I accepted the definition of naturalism which was essentially given by its enemies and by major writers who were struggling with its difficulties or frustrated by certain of its restrictions: that is to say, the essentially technical definition of naturalism as the reproduction of real contemporary life on the stage. Like everyone else, I saw this project in terms of the difficulties it subsequently encountered. Firstly, as many had said, it was impossible within this mode to represent experience which was not a subject for probable conversation. Yeats remarked that when modern people have strong emotions, they do not say anything, they stare into the fire. All sorts of problems of subjectivity, or of the representation of thought, could be handled only in a very awkward fashion, if at all, and were mostly evaded. Secondly, as I came to stress, naturalism was simply unable to move outwards to society and history: it could not extend its focus. So I traced the two forms which replaced it in practice – the movement towards a subjective expressionism which reconstructed the site of the dramatic action as consciousness and not action or behaviour, and the movement towards social expressionism which reconstituted the site in society in a very generalized way. The analysis of the transition was absolutely right. What was wrong was my misunderstanding of the original project. For naturalism was part of a necessary and progressive secular social movement. The whole point of naturalism was its opposition to super-naturalism. Its thrust was threefold: a stress first on the secular, second on the contemporary, third on the scientific procedures of natural history. In other words, the work that the naturalists introduced belongs decisively to a liberating project and in that sense seems to me analogous, within its narrower scope of success, to realist work in the novel.

Now there is one founding proposition of naturalism as an intellectual movement which also yielded two very powerful generations of literary production. It is that character is inseparable from environment, in the weaker version, and is determined by environment, in the stronger version. The great emphasis of dramatic naturalism on the creation of accurate settings, the endless reproduction of life-like rooms, was later supposed to be an attempt at verisimilitude, to induce the illusion in the audience that they were watching a real room. Its actual significance was very different. The real impulse behind it was that the environment must be physically present because it is a crucial part of the action. It is not a setting. There is no such thing as a naturalist set, as is very clear in Ibsen's naturalist plays, where the characters have produced this environment by living in these rooms which are always the physical centre of attention. They have soaked into this environment which in a sense materially reflects back at them their lives; yet at the same time the environment is crucially active in their lives – the actual physical restrictions of the room, the sense of a particular kind of fixed landscape. Now it used to be an absolute commonplace, which can still be found in the textbooks, that the only reason those realistic sets were constructed was because of technical advances in stage carpentry and lighting which enabled exact replicas of rooms to be put on stage. This is of course absurd, since a room could have been built in a Greek theatre in the classical period if anyone had wanted to do it. The real purpose was to create the physical environment as an agency and not as a setting. At the same time, this was a movement within bourgeois society and therefore the environment that was created defined the centre of society as the family and private life. So that by contrast to the earlier drama it not only rejected the metaphysical religious dimension, but it also narrowed the whole sphere of public action down from the court, the forum or the street, to the room in a family house. It was there that important things happen between a few people. The result was that the proposition of a determining relation between character and environment suffered a peculiar qualification, that was not inherent in the original project, as the environment became socially limited and in its most extreme development static. The most powerful physical image created in the period of major naturalist drama is the living room as a trap. People look through the window to see what is happening in the world beyond, which cannot be shown. Messages come through the door from the world outside, but the centre of the dramatic interest is inside. A passive sense of the environment, not merely as forming – which in my view is a progressive notion – but as totally determining – which in my view is not – is eventually embodied in this immobile, trapped form.

By contrast, the Marxist definition of realism starts talking about society or history, instead of the bourgeois notion of 'environment'. That is in itself an advance, because it introduces a necessary mobility. This was precisely what the dramatic form that had been most extensively developed within naturalism could not handle: the movement of history. It could at most seek a typical moment of crisis in which social history erupts into the closed space of the drama – the end of Chekhov's *The Cherry Orchard* is a classic instance – but as an action which is essentially played off stage. So to realize the full possibility of the naturalist project, as a new secular view of personal character and social relationships, drama had to move on to other forms. This necessity underlines the difference between what was possible within the dramatic forms and within the fictional forms which were the product of the same impulse. For a deeply detailed description of the physical and social environment, a fully presented account of character, could pass relatively unproblematically into the novel. The exclusion of them in a whole area of modernist fiction seems to me unquestionably a regression at the major level – although of course this exclusion has allowed certain minor advances of another kind. But in drama, because of the very particular form of bourgeois constraint it underwent, naturalism in the technical sense had to be rejected. However, the forms which succeeded it tended to be in their majority attempts to realize more adequately its initial project. The one important exception is the drama of Yeats and Eliot. That is why it was really wrong not to have seen the character of the Eliot-Yeats attack on naturalism. For what they were opposing was not the technical restrictions of naturalism, although they could speak eloquently enough about them. What Yeats and Eliot were trying to accomplish was a restoration in the real sense – a return behind naturalism to a pre-secular and metaphysical conception of relationship and character. Their aim was a dramatic counter-revolution. I should have been able to separate the technical issues which they pin-pointed quite accurately from the ideological themes they were advancing, which I was only later able to define.

That is very clear. It leaves one further question, however. In your revised conclusion to Drama from Ibsen to Eliot, *written in 1963, you register the collapse of Eliot's drama and express your own disillusionment with it. But the main burden of your critique is that what went wrong with it was essentially that it compromised with naturalism. 'What in fact had happened, in the verse-drama, was that a new principle collided with a major habit [of naturalist theatre], and it was the principle that was now in retreat.'*[15] *You then go on to say: 'The disappearance of the left-wing theatre of the thirties led to an identification of verse-drama with one doctrine only; an unusually bleak Christianity. Coming on top of its technical difficulties, this doctrinal isolation was too much for it. It was very exposed, and was easily attacked.' The crippling mark of this identification was that 'when people thought of English verse plays, from the mid-1950s, they thought of religious or quasi-religious themes, or fragments from a classical education, all declined into mannerism.'*[16] *The question that has to be asked is this: is it not possible that there was an intrinsic connection between the doctrinal isolation and the very project of verse-drama in the first instance? Were the two ever really separable? You present verse-drama as essentially a technical solution to the problem of the low*

[15] DIE, p. 302.
[16] DIE, pp. 302–3.

intensity of contemporary speech. Your argument was that verse-drama is capable of quickening or heightening the ordinary range of expression in conversational exchange, to a point where a quite new depth of experience can be embodied on the stage. However, might it not be that by the mid-20th century the very idea of using verse on stage as a medium of speech had an inescapably hieratic and ritualized cast which would inevitably tend towards a clerical or conservative outlook? In other words, perhaps the conjunction between technical solution and ideological orientation was not so contingent as you have just suggested. Could even gifted poets of the left have taken this sort of dramatic project very far?

I did eventually understand this difficulty, when I realized that the real question was not verse or prose, but what kinds of verse, what kinds of prose. The biggest single mistake that Eliot made was his attempt to find an all-purpose dramatic verse which could function as a substitute for conversation. For the whole case for verse as capable of greater precision and intensity of meaning collapsed when characters had to ask whether someone had bought an evening paper, a perfectly ordinary conversational exchange, in a uniform poetic mode. Now if you look at the verse experiments of the thirties or in some other forms of post-war drama, the whole point is that verse, or song, are used for intensification, but they do not attempt to impose what is necessarily a false unity. All the different levels of exchange and interrelationship cannot be contained within a single rhythm.

Our point is still somewhat different from yours. What we are suggesting is that even if the action of the play never dropped to the level of the banal or mundane, a verse-drama would probably still remain unacceptably archaic and regressive. There is one very suspect absence in your book. It is a comprehensive work about the European drama, but one name that cannot be found in it is that of Claudel – who actually is the pioneer of verse-drama on any major scale. Claudel's plays are absolutely hieratic and religious, and they make no concessions to small talk whatever: the action is sustained on a high, heroic tone throughout. The results of Claudel's practice should have been a warning about the direction any attempt to reintroduce full-scale verse against the current would be likely to take.

Yes, but this is still a formalist analysis – you may say justly so, since my original argument was couched in formalist terms. The problem, however, is that any definition of verse-drama depends on a prior definition of prose drama. Yet as Eliot himself pointed out, Molière's Monsieur Jourdain was entitled to be surprised to be told that he had been talking prose all his life, because of course he had not. In fact, very little of dramatic speech writing is prose in that sense. The whole point of drama is that it is a very specific mode of writing for speech; not writing of speech, but writing for speech. The particular novelty of naturalism, which is quite separate from the question of verse or prose, was that it was for the first time the reproduction of conversation. The writing of conversation became in time extraordinarily skilled, as you can see in Ibsen, whose use of it is a major innovation in European drama. That technique later became a naturalist habit. By the time you get to the television drama of the sixties, the technical ability to reproduce conversations even to the point of emphasizing their inadequacies – the characteristic inarticulacies, false starts, unfinished sentences – is startling. At one period, every episode of *Z-Cars* had policemen speaking like characters out of late naturalist drama, where inarticulacy as such is being communicated rather than conversation being inarticulate.

Now if writing for speech is the problem, it is clear that if you impose a uniform verse form over an entire play, you are committed to a certain position towards, in effect a distance from, the reality represented. Other kinds of experiment can use verse successfully by integrating a multiplicity of levels within the drama. It would be quite wrong to exclude verse from certain kinds of writing for speech, on general theoretical grounds. What becomes intolerable is either the adoption of an overall verse form which pitches everything at the level of myth, or the descent from the metaphysical to the trivial within a uniform verse medium, such as you find in Eliot's later plays. On the other hand, the opposite course paradoxically produces the same uniformity, not of prose, but of representable speech. The result is a very similar effect of closure. For once a certain level of conversational speech is set, you can never move beyond it: people are confined to its limits at moments when a greater intensity of expression is needed, and the result is a corresponding kind of failure. I commented on some examples of this in early English naturalist drama, where characters move into a more intense diction and then have to make an embarrassed withdrawal, saying things like: 'Shall we finish the conversation in prose?' By contrast, if you look at the way represented speech is written in realist fiction, it varies quite extraordinarily from the level of simple exchanges when people are asking the way or talking about some immediate bit of business, to the most wrought kind of writing when some crucial experience is at stake. The convention carries this range perfectly easily, because it is unified in the novel by the overall narration. Now I am by no means convinced that this kind of variation of level has to be ruled out in drama. Its means will of course be different. But take verse not in a formalist sense but as the employment of certain devices of rhythm to intensify certain kinds of writing for speech, and then look at *Sergeant Musgrave's Dance*. It is a very successful instance of such an experiment, precisely because of the great variety of levels within it.

That is an interesting example, because Arden makes such effective use of song. For song is in a certain sense closer to ordinary speech than verse, because people do actually sing in everyday reality whereas they never speak poetry. Singing can be curiously less of a break within the texture of a drama than declaiming. It is surely suggestive that Brecht, although himself a major poet, generally resorted to song rather than to verse in his plays. Most of the heightening devices of which you have spoken would probably prove to be closer to ordinary song than to traditional verse, with its set range of classical metres.

I would not want to make a theoretical foreclosure of verse forms. If one were to take the position that realism involved a commitment to probable everyday representation, which should only be broken where probable everyday action itself breaks, as to the new and shared experience of song, one would be in serious difficulties. For certain areas of silence or dominant codes can only be broken by something which is unquestionably an alternative convention in writing for speech. Whether that will be verse is another question. It is true that actors who are not trained to speak verse, as happens even when they are playing Shakespeare, tend to pull the poetry back towards other rhythms and so make any break very severe. I think in any case that the general situation has been transformed by the mobility of dramatic forms which has come with the camera. The theatre is now far from being the only site of major radical experimentation. For visual imagery is now continually functioning in some of the ways that verse once did: not just establishing shots which correspond to a naturalist setting, but imagery of a consciously extending kind.

My own view is that it is crucial within the broadest social-cultural perspective to retain the principles of the original naturalist project – I do not apologize for using the term although it may now be more convenient to call it realist. By that I mean the project of a drama attached to history, society, and secularity. At the same time, such a drama must always resist the pull towards the reproduction of everyday reality on its own apparent terms – which has had baneful effects even on some of the strongest and most necessary writing in the novel. In that sense fulfilment of the naturalist or realist project demands openness to many conventions rather than reliance on any single one.

That position is not incompatible with much of classical naturalist drama, which was never confined to a mono-representational diction. The late Ibsen, as you show very well, had a remarkable ability to change keys in the speech of his later plays.

Ibsen could effect breaks from people speaking in the conversational exchanges of the time to the most extraordinarily intense articulations of things that would be very improbable ever to be said. These breaks were very difficult to achieve, but he could control them.

Another central case would be the language of Büchner, which possesses a poetic power of astonishing intensity, within the most relentlessly naturalist dramatic project conceivable, in the strict definition you have given the term.

Yes. The great interest of his work is its use of multiple conventions, which came from the fact that he saw society so clearly as a class order. Büchner sought to represent alternative modes of speech, not only between different levels of personality – which is the usual context of the formalist concern – but between different levels of society.

Between the publication of Drama from Ibsen to Eliot *and the major revision of it in* Drama from Ibsen to Brecht, *you wrote* Modern Tragedy. *This is obviously a book of far-reaching importance in the development of your work as a whole. Despite its title, only a part of it is actually devoted to drama – it also discusses novels, philosophy and political history. We will have to come back to it in those other contexts. For the moment, can we just ask you what were the origins of* Modern Tragedy *as an intervention?*

It was never a book I had foreseen writing. Most of the books I have written were projected a few years earlier – a lot of them worked out very differently, but they were envisaged in advance. This one was simply a response to the shock of returning to Cambridge and encountering the course on tragedy there in a much more ideological form than it had been when I was a student. The surprise was the greater for me because, after all, I had taken from that earlier study of tragedy a lot of impulses which had gone into my own work in drama and I didn't think I would be working again in that area. My initial reaction took the form of the short 'Dialogue on Tragedy' which was published in NLR.[17] At first I didn't intend to go much further than that, but in the process of arguing it out, the question took on new dimensions. I still didn't think this would be a book, just a few essays. Then a curious thing happened. I was giving a course on modern tragedy and I thought well, I don't really have to prepare particularly for it, because I've got *Drama from Ibsen to Eliot*, I'll take my lectures from that. But in the process of giving the lectures, with a particular awareness now of the more general debate over the nature of tragedy, they became transformed. It was as if I went into the lecture room with the text of a chapter from *Drama from Ibsen to Eliot* in front of me, and came out with the text of a chapter from *Modern Tragedy*. The same authors are discussed in the two books, the same themes developed, the same quotations used – which is the key point of continuity. But the discussion was now in a different mode. Where much of the earlier work had been rather technical, concentrating on dramatic conventions and the relationship to theatrical staging and individual playwrights, the new work was closer to ideological criticism.

Modern Tragedy *has a strongly committed tone, politically and culturally. In fact, the chapter entitled 'Tragedy and Revolution' is probably the most militant text you had published since your student period at Cambridge. What was the reaction to the appearance of* Modern Tragedy? *What was the conjuncture in which it was published?*

This was a period of more conscious writing against an opposition, after the very hostile reception of *The Long Revolution*. A very particular

[17] *New Left Review*, 13–14, 1962.

formation, around a teaching situation, a cultural and political situation, was in my sights when I wrote the book. The chapter on 'Tragedy and Revolution' was written quite late and was directly related to the conjuncture of the mid-sixties. For there was enough activity in the universities even then for the idea of revolution to have – if not the impact of the late sixties – already a significant resonance. I was invited to give a lecture; I chose the subject of tragedy and revolution very specifically to speak to what was predominantly a left student audience. *Modern Tragedy* as a book was a breach of the conventions in every sense. After *Culture and Society* the reception of my work changed completely. It is a curious fact that I was being a relatively sound academic before I was in academia. Once I was in it . . . I think the connection isn't accidental.

You write that one major basis of the contemporary idea of tragedy is 'the assumption of a permanent, universal and essentially unchanging human nature'.[18] *You criticize this notion very convincingly and demystify its component elements: the persistence of evil, the heroic flaw, and so on. But if one rejects a general account of tragedy as completely as that, what reason remains for speaking of 'modern tragedy' as such, which suggests a specific variety of a larger category? Was the word more than a lexical or procedural convenience for you?*

There are two levels of answer to that. One is that many of the writers whose work I discuss thought of it as tragedy – there was a continuity in their consciousness of their own aims with those of their predecessors, as well as radical differences. That's the simple answer. The more substantial answer is that the concept of tragedy still represents a reasonable though very difficult grouping of works in a certain mode around problems of death and extreme suffering and disintegration. I say in a certain mode because there are ways of writing about these problems which are not reasonably grouped with tragedy. But to the extent that death is a material constant in social life, that there is a common quantity of various forms of extreme suffering and dislocation, which may have highly disparate causes, and that these experiences are both interpreted and ideologically captured in successive forms of meaning, it is possible to speak of tragedy as a general category. I was concerned to show the very substantial

[18] MT, p. 45.

relativities operating on certain permanencies in the material situation, even in the case of the inevitability of death. The physical constants are there, but they always undergo a highly variable cultural, philosophical or sociological interpretation in the works of art, that constitute them as tragedy.

2. Brecht and Beyond

We have not yet discussed the big change that occurred in your whole view of modern drama, symbolized by the alteration of the title of your book to Drama from Ibsen to Brecht. *It is clear that your encounter with Brecht's plays led to a revaluation of your earlier positions. There are two questions which we would like to ask. One is simply why Brecht is so completely absent from the first edition of the book – whether you just had no opportunity of reading or seeing Brecht? If so, when did you first become acquainted with Brecht? The second question returns us to the centre of our previous discussion. It is this. Your account of Brecht's drama is now certainly the most brilliant analysis in the book. Your argument is essentially that Brecht broke with naturalist drama by introducing history and producing an action, where naturalism had characteristically been concerned with a passion, in a technical sense, that is with people suffering some process determined beyond the space of the stage. Yet at the same time you demonstrate that Brecht retained the central knot of the naturalist structure of feeling, for the two terms of his drama remained the unmodified pair of the isolated individual and the overwhelming society ranged against the individual. Thus while the late plays like* Galileo *and* Mother Courage *are direct critiques of the myth of the autonomous individual, showing the extent to which he or she is subject to all the changes and determinations of society, they never show the real composition of the latter, since Brecht was 'hardly interested at all in intermediate relationships, in that whole complex of experience, at once personal and social, between the poles of the separated individual and the totally realized society?'[19] Equally, you point out that while Brecht was committed to revolutionary socialism, he could never actually represent any positive social liberation in his plays. Instead their real force comes from an irresoluble opposition between the satisfactions of immediate sensuous experience and the abstract organizational exigencies and sacrifices of politics.*

[19] DIB, p. 289.

Unable to underwrite immersion in the material pleasures of immediate experience, yet aware of what the dictates of Communist politics involved in the epoch of Stalin, he could never situate his major actions in the present, setting them in the far historical past. You conclude: 'Because the polar relationship is still there and decisive, the drama is retrospective, in a deep sense: the intolerable isolation is a fact, and when we see men producing themselves and their situations it is this, essentially, that they produce; that is seen as inevitable and yet is rejected. The dramatic form is not oriented to growth: the experiences of transforming relationship and of social change are not included, and the tone and the conventions follow from this: men are shown why they are isolated, why they defeat themselves. . . . It is a major originality, not because it enters a new world, but because it values an old world differently: the world created directly, in drama, by Ibsen and Strindberg and Chekhov – a world of defeat, frustration, isolation; a world rationalized by Pirandello and the absurdists to a total condition, an inherent insignificance and loss of values; a world purged now, by Brecht, of pity and acceptance – held at arm's length, criticized, explained.' Then you say: 'The power of this different master is conclusive. With this last shift, a particular dramatic world – that of the individual against society – is now wholly seen. Without the substance created by others, Brecht's critical epilogue – his dramatic negative – could not have been written. But now that it has been written, in two or three great plays and in a wider achievement of a powerful and unforgettable dramatic consciousness, we have to struggle to enter, as Brecht himself insisted, a new kind of world.'[20]

That appears to be the new programmatic ending to the book. In effect, you are suggesting that a future drama lies beyond Brecht's theatre, which would at once reach past the polarized versions of individual and society, to the intermediate relationship of concrete class structures, and would represent historical actions no longer paralysed by the opposition of hedonism or authoritarianism, capable of transforming our present world. Was that your intention? If so, has there been any drama before or since which you would regard as approximating to the horizon you evoke?

First, let me explain why Brecht was not there in the original book. This was simply ignorance. Brecht had in fact appeared in *Left Review* in the thirties, and if you care to look back there were ways of knowing about his

[20] DIB, pp. 289–90.

work, if distant and specialized ones. But I think my lack of awareness was very common at the time. It was only in the mid and late fifties that most of us got to know Brecht, and even then it was presented in very ideological ways: as political drama, correctly, but also as an unproblematic supersession of naturalism, and as the enthronement of the critical spectator. For many people, it was and has remained very difficult to detach this position, which they immediately underwrote because it was where they wanted to live themselves, from the actual dramatic actions in which it was embodied. But the more I saw of Brecht's work, from *Baal* through the *Threepenny Opera*, and the very crucial transition in *Saint Joan of the Stockyards*, the more it seemed to me that this drama was a very powerful kind of critical negation whose effect really depended on the presence of what it was negating. That is connected with the fact that much of Brecht's output was a brilliant adaptation of other writers' work – Shakespeare or Marlowe, whom he could react against. Then the exile plays, as I came to think of them, because Brecht's emigration does underlie the whole cast of his later work, always reverted to the isolated individual and the total society. They did not seem to me at all what everybody was proposing – that this was revolutionary drama. The drama was really not that. Although one can read with interest Brecht's attempts to deal with fascist Germany in the thirties, it is quite clear that his creative power went into works like *Mother Courage, The Good Woman of Szechuan* or *The Caucasian Chalk Circle*. The notion of complex seeing, which becomes so important, is not to be associated with revolutionary entry into a new world, because that repeatedly in the plays does not happen. There is no transformation – there are modes of evasion, necessary to protect yourself against an oppressive society. That is a preoccupation to be deeply respected, given how much people have to do so. But it is notable how much he had to distance even this theme, setting so many of his major plays back in time. When the plays began to be produced, the Berliner Ensemble visited London and so on, and I got to know Brecht's drama, even then it was some time before I could see a sufficient range of work to be able to pose any questions about it, because the mode of that particular introduction of Brecht to England also presented and tended to reduce it to a new method of staging. English drama was so dominated by preoccupations with theatrical production that it was quite difficult to push through these to the body of work itself. Of course, it was fashionably interpreted as an attack on 'naturalism', because every new season a theatre stages what is announced as some new version of anti-naturalism, even work which is clearly a reproduction of the naturalist habit. Then when I first read Brecht's extremely interesting critical and theoretical work, what most struck me was then his curious description of what he called Aristotelian theatre. Brecht's account of it would have very much surprised Aristotle, given the possibility of an encounter across two millennia. What he was really referring to was naturalist theatre, and what he was concerned with was the problem of empathy. He developed a political position out of this theory, based on some real continuities, some real breaks, but also several evasions and obliquities. Thus *Galileo* is a very powerful evocation of the problems of an alienated science, which he himself related to the question of the atom bomb, yet it is a drama about the seventeenth century, as is *Mother Courage*. There must have been something in the nature of contemporary reality which prevented another project. But since it was becoming a new radical mode to use Brecht against realism, as a bourgeois form which he had shown how to transcend, it was necessary to point out the negative continuity of his work with naturalism and the relative absence of the transformation at which it aims.

The question of the possibility of moving beyond the limits of Brecht's drama, to show transforming relationships, has to be considered in very precise contexts. I think that there is very little normal such work in the theatre. A consciously minority metropolitan art is not going to be the medium through which that kind of move will be made. The development of television drama has in this respect been much more interesting. But here one comes upon a paradox. The original naturalist project of showing the determining pressures of the environment on character flowered within bourgeois drama in the last quarter of the 19th century. A hundred years later we are now seeing the entry into production of a whole body of writing, if not by, at least of the working class. Now it happens that certain of the original naturalist formulations could go quite a considerable way with this quite new area of social experience, before the same technical problems were encountered yet again. I am very struck by this unevenness in time. The working class had historically been much more excluded from drama than from fiction, so that its break-through into naturalist forms was in a sense very much like the position in the bourgeois theatre in the eighties when there was a whole body of material waiting to be dramatized. Works like *Days of Hope*, or early episodes in *When the Boat Comes In*, were clearly able to operate unproblematically with their new material before the same problems were hit again. Characteristically the focus of this naturalism was retrospective, filling the gap where the historical experience of the working class had never before been represented: its impulse was contemporary with the significant new works of history which were similarly reconstructing the past of an unwritten class. So in a way the people who might have been moving on had this urgent and necessary task to perform, which however left the whole situation of dramatic form where it stood.

For you cannot show transformation within a realist framework unless you introduce the kind of distinction for which Brecht's drama does in fact contain a good precedent, that can perhaps be best put as the difference between indicative and subjunctive modes within the dramatic form itself. A dramatic form which is indicative states that this is what reality is like, these were the impulses that emerged and these were the impulses that were thwarted. It may have to represent a social situation in which at one level or another all roads have been blocked; or even if certain limits are being pushed back, they will still by definition subsist so long as this class society remains. It is at that point that the notion of a subjunctive mode needs to be introduced. I use the term deliberately, rather than utopian or futurist, which have other connotations – whereas subjunctive precisely captures the most important Brechtian intention. For what suddenly started to interest me were those scenes in Brecht that are played and then replayed. This is an incredibly powerful innovation. A typical and less interesting pattern in Brecht's works is a certain fatalist outcome of the action, redeemed only by the spectator's perception that the people on stage were wrong: they are defeated but you can see why they were defeated, so it is your job to go home and make your own revolution. The subjunctive mode allows another sort of resolution. There is a striking example in *Fears and Miseries of the Third Reich*, where a scene is played with this sort of outcome and then it is replayed with the introduction of some other element and the result is a different outcome.

This sense of subjunctive possibility is the main ground of my dispute with those who attack realism as a bourgeois form yet propose no particular alternative to it except a different kind of criticism. Let me take the television play *The Big Flame* by Garnett and Allen as an illustration. For that starts out as a wholly indicative drama in the realist sense. Indeed it reproduces the enclosed world of Liverpool dockers at the time of a very critical reorganization and movement into a strike, in a way that is almost too internal and dependent on identification with it. The play then shows the frustrations of any militant fight for the improvement of conditions within the present social and political order, so long as there is no question of transforming that order. So what can you then do? You can represent the strike as winning heroically or as losing tragically. But in *The Big Flame* there is an attempt, even if it is not adequately sustained, to do something different. At a certain point the strikers say: suppose we went one step further, suppose we occupy, suppose we assert our own control over the docks? The whole sequence which follows is a really subjunctive one. Its form is: if we did this, what would happen next? The occupation occurs. In the event the workers are defeated, as the army invades the yard. Nevertheless what the play successfully presents is an experience which is not realist in the indicative sense of recording contemporary reality, but in the subjunctive sense of supposing a possible sequence of actions beyond it. A utopian or futurist drama, by contrast, would make a completely false jump to a socialist docks run by the workers in which there was no more conflict. In that kind of mode, there is no way of getting from the present to the future, which was always what was wrong with the Stalinist definition of socialist realism.

Reflecting on the play and talking to Tony Garnett about it, I said to him: suppose you had dropped a lot of the earlier material which simply establishes that these are dockers and this is the way they talk and think, because it is too long and enclosed, and you had brought forward the as-if situation of the occupation, which through betrayal or lack of preparation is defeated by the troops. You might have then re-run the whole action of the take-over of the docks, with the workers now making other dispositions leading to another outcome. That would have provoked an outcry from the ordinary critics about lack of realism – they would have said it was ridiculous to play an action and then go back to the beginning and play it again. But this movement is precisely, it seems to me, what the realist project would now be. The notion of the dramatic hypothesis is perfectly compatible with the realist intention. Indeed in this case, as I've suggested, there is no reason why the hypothesis should not have been clearer from the outset. It is ironic that *The Big Flame* should have been attacked on the other side, by people on the left claiming Brecht's authority. For although it is curiously not in any sustained way what Brecht does, he gives more actual examples of subjunctive action than anyone else I know.

You have focussed very helpfully on that aspect of your critique of naturalism which concerns its essential passivity – the external determination of the characters in the drama by forces that remain permanently beyond them. What you have now suggested is the way in which a shift of form from indicative to subjunctive can allow all kinds of alternative futures and dynamic actions to be enacted, without breaking with the realist intention. However, there is another count on which you criticize naturalism – its polarization between individual and society. In effect you argue that Brecht never broke with this essentially liberal dualism – his schematic drama missing all intermediate relationships. Now if one looks at that problem, the issues of naturalism and realism can be posed in a slightly different way. There seem to be two possible readings of the opposition realism/naturalism in your work. One would be Lukácsian, in the strict sense, the other possibly more formalist. The Lukácsian version would be this. Realism, which Lukács defined in very similar terms to your own as a kind of synthesis of the personal and the social, is in effect the great aesthetic achievement of the bourgeoisie, when it is still in its historical ascent. Naturalism is a decadent successor to it, which has ruptured the dynamic linkage between men and women and their society, indeed projects society into a kind of second nature. Characters in naturalist fiction become essentially passive – the hero of L'Education Sentimentale *is the archetypal example. Lukács argues that naturalism sets in as the bourgeoisie ceases to play a progressive historical role in 19th-century Europe. 1848 is of course the turning point in this interpretation, after which Flaubert emerges and is followed by Zola and Maupassant, in a curve of increasing aesthetic decadence. Here the opposition between naturalism and realism is founded historically and corresponds to the variant social destiny of a class. Now it is immediately noticeable that your use of naturalism fits this chronological scheme quite closely, because it starts in the epoch which for Lukács is already the period when the bourgeoisie on a European scale is starting to spiral downwards: behind the 1880s and 1890s lies the watershed of the Commune, which for him represents the further stage of its reaction after the great turn of 1848. Such a reading also appears compatible with your own account in that you lay great stress on the fact that naturalist theatre, even at its height, is unable to re-create or embody a dynamic interrelationship of persons and societies: the greatest masters of naturalism do not achieve that, whereas the masters of the realist novel did. On this reading, one could argue that at the end of the great crisis of the naturalist form one would expect the writers of a new social class – of which Brecht might be a premonitory outrider – to attempt a new realist synthesis. At least there would be nothing directly impossible in this prospect. One of the tokens of such a new realism would presumably be a breakage of the liberal-naturalist deadlock, not just at the point of action and change, but at the point of interconnection between the social and the personal. That is to say, there would be characters on the stage who would be at once bearers and transformers of determinate social relations, but these would be the essentially intermediate relationships of a concrete class structure rather than the abstract polarities of naturalism. On the other hand, another reading is possible, which you seem to have suggested earlier on – that the theatre as such is inherently unable to reproduce the realist synthesis in the sense of the interconnection, if not in the sense of the action. You could envisage a realist theatre which has dynamic and transforming actions and yet in which the persons on the stage necessarily remain schematized well below the threshold of their embodiment in the realist novel. Which of these two versions corresponds most to your own position?*

Let me first say a word about the very interesting question of the relations between forms of art and phases of a class. I was very struck, of course, by Lukács's account: it would be much easier if one could hold to it. But there are serious problems. Naturalist drama, in spite of the limitations we have discussed, still seems to me to be committed to what Lukács elsewhere describes as the classical realist project: showing a man or woman making an effort to live a much fuller life and encountering the objective limits of a particular social order, and depicting the creative contradiction between the impulse towards another life, seen not as an individual but as a general aspiration, and the structural constraints of a society. That description precisely fits the drama of Ibsen and early Strindberg. Yet it cannot be related to different phases of the bourgeoisie, because we are not talking about central ideological representatives of the bourgeoisie at any point. What we are witnessing is the strange phenomenon of the last hundred years of bourgeois culture, of very significant groups breaking from the bourgeoisie, so to say, within its own terms. There is no question of saying they are not within its terms, but they break from it. The whole social formation of this drama, even at the institutional level, suggests that sort of movement. There existed a bourgeois theatre which was very powerfully reproducing society as an unchangeable order, inside which there were only problems of adjustment and attitude. English naturalism was a perfect example of this. Then a break came, curiously within the space of the same ten or fifteen years in so many European countries, to new minority, consciously avant-garde theatres. These were all bourgeois in their social composition – yet the drama which arose out of them proclaimed that social life was stifling, and affirmed the validity of suppressed desires and impulses to a point where it questioned the whole order, though by definition the work did not get through to breaking with it. This is what is usually called naturalism, which has produced a great confusion of terms. Perhaps it would be simpler if we called it realist drama. But that would leave unaddressed the problem of the different historical phasing of the novel and drama. Lukács's periodization of the novel seems to pivot on the contrast between Balzac and Zola: one notices that most of his constructions are in fact from French literature. I think that the English novel has its own specific development.

But it would not be difficult to rewrite Lukács's paradigm as the difference between Dickens and Gissing?

That is right. But on the other hand the movement from George Eliot to Hardy would be different. *Felix Holt* concludes that when an impulse reaches certain limits, it is human wisdom to accept these, and to learn a kind of mature resignation. The limits are even more dreadful in *Jude the Obscure*, for they are totally destructive of the carrier of the impulse, yet the whole action of the novel is subversive of the social order which has produced those limits. Hardy is remarkably contemporary with Ibsen in his presentation of a wholly valid and never questionable desire, which is quite tragically defeated without cancelling the validity of that impulse, and which reaches the point of questioning the social order that has defeated it.

You seem to be using a new definition of realism now. The action of a man or woman who seeks a freer life with a greater attainment of value in it and finds the society an insuperable barrier, the ratification of the quest, yet at the same time the representation of the society – this is not what Lukács called the realist project. It is rather the leit-motif of Theory of the Novel, *before he was a Marxist critic at all. At that time, Flaubert – not at all Balzac – was actually his aesthetic model. Goldmann was later to take over these ideas of Lukács's early metaphysical work, but Goldmann of course never accepted Lukács's later literary theory or espoused the category of realism. The struggle of isolated individual desire against a society that thwarts it is a thematic figure which is common to a vast number of different sorts of 19th-century works. It does not really distinguish any particular form or phase. What you describe so eloquently in Ibsen, for example, exists term for term in Stendhal. You yourself have cited the case of Hardy. The question we are asking is another one: is there a substantive difference between the achievement of Ibsen and that of Hardy, corresponding to the two terms naturalism and realism, or is there only the formal difference of the two modes in which they worked?*

It is very significant that Hardy stopped writing novels after *Jude the Obscure*. One can speculate about the reasons, but I think he had reached a certain limit within the form of his fiction. Let me, however, try to answer your question more generally. It seems to me that there is not only the possibility but the necessity of the resumption of the realist project today. But it will involve the sharpest distinction from naturalism in the conventional sense in which it has settled down. If you look at the majority of fiction about the working class and even to an extent by working-class writers, or the drama which has emerged with the increasing working-class contribution to English culture, it is clear that they remain overwhelmingly in that mould. They convey a sense of complaint and injustice, often retrospectively, and they tell the truth within these naturalist terms, which always demands respect. But they do not represent an alternative perspective. Now I do not see how the realist project can be resumed within any theatrical forms that I know, but this is not to say within any dramatic forms. However, I think that the keys to change are not only a matter of form but also of audience relationship. One can never in the end define a form without defining the actual productive relationship within which it is generated. In a recent essay on English naturalism, I have argued that in a country where it should have been very strong, high naturalist drama was never achieved precisely because of the constriction of the form by the nature of the London theatres as institutions, and the class character of the audiences they represented. Today, however, in television there is a totally different organization of audiences, especially developed in Britain, which completely overpasses the extraordinarily limited relationship of drama to its audience which has been stabilized in the metropolitan theatres. At the same time, far more mobile forms are possible within film and television, as distinct from theatre, because of the camera. I earlier pointed out the technical difficulty of any dramatic form in the theatre finding the equivalent of that intense location and realization of people and place which is so superbly achieved in the realist novel. But the camera now precisely allows television or film to do what theatre in the 19th century could not. It permits the resumption of public actions in fully realized locations of history, moving drama out from the enclosed room or the abstract plain space to work-places, streets and public forums. It is in the combination of three directions, the more mobile dramatic forms of the camera, direct relationship with more popular audiences, and development of subjunctive actions, that I think the future of a new realism lies.

Isn't there a danger here of exaggerating the limits of the theatre, and overestimating the possibilities of television and cinema? At least in Britain, there has been an extraordinary development in the last few years of different types of theatre and theatre groups, while at the same time it has proved extremely difficult to develop equally original work in the cinema and even in television, despite some successes. There are a number of reasons for this. One of them is the fact that television and film remain extremely expensive media, demanding large capital resources which bourgeois companies or bureaucratic corporations naturally control quite tightly. Current developments in technology hold out a different potential – a situation where equipment for immediate visualization is within the reach of every school budget, video-tapes can be re-used, and so on. But this is far from the case at the moment. Even modest attempts to found cinemas outside the commercial circuits of distribution are proving very difficult in Britain. Yet at the same time, with relatively small grants from the Arts Council, there are now perhaps over twenty theatre groups active in various parts of the United Kingdom, which are socialist, feminist, anarchist, or populist. A good example of this phenomenon, although there are many others, is the 7:84 Company, which mainly produces plays by John McGrath, who is himself of working-class background, and previously worked precisely in television and then in naturalist cinema. The central organizing principle of the company is that it does not spend long periods in the capital and it never goes to the West End; it essentially plays in theatres, halls and clubs in the provinces, which have working-class audiences. One of its plays, The Cheviot, the Stag and the Black, Black Oil, *is an attempt to trace the history of Scotland from the clearances of the Highlands to the coming of the oil companies. It certainly meets your criteria of active historical movement and multiple conventions –*

using song and music particularly effectively. Probably over a hundred thousand people in Scotland saw the play live. It was subsequently televised with great success, but it is specifically a creation of the stage. A work like this seems to represent a development which has not received its equivalent in cinematic or televisual form.

I have been telling people all over Europe that *The Cheviot* is the most important recent play in Britain. I don't have to be persuaded of that. But I think it is a rather special case. For the play enjoyed the advantage of a precise cultural location in Scotland which not only ensured the very specific relation of the audience to the form, but also made available certain materials for use as new conventions – that is to say, the continuity of a body of popular song. It was a very considerable part of the rapport between the company and the audience that the songs were shared: they did not have to be produced to be learnt, they already in a sense existed as a bond. *The Cheviot* in that sense benefited from one of the relatively isolated cases of continuity with a traditional culture that is at once working-class and nationalist. There is a possibility of this kind of link in Welsh culture. I had thought these links were much less available in industrial England – they're obviously more difficult – but McGrath himself has recently persuaded me that they may be there if actively sought.

More generally, one of the most interesting and heartening developments of the sixties was the emergence of new groups which were able to by-pass some of the blockages of the dominant culture and perform in different ways – the Street Theatre, the Basement Theatre, the Lunchtime Theatre. These were the equivalent of the extraordinary outburst of new periodical publishing, which also depended on a cheapening of available techniques which is going to come in video as well. Yet while these alternative projects are crucial, the left can never content itself with a cultural policy that does not attack quite centrally the dominant means of production. So it is perfectly true that many people are now getting their experience in underground arenas, but the fact is that these are operating within an increasingly centralized capitalist culture, which has this margin that is partly tolerated and partly even supported in a rather distant and eventually complicated way. For major projects you do have to appropriate the major means of production.

Yes: if the power and the opportunity are there to achieve such an appropriation, you are certainly right. But in the meantime there is one argument that could be made against you. To take the most dominant single means of cultural production today, there may be something specific and unalterable within a given society about the television audience itself. You have stressed very eloquently the nature of the bourgeois theatre as a room. You write, for example: 'Any break from naturalism is a break from the room: from that representative room, above a capital city; from that trap of a room, in which the victims torment each other; from that everyday room, in which the menacing agents arrive unexplained. It is not, of course, mainly a question of staging, it is a question of consciousness. What is enacted in the room is a state of mind in which these things happen to people from a determining world beyond them.'[21] *In your inaugural lecture you refer to the theatre of the room in which the auditorium is so to speak the fourth wall.*[22] *Now there is a way in which that argument applies in reverse to television. For one could think of the television set as the fourth wall inside the real bourgeois room. Of course, much of the population watching it is working-class, but the striking point is that virtually the same terms can be retained for the relationship of the audience to the form. However much you use camera mobility or differential location and time, even the most advanced techniques of television are still received and absorbed by spectators cut off from each other in innumerable private rooms, literally receiving alongside or just after your development of realist plays other programmes which arrive unexplained, as the messages of a dominant and determining world which comes from the outside to them through this opening in the wall. The television audience is in Sartre's terms archetypally serialized – an object, if you like, of 'roomification'. Whereas people who go out of those rooms to theatres or clubs or to performances in factories or village halls or local schools, as you must have done on occasion, enter a completely different atmosphere through their common relationship with the other spectators. The energy and mobility of the drama, very intimate because it is on the same floor as yourself, can communicate itself to two or three hundred people with remarkable power. Might it not be argued that this type of drama is now a more effective form than the television play, because of the social organization of its audience?*

I do not at all want to deny the access of energy that comes when the

[21] DIB, p. 325.
[22] *Drama in a Dramatized Society*, Cambridge 1975.

companies and the spectators put themselves in deliberately altered social relations – a new kind of drama results. Nor do I disagree that to understand television as a medium one must have grasped the function of the stage as a room – it really is a realization in a different technology of much of that same set of social relationships. But the fact that television was developed as a domestic receiver was not an effect of the technology, it was a consequence of the particular investment decisions made by capital. The experiments which some radical groups are making with split screen television, with large screen television, which is after all a general possibility within ten years, are now creating the possibility of taking television out of the living room.

In a genuinely socialist society, television would obviously have a different potential. But if you want to combat the social relations that exist today, you have to take into account the way it is organized at present.

Agreed. But after all even that organization has allowed the emergence of a run of working-class drama in television that already seems to me a significant achievement – the work of Garnett, Loach, some of the Wednesday Play productions or *When the Boat Comes In*. Whatever their limitations as a renewal of naturalism, these represent quite a substantial quantity of work. Whereas, while it seems to me perfectly possible for radicals to work in the unoccupied fringes of a culture, I do not think that on the whole the realist project is being much resumed there. What you see is a very effective use of certain theatrical modes for political satire or mobilization around specific issues, for new kinds of audience. Ironically, some of the people involved in this radical theatre are as hostile to the notion of realism as the avant-garde bourgeois theatre. Much of this movement is as distant, rightly or wrongly, from the project of resuming realist drama at a higher social stage, as really any other part of the theatre.

Do you think that there is any intrinsic connection between what you call the resumption of the realist project, and revolutionary politics? Is there a necessary class direction to this form?

Ultimately yes. I think that there must be such a relationship in the sense that the only possibility of overcoming the individual-society or family-environment polarity is at once a socialist and a working-class bearing. But the difficulties of the project are enormous. As a matter of fact I myself now think that there are more practical possibilities in the whole range of drama, including for me especially film and television, than there are in the novel where the problems of cultural production are very severe. It is very tiresome to hear people complain about the thinness of novels today, when they overlook the elementary fact which anybody faced with pieces of paper on a desk knows from the outset, that the characteristic length of the modern novel which can find a publisher is about that of one section of a Tolstoy or a George Eliot or a Balzac novel. Although there are possibilities of exceeding this by trilogies or series, the result is not in fact the same since these involve a basic difference of formal organization. I do not mean that realism is achieved by bulk, merely that it demands scope for a complexity and alternation of perspective which are simply not materially negotiable within 80,000 words. In certain ways film and television can move much more quickly. But there too it is much easier to dramatize extreme situations of a polarized kind between the individual and the society than to show the interconnections between them or to explore the intermediate relationships which are proper to the realist project. All these need space, which the pressures of a capitalist culture at this stage do not ordinarily permit.

It is noticeable that right from the start of your account of modern drama, you say of the very first plays you discuss – especially Ibsen's Peer Gynt *– that they are reaching for effects which cannot really be attained on the stage but are actually promonitory of film. You repeat the same comment on Strindberg somewhat later.*[23] *Extrapolating your argument, one might say that the visual condensations in film can perform something like analogous functions to the lengthy physical descriptions or development of character through a great deal of reported speech in the realist novel – precisely the element that you have suggested is by definition impossible for the theatre. If that were so, one could perhaps regard naturalist drama as a transitional form in a larger epochal sense. For after all it arose, a point which you don't really ever discuss throughout the book, quite some time after photography had already deeply changed what must have been a very large area of European consciousness about what visual accuracy of reproduction or representation meant, and its course overlaps for fifty years with the genesis and development of film. In that*

[23] DIB, pp. 43, 76, 93.

perspective would it be possible to argue that of the two elements of the naturalist deadlock, the limitation of action and of interconnection, the problem of historical action could be resolved on the stage – as the work of Brecht was at least partially to show, whereas the solution to the problem of intermediate connection lay beyond, in the relative plenitude of the new imagery of film or television?

That may be. One is bound to be struck by the recurrent attempts within the general crisis of the last thirty, perhaps forty years, to create new forms which are extremely difficult to classify in older terms. There have been endless discussions within television, for example, of the relation between drama and documentary, including official fiats that it should be always clear to the audience whether it is watching a documentary or a play, which are being resisted by progressive producers. What could emerge from these new forms, which would not resemble much that now passes for realism, need not in a conventional sense be dramatized or narrated at all, but could yet be realist productions.

Could we ask about the development of your views on the cinema? How did you come to write Preface to Film *after the war?*

The book was prompted in two ways. One was my own interest in teaching film at this time in adult classes. The other was a proposal from Orrom – with whom I had been out of touch for a few years – that we collaborate on a film, introducing our approach in the form of a book. What happened, of course, was that the book got out but that the project for the film was never realized, for lack of funds.

The aesthetic argument of Preface to Film *culminates in the category of 'total expression', which you define as 'the ideal of a wholly conceived drama' in which 'each of the elements being used – speech, music, movement, design – bears a controlled, necessary and direct relation, at the moment of expression, to any other that is then being used.'*[24] *Historically, phrases like this have been associated with aesthetics that have very little to do with realism, given the subjectivist overtones of the term 'expression'. They evoke rather the symbolist idea of synaesthesia or the* Gesamtkunstwerk *of Wagnerian opera. What did*

[24] PF, pp. 52, 54.

you intend by this notion?

The idea is inadequately put there: I should have spoken of total form. Its rationale was this. There has been an incredibly problematic relation in modern drama between the writer and the production of his work since the advent of the theatre director. In England that arrived in the 1860s with Robertson. The director intervened more and more powerfully as the real producer, while retaining an increasingly ambiguous link with the original producer, the writer. The characteristic ideological formula was that the writer provided the 'script' for the 'production'. This then became the standard working relationship in the cinema industry. Dramatically the consequences have usually been disastrous. There does not, of course, have to be a single author for a work, but in this system writing is reduced to the provision of raw material processed somewhere else. On the other hand, if one takes the classic case of Chekhov bitterly protesting about what Stanislavsky had made of his plays, it is obvious that Stanislavsky had to do something to them because what Chekhov had written was not a performance. It has been the complaint of dramatic authors for the last eighty years that they lose the results of their labour in the next stage of the production process; yet ironically what is lost – the text – survives, while what is achieved – the performance – does not. The real problem then is, how can you find a notation for writing, not simply dialogue, but a whole dramatic action? The idea of total form was designed to indicate that all the elements of a dramatic work should be under coherent control, rather than vagaries of the dissociated process typical of capitalist relations of production. The specific interest of film was that it held the technical promise of a total performance, while being as durable as a written text. Hence my interest in Bergman, who published his own scripts – *Drama in Performance* ends with an analysis of the problems of notation and physical realization in *Wild Strawberries*.

It is certainly one of the most striking aspects of Drama in Performance *that it concludes with a kind of manifesto for the primacy of film today. You advocate throughout the greatest possible fusion or unification of the written text and the active performance in drama. So it is in a way logical that you should end with a discussion of the characteristic figure of post-war cinema, the director who writes his own script and oversees down to the last detail every single aspect of the final production of film, in so far as commercial pressures allow him –*

ideally the complete controller of the ultimate artefact. Were you actually maintaining that a total performance can be achieved in film in a way that it could never be in the theatre, where the staging tends to be a more or less poor or adulterated version, a rough imitation at best, an outright betrayal at worst, of what the dramatist has written?

No, that need not happen to the text in the theatre. The problem is one of notation. There was a unity of text and performance in Greek or Elizabethan drama, so far as we can reconstruct them, made possible by a set of shared conventions, which controlled not just the writing of the dialogue but also the movement and grouping of the actors on the stage. Something similar exists today where a play is written for production within a particular company, such as Brecht's works for the Berliner Ensemble. In that case, there are either the known habits of the company or there is a body of shared if unwritten knowledge that will be brought to bear on the production, so that it can be assumed that the complete text will be realized – indeed will be actualized – in performance, without disparity. The problem arises when the modern dramatic text is treated by directors as simply a script, which really means just dialogue. The look of a text with forms of notation for scene and movement would be quite different. That was the great interest of the work of Bergmann. It did seem to me that certain of the current problems of the theatre, with its lack of adequate notation, could be by-passed in the cinema where a definitive performance of a text was possible, theoretically subject to integral control.

However, to avoid misunderstanding, I should emphasize that I did not mean any project of individual control. A total performance could quite clearly be controlled by a collaborating group. Nor did I mean to suggest that film was in practice necessarily an easier form in which to aim for such a performance. On the contrary, the cinema has typically reduced the writer to script-writer more radically even than theatre. Television has not been much better. I once really followed through this experience myself. Having written a television play, I was invited to go along to the production – only to find that the author is a damned nuisance there, unless you've got to cut ten minutes out of a scene and need a quick rewrite, or a few new lines have to be written into another scene. Even with a very sympathetic director, the writer is a sort of adjunct, witnessing the production of something he had not intended to produce.

You've said that the most intense cultural experience of your student days was the cinema. You later thought that at least in principle film possessed the potential privilege of a complete unification of text and performance, such that the distinction between the two would cease altogether and that the final product be equivalent to a poem or a novel. Yet in Preface to Film *you don't cite actual examples of what you held to be the creative achievement of the cinema. That raises the question of what sort of films you were seeing in the post-war period. Which approximated nearest to the realist possibilities of a cinema capable of accomplishments beyond Ibsen or Strindberg?*

I saw far fewer films in the period from '46 to '60 than at any previous time, essentially because I was living in a small provincial town and teaching in the evenings. The early Soviet cinema always seemed to me the major work that took up the original naturalist project of the secular, the contemporary, the socially extensive. But it had broadened its movement out into public and historical action by the application of new concepts to the process of production. In that respect, the Soviet cinema of the twenties was crucially superior to, say, the Italian neo-realism of the forties and fifties. I was sympathetic to neo-realism because of the new social material it presented, of which there were many decent examples after the war. But its form seemed to be a step backward, much like the later English drama of working-class experience of which I've spoken. The conceptual innovations of Eisenstein's cinema, which can be related to Brecht's complex seeing, are missing. In the sixties, on the other hand, there was a development of incredibly complex seeing, but of nothing very much. The complexity became a fetishized concentration on the point of view at the expense of what was viewed. This cinema could genuinely be described as formalist in the sense that it was preoccupied with problems of the medium without any adequate relation between its methods and the kind of content these were supposed to interpret. In the late thirties admiration for *Dr Caligari* or *Metropolis* was virtually a condition of entry to the Socialist Club at Cambridge. When I see them now, what I feel is 'here comes the sixties'. The thematic preoccupations are very similar, making allowance for the technical differences between the epochs of expressionist and contemporary cinema. There is also much the same interesting confusion in the sixties and in the twenties of a kind of formalist radicalism and a socialist radicalism, which for historical reasons got mixed up together. Eventually the two had and will have again to be separated.

What was your attitude to the American cinema after the war?

In the end the biggest argument I had with Orrom was over Hollywood. When we were discussing what we meant by a film of total expression, I asked him to cite an example of his version of one. He answered: *Singing in the Rain*. At first I was completely uncomprehending – I thought it was a joke. Then the emphasis on technique, abstracted from any content, totally turned me off. My own thinking was derived from the cinema of the twenties, which made my ideas seem reactionary, in the sense that I was ignoring the quite different productive conditions of the time. The scenario I actually composed was an attempt to rework a particular Welsh legend in terms of a contemporary situation. It may have been a better direction than *Singing in the Rain*, but it was not exactly an overwhelming alternative. Anyway, I only got as far as writing it.

Did the development of television modify your notion of total performance subsequently – or do you regard its technical possibilities as still too limited? One of the most forceful arguments in Television: Technology and Cultural Form *is that the television screen is not just a miniature version of the cinema screen, but that the reduction in the scale of the image produces a qualitatively different, more restricted medium.*[25] *Do you regard that as an intrinsic feature of television, which will prevail in the future as well?*

Not necessarily. Far larger screens are technically possible. Even today, of course, many films are really made for television transmission. There is still the problem of the technical reproduction of the image, but I think in the present situation you have to be prepared to accept certain losses if you can also achieve certain gains. Whereas it is very difficult to see any short-term prospect of a revival of active film production in this country, we now have fifteen or sixteen years of major contributions to television drama. When I talk in Europe about contemporary British drama, I am typically asked about theatre dramatists whose texts have been translated or whose

[25] TTCF, pp. 62–3.

productions have been toured; when I reply that there is really much more important work on television, they usually think at first that I am joking. To an Italian, for example, it seems incredible or ludicrous that this could be so. On the other hand, when they say, all right – show us, what can I do? I can't show them. There are such tight agreements about the re-showing of television productions, especially with Equity, that it is extremely difficult to see any of this drama – that is, even where they are not wantonly destroying work which could quite easily be stored. For example, to view *The Big Flame* again for a collective discussion of it, the most extraordinary subterfuges were necessary: in effect it had to be smuggled out.

It is difficult to imagine television drama founding a cumulative tradition anywhere until there is an elementary level of re-seeability of its work. Surely that is essential for any ongoing process of development, with a dynamic interaction between a number of different styles of work in the same form?

The present situation is an alterable one. I am involved in a campaign right now to get it changed, which would not actually involve any very great transformation of social conditions – just a sensible renegotiation of copyright and union agreements, which were once quite rational: nothing compared to the scale of the problem in altering the nature of capitalist film production. It will no doubt take time, but it can be done.

IV

Literature

1. Reading and Criticism

When you wrote Reading and Criticism, *were there any substantive divergences between you and the* Scrutiny *tradition? Looking at the book today the two seem very close, but perhaps there were unexpressed differences?*

I was conscious of one difference which may not appear obvious now, but was important then. The normal *Scrutiny* practice in the criticism of fiction was to judge the quality of a novel or of a novelist by analysing a sample of prose which was assumed to be a representative pattern of the writer's work as a whole. This method was developed essentially for the analysis of the single short poem. I didn't think it would work with the novel. Already in preparing for the Tripos I searched for a long time to find paired examples of prose by George Eliot and Lawrence that would demonstrate the point. The cases I chose showed that one pair would make George Eliot a better writer than Lawrence, and the other pair would make Lawrence a better writer than George Eliot. At the time I felt this to be a challenge to the critical orthodoxy. Later, of course, I would have said that the very selection of a passage for close analysis usually presupposed an unexamined judgment of the work from which it was taken, derived from other sources.

Your comparison of the passages from Eliot and Lawrence in Reading and Criticism *remains very effective. The practical conclusion you drew from it was the need to analyse, not arbitrarily isolated passages, but complete works. You went on to attempt this with an account of Conrad's novella* The Heart of Darkness. *How do you feel about that chapter today?*

I think that it was moving in the right direction, although it was again taking a relatively short work. Yet what the chapter shows is the limits of that kind of critical analysis – what it can and cannot do. For ironically Conrad's text poses quite crucial issues – about imperialism, for example –

which concerned me greatly later on, but which I did not discuss at all then, and which in a way could hardly be discussed within a procedure so completely focussed on use of language or thematic organization.

That raises the question of your general theoretical position at the time. Reading and Criticism *contains some aggressive restatements of wider Leavisian intellectual tenets. For example, you scout very boldly and deliberately the idea that literary judgments are in any sense subject to, let alone could benefit from, wider theoretical perspectives. You write: '"What are the standards?" This question could be treated theoretically, but a preoccupation with theories of literary judgment and value seems quite frequently to be of little relevance to the actual judgment of literature, however useful it may be to other branches of knowledge. Often, indeed, one has seen a theoretical interest of this kind distract attention from literature.' Then you go on to say: 'To the questions, "What are literary values?" and "What are literary standards?" one could only reply "They are literature itself".'*[1] *Isn't that the classic Leavisite argument, at its most circular?*

Yes, this was more or less a statement of the orthodox position. However, I wasn't thinking so much of the theory of literature as of the theory of literary judgment. Actually, although I wouldn't put it that way now, I still hold much the same opinion of what is called critical theory, which is a very different matter from literary theory or cultural theory. There is a good deal of apparently theoretical discourse about the process of making judgments which as an isolated activity repeats the limitations of the isolated critical practice itself.

At the end of the book, you say that literature is 'valuable primarily as a record of detailed individual experience which has been coherently stated and valued'.[2] *That seems a very surprising formulation for you to have penned, even at the time?*

That's right – obviously I wouldn't use those terms now, although I would retain the elements of 'detail' and 'experience'. It is 'individual' that destroys the emphasis. The intention of the word was to reject the idea of

[1] RC, pp. 25–26.
[2] RC, p. 107.

society as a literary abstraction. In fact, as I later argued, a social system can only work itself out in quite specifically detailed lives and relations; if that is not said, literature is displaced towards forms of discourse which are more appropriate for studying the structure of the system as such. But what I did not see is the deeply ideological presumption of the use of the term individual, in the other direction. I wanted to assert that a social system is also a human society, but the forms of my definition perpetuated the false contrast between the individual and the social.

One final problem posed by Reading and Criticism *brings us right up to the present. For a new reader today, the most striking single theme of the book is in some ways your general plea for criticism and the terms in which you make it. For you write: 'Criticism is widely resented, and the hostility which it provokes is so frequently intense that it is clear there are very large emotional forces involved. It is a little difficult to understand why this should be so.'*[3] *You attack the treatment of criticism as a mere 'nagging, fault-finding activity',*[4] *designed to take away one's pleasure, and declare that criticism is actually the legitimate process of evaluation and comparison of standards in mature reading. Thirty years later, you take up the very same terms in your entry on criticism in* Keywords *and in your discussion in* Marxism and Literature, *and you now appear to endorse the very equation between criticism and fault-finding which you once denounced. In* Keywords *you write expressly: 'The continuing sense of* criticism *as fault-finding is the most useful linguistic influence against the confidence of the habit [of judgment].'*[5] *Did you intend this to be a complete and calculated reversal of your previous position?*

Of course, it was very conscious. The change, however, has to be related not just to the development of my work, but also to the evolution of the cultural context. The fact is, and it is a point of general importance, that the early stages of practical critical activity were linked to a corresponding advocacy of certain kinds of contemporary writing. The force of the new criticism in the twenties was directly related to the new poetry and prose of Eliot or Joyce. The literature of the past was of course often invoked by these critics, but they had a sense of connection with literary practice in the present too. When we took up their watchwords immediately after the

[3] RC, p. 3.
[4] RC, p. 2.
[5] K, p. 76.

war, we felt there was a cultural battle to be waged. There were certain figures or styles of writing we wanted to attack; for example Priestley, who precisely responded with the lofty tone of the creative writer – 'Who are these young Cambridge people nagging away?' That was what we meant by resentment against criticism at the time. On the other hand we were much less clear about alternative positive directions for contemporary literature. That uncertainty was later succeeded by a general indifference in the fifties, when very little critical practice was in any way alive to even qualified advocacy of any tendency in current writing. The two became quite separate. Leavis was a key influence in this change, rejecting everything after the war but a few surviving writers of the earlier period. The implicit standard by which contemporary work was now judged was simply work of the past. The result was the emergence of the familiar socio-cultural doctrine of past civilization and present chaos, combined with the assertion of the priority of literary criticism over any kind of literary practice. By the early sixties, it was widely assumed that pointing out flaws in contemporary writing was a much more important activity than attempting any such writing itself. At that point, it could more justly be said that fault-finding was being elevated into a central discipline of English studies – something qualitatively different from the original character of practical criticism.

Today, when I see young Marxist anti-realists making very severe points against people of their own generation in television or fiction, rejecting all the premises of the Leavisite critical tradition and proceeding from quite different philosophical bases, but responding to the work of their contemporaries in a remarkably similar spirit of hostility, I cannot help feeling that this culture is rotten with criticism. That is why I now think it is important to restore the sense that unless critical practice is related to some advocacy of literary practice, it is going to be much nearer to what is described in a philistine way as merely nagging and fault-finding, and is inevitably going to provoke the crude reaction that if you think you can write a better novel or make a better television programme – do it, we'll look at yours too. Of course it's true that this response is often philistine bad faith, when it comes from people who are busily preventing anyone from doing that kind of work. The recent television festival at Edinburgh was an occasion where these two attitudes were prominently displayed. On the one hand, you got the most complacent kind of 'creative' people telling the young critics: 'Of course, you are just critics, we are the people who make the programmes.' That sort of reply takes me back to my 1947 position – against it I would write the same defence of criticism again. On the other hand, when I talk with many of the critics who are dismissed for not understanding 'us creative people' about the direction of their criticism and its relation to contemporary work, it is impossible not to notice its disconnection from any alternative practice, which should be a condition of its health.

Moreover, you cannot see the institutionalization of criticism as a prolonged educational practice in examination papers or university essays without getting a very strong sense of what it does to a generation that is trained to an assumption of critical privilege. The incident which crystallized my conviction of this was when I read a whole set of examination answers on Johnson's epitaph to Levet, which describes Levet as 'officious', in the second verse, as well as 'innocent' and 'sincere'. 'Officious' was often positive in the 18th century, meaning conscientious, whereas now of course it would mean bossy or interfering. One could forgive anyone for not knowing that. But one would expect some openness in the undergraduates who found this problematic word in a list of virtues, some willingness to admit 'There's something puzzling here even if I can't explain it.' What struck me as extraordinary was the confidence with which the answers either fell back on the technical mystification that came out of practical criticism – that this was an interesting ambiguity: nice and officious at once; or simply declared that Johnson was muddled and confused, unable to make up his mind. That un-selfcritical habit takes hold incredibly easily, and does no good to man or beast. A style develops – the more institutionalized, the more confident it becomes – which is profoundly unproductive. In fact, it is now a crucial ingredient in a certain kind of anti-political cynicism. Critics like this are so attuned to faults that when there is an industrial dispute, they would rather be analysing the militants' language, which will always include some errors or clichés, than giving a damn what the dispute is about. It's at that point that the sense of criticism as merely fault-finding has to be articulated, in however qualified a way. That is why I consciously revised my judgment in *Keywords* – to protect people who need some protection.

Every socialist should have the strongest sympathy with that. Your reply is actually a reminder of one important feature of Reading and Criticism *which isn't easily inferred from a simple comparison of texts, but which should be part of any retrospective judgment of the book: which is that you were trying to transform the social relations of Leavisian-Richardian criticism. Richards's audience was factually a social elite; Leavis's audience was programmatically an intellectual elite; whereas your direct audience was in principle working-class, largely taught by committed socialists who saw their educational practice in that light. So in a way the book did actually stand outside the development you have been talking about – the professionalization of the discipline.*

That is objectively true. But I don't think I was so conscious of the difference as that. Then, of course, as I've explained, since Adult Education was a mixed movement, there was a sense in which it was only an expansion of an elite. But the presence of working-class students was the other part of the mixture, and taking the practice of criticism to them inevitably led to its modification: the altered social relations necessarily produced an altered social tone.

2. The English Novel from Dickens to Lawrence

We would like to ask you a general question about the role of literary criticism in your own biographical development. There is a very long lapse of time between the publication of Reading and Criticism *and* The English Novel from Dickens to Lawrence. *In effect, you were teaching literature for fifteen years in Adult Education and then for another seven or eight years at Cambridge before you published a book directly in English Studies again. That is a striking gap. What was the relationship of literary criticism to the rest of your work in that period? Were you intending to produce a full-scale work in the field or not?*

No, I wasn't particularly interested. When I was teaching in Adult Education, I used to devote up to two-thirds of the course each year to work that I had either never read before, or knew only superficially. So I spent a lot of time simply reading more widely. I didn't want much to write about it. I was more preoccupied with *Culture and Society* and *The Long Revolution*. From somewhere in the early 1950s I ceased to see work in criticism as the sort of book I wanted to produce. I didn't keep up, for example, with what they call 'the literature'. When I came back to Cambridge, I was quite out of touch; I wasn't a professional literary scholar. I had to read all the publications on the major authors which had appeared since I was a student, to bring myself up to date. Even on authors I had been constantly thinking about, like Dickens, I hadn't read those sorts of book, let alone the articles.

When I got back into the academic atmosphere, it was assumed as a matter of course that criticism is what you would be doing. 'What are you working on?' people would say. I would answer vaguely, 'I don't know, on Godwin or Herrick or something.' In actual fact, however, the return to Cambridge produced two works which include literary criticism but also other kinds of attention and argument. They were *Modern Tragedy*, which I wrote because I was appalled at the ideology of tragedy in the university, and *The Country and the City*, which had its origin in discussions of country-house poems at the same time. The impulse for these books came in a sense from re-entering this literary critical atmosphere. But then neither of them was called a literary critical book. In the end, I only published the book on the English novel, which was originally a series of lectures, because the spin-off from them in other people's work was occurring at such a rate that I thought I'd better make my own position clear. It wasn't a planned work, and it was done very quickly. I just found my old notes and transcripts and wrote them up into a short book.

Many readers must have felt that the book has a particular clarity and urgency of diction, perhaps because it was first spoken. Is the final text very close to the original form?

Yes. I became very involved in the course I was giving on the novel, after I came back to Cambridge: it met with a lot of response and over the years several post-graduates started developing their own work from it – Terry Eagleton, Pat Parrinder and others. Many of the ideas occurred while I was actually speaking. I remember for example the moment when I linked the analytic composition of *Middlemarch* to George Eliot's loss of her earlier social perspective – a connection which hadn't occurred to me till then. Terry Eagleton, who was sitting in the front row, sat bolt upright because he was so inside the argument – we talked all the time – that he could see immediately the shift of judgment that had just come out of the logic of the argument. When I went through the recordings, I maintained the way the lectures had been given. I deliberately kept the book at about that level. I wondered whether I shouldn't, but then I thought that if I were to produce what would be called by my colleagues a proper book on the English novel from Dickens to Lawrence it would be an enormous job that would take years, and the end-result would be something entirely different. If it had been a work conceived in current academic styles it couldn't even have been written. For myself, I felt that a period was over and it was now time just to have it on the record.

One feature of The English Novel from Dickens to Lawrence *that cannot fail to strike anyone familiar with Leavis's work is its apparently sustained, virtually symmetrical inversion of the authors, evaluations and emphases to be found in* The Great Tradition. *In each case the books begin with Jane Austen, who doesn't get a chapter to herself but figures as the starting-point of a tradition; but whereas Leavis writes Dickens out of his tradition, you instate Dickens very firmly as the first author you discuss at length in yours. Moving on to George Eliot, Leavis puts all his emphasis on* Middlemarch *and* Daniel Deronda *– the later work, which you precisely deprecate at the expense of* Adam Bede *and the earlier work. Then when he jumps straightaway to James, omitting Hardy, you go straight to Hardy and delete James. Even with Lawrence, where Leavis holds* Women in Love *to be the peak achievement, you single it out for censure – praising by contrast* Sons and Lovers *and* Lady Chatterley, *which he neglects. It looks as if at nearly every point you are joining issue with him and seeking to overturn the map he drew. How deliberate was that on your part?*

At certain points very deliberate: the different judgment of the relationship between Jane Austen and George Eliot, or Jane Austen and Emily Brontë; the assessment of Dickens (which by this time he had amended anyway); the transition from George Eliot to Hardy rather than James. I couldn't fail to be conscious of this process. It was not merely that I knew *The Great Tradition* by heart. One must remember that by this time, although Leavis still thought of himself as an outsider in his last years, he had completely won. I mean if you talked to anyone about the English novel, including people who were hostile to Leavis, they were in fact reproducing his sense of the shape of its history. So I couldn't but talk to that situation. I think it even influenced me wrongly, because I wouldn't start now at the 1840s but in the 1790s. That would have been the correct decade, the time of the suppression of the attempt at a new kind of novel by writers like Godwin. I think this would probably have yielded a different perspective on Jane Austen and then on the re-emergence of a similar kind of fiction in the late 1830s and 1840s, which should have been related to a social history going much further back. I failed to see this, because the 1790s weren't on the conventional map of the novel at all.

So far as Leavis himself was concerned, what I thought and still think most strongly is that even making the most generous judgment of Leavis and all his values, which are real, he should not have done that to Hardy. His attitude to literature in the middle of the 20th century I can understand, although I reject it. But I still cannot understand, except on the very worst judgment of him, why he should have adopted that particular tone towards Hardy. Even the faults in his formulations – his emphasis on Englishness or on particular kinds of rural community – should at least have directed his attention towards Hardy, rather than to excluding him from the very tradition in which they were being urged.

Isn't the answer that he must have felt very threatened by the radicalism of Hardy? You domonstrate very clearly in your book that in many respects Hardy is the main ancestor of Lawrence. But in a way Lawrence is more easy to take. If you don't want to look too closely at the realities of class and power, Lawrence is curiously less explosive than Hardy, although he comes after him.

That's right. But it is still ironic that Leavis should have listed Hardy as one of the Great Names in his *Minority Culture* pamphlet of 1930, whereas by the time of *The Great Tradition* he treats him patronizingly, almost as a country yokel. I think you are right that the explanation of the paradox is that Hardy is very disturbing for someone trying to rationalize refined, civilized, balancing judgment. Hardy exposes so much which cannot be displaced from its social situation, particularly in the later books. The most immediate effect of the course at Cambridge was probably to start that kind of reassessment of Hardy, and perhaps Wells. It was assumed that Wells had been finished off by Virginia Woolf – 'Nobody reads that sort of thing.' I sought to show that the Wells-James controversy was a very open argument rather than decisively won by James, with no more to say.

You mention that in the twenties Leavis made approving references to Hardy, of whom indeed there is quite a positive evaluation by Frank Chapman in an early number of Scrutiny. *It is interesting that there is one other novel of which both the Leavises thought highly and yet neither was ever able to write about, and that is* Ulysses. *May there not have been something in Hardy's writing strategy, in particular his weaving of discourses, a strategy much more manifest in Joyce's novel – which from your different position you're able to analyse very effectively – that in the strictest sense actually defeated Leavis's aesthetic conceptions of concreteness? Perhaps it was also for that reason these novels were frustrating to him.*

I think that is probably right. In terms of Leavis's stated positions of colloquiality and lived experience, *Jude* or *Ulysses* should have been works that *Scrutiny* attended to. But in fact there was an increasing movement towards precisely the alternative tradition, towards the more formal, the more consciously educated, the more unified literary forms. When these critics found themselves in their own time confronted with a colloquialism and everydayness which was not merely an abstract value but was there in your own room, and among other people, their whole programme ran into difficulties. You can't extol these virtues in the past and then lament them in the present without the extraordinary cultural map which Leavis had to draw: once all these things had been part of real life, now they were a simple vulgarity. This is where it all ended.

The concept which is crucial to much of your discussion of Hardy is the idea of the knowable community. This category, which is at once social-historical and literary-textual in its references, is the organizing principle of the book. Nevertheless there is no direct exposition of it as such in The English Novel. *Could you give us an abstract definition of the knowable community?*

Those novels which can attain an effective range of social experience by sufficiently manifest immediate relations possess a knowable community. Hardy has often been described as a regional novelist, but the term is mistaken. A regional fiction is one which does not include the conflicts of the larger society of which the region is evidently a part. There is a lot of 20th-century rural fiction, from which you could not guess any of the major movements within English society, and the fiction is regional in that sense. That is absolutely not true of Hardy, whose novels reveal the major crises of late 19th-century England. He could reach a very wide range of social experience through a series of relations which were wholly knowable to him in manifest ways, and which he could render concrete in his fiction. That was not possible, for example, for Dickens, who had to devise different fictional strategies for a much more complex urban world, increasingly dominated by processes that could only be grasped statistically or analytically – a community unknowable in terms of manifest experience. The contrary notion of the unknowable community is very important for the argument of the book, since the idea of the knowable community alone might suggest that novels could not be written, except in very special circumstances, in the 20th century. That conclusion would, of course, go against everything in my own writing, where these problems are very directly posed for my own practice.

There are a series of specific judgments in The English Novel *which raise a number of general theoretical questions, which we should perhaps explore. The first concerns the way you treat the relationship between Jane Austen's literary achievement and the class conditions of its creation, or putting it another way, between the code of morality in her novels and the class selectivity of her world. You argue in effect that the extraordinary unity of tone in Jane Austen's novels is due to the fact that moral improvement was for her in some way connected or even consubstantial with economic improvement – in other words, that the virtues of the modernizing British agriculture of her day were latently connected with the virtues of personal self-discipline, refusal of crasser forms of selfishness, and the other values which inform the world of her novels. You contend that this unity was actually an illusion, and that what actually happens in her novels is a separation of the two sorts of improvement as she develops a kind of moral discrimination of such intensity and autonomy that it becomes ultimately a standard from which the economic society can itself be judged – a step later taken in the early work of George Eliot. You write: 'What happens in* Emma, *in* Persuasion, *in* Mansfield Park *is the development of an everyday uncompromising morality which is in effect separable from its social basis and which, in other hands, can be turned against it.'*[6]

Now the difficulty here is whether it is not idealist to try to separate the aesthetic achievement of a writer like Jane Austen from the social code of her class. Can one actually extricate a non-class morality from her work in this way? Isn't it possible that the particular aesthetic value of her novels is on the contrary in some sense the product of the particular type of social domination of the English landed class of the time? In other words, might there not be a closer relationship between the social position from which the novels were written and their literary merits than you allow?

In my view, Jane Austen makes a very strenuous attempt to unify what was not unifiable – that is to say, the necessary processes and structures of a class to which she was committed, and the universalist values of a moral tradition which were overtly defined as honesty, kindness, responsibility. That is why I used the phrase that she has to guide people towards the reconciliation of property and virtue like a supernatural lawyer: by which I meant that her settlements are an artificial solution. When the early

[6] ENDL, p. 23.

George Eliot applies the same values to a wider admission of actual social relations, for example between landlord and tenant, the confidence of Jane Austen's remarkable unity of tone breaks up. I think this is a frequent pattern in the period after an apparently successful unification of an ideology and a practice within a dominant class: the values concerned provide the initial basis of a critique of the practice with which they have been merged.

Granting all that you have said about the relationship of morality and social class, there nevertheless seems to be a tendency in your treatment of Austen to counterpose the specifically aesthetic achievement of the writer, which in the case of Austen is obviously related to a clarity of moral perception, to the class from which the literary form came – in other words to suggest that there was a surplus of creative vitality, intelligence or sensitivity in the individual fundamentally at variance with the class of origin, that permitted the production of the work. Tentatively put, the more classical Marxist view would be that every ascendant class in history is likely, in the course of its development, to produce major works of art which embody its experience of the society of its time. That is, we should expect a causal rather than a contrary relationship between the two: for example, precisely the experience of acquiring a ruling position, together with all the domination and exploitation inherent in it, also involves achieving a real mastering of the world and of social relationships. The literary poise of Austen is very remarkable in any European perspective: what it seems to reflect is the extraordinary confidence and maturity of a class that had by then 150 years of post-revolutionary existence. In that sense Austen should be seen as, if you like, the best product of her class and not as a deviant one?

I wouldn't want to deny at all that, putting it in a more familiar way, the artistic achievements of a class belong to its rise. This is a classical Marxist proposition and there are many examples to confirm it. But I think that there is a very interesting other type of case where the achievement of a particular kind of work occurs at a very late stage in the history of a class – even when it is in open crisis. Goldmann's analysis of Racine explores an instance. Another curious example is a 'Restoration' play like Congreve's *The Way of the World*, written in 1700 when the social basis for that kind of work had apparently disappeared. In these cases, we find a certain perfection of form at a very late stage, not associated – as we usually and rightly do – with the rising vigour and mastery of a class. The latter relation would be true of the earlier 18th-century novels in England. But then these are radically different from the art of the early 19th century. They correspond much more to the real activity of the bourgeoisie: the novelists themselves are exploratory, possessive and opportunist as well as the activities they describe. They are not composed, they are vigorous. Another kind of correlation is involved when you come to the particular kind of work, like that of Jane Austen, which is quite extraordinarily composed. You can't use the term confidence for both, or if you do it is a different kind of confidence. One is the energy of a will to win and of the excitement of victory, the other is the calm of a set of assumed values unifying the whole social process, which provide the basis for specific imaginative innovations. I have often been tempted to think that it is a regular pattern that a particular kind of formally perfect work emerges at the end of a period in the history of a class, although not necessarily that of its defeat – clearly not in the case of Jane Austen's time. I think we have probably paid too little attention to this recurrent phenomenon, because the other proposition – that major art is connected with the confidence and vigour of the ruling class – takes us a good way. In fact there can be an especially perfect kind of art at a time when its social positions have become impossible.

Your general argument is very interesting, but the specific periodization of Austen's work seems questionable. It is too often supposed that there is either just the historical rise of a class or its decline, when in fact there are characteristically plateaux of stable, achieved rule when the class is not rising and is obviously not falling. England in the Napoleonic epoch is surely such a case. The capitalist landowning class was at the apogee of its political power, nationally and internationally – after Trafalgar and before the Reform Bill. It wasn't a period of rise, but nor was it so late.

Well, what pleased me most in the chapter on Jane Austen was to establish how much of exactly that English history is there in her novels, which were always said to be just about personal relationships. We don't disagree on the main issue. In cases like Racine or Austen, you can't separate the extraordinary achievement from the social position. The question must be put in a different way: if there is a relation between the two, then one must analyse its conditions. In Austen's case, I would now say that two special conditions of her ideological stance were decisive. She was doubly marginalized in relation to her class, as a dependant within it, and as a woman.

Turning to Dickens, you have repented nearly as drastically as Leavis. In Culture and Society, *your strictures on* Hard Times *were very severe. You wrote:* 'Hard Times, *in tone and structure, is the work of a man who has "seen through" society, who has found them all out. The only reservation is for the passive and the suffering, for the meek who shall inherit the earth, but not Coketown, not industrial society. This primitive feeling, when joined by the aggressive conviction of having found everyone else out, is the retained position of an adolescent. The innocence shames the adult world, but also essentially rejects it. As a whole response,* Hard Times *is more a symptom of the confusion of industrial society than an understanding of it.'*[7] *Your criticism of the pre-adult elements in the art of Dickens – the theme of 'innocence' – is particularly striking, since in* The English Novel *you endorse Dickens precisely where he exalts a fictional innocence in defiance of the normal terms of accurate social observation, and justify what is generally regarded as the weaknesses of implausibility and fantasy that result from it. You now assert: 'It is easy to show that having defined a social condition as the cause of virtue or vice, Dickens then produces virtue, almost magically as in* Little Dorrit, *from the same conditions which in others bred vice. . . . We may or may not believe in it, as social observation, but though it has the character of miracle it is the kind of miracle that happens; the flowering of love or energy which is inexplicable by the ways of describing people to which we have got used. There is no reason, that is to say, for love or innocence, except that almost obliterated by this general condition there is humanity. The exclusion of the human, which we can see operating in a describable system, is not after all absolute, or it would make no sense to call what is alienated human; there would otherwise be nothing to alienate. The inexplicable quality of the indestructible innocence, of the miraculously intervening goodness, on which Dickens so much depends and which has been casually written off as sentimentality, is genuine* because *it is inexplicable. What is explicable, after all, is the system, which consciously or unconsciously has been made.'*[8]

The rhetoric of this paragraph – the authentic is what is inexplicable –

[7] CS, p. 107.
[8] ENDL, pp. 52–3.

inevitably arouses one's resistance: it is much too close to the logic of mysticism. But there is a more important objection to it even than that. Your whole theoretical argument in The English Novel, *as in* The Long Revolution, *depends on the interrelation between personal qualities and social relations in the realist form. The divorce between the two is what you indict as leading to the breakdown of either the psychological or the sociological novel. One might say that the notion of the integral interconnection between the personal and the social is the fulcrum of your whole literary theory. Now surely your account of Dickens flatly contradicts this principle, because you in effect credit Dickens with precisely abstracting out a human quality which is not in any sense social: on the one hand there is the system, and on the other there are people who defeat the system?*

There is a simple point, and a difficult point for me here. The simple point is that the tone and pitch of the passage tell me that it is arguing against the grain. It is the sort of exalted pitch that comes from undue immersion in a writer, and assimilation of his own way of seeing the world: I mentioned this danger, of an unconscious ventriloquism, in the case of Carlyle earlier. I certainly wouldn't want to defend the terms of that passage now. They mask a more difficult issue, which I think I understand better now. If you base your work, as I do, on the indissoluble unity of individual and social experience, then you do have a problem explaining in non-metaphysical terms those acts and responses which are not, so to say, prepared by social circumstances or relations as we can ordinarily assess them. My present position, which I develop in *Marxism and Literature*, is that however dominant a social system may be, the very meaning of its domination involves a limitation or selection of the activities it covers, so that by definition it cannot exhaust all social experience, which therefore always potentially contains space for alternative acts and alternative intentions which are not yet articulated as a social institution or even project. I would much less want to apply this notion to Dickens now, however. I think he *had* to produce his values inexplicably, because to have presented them in any other way would have meant alliance with forces with which he did not want to have anything to do. But that does not make the impulses and energies of his response, however ideological their final form, in any way negligible.

No, the values are real, it is the magical procedures that are false – Dickens cannot be defended as a novelist on their grounds. The generosity of feeling and powerful desire to re-create in the novels certain fundamental and liberating impulses are undeniable: but they are dislocated by the structures of the fiction. Your highest praise of Dickens is for his ability to totalize the social system as a whole in a way no other writer could do, by a quite new formal use of metaphor and symbol. You also concede that he was curiously unaware of the forces that were seeking to reform the system in his own time, but you discount this as a serious qualification of his vision. Isn't the real problem of Dickens's work, however, that there is actually an overtotalization of the system – essentially the brute early industrial capitalist mode of production in England – on the one hand, which then generates a resort to positive completely outside it, magically overindividualized personal qualities on the other hand? But in fact, of course, the capitalist system in the strict sense of an economic mode of production never exhausted the social experience of England of the 1840s, even apart from its own repressive selectivity, because other modes of production and class relations subsisted as well. The social formation was much more complex than the simple schema of Coketown – although that is a very extreme example in his work. But if Dickens had possessed a fuller vision of English society, with its various and differentiated points of resistance to the order of capital, isn't it possible he would have achieved a much more aesthetically persuasive incarnation of the values he sought to represent?

I think this is right – it is exactly what I felt was wrong with *Hard Times*. You have the classic contradiction inside the text – the novel begins with a description of a town where all the people are exactly like each other, and then inevitably, because of the kind of novelist Dickens is, it goes on to show people who are totally unlike each other, moving in different directions and against each other. But the initial statement of the work is never revised. I felt this less strongly writing about *Dombey and Son* and *Little Dorrit*. But in reality there were other social experiences as possible sources of opposition or alternative direction in the society of Dickens's time. A very precise historical analysis is needed to establish them, which would not be easy to carry over into fictional analysis. But I would like to see it attempted, because as a matter of fact there are a number of non-capitalist relations in Dickens, although he much more usually turns to certain conventions like childhood, or rural idyll, or sickness, or physical disability as the saving element in his world. However, if certain values could be non-magically retraced to social sources, there remains the possibility that others emerge outside the established range of modes altogether. The same problem comes up again if we try to locate the origin of alternative conceptions of relationship in *Wuthering Heights.* When people are living under a dominant system, you both get alternative sources of social experience in other modes which have survived from the past or are in active opposition to the system, and you seem to get other impulses which have not been produced by the known calculus of forces. But one should never then say that because they have not been produced by the known calculus of forces, they have not been produced by any forces at all. That was what I was trying to say, but inadequately, in the passage you quoted. But in my attitude towards Dickens, there has been this swing. I won't ever get it right, somebody might.

You mention a comparable difficulty in Wuthering Heights. *In effect, your discussion of Emily Brontë could cause a similar perplexity in a reader. For your main focus is the nature of the relationship between Catherine and Heathcliff, of which you say: 'that kind of bond, that sense of absolute presence, absolute existence in another, in one another, is indeed an ordinary though of course always a transforming experience . . . not desire* for *another but desire* in *another'.*[9] *You go on: 'In its quality as given, it is where social and personal, one's self and others, grow from a single root.'*[10] *What you seem to be pushing towards here is a description of a relationship which is prior to any distinction between social and personal at all. The image you use evokes the growth of a plant. But if you look back at how Emily Brontë formulates it, she negates precisely that image. What Catherine says is: 'My love for Linton is like the foliage in the woods: time will change it, I'm well aware, as winter changes the trees. My love for Heathcliff resembles the eternal rocks beneath.' In other words, the relationship is not naturally grown, but praeternaturally given. The metaphysical charge of the language is very evident. Yet your commentary and interpretation appear to be endorsing something which seems very difficult to negotiate within the terms of your general account of relationships within the novel.*

I see that. I accept that the metaphor I used could be taken as contradicting hers; and that hers is anyway very difficult – what could this underlying

[9] ENDL, p. 86.
[10] ENDL, p. 67.

stratum be? It should either represent something wholly physical, which I don't think it can only be; or a configuration of grace, which would presuppose a totally determining pre-nature which would then control all personal and social development, which I don't think it is either. Emily Brontë does actually show the movement of the relationship through time, from childhood onwards, which is certainly in that sense growth. My own image of the single root was only meant to suggest that the relationship and the most substantial kind of personal identity come from the same experience – not that the experience is pre-social, but that it emerges before the separated categories of social and individual are relevant. All these questions revolve around a single problem which still preoccupies me to an extraordinary extent. How are we to explain the possibility of liberating responses to a system that do not seem to have in any obvious ways been prepared by social conditions? Certain relationships occur which are very difficult to understand by normal canons, and which give force to metaphysical or subjectivist explanations because these remain virtually the only terms to hand for them. I am very keen to find alternative terms. But I am also determined, and this accounts for my overstatement, not to go along with the way the left has ordinarily tried to solve this problem. In the case of *Wuthering Heights*, for example, you have the classic attempts to read Heathcliff as a figuration of the proletariat. It can't be done in that way. The other danger which I've noticed is that, understandably feeling the need to resist metaphysical or subjectivist explanations, people put more weight on a quite proper identification of the ideological evasions which are always there in a work – more so in Dickens than in Brontë – than on an exploration of the issues presented through the ideology: the real problems then remain, often forgotten or put aside or postponed behind the confidence of the class account. I think this is related to the general neglect within a powerful Marxist tradition of questions of sexuality and primary relationships. The sense of the deep problem, the deep flaw and yet at the same time the deep possibility of this level were as much a part of the social crisis of the 1840s as any other. Indeed in the late 1960s, the social crisis of our own late capitalist society was being interpreted through at that level with much more passion than in the more received terms, producing a great deal of confusion between political and sexual liberation, in fact: there I was on the whole on the other side of the argument. But I would still insist that the social crisis erupts there too. Yet while I can say *that* it does so, I am not sure *how* it works.

I've tried to draw attention to the problem, as you can see from each example you've taken. In Hardy or Blake I can tie it down more to its sources, but I'm not sure in certain other cases I can. The same problem recurs with the heretical radicalism of 17th-century politics. How much of it is explicable in terms of the known social conditions of an excluded class? How much of it remains a quite inexplicable project of sexual liberation, which ranged all the way from lunacy to extraordinary imagination and insight? I think there is a particular danger of dismissal now because this is the sort of phenomenon of which a Marxist structuralist criticism is particularly impatient, from which indeed it consciously dissociates itself in its version of scientific analysis. Yet the problem of these non-traceable, or not immediately traceable, liberating impulses is in the most emphatic sense not only a question of literary analysis, but a very urgent contemporary political issue.

Moving forward within The English Novel, *there is one major point at which the impetus of your polemic against Leavis does seem to result in a damaging one-sidedness in the book: that is your account of James. It's as if your treatment of James is your revenge for Leavis's treatment of Hardy, which isn't really the best way of responding to either. Your remarks are very brief – peremptory in fact. But your essential charge against James is that he is uninterested in history. 'What he has really excluded is history: that other dimension of value which from Scott through Dickens and George Eliot and Hardy to Lawrence (but not to Joyce) has transformed prose fiction.'*[11] *This is a very surprising judgment. After all, it is you yourself who have shown that there are multiple social processes of a manifestly historical character in the work of Jane Austen, whose fiction is instinct with her time in a much more direct way than is usually thought. Your central argument is that she is not at all unhistorical – she's a highly historical writer. Surely by your own criteria the same can be said* a fortiori *of James? His whole work is marked by an intense materialist interest in patterns of wealth and the social relationships that are generated by them. These patterns are traced over a much longer time-span than that of Jane Austen, involving many more successive historical changes: one need only think of all the complex real social history that supervenes between* The Europeans *and* The Golden Bowl. *Moreover, the dimension of history that dominates much of James's work is actually*

[11] ENDL, p. 133.

fundamental to the whole epoch: the evolution of the relationship between American and English or European societies. This was an immensely important part of the history of the late 19th and early 20th century. One might say that James's world is the other side of the coin to the universe of Conrad. The colonial exploitation of Asia, Africa and Latin America was being accompanied by a rearrangement of the metropolitan relationship between English and US capitalism. The whole future of the imperialism described by Conrad lay essentially in the modulation of power within the Anglo-American partnership that absorbed James. Even today the latter process has never been very thoroughly explored on the left. There are many criticisms to be made of the middle or late James, but inattention to history is surely, in any balanced account, not one of them?

I think this is a useful correction – my comments on James were affected by their polemical context. The main case for James should be made as you put it: I particularly accept your emphasis on the Anglo-American relationship, which has never really been followed through adequately in work on James. The only qualification I would still enter is that there is something in James's fiction which moves from history towards spectacle. At a crucial moment in the evolution of the novel, he leads towards a preoccupation with the processes of the spectacle and with the processes of observing the spectacle. That may be connected with certain ideological blockages, which prevented him taking his characteristic insights right through. Other symptoms would be the cases in his work of miraculous innocence or predestined virtue, as blatant in their way as those of Dickens. For they occur in the midst of what is in general a cold-eyed and quite undeceived observation of what money and its social relations does to people. After publishing *The English Novel*, I started working with someone simply on money in James. I was continually surprised at the closeness with which James addressed himself, not only to the relations between capital and power, affluence and consumption, but to the relations between money capital and other kinds of capital. That should be quite central to an assessment of James.

Yes. You reproach him with allegiance to Flaubert in your book, but actually he always said his great master was Balzac – certainly a more historical and perhaps a more materialist writer than Dickens. James is very closely related to Balzac in his sense of money as a force of corruption. The ramifications of his vision are sometimes so wide – the consequences of wealth as the fatal gift of freedom to Isobel in The Portrait of a Lady *– that one is uncertain how aware he is himself of what he is actually displaying.*

I was extraordinarily impressed re-reading *The Spoils of Poynton*, not merely by its treatment of money, but of money as conspicuous display. Although it is presented as a spectacle, there is absolutely no deception possible for the spectator. It's an incredibly powerful demonstration of a certain kind of fetishism. One might even say that after the first chapter of *Capital*, people should be sent to read *The Spoils of Poynton*.

Your chapter on Lawrence takes up an interesting earlier discussion of him in Modern Tragedy, *in which you compare* Women in Love *with* Anna Karenina. *The two accounts touch on an important submerged theme in your work – the continuities of generation and of life, of family and children. One of the pivots of your criticism of* Women in Love, *as compared with* Anna Karenina, *seems to be what you call Lawrence's rejection of 'that whole body of personal life which is more than a relationship in a single generation.' You write: 'Lawrence, in all his later work, reduced the definition of personal life to a single generation, over and over again, and he has been widely followed. Parents are distant and meaningless . . . [there] is an effective rejection of children.'*[12] *Elsewhere you speak of Lawrence portraying 'feelings without consequences' in a context which suggests that by consequences you mean children. Isn't there some danger of overstatement here? Your general criticism of* Women in Love, *that it extrapolates personal relationships out of any real social context and then develops them in a kind of crystalline isolation, thereby effecting a damaging break with prior traditions of realism – including Lawrence's own earlier novels, is very persuasive. But to what extent does it need to be specified to the limitation of the narrative to a single generation? One reason for feeling a qualm about your argument is the disquieting precedent of Leavis's* ad hominem *attacks on Lawrence for not having had children, allegedly the cause of his decline as a writer and a man. More importantly, however, literature – including that of classical realism – is surely replete with representations of relationships, often very perfect ones, that are confined to a single generation: one need only think of Stendhal. Doesn't your phrase 'the whole body of personal life' have too integrist a connotation?*

[12] MT, p. 135; cp ENDL, p. 181.

Let me say at once that my comments on the novel and the single generation referred to a very particular context: the prolonged and important attempt that Lawrence made to define a sense of life and relationship as part of a whole process of change, from the starting point of a demonstrably shared world. The extraction of a single generation has a very specific effect upon that search in a way that it wouldn't, for example, on the working out of other very complicated processes of relationship which could, of course, be wholly run through in a single generation. I certainly would not want to suggest that the consequences of personal relationships can be only other beings, other times. But in the case of Lawrence, the concentration on the single generation in this patterned way creates too vast a gap between the intense personal relationships and the total life process, conceived in terms of creative and destructive principles in nature. That gap is too broad to bridge and it puts both levels of the novel in question. If it had been simply a history of four people in their relations without the larger consciousness which Lawrence introduces, it would at least have been more coherent in its own terms. The abrupt jump Lawrence made in *Women in Love* becomes very clear when you compare it to *Anna Karenina*: the difference is not specifically to do with children, but it is to do with processes of work, including a sense of nature, not just as a milieu of work, but also as a milieu that we work in. In other words, what has happened in Lawrence's novel is that individual relations are explored to the point where at least some of them are felt to be negative and destructive; then a huge leap is made by projecting the same vision onto an absolute and universal plane. Nature here functions in a quite different set of relations. The gap is not so wide in *Lady Chatterley*, which tries to rework the same problem. It is remarkable that in one of the versions of *Lady Chatterley* Lawrence should have attempted to relocate the process in industrial England rather than where he ended, a rural England which permitted a more plausible transition between the intense personal relationship and the cosmic natural forces. But by then it was very late for him. Afterwards, the ideological jump from the relationships of the limited group to the pattern of cosmic forces, the equivalence of the creative and destructive poles within each, proved very influential. That was an extraordinary narrowing of scope from *Anna Karenina* or indeed from other realist novels which attempted the same kind of continuity.

One of the most powerful and central passages of Modern Tragedy, *in fact, relates these themes of nature and generation directly together. Criticizing Camus and Sartre for their philosophical treatment of death, you write: 'The reasoning mind is only* contradicted *by the universe when the supposed irrationality is not merely indifferent but hostile – an assumption about nature that is very near the creative roots of all this writing. The life-death contradiction is limited, in fact, to the kind of individual consciousness especially characteristic of bourgeois philosophy. "I exist – I die" seems absolute, within this experience'.*[13] *To which you object: 'Life is not only negated by death, but is also renewed by birth.' You then go on: 'Just as the experience of life and death is limited, by the unnoticed assumption, to individual and even isolate experience, so, by a related assumption, nature is converted into a kind of theatre . . . Whether in the bourgeois or bourgeois-marxist version of nature as matter to be dominated, or in the existentialist version of nature as indifferent or resistant, there is no sense of common process or common life, and this, itself an analogue of individualism, leads inevitably to despair.'*[14] *There is, of course, one Marxist tradition which has rejected the whole theme of our mastery over nature, stressing our affinity with it – the Frankfurt School; while another, represented most eloquently today by Timpanaro, has emphasized the dominion of nature over us, in a materialist regrounding of the problem of death. Neither, however, has any notable sense of what you call common process or common life. To what extent did you feel at the time that your argument was an unusual one for a socialist writer?*

In terms of the immediate tradition behind me, I felt it to be unfamiliar. I hadn't read, for some time, anyone on the left connecting natural processes with the politics of socialism. I simply didn't know the Frankfurt School except in incidentals and by account; it was surprisingly late in coming into focus. At the time, I myself was particularly aware of a sense in which the socialist perspective was confined within a wholly urban industrial landscape – quite arbitrarily separated from that of nature. So I felt very much that this was one of those extreme cases where, as I said in *The Country and the City*, I couldn't see where the tradition which would include that kind of consciousness was to be found; one would have to say 'leaving that aside, I'm a socialist on this and this' and it wasn't something one could easily leave aside. I think it is much easier to argue out this

[13] MT, p. 188.
[14] MT, pp. 188–9.

problem now and I am extremely impressed to see attempts to work it through from a very different position, starting from some of these profound feelings of negation and indifference. Sartre's theory of scarcity is an example. It might be thought I would be very hostile to it, since it proceeds from that polarization of man against nature. But on the contrary, I think it is very important. Not that it is the way I see or feel the problem, but it is a way of beginning to confront it as other than a subjective datum – the complex of feelings which could so easily be exploited not just in the earlier existentialist fiction, but in all kinds of lesser triviality and barrenness.

Returning to the English novel, one of the major historical problems posed by your overview of its development is the causes and timing of the scission that you argue occurred between its social and personal dimensions, leading in the 20th century to the contrasted forms of the purely sociological or documentary novel on the one hand and to the psychological novel on the other. You date the division to the 1880s and 1890s, and suggest that Wells and James represent in their different ways a hardening of positions towards the two alternatives. Now, you do not really explore the reasons for this decisive change, but you seem to hint at two explanations. At one point you remark: 'I'd settle for saying the formed self-confident insulated middle class – that class you could see coming, hear coming, all the way through the century, [had] now arrived . . . the English *middle class, English in a new sense – insulated and strong in their insulation just because, perhaps, that island within an island ruled an empire, ruled half a world.'*[15] *The operative clause in this rather cryptic comment appears to be imperialism, which insulates the new middle class from the generous openness to experience which had permitted the integrated realist novel. How much weight do you attach to this indication? Imperialism does, of course, become a manipulated mass ideology in a much more explicit and systematic form in the 1880s and 1890s. But structurally the heyday of British imperial power was probably the 1850s, while widespread imperialist consciousness certainly extends right back to the Napoleonic Wars or earlier in England. The one other passage where you allude to a possible explanation of the rupture you are describing broadens the range of factors which may have been responsible. You write: 'It wasn't only a crisis within a single society, a nation; that specific Englishness which was a strength, a focus, in the*

[15] ENDL, p. 122.

generation from Dickens to Hardy. Much wider issues, implicit before, now became explicit: war and imperialism, which then had been distant or marginal; poverty and revolution, which had new international bearings. It was a very much longer way – impossibly longer it seemed and can still seem – from those human crises, crises that do decide life, to what can be known directly and particularly as . . . the texture of what James so rightly called, emphasized as "felt life".'[16] *Here again, it is very questionable whether imperialism had been distant or marginal in the generation from Dickens to Hardy. Throughout the period Ireland after all was very close. Poverty was not less in the 1840s than in the 1890s – it was measurably worse in England. Revolution was more present to Europe in the epoch from 1848 to the Commune than in the long stabilization from 1872 to 1914. War acquired its modern technological forms at Sebastopol, Magenta and Sedan: thereafter there was a European peace for forty years. Your reader is left with an insistent question. You mark a caesura in the form of the novel, which coincides with the break in the tradition of* Culture and Society *which you call there an interregnum. But the explanations you suggest for it leave one unsatisfied. Could you qualify or specify them further for us?*

Well, they were tentative. I noticed the changes in the novel and in cultural thinking before I knew what they could be related to in any social history. The two developments which I would now single out for emphasis, I think, are the political emergence of a new working class, and the cultural segregation of a new bourgeois order, after the 1880s. To take the first: it is extraordinary how localized the thinking about poverty is in the Victorian period proper, precisely because there was no perception of a fully contemporary and active alternative system to capitalism. I think that it is possible – I throw it out only as a hypothesis – that the arrival of an articulate, newly organized and modern working class presented qualitatively new problems to the kind of integrated and extended social vision which had been the achievement of the bourgeois realists. It meant that many issues immediately went into terms that were going to be uncongenial to precisely the learnt mode of that realism. In the last two decades of the 19th century, although the cultural contribution of the working class seems to be less than in an earlier period, it is organizing politically in a way that poses a radical challenge to the older vision – that

[16] ENDL, p. 131.

was really what I had in mind when I referred to poverty and revolution. Now in the same period, there had also been a very deep and successful reorganization of bourgeois cultural and educational institutions: the creation of the new public schools, the renovation of Oxford and Cambridge, the development of a fully extended bourgeois press, the modernization of publishing. Together with these changes went an increasing centralization in London, which now functioned much more as an imperial cultural capital. The result was an integrated and confident set of bourgeois cultural institutions such as had never existed in any previous period of English history. The social base of the writers from 1880 to 1930 is much narrower and more standardized than from 1830 to 1880. That is why I used the term insulated – the writers themselves now had a much more limited experience. The characteristic change is from a George Eliot to a Forster. Now Forster proclaims the same aims as George Eliot, but there are areas of social experience to which he is no longer open. The vision of Englishness itself changes: whereas earlier it is really internal to England, in the 1880–1920 period it is far more defined in terms of an external imperial role. Tom Nairn argues that England was deprived of a modern nationalism by imperialism. That is linked to what I meant by Englishness becoming problematical in this period. From now on what it was to be English was quite new. It was defined in very insulated ways, within these very hard trainings, within increasingly standardized and masculine institutions. I repeat that these are only suggestions. It is much easier to see the historical pattern after 1914, but what is interesting is that there was such a radical shift in the culture from somewhere in the 1890s, which preceded the major political and social upheavals.

There is another question we would like to ask about The English Novel from Dickens to Lawrence *as a whole. At no point in the book do you propose to the reader anything like the programme that was the innovative element of* Reading and Criticism, *that is to say an analysis of a complete work. Characteristically you take one passage or a number of passages from a novel which so to speak figure as condensations of the novelist's work as a whole, on which you then comment. But there is an absence of analysis of the structure of any novel as such: you never mention narrative, for example, and only in one case, Hardy, do you stop to look closely at the texture of a writer's prose. Is an underlying emphasis of the book an attempt to get the reader away from too much preoccupation with traditional problems of form? It is noticeable that when you do mention problems of form a recurrent rhetorical trope appears. You start by remarking that a given novel has a very perfect or crystalline form: examples would be* Middlemarch, Women in Love, *or James's work. The adjectives you use are superlatives: 'superb', 'brilliant', 'crystalline', 'perfect'.*[17] *Then you invariably go on to criticize or dismiss the work in question as being too formal:* Middlemarch *is cold,* Women in Love *is detached from the problems of living in society, James's novels convert life into spectacle. On the other hand novels which are generally held to be much less accomplished, much less worked through in terms of form, receive your unstinted approval:* Lady Chatterley's Lover, *or the early works of George Eliot, to which you give much greater emphasis and value than to her later novels. Was this a deliberate emphasis on your part and one that you would defend, or was it more an accidental by-product of the fact that you could only say a limited number of things in the book?*

I think the main reason is that the book was essentially a transcription of a series of lectures, and with a large audience you cannot get down to sustained analysis of whole forms. However, I was also conscious of a curious alliance between Leavis's map of *The Great Tradition* and a developing formalism derived from American New Criticism, which I was seeking to reject. A major theoretical problem is involved here. Form is ordinarily perceived only in a rather integrated classicist sense. Yet the formally disturbed novels of early George Eliot or the essentially confused forms of Dickens's novels are related precisely to the problems to which their fiction was addressing itself – a far more powerful fiction than that, say, of Trollope, who had no difficulty in reproducing known forms. The same is true of Hardy. When people say that Hardy wrote badly, the problem is not one of form but of received literary judgment. Why does he write on two or three different levels of discourse, and how does he try to unify them? The diversity exactly corresponds to the range of his social address. So although the lectures don't systematically consider problems of form, if I were analysing forms in the English novel, it would be a different sort of book, but there would be very few judgments that I would have to change.

The difficulty with the lecture mode you adopted is that at times the way you

[17] ENDL, pp. 91, 135, 179.

argue seems not so dissimilar from the procedure of Leavis which you earlier criticized: the extrapolation from one passage of a novel to a judgment of the work as a whole, without a demonstration that the passage is really representative. The relevance of form here is that by contrast it refers the reader to the total effect of the work: where one part or element of a novel must be responded to in relation to the others, so that each provides a control on the final judgment made. The absence of this control is perhaps related to the fact that you appear to be sheering away from any comparative evaluation of novels as works of art in their own right. Would it be right to say that you weren't directly interested in that?

Entirely. So far as the question of passages is concerned, the only time I analyse one for evaluation occurs in my discussion of the different levels of Hardy's prose: a close reading was relevant there. In the other cases, the quotations are all used for illustrative rather than analytic purposes – as indications of the central preoccupation of a work, rather than as tests of its literary value. For that after all was not the question I was putting.

Yet powerful general evaluations are in fact conveyed in the book. The legacy of practical criticism and of the tradition of Leavis is still present in the sense that major presumptions are made and judgments are enforced, yet not often directly defended by demonstration of the quality of specific works. A salient example is the way in which you assert the importance of the connection from Eliot to Hardy, rather than from Eliot to James. You just say categorically: 'the development that matters in the English novel is not to James: it is to the novels of Hardy'.[18] *This is an authoritarian – and tendentially subjectivist – style of formulation. It invites the replies: matters to whom? why does it matter? why should there be only one development that matters, anyway? Wouldn't it have been preferable to declare your evaluation directly, and justify it from the texts?*

That was a polemical attack on the traditional, opposite evaluation. It is a flourish. I couldn't attempt analyses on whole forms in the lectures. I have done one or two detailed accounts in classes – the class on *Middlemarch* actually folded up because it went on too long. But it isn't something I would want to give a lot of my writing time to. I am not against it – I

[18] CC, p. 181; cp ENDL, p. 95.

consider it important. But if you only do that, you misdirect the centre of interest, which is the *project* of a work. Once you have the sense of what the Dickens project was, or what the Eliot problems and project were, or the Hardy project was, then you can put the questions about form – which may require the most technical sort of analysis. People on opposite sides of the critical battle will often use the same techniques, but there is a qualitative difference in the ends for which they are using them. The handbooks of fictional technique which started coming out of American New Criticism may look fairly impressive, but actually cannot even be called formalist, because the Russian Formalists had a much stricter sense of what the literary project was than this quite unrooted academic analysis. *The English Novel* was an attempt to clear the ground by challenging this whole approach. Its greatest value is probably the four or five books by other people which took their origin in the questions that it asked. What these do in a lot more sustained way is infinitely more useful. But the focus of interest had to be shifted to a different kind of question: what had these novels been about? There was a certain novelty in the notion, not to the writers, but to their critics meanwhile.

Turning finally to problems of the recent past and present, you ended your chapter on the realist novel in The Long Revolution *by remarking that: 'The realist novel needs, obviously, a genuine community: a community of persons linked not merely by one kind of relationship – work or friendship or family – but by many, interlocking kinds. It is obviously difficult, in the twentieth century, to find a community of this sort.'*[19] *Here you evoke a crisis in the development of realist fiction due essentially to a growth of industrial scale. Just now, however, you suggested it was the emergence of the organized working class which may have disrupted the manageable social world of 19th-century realism – a rather different explanation. In* The English Novel *itself, you contend that there has not been a significant decline in the quality of the English novel in the mid-20th century: but what is needed and what is difficult to find is a contemporary grammar for the presentation of community. How far do you link the discovery of such a grammar to the representation of the working class in modern fiction?*

The way forward which I learnt in the thirties was to shift realism to the

[19] LR, p. 312.

working-class novel. I still have great respect for the literature that effort produced – from the work of someone like Grassic Gibbon who didn't stay in the working class, to some of the Welsh and London proletarian novelists of the 1930s. I think it has been seriously undervalued: even left students of literature don't seem to read it today. But the problem is that the working-class novel can very easily become a regional novel in the sense in which I have defined it. It depicts a very interesting, vigorous and autonomous community, that has as much claim to be taken as a whole world as a Jane Austen community, or for that matter the community of *Middlemarch* which was more socially extended but still highly selective. Yet curiously the very stress of this autonomy often denies the essential problem of what working-class fiction should be about – the lived experience of the immediate producers within a class society, and therefore specifically in relation to other classes. It is extremely sad to read proletarian novels which are totally authentic and have something of the breadth of interest of 19th-century bourgeois realism, yet to feel at the end that they are profoundly regional in the sense that the very forces which operate from outside on the formation and destiny of the class itself, which make for suffering and exploitation, cannot be represented within them. The most that can be introduced is the occasional class visitor or class enemy. Sometimes you even get a propagandist attempt in the last chapter, in which joining a particular party is the solution. But the crucial problem for working-class fiction is not finding the way out, difficult as that is, it is finding the way in. Even where the focus is smaller, as in the case of novels from Wales in the 20th century, this is true: by definition you cannot write a fully realist novel about Wales without writing about England.

This issue brings us to the major change in the subjective situation of the novelist since the 19th century. Since that time there has been a qualitative transformation in the awareness of alternative modes of information and analysis. Statistical evidence alone, for example, can reveal certain processes in an otherwise unknown society. The contemporary novelist is inevitably much more conscious of that kind of information. At the same time, the availability of alternative theoretical explanations of social relations differentiates the situation of the writer today markedly from that of a century ago, when these philosophical systems were not present. Now I do not believe that you could write a realist novel about, say, a British working-class community unless you were able to include within your fiction the kinds of knowledge to which those innovations relate. I'm putting this rather carefully, because I'm not sure we should try to integrate theoretical arguments themselves, for example – although that may be a possibility. The contemporary difficulty, however, is that bourgeois novelists have not sought or wanted to solve the problem – the contrast with the rapid fictionalization of the Blue Books by Dickens or Disraeli is very striking. The modern formation rigidly excludes these areas as abstractions, whereas novels are about people. But for the socialist novel, it is crucial to be able to include them. It is easy enough in general to say that these kinds of evidence must be capable of representation in fiction: the problem is to know how.

If that is the problem of a grammar of community, there is also the question of a vocabulary. Many of the most provocative and stimulating passages in The English Novel *concern the relations between what you call educated and customary speech, in the work of successive writers. That forms one of the main themes of the book. Do you feel that the gap between the two is potentially smaller today than it was in the 19th century? You argue Lawrence achieved in some of his work a unity of idiom – the narrator and narrated characters in effect speaking the same language – that was unattainable for Eliot or for Hardy. Would you say therefore that the problem has on the whole decreased in the novel since then?*

It should have decreased. In fact it has decreased, but the danger is that the shared discourse is often no more than that of the communications system. On the other hand, there is now a much more extended vocabulary across class situations – in that respect the writer is in a totally different position in the 1970s from the writer in the 1870s.

Logically that should be so. But is it actually? Cobbett or Dickens deploy a very large vocabulary, probably much wider than that of most writers today who have anything approaching their readership, not just in numbers but above all in class background. You say that what was profoundly novel about Dickens is that he wrote from a popular culture. If so, the lexicon of that culture comes as something of a shock. Is there any contemporary equivalent?

Yes, Dickens's vocabulary is very surprising. Of course, it was a small section of the working class that was included in his readership. But it had learnt to read and write from classics: it was very articulate and its vocabulary was highly formal. It is true that after the epoch of Lawrence's achievement, a general argot has been created for consciously co-optative purposes, a *Daily Mirror* cross-class language, which is in some senses a more deprived vocabulary than that of the mid-19th century. An artificial idiom has been established, in a very concentrated and professional fashion, which is much more limited – it is the opposite of the vocabulary needed for an extending attention. Nevertheless, I think that the possibility of a much more effective common language is there today. In Dickens, the conceptual terms are often formal equivalents for colloquialisms, the long word for the short thing: a lot of his jokes are around this sort of usage. Today, although I may be deluded, I think that certain concept-carrying terms are losing their technical unfamiliarity, and can be assimilated into the language of a novel. If one were to try to resolve the problem of a fictional method capable of the equivalent of statistical information, for example, it might be on concepts like these that a solution would depend. I am talking now in an entirely speculative way, because you have only to state the problem to realize how extremely difficult it is: most people would rule discussion of it out as absurd in any case. You can see the difficulty in the current arguments about television drama that I mentioned. The critics of this neo-realism contend that to re-create the apparently experienced world of the working class is a form of naturalization which renders it impossible either to explain that experience or to show that it could be otherwise: the diction of this drama, they say, is only a left version of the miming of working-class habits in advertising. The criticism has a lot of force: the trouble with it is that its alternative usually gets no further than one word, Brecht, and that powerful word is not even glossed – Brecht, as I've said, being the outstanding example of someone who didn't, with rare exceptions, solve the problem in his own work. However, the only point in talking about the problem is in terms of possible solution. In the novel we may have to learn a mode, which seems to me not an impossible one, which combines chapters of fiction with chapters of what would be more like social analysis or history. We may have to consider that as a potentially integrated form. At the moment, it might seem strange or absurd. But as a matter of fact one writer who would have understood this is Tolstoy, who is not far from doing it himself at times.

One last question: why did you confine your book on the novel to England? The contrast with your work on drama is striking.

The book owes its national boundaries to the circumstances of a lecture course in the English Faculty at Cambridge. They are paradoxical in the sense that in Adult Education I taught at least half my courses on non-English novelists: key-points of my map of the novel would still today include Balzac, Dostoievsky, Tolstoy, Thomas Mann, Kafka or Proust. I now wish that in the fifties I'd done the sort of book on the novel that I did about drama. I could have done it then – it would have been no more than consolidating the teaching I was doing in adult classes. But it is a young man's project – as was writing about European drama in the last hundred years, which really is no less ambitious than writing about the European novel in the last 150 years. Living in an academic environment is very bad for such ventures, not that I worry much about that. A more serious reason why I've felt reluctant to attempt a general book about the novel is that I find it very difficult to write about the subject as a critic, while trying to solve any of its problems as a novelist. I would say, however, that I think the first work to be done on 19th-century literature is always within specific national traditions, from which one should then move to comparative studies. But in the 20th century one should proceed the other way round – from a general thematic and formal exploration of the international range of literature to the national or domestic novel.

3. The Welsh Trilogy; *The Volunteers*

Can we start by asking you something about the position of your novels within your work as a whole? From your own account, there seems to be a discrepancy between the proportion of fiction in your publicly visible work – so far four novels out of a total of twenty books published – and the amount of moral and intellectual energy you must have invested in your work as a novelist. Looking at your biographical dates, it seems that between 1947 and 1960 you wrote something like seven successive versions of Border Country *alone, together with three other unpublished novels. The same pattern seems to recur in the later sixties and seventies:* The Fight for Manod *going through five versions over twelve years from 1956 to 1977, and* The Volunteers *taking six years to complete. Is there a major difference for you between discursive and fictional works in your practice as a writer?*

It's certainly true that I have given relatively far more time, in comparison with what became visible and valued, to fiction than to any other form of writing. In the late forties, I regarded the novels as the work which I most wanted to do. Now I feel differently about them. All along there have been certain things pressing on me, which I could simply find no alternative way of writing; today, however, fiction is something I'm prepared to work on a long time without feeling any urgency to finish quickly.

But the reasons for the peculiar chronology of my writing involve more than that. I've been aware since *Border Country* that I've been living in a time where, for my kind of interest anyway, the basic forms of fiction are against any simple connection of a writing intention and a relatively rapid or available completion. To this extent I have been conscious of writing against the grain of the forms. The 19th-century forms of the novel were shaped within a bourgeois world. So the first modes of access to working-class experience in fiction were often those of some distanced observer. Then between the wars writers emerged who had grown up inside a working-class community and sought to re-create its world – typically the world of childhood or of the family, while cancelling their present selves from this original situation. The result was the separated novel about the working-class community, which became a kind of regional form – the enclosed class as a regional zone of experience. It was very characteristic of all these novels that they were retrospective – a recapturing of an early experience from another social world. The early versions of *Border Country* were continuous with these kinds of writing. But I was dissatisfied with that form, initially without quite knowing why. Then I gradually realized that with the degree of change after 1945 the problem was to find a fictional form that would allow the description both of the internally seen working-class community and of a movement of people, still feeling their family and political connections, out of it. That change of experience was exemplified in so many individual lives that it seemed to have a certain social importance. But the forms for it weren't easily accessible. The new forms of the fifties, to which many writers quickly turned, were usually versions of the novel of escape, which one part of Lawrence had prepared. Their theme was really escape from the working class – moving to the room at the top, or the experience of flight. They lacked any sense of the continuity of working-class life, which does not cease just because one individual moves out of it, but which also itself changes internally. Often these novels would display very rude attitudes towards the world where they were arriving, and sometimes sentimental recollections of the world which they were leaving. But they were not about what interested me most, which was a continuing tension, with very complicated emotions and relationships running through it, between two different worlds that needed to be rejoined. There was no form for this. I found that what I was writing was an experience of uncertainty and contradiction, which was duplicated in the problem of discovering a form for it. So I learnt the hard way the theoretical lesson that if a writer in a certain mode does not have social forms available to him for development, then his writing experience is likely to be prolonged and difficult, and the work very much more problematic. The actual process of composition was never so halting: the problem has always been in the form, of finding some shape with which I can be satisfied.

Of course, there were probably all sorts of other reasons in myself for certain of the delays – when I got blocked on one work I would move on to another, and so on. There was a long alternation between *The Country and the City* and what became *The Fight for Manod*. In fact *The Country and the City* went through much the same process in that it was laid aside for three or four years while I worked on something else. But in general I have found in the last ten or fifteen years that I can plan a theoretical book and execute it fairly straightforwardly, whereas the novels have always been written this other way – even if someone could once say to me, meaning it to be kind and complimentary, that he had sat down of an evening and read *Border Country* straight through, as if it had just flowed from the pen, which was so very different from the experience of writing it.

Did you have any literary reference-points or previous models in looking for appropriate fictional forms?

I was aware of the Welsh writers about the working class of the inter-war period, who produced a distinct body of work which is very varied, although not much read now. They too had been trying to find a form. But the problem was always that those writers who stayed in the working class had great difficulties with the novel as such, tending to move towards the autobiography or political pamphlet or a curious panoramic genre like Jack Jones's *Rhondda Roundabout*; while those who moved out of it, like Gwyn Jones who was a university teacher when he wrote *In Times Like These*, produced novels of an enclosed working-class world in which the movement outwards was not made part of the fiction – people continually have to get away for economic reasons, but the experience of combined continuity and discontinuity didn't enter as a theme. Of course, where it did enter was in Lawrence, but to an excess of discontinuity, as his later work developed away from full social relationships. I only really felt easy when I could establish the difference between the two worlds and explore the problem of rejoining them; crucially, when I could get the sense of the tension inside that working-class life by splitting one of the central characters to illustrate diverging roads.

In the 19th century, as a matter of fact, I found some important precedents for what I was trying to do – successful studies of one kind of mobility, the uncertainty of moving between two kinds of life. But what I then noticed was the almost embarrassingly practical point, that the simple physical space enjoyed by 19th-century novelists was so much greater than that available within post-war fiction. If you are trying to depict two different kinds of social life and people moving between them, the scale of the canvas on which writers of the last century could work was about five times that which any post-war British novelist could realistically expect. The economics of commercial publishing now impose extraordinary restrictions on writers. The first reaction of a publisher to a novelist these days is: 'Fine, but not more than 80,000 words.' This was a major problem for me. I kept building up something which I thought was the right pace, and then found that what was intended to be one movement in the novel was already longer than anything a publisher would accept. So much of the work was then looking for condensations or formal solutions to knit the materials together in some more economical way. This was another sense in which I felt I was writing right against the grain.

One way round the diminution of scale in contemporary fiction which has been taken by many 20th-century writers is the serial novel, which can re-create a comparable space across a number of books. Did you ever entertain this solution yourself?

The series has been the most significant response to this difficulty, but it has its own internal problems. First, you can never guarantee that people will read the novels either in any particular sequence or as a whole. You therefore have to establish elements in each individual novel to stand on their own, which you wouldn't in a longer single work. Then you tend to be forced into a kind of recapitulation of the past of your characters in summary form, unless you adopt the convention which is quite common now of presenting people unexplained, without a history. The nearest I've come to the serial form are certain character continuities between *Border Country*/*Second Generation* and *The Fight for Manod*. I kept finding that I wanted to assume that the reader would know these characters, yet of course I realize that this usually won't be so. But I think the series is the only technical solution which is open to a contemporary novelist who is interested in a broad band of social experience. I should add, however, that I am not convinced that the economic problems of a long novel are as difficult as publishers make them out to be. When long novels arrive from America or Russia people say how wonderful it is that at least somewhere writers still have the necessary breadth and depth of imagination. When you've been compressed, that's hard to hear. The situation may be unique in Britain, because of the peculiar dependence of fiction on the public library system.

Economic constraints have certainly led to a contraction in the scale of the novel in England. But surely there are social and ideological reasons for the difficulties of the realist form as well?

Of course. To begin with, there is the problem of narrative location. You can move very much faster, more economically, if you adopt a single unproblematic narrator. But the single unproblematic narrator is precisely in question today, especially in the sort of novels that I have tried to write. The conditions of movement between different worlds are much more complex than in the large-scale realist novels of the past century, while the space for realizing them has conversely diminished. That is one difficulty. Another is much more directly ideological. In most modern fiction a character appears without much explanation. He or she is given a name, usually presented saying or doing something; not much is learnt about their social or personal identity beyond what is made evident in the subsequent action of the novel. By contrast if you look at a 19th-century realist novel, when people are introduced, they are given a whole network of history – all sorts of minor technical variations are used to ensure this. In the same way when a place is introduced, it is not just the site of an event as is typical of contemporary fiction, but the materialization of a history which is often quite extensively retraced. This is precisely the kind of thing for which there is ordinarily no room today, and which seems easiest to cut. But the omission is actually a crucial change. For what these formal devices corresponded to was the highest moment of bourgeois cultural engagement: a moment from which historical materialism is itself a development. In the dominant pattern today, there is no longer any effective history. At any moment a person is a free-floating individual who makes his life through a series of encounters, which are really quite undetermined by any larger forces. If you're interested in those, they say, you should write sociology or history, not novels. The dropping of these principles of presentation has an ideological effect. The result is a late bourgeois fictional form, which maybe we cannot escape anyway. But at least it should not be taken as unproblematic.

These modifications within contemporary conventions are clearly inimical to the writing of socialist fiction. But there is another and deeper question. Are there any inherent difficulties in reproducing the achievement of classical bourgeois realism in the 19th-century from a working-class standpoint in the 20th century? That in turn breaks down into a number of interconnected issues. Firstly, does such a shift in actual social stance itself involve in certain crucial respects a different compositional way of looking at society? To what extent are the accomplishments of the 19th-century novel directly continuous or germane to the problems posed for another social class in the 20th century? Secondly, there is the question of the change in the structural dimensions of capitalist society – not only within each national framework but perhaps especially in the internationalization of so many of the determinant processes of common life. Could the canons of 19th-century realism hypothetically cope with the increased complexity of 20th-century industrial capitalism, whose much greater anonymity and impersonality – it is often argued – preclude the kind of totalizing imagination classically to be found in Balzac or even Dickens? Then thirdly, it may be wondered whether the confidence of bourgeois realism in the 19th century was not inseparable from its theoretical innocence of the analytic discourses which eventually developed into the social sciences in the 20th century. Did you feel any of these problems acutely yourself?

The general problem, which has exercised many producers – perhaps more often in plays than in novels – is whether to break with the realist tradition altogether or to try and extend it. I think there is a case for seeing how far certain areas which the bourgeois form typically excluded could now be integrated in the novel. The experience of work is a good example. Before Hardy the work of the majority of people never got into fiction as an important experience at all. Of course, the work of the bourgeois world is sometimes rendered as in Balzac's fiction, but not that of the labourer, the industrial worker. Their experience still offers the possibility, with all sorts of difficulties, of seeing whether the realist form is capable of extension and transformation. I myself think the project is worth attempting, and I've tried to explore it in my novels.

The question of internationalization raises an absolutely crucial issue here. For some of the most faithful documentary novels of working-class life did become, as I said earlier, in effect regional novels. Although this in a way expressed what was happening to certain important parts of the working class, it's not possible to underwrite that form. The rural novel became regional not because the Lake District is less important than Central London but because you cannot conceivably write a realist novel about the Lake District in which the much broader economy outside it is absent. That has produced extreme complications for the traditional form because it did depend, in my view, on the idea of a knowable community, and now we are faced with the fact that this cannot be called a community and is not knowable in the former ways. The result is an extreme crisis of the form. I find it interesting that so many writers, of course for other reasons as well, have turned to the essentially different form of drama to write this experience, rather than to fiction.

So far as the development of separate discourses is concerned, if you look at the classic example of George Eliot, she was the reverse of innocent of them. She was not only aware of other kinds of discourse, but in a very interesting way used some of them in fictional form. There are very strong presuppositions in English culture that the writer should not think too much, because ideas cannot be accommodated in fiction. But by no means all English novelists have respected them. There are obviously difficulties in incongruity of idiom: I find that when I am revising a novel I often cut out phrases which quite clearly come from a different consciousness. But I think that a much more extensive theoretical discussion of the possibilities in *all* the available forms is necessary, because I don't think that in the end the ready move to a certain kind of television drama, which on the whole is the most interesting option recently made by socialist writers, can do more than a certain small part of the job which has to be done. Alongside this theoretical debate we need a lot of examples of practice, so that people can see how far a particular form can be taken. We must be very experimental about it.

How did your own experiments in writing novels develop? It was a decade before Border Country *was completed and published. In the same period you wrote three unpublished novels. What sort of books were they?*

The first, which I wrote in 1948, was called *Ridyear*. It was a curious attempt, which I can now see was greatly mistaken, to get across certain ideas about contemporary social and political experience by taking a fairly rare account I had found of an Englishman who had gone to Klondike. It described his journey there and his experience in the gold-fields – where he made a strike but eventually ended up with nothing. The form I chose was an adventure story, but I was trying to make the novel a sort of parable as well. *Adamson*, written two years later, was again an attempt to use an available convention – this time of the man who reaches a crisis of identity and disappears from his old life, re-emerging elsewhere with a new identity. The third experiment with a simple form was called *Grasshoppers*. Today, I'm glad it wasn't published, although at the time I wanted to see it out. The novel isolated a group of people unable to reconcile their feeling for the urgency of change with the rather inert society around them, who set themselves up as a comic commando travelling around to institute certain changes. If a town was trying to reorganize its public transport system and was bogged down in the usual bureaucratic delays, they would simply go out one night and move the road signs. The title suggested both their mode of intervention in local political deadlocks and also what I felt about that kind of activity. Looking back, I can now see that if it had been published people might have said it was a fairly characteristic novel of the fifties, or an anticipation of the sixties, and so it was. It was the only one of these early novels I tried hard to publish.

You've said that as a young man you very much wanted to write fiction, and not to be a university lecturer or a critic. Talking of your literary formation in the thirties, you remarked that the work which most interested and attracted you was Finnegan's Wake – *the farthest shore of inter-war modernism. Yet the texture of the first novel you published is not at all what one would imagine from an admirer of Joyce. At a purely verbal level* Border Country *is quite austere, making very little use of either metaphor or simile. The style of the book is extraordinarily sparing. Intensity is nearly always achieved through the rhythms of spoken dialogue, without any recourse to rhetorical figures. Was there some major change in your literary sensibility after the war? How deliberate was your writing strategy in* Border Country?

I can remember, like most of my contemporaries, producing exercises in the manner of Joyce, which was an incredibly impressive method of writing for us in the forties. At that age, you have an ambition to write which is very generic and unlocalized – it's not yet the case that, as I would now put it theoretically, what you write is in a very wide sense of identity and social relationship what you are. Nearly all socialist writers of the time were excited by Joyce, but I would think that few were later influenced by him, unless the impact went a long way – not their own way. Joyce's personality is too strong; you can be influenced by other writers but the danger is of being overwhelmed by him. I discovered in the end that what excited me in Joyce belonged to a very specific and very relevant kind of consciousness which happened not to be my own. So that once you have worked past the formal fascination you realize that your own projects can coexist with admiration for another kind of writing which you don't want to do yourself.

In writing *Border Country*, on the other hand, I was conscious of wanting to be very careful not to write in what had become identified in England as a 'Welsh style'. This was a general reaction among most of my contemporaries. The Welsh style that got established in England as a popular mode did, in fact, have certain relations to Joyce, in its extreme verbal exuberance – everything from free-association to extraordinarily vivid metaphor. Dylan Thomas was the most notable example of this period of Welsh writing, which had the effect of making Welsh people into the characters which the style demanded – garrulous eccentrics. The fact that it represented a development of observable forms of Welsh social habit made it all the more necessary to draw back. It is not that I don't admire it. But when Welsh writing became fashionable between the late thirties and the early fifties, I shared with a lot of my contemporaries the feeling that it was necessary to get away from the perception of the Welsh that it seemed to project to the outside world. Many people now say – some much more strongly than I would – that its language was a form of cultural subordination, the only – slightly degraded if subtle – way the Welsh could present themselves to a London audience. At all events, I was certainly determined to avoid that.

If you were in partial reaction to a traditional Welsh style, was your writing practice in Border Country *fairly deliberate?*

Writing fiction is a quite different experience from any other forms of composition. You do not really know what you are going to say. To give this a more secular explanation than the usual way in which it is presented, I think that what probably happens is that writers commit themselves to certain rhythms – in my case the rhythms of certain kinds of ordinary Welsh speech. At the same time I was very aware of the problem of the distance between the language of narrative and analysis and any language of speech which is other than the most tidied up standard English. I didn't want there to be a contradiction between the two in the novel. But in general the process of composition was much more unpredictable than with other kinds of writing, where I find that I have in front of me on a piece of paper the outline of what I am going to write – unexpected things may happen, but broadly you know where you're going.

Did you revise successive drafts of Border Country, *or rewrite it largely afresh each time?*

No, it was never quite starting afresh although in fact in the last unpublished version, I put the lot away, but by then I knew most of it from memory. It was more a case of revising drafts – a very complicated business in the last stages of *Border Country*, when I remember adopting the undignified procedure of walking between piles of paper on the floor, arranging and rearranging them to get the right shape. Once I'd done that, then I rewrote them to get the proper sense of flow into the novel.

The central figure of Border Country *is the railwayman Harry Price. The portrait of him is a very powerful one. Its effect is achieved partly by the contrast with his friend Morgan Rosser, who becomes a small manufacturer, and his son Will, who becomes a university lecturer. Morgan and Will are in quite different ways more restless and uncertain personalities. Harry is presented as someone with a wholeness of character that commands an absolute respect: his life appears the dominant centre of value in the book. Now although the characterization of him is credible and moving, the thematic significance attached to it seems more problematic. In effect, Harry is seen as a figure virtually without contradiction; even the physical descriptions of him emphasize a singleness of being which appears to have a normative force in the novel. In the key scene where Morgan attempts to persuade Will to join him in running his new factory, Harry is asked for his opinion on the matter and says: 'You set yourself a job, you finish it; agreed the job may be wrong, you might have done better. But get the habit when it's difficult of stopping and going off somewhere else, then it's not the job's useless, that may not matter, but you, yourself. Nobody sets himself what he doesn't want. What you set yourself you wanted, or seemed to want it. And now it isn't the chance you'd be missing, I don't care so much about that. Only once turn aside from what you've set yourself, once keep back just a bit of your strength, then whatever happens, succeeding or whatever it is, whatever the others say, still it don't matter what you get, you're finished with yourself.'*[20] *What is surely wrong with this is that after all people have very conflicting desires, impulses and aspirations; they do set themselves aims they later don't want; they are always liable to crises and change. The very possibility of areas of acute strain, which seems to be the*

[20] BC, p.

normal condition, is discounted in Harry's credo. Such a moral integrism – character either given as one bloc, or if not, fissure seen as a flaw – is not persuasive novelistically or in real life.

I agree with your criticism of that way of seeing things. My intention in the novel was to show that it produces both an undoubted strength and an illusion. For the idea that nobody sets himself what he doesn't want is untrue about him as well as about most other people. Harry Price has not set himself a life, he was set into a situation where he goes through a process of adaptation and integration as well as clearing a certain space for living in which he can feel that more of himself is there. The central thrust of the novel is actually that the kind of strength which that apparently integrated view of moral value gives is insufficient. In Harry's case, it fails in the end when death approaches, which sets a term to any perspective. There is a sense of total bewilderment in this otherwise very strong and confident man, when he becomes ill, when he can no longer work, when he's dying. What had seemed like a connection between an integrated view of life and a force of character falters once the conditions which were carrying it really go, his own physical strength, health, and the place to which he's got used. The effect of the scene where his mind is almost disintegrating is that the meanings which had seemed so powerful are losing their power. His son sees not only the physical nearness of death, but also the confusion and withdrawal of interest as it approaches. This is the reason for the son's great difficulty – he is bound to respect his father's example, and yet he is bound to feel that it isn't complete. That is the crisis in his response.

You've explained your purpose very clearly. But does it come through so definitely in the novel? Death, and the fatigue and bewilderment that precede it, is a general biological limit which can cancel any project. Can the reader easily construe the specific significance of it of which you've just spoken?

Will's final comment is meant to convey his experience. He says: 'It was as if I stared straight at the sun. A sun that was blinding me, as I was learning to see'.[21] The image is of a light that is literally a source of life, something acknowledged to be extremely powerful, but which can also blind the

[21] BC, p.

beholder. The normal sense of a son getting his notion of identity and life from a father is here intensified by the sight of an unusual kind of self-sufficiency which in the end had proved insufficient. The decision to treat the character of Harry Price in this way was one I took after several rewritings, and was not based on my own experiences. Harry is not my own father, because a lot of him went into Morgan too. It would have been possible to combine his contradictory impulses in the same character; I tried that but in the end decided to separate them out by creating another figure who represented the much more restless, critical and self-critical side of my father's nature. I realized the danger that if I took away those characteristics I might be left with too single a character. You may be right that, as often happens, the strengths of one particular way of looking at the world are so communicated in the novel that the qualifications or limits set to it aren't fully noticed.

One of the overt exchanges between people in Border Country *which seems to run against your intention is a conversation between Morgan and Will after Harry has fallen ill. Morgan says: 'Harry's different. He changes a thing because he wants the new thing and he settles to it because he wants it right through, not because the rejection is driving him', Will answers, 'It comes to the same thing' – to which Morgan replies: 'No , Will, it's coming to a different thing. Take a look.' Then Will says: 'Yet in the end he's lying up there, on the edge . . . If it was right, he'd be right, that's why I get so impatient. . . . We take good care not to live like him, we take good care of ourselves.'*[22] *Now the suggestion here is that Morgan is making a self-criticism of his own equivocal compromises, as someone who was moved by dissatisfaction, who did negatively reject his circumstances, and whose desire for change took him from work in the signal-box to ownership of a jam factory – a shift of class position that is certainly presented in a critical light. On the other hand, when Will takes his distance from his father's position, the sense of his reply is that it represents an unobtainable standard of value, that will break anyone who tries to match it – but the force of the ironic 'We take good care of ourselves' is surely that to renounce it is a form of self-protection. In other words, the suggestion here seems to be not that Harry's way of living is insufficient, but rather than it is too demanding. Would that be a misreading of it?*

[22] BC, p.

The idea of settling to do the new thing because you want the new thing rather than because you don't like the old thing is underwritten. It is a difference. But when the son says, 'If it was right, he'd be right', the sense is not only that the father is dying, but that if it was right then it would be a good way for us all to follow. Saying 'we don't usually put ourselves that much at risk' is also a way of asking: if we *did* put ourselves that much at risk, would it be right? Would it be something which could sustain itself against all the forces which are inevitably much larger than the strongest possible kind of man? That's what I had in mind.

A small biographical question – did you take the dual naming of the son, Will and Matthew, from your own experience?

Yes. All the people who knew me till I was eighteen called me Jim. I adopted my legal name Raymond at university. The two names in the novel, and in my own experience, point up the problem of being two persons to know, and of negotiating between two different worlds. Yet I always find it strange how quickly one adjusts to being called a certain name in a certain place.

Border Country *is in the widest sense a novel about class relations in Britain. One of its major episodes occurs in the vortex of the General Strike. The representation of class struggle, however, poses a particular problem once the class position from which the realist novel is written changes. For in the 19th century, an inclusive movement of the fictional imagination could be achieved by certain authors – Eliot, Zola or Hardy would be examples – looking downwards from a familiar bourgeois or bourgeois-assimilated world in which they were living and working, towards the world of the exploited and oppressed. Impulses of social sympathy – most evident in Zola, very clear in Hardy, not to be underestimated in Eliot – permitted a comprehensive exploration of the social hierarchy in their novels. The world of manual work, which you mentioned, is emphatically present in Zola as much as in Hardy, but political revolt as well. At the same time these writers had no difficulty in representing the possessing classes. The question arises, however, whether that inclusiveness is ever likely to be reproduced in reverse in the 20th century. Isn't it improbable that working-class writers, attempting to connect the experience of their own social class with the totality of the structures that determine it, would be able to extend their imagination with anything like the same degree of sympathy, for very good reasons, to the oppressor world? In that sense, one could conjecture that the span of concrete re-created life – to use* Scrutiny *terminology – is likely to be much more uneven in a 20th-century realist novel written from a proletarian stance than in certain 19th-century novels, although it was very uneven in most of them too, of course. In* Border Country, *the bourgeois world is very remote – scarcely impinging at all on the village of workers and farmers. But this is a very special case, since the community which the novel describes is one without a major local exploiting stratum, for the biographical reasons we have discussed. But had there been a powerfully entrenched local ruling class, wouldn't the movement to capture it in the novel have posed severe problems for you?*

Yes. The class relations in *Border Country* come through literally at the end of the line, in the way the railway company tries to treat the workers after the General Strike through its remote telegrams and notices. The capitalist world is not a presence, it is never directly introduced in the novel. If it had been, I would have felt in a quandary. If you read the sympathetic 19th-century novels, which go down from the mill owner's house to the mill-hands and then back to the house, what you notice is a certain sense – however fraught it may be as in George Eliot – of being able to settle in that house and treat the people in it familiarly and fairly. That would now be extremely difficult. For one thing, the mill owner's house and the mill below were more characteristic of the 19th-century form of close and immediate class oppression. Where would capitalist power be exercised now? In offices, through structures whose description would need something other than physical observation. To follow the processes of an accountant's decision to close a particular works would involve a very different problem from the imaginative seizure of a more local kind of capitalism. In *Border Country* I was writing about a social situation which could be described in smaller scale because it was more visible. I am aware that the different kinds of relationship had not so wholly separated out as more characteristically in a modern industrial community. I found when I was writing *The Fight for Manod* that I had to go back up to Whitehall, where ministry meetings make long-distance decisions. It is a world I now know better, but it still may not be adequately realized.

Second Generation *appears to have been an exception among your novels, in that it seems to have been written in one burst between 1960 and 1962. Does that mean that you found in* Border Country *the impetus for its successor?*

It did go fairly consecutively, although it started out as a quite different novel. My original idea was to take a group of students in Oxford and follow their different paths for five years or so afterwards. The son of the car worker, who eventually became the central character of *Second Generation*, was simply one of the group. I then found the familiar problem that if I was to pursue this project with enough people, the result would be an impossibly long novel. So I got more and more interested in this character, as a way of contrasting worlds within a single city. Once I'd fixed on that, I wrote the book fairly quickly.

Did the conception of Second Generation *develop out of your completion of* Border Country, *or was it entirely subsequent?*

I had some idea of the theme at the time of writing the earlier book. I wanted to set the next novel away from Wales and to bring in the experience of the university. But the actual shape of *Second Generation* only emerged after *Border Country* was finished.

Did you feel the same kinds of difficulty of form or not?

Some. The basic problems were different, however, because the notion of the intermediary figure moving between one kind of life and another was now more complex. In *Border Country* the movement was a physical one, in the journeys of Matthew Price from London to Wales, and so in that sense was simpler. In *Second Generation* I found I wanted more room. The novel in the end came out much too long. The helpful suggestion was then made that it might be difficult for me to shorten it but one of the publishers' editors would be very glad to have a try. The editor turned out to be C. Day Lewis. He did produce a masterly condensation, which succeeded in reversing the whole meaning of the novel. I couldn't bear to read it after the first ten pages, but my wife did: every time there was an argument between the car worker's son Peter Owen and his academic supervisor Robert Lane, in which Lane pointed out the need for a balanced view of English society and Owen made a radical criticism of it, Lane's cautious speeches would be left in and Owen's replies taken out. The result was that I had to take the manuscript back and shorten it myself. The episode is worth noting because the editor was Day Lewis: the irony of this continuity from the thirties didn't escape me.

Second Generation *is a much more directly political – one might say intransigently militant – book than* Border Country. *It is not surprising that it was attacked nearly as widely as the earlier novel was praised, given its portrait of class struggle in the motor industry and of compromise and corruption in the academy. There is, however, one pattern that seems to be common to the two books, which could be questioned from the left. This is the opposition that they appear to suggest between personal and social integrity on the one hand, and intellectuality on the other. In* Border Country *Morgan Rosser initially demands more urgent and sweeping political change than Harry Price; but when his hopes are disappointed with the defeat of the General Strike, his restless and outgoing energies end in pursuit of a somewhat dubious commercial advancement. In* Second Generation, *two working-class couples, Kate and Harold, Gwyn and Myra, represent very much the same contrast. The stress is again on the personal costs of a wider commitment to politics or ideas, taking the different forms of a kind of deadened fatigue in the case of the shop-steward Harold, and of inconstancy and incipient disregard for other people in the case of Kate. Whereas Gwyn and Myra, the other couple of the same generation, exemplify a more limited range of hopes and interests, in the case of Myra with some elements of prejudice, and a relative immobility and refusal to engage in wider issues, except in times of common crisis; but it is they who are undivided and preserve the values of immediate feeling in their home. Do you think this is a typical or necessary tension within the working-class experience?*

I thought so then and didn't change my mind. *Second Generation* was written at a time when I felt there was a profound crisis inside the class. There was a widespread settling for a narrow area of private experience – certainly not with any anti-union attitudes, but essentially living outside that world of work altogether. The kinds of engagement which can operate at different levels, whether it's the hard work of a shop-steward, or a more intellectual horizon, were beginning to come apart from that. An internal division in the working class was occurring, separating the politically and industrially active sectors of it from the rest of the class, which had not withdrawn its general and rather occasional sympathy, but was not living in those ways and was therefore recruitable into quite different social perspectives. I suppose I may have taken that as a general situation more than perhaps I should have done, though it has since greatly strengthened. But it was a process of which I was very conscious from watching a number of people I knew. There was also the special dimension in the novel of the different kind of politics in the university. Perhaps I was over-influenced by the experience of seeing people burnt out after active involvement in politics in that period. However, the emphasis on the costs of engagement was not intended to indicate that some other choice would be preferable. For withdrawal from that world to make an even safer enclosed area, where you can concentrate entirely on private life, doesn't work. But the implication of the contrast in *Second Generation* is not, any more than I intended it to be in *Border Country*, that if you keep to that which within certain constraints you can get under your control, you can live a more integrated kind of life. The form of *Second Generation* should make that clearer than *Border Country*, because there are more differing characters and situations in it – there is no one central or dominant character. The meanings and values of the novel are more distributed.

Counterposed to the different working-class families in the novel are two figures from the university milieu – Robert Lane, a sociologist who is Peter Owen's thesis supervisor, and Arthur Dean, a lecturer in politics who has an affair with Kate Owen. Each represents, with a contrasted tonality, a combination of political conformism and moral corruption. Lane counsels his students towards a wise academic moderation, and exploits his long-suffering wife. Dean enters a manipulative relationship with Kate Owen, while cynically denying any working-class ability to struggle or change society. One in effect preaches a resigned quietism, the other an active nihilism. Now the pairing of qualities in these two characters arouses some misgivings. The direct equation of political reaction and personal hollowness or corruption seems empirically doubtful. There are surely upholders of the bourgeois order, whether in the economic, political or cultural domain, whose private lives are of reasonable rectitude – say, the Keith Josephs of this world? To identify the presence of social reaction with the absence of sexual integrity appears to be a dangerous aesthetic simplification.

As a generalization, yes, but I had watched one particular highly educated socialist, who was 'liberal' in these deliberately identified senses. There was a very characteristic kind of left figure (you know what sort of a left it turned out to be) who was intellectually active in the Labour Party, representing a type of political affiliation which had nothing to do with the militant working class, indeed was objectively using and betraying it. Now, I didn't feel that about Lane, who many people have said to me they find unsympathetic as a character. I did mean him to be a smoother-over of conflicts – this was the whole sense of his relation with Peter. But I didn't intend him to be corrupt, but only to be that again fairly familiar figure of the man who so much wishes everything were better than it is. In that respect you could say that I took a lot of his reactions from elements I could feel in my own personality. There is a contrast with Peter, of course, where I wanted to get the sense of a different and I hoped unidealized kind of commitment coming through – of someone who experiences various kinds of dreadful confusion, but ultimately makes another kind of choice, not an option that is sustainable where it ends, but at least one that is symbolically correct. But he also represents a radically different generation.

On the more general problem of the connections between personal and social corruption, I think I felt in the late fifties and early sixties that what had happened to the left and to the working class involved a deeper kind of disturbance than was generally admitted. The rhetoric of the time was of breakthrough and liberation, which seemed to me much too simple. Just watching a fair number of people, I got a sense of considerable danger – of the costs of different ways of trying to live under the pressure of an order that systematically frustrated them. More than any other novel I've written, *Second Generation* was based on direct observation. In that respect it is an impressionistic account, which I wouldn't say however seems wrong when I look back. But I hoped that by taking something as basic as the division between intellectual life and manual life, coexisting within one city, I could at least show the real theatre in which these confusions were occurring.

The compositional integration of the conflicts within the intellectual and the industrial worlds is very effective. But there is one significant absence, which perhaps leads to a serious displacement of emphasis. It is noticeable that the struggle of the car workers within the factory never encounters the capitalist enemy itself. The real centres of industrial power remain entirely abstract in the novel: the highest figure ever shown in the company hierarchy is the local personnel manager, whom Harold sees in one memorable but fleeting scene, in

which he reflects on the possibility that the man opposite him might have come from a working-class background himself. In general the factory is presented exclusively through the experience of the workers on the assembly line – the reader never sees the controllers of the order against which they are struggling. On the other hand, what is powerfully materialized in the novel is the university. The two lecturers, Lane and Dean, thus tend to function unduly as structural substitutes for a depiction of the employers. The result is a kind of over-signification of them as epitomes of bourgeois Britain. In a climactic scene near the end, Peter denounces Dean publicly with the resounding phrase: 'You rule England.'[23] But actually, although the universities certainly serve the dominant social order, they are by no means the seat of real political or economic rule, and moreover – partly for that very reason – possess a relative intellectual autonomy as centres of teaching and research. To displace industrial to cultural targets involves an element of false consciousness, surely?

I agree with this. The problem is related to a more general limitation in my own social formation and within working-class experience as a whole. The farthest outer scale of social power with which the working class normally comes into direct contact is the level it encounters in a local confrontation. Now clearly one move that a fiction committed to a political perspective is going to make is to look at the higher levels of decision-making in the economy and society. How far up do you then go? Suppose I had gone to – what? – the board of the motor company, to the whole interlocking between it, the banks and the state machine. This would have been better, but it is precisely what fictionally is not easy to do. I still mainly know the actual ruling class only by reading about it. But it's incredibly difficult to create characters who you don't feel in the gut; at some level if you don't know who they are you perhaps don't have sufficient energy to project them. It is then that the university often functions as a displaced perception of the ruling social order. It seems to me that at least in that period, and it may still be true, the organized working class tended to see academic figures as pre-eminent examples of the ruling class precisely because they are at somewhat closer range to it – especially given the typical British characterization of class by external traits of accent, appearance, minor habits, rather than by the exercise of social and economic power. So in a way *Second Generation* has some of the faults of

[23] SG, p. 318.

the working-class perspective, which however are not only mine but are part of the way the system operates – that the farthest the ordinary perception of power can reach is some middle functionary. I have been continually struck by this limitation of horizon in working-class experience, as if that whole world of big corporations and banks is too remote to be really registered. I share in that. Not that I don't know the realities of power intellectually, but when it comes to writing about them imaginatively, it's a problem.

It should be said that there are very few novels which attempt to range through a complete social and political scale of power. One work that can certainly be admired in this respect is The First Circle, *which does explore a dramatically hierarchical regime from top to bottom. But of course the USSR is very different in nature from a capitalist society, its social order is at once more uniform and its structure of power more transparent – in that sense it may be imaginatively more accessible. It is probably also of some significance that Solzhenitsyn seems to have been a convinced Stalinist in his youth, so that the problems of projection would be less in his case.*

What seems to me extraordinary in *The First Circle* is the perception of a system running right through all the relationships of the novel: finally when you arrive at the summit of the system with Stalin, he is still seen as part of it himself. That is an incredibly impressive achievement. One wishes for a similar integration in British terms, but the world of rather elegantly concealed power which is characteristic of ruling-class relations in this country is much more difficult to get at.

The Cecil King Diaries *give a pretty startling impression of what the upper reaches of this world are like. The two most striking features of it, as they emerge from King's account, are the direct and unmediated personal relations between newspaper magnates, top civil servants, cabinet ministers, big businessmen and service chiefs; and the shedding of polite hypocrisies for brutally explicit discussions of the day-to-day realities of class struggle. Of course, King was something of a rogue elephant in this world, which is normally concealed.*

These are the equivalent of the sort of documents which Disraeli read to find out about the working class in the 19th century – novelists like him didn't know about workers from having broken bread with them. King's *Diaries* aren't the only such revelations. Thomson recounted travelling back from a banquet in a limousine with Wilson during the crisis over the old cooperative paper, the *Citizen*, and Wilson trying to persuade him to buy the paper. His comment was: 'Harold, I can't get it through the Monopolies Commission' – to which Wilson replied: 'I'll give you a written guarantee'. Such exchanges are probably typical. When these people move outside their own circles, they are more careful – the shutters are put up. In fiction, I suppose that to some extent you've got to enjoy even wicked people to be able to write about them – to make them more than the cut-out of who we are against. It would be necessary to see the function of the pleasures of food, drink and company in the tone of their arrogant decisions about how to dispose of everything from a factory to an army. If you can't convey how their relish in these generates the good feeling with which they are on occasion capable of conducting their affairs, you won't create credible characters. That ought to be compatible with seeing quite clearly what they do – but it is very difficult in practice.

The Fight for Manod *took you over a decade to complete – longer than* Border Country, *in fact, although by the mid-sixties you were already an experienced novelist. Why was its composition so protracted?*

Well, to begin with it went very quickly. What are now the second to the seventh chapters seemed just to flow. And I had got not only the village and the valley but the prepared lines through to Birmingham and Coventry, as well as to the Ministry in London, so it was all shaping in that form. Then I did a count. I had done six out of a projected thirty chapters, moving at the only pace at which I judged it could be properly done. It would be well over two hundred thousand words. And then it wasn't only the problem of publishing length; it was that on top of the reaction to *Second Generation*. I tried compressing, but that didn't seem to work. I left it for some time, and then so much else started happening: the decisive political break in 66 and the beginning of that very absorbing work on the Manifesto. Also a television producer who had read *Second Generation* came and asked me to do a play. I found the form interesting, though ironically the first play, *Letter from the Country*, eventually got acted in thirty rather than the original seventy-five minutes, but the second, *Public Inquiry*, was produced at the normal length. I welcomed the form because an action could be isolated, but I still felt, and feel, that the connecting composition of the kind of novel I had planned had more of what I wanted to say. So whenever I had a clear month I would go back to the chapters and try again; and it kept expanding. I had now a couple of additional chapters in Brussels, where one of the main characters goes to track down the source of the corporate initiative to create a new urban settlement in a Welsh valley. All these were ordinary writing difficulties – well ordinary nowadays, though the constraints of length are historically extraordinary – but by the late sixties I became increasingly aware that there was another set of problems, which amounted to a shift in perspective, though there seemed no discontinuity at the time. I saw the whole country and city relation, which from the beginning had been the general theme, as for me the crucial relation in contemporary social analysis. I'd also started, remember, *The Country and the City*, but that had been foreseen as a smaller and more specifically literary book. Now it seemed to run through everything. I expanded its scheme and started a whole new programme of reading. For some time it was my only large-scale project, but then in turn I dropped it, feeling blocked. I did some smaller things, and then suddenly wrote the whole of *The Country and the City*, in its new form, very quickly. And that was all right, but still I would go back and look at those novel chapters. I didn't want to abandon them, but now much of the wider project of the novel had gone into the other book. I kept thinking it through and then I thought I saw an alternative shape. I let it lie a few years but as it continued to make sense I eventually took it up again and completed it without difficulty. Except that it's not, of course, for better or worse, the novel I originally set out to write.

Did you conceive the novel as closing a trilogy from the outset? What were your aims in drawing on the first two, technically unconnected, books to create a related trio?

Yes, I had a trilogy in mind from the beginning. The first two were locally unconnected, but the links between Glynmawr and Trawsfynydd – a few miles apart – had been put ready for use. And thematically the shape of the trilogy was clear. They were interconnecting versions of a specific kind of change, across borders. *Border Country* was the present, including and trying to focus an immediate past; *Second Generation* a true present; *Fight for Manod* a present trying to include and focus a future. There was even a linkage through the successive means of mobility: *Border Country's* railway; *Second Generation's* car traffic and factory; *Manod's* potential electronic technology. And in each, through these different situations, the decisive problem of the relation of learning to labour, taking different class and political aspects. All this, of course, as the infrastructure of the trilogy; the human specificities had to be dominant at each stage. Incidentally that was another reason for the special difficulties of *Manod*. Much of it is about projecting and imagining a future, but deliberately not as futurism, rather as a future that has in some way to come through from a rooted present. This made a more difficult balance than usual between the lived experiences and the projected – in fact thwarted – historical movement. The novel ends with the sense of a possible direction – I think the main good direction – but only just held on to, beside the heavy certainties of present and past. That precise feeling, of course, was the shape I eventually saw for the novel, as distinct from the larger interactions of the original project.

Much of The Fight for Manod *is constructed around the contrast between a character from* Border Country, *Matthew Price, and a younger character from* Second Generation, *Peter Owen – whose different reactions to the discovery of corruption and speculation in land-use in a projected new city-development in Wales, largely determine the resolution of the action. But there is a persistent asymmetry in the treatment of the two. Matthew is unquestionably the central figure in the novel; the portrait of him has a depth and inward quality which is not really granted to Peter, who – for all his structural importance – is nowhere given the personal consciousness of even some of the secondary characters among the local country-people, who are very finely realized. He is mostly seen from the outside, through his wife or others. Do you think this is a criticism of the novel?*

Yes, it could be. Though he is also, in *Second Generation*, presented mainly like that. I wanted a character whose deep internal life is in a way inaccessible to him, though of course all the time he thinks and reasons and acts. I wanted someone whose inner life is in a way only sensed by others and who then continually disconcerts them. I think I have known him but of course I can't say whether I've realised him. I feel sorry I had to let the Brussels chapters go: his combined flight and productive knowledge were there. But as I saw the eventual shape they were in too different a dimension. I might, though, sometime put them back. More generally, of course, there's a constant problem of asymmetry in these kinds of internal access: a very difficult problem of conventions because in one sense, as Gogol observed, there is always asymmetry in the persons of a fiction, and it is always from one point of view indefensible, though on the other hand if you go for full symmetry you break the bounds of possible fictions. The Matthew-Peter contrast is important, of course, and Peter is absolutely not intended to be shown as in any way, including comparatively, wrong. On the Manod people, it was crucial that they should be full subjects; Gwen Vaughan particularly, and Modlen Jenkins, and Trevor and Gethin, even Dance; their autonomies are vital.

The title of the book has an element of paradox. The present straits of the valley community at Manod are etched very sharply, and the fate that will probably overtake it should Anglo-Belgian corporations move in is also vividly conjured up. But there is surprisingly little actual fight demonstrated in the narrative itself. The press exposure of the governmental plan and its interlock with corporate interests, and the potential aid of Welsh radical groups – these occur so to speak putatively, off-stage. No force is really presented within the action proper that seems capable of resisting or changing the overall course of events. Compared with either Border Country *or* Second Generation, *the absence of collective scenes is striking. There is no equivalent of the solidarity of the railway-line or the car-factory. A wedding is the only occasion where a significant group of characters comes together. Was this thinning-out deliberate? It seems to give an undercurrent of sadness to the book that is unlike its predecessors.*

Well, I've given part of the answer to this. The eventual shape was indeed a certain sadness: not the restrospective sadness of so much rural fiction, but a specific contemporary sadness: the relation between a wholly possible future and the contradictions and blockages of the present. There's no term for it, as with nostalgia in the case of retrospect. It's the opposite of that, and of course it's distinctively different from the kind of confidence in the future many of us have had, and that I've often written to try to restore, because it is crucial, and yet to get it again means passing through the shadows of the devastating experiences of war and what happened to the best revolutionary societies and then, here, the terrible disintegration of what was once a labour movement with apparently unproblematic perspectives: all the sadness that came when we began to understand reproduction and incorporation, not just as concepts but as the wearying and displacement of flesh and blood. I wanted to seize that moment, when the common actions are latent, indeed quite precisely latent, but through a whole set of contradictions are not actualizing. The original shape, by the way, had the inner-city and Welsh protest actions which in broader terms are relevant and even decisive, though as we know, the broader you go, the more they don't yet link. Two other elements decide the later shape. First, the quite specific sadness of rural Wales today – the Welsh writers I most respect, Emyr Humphreys especially, have this much more strongly. Then second, the experience of ageing. I don't so much mean in myself, though I've felt it at times, but in a few people I know very well and deeply respect, who have fought and fought and quite clearly had expected that in their lifetime, their active lifetime even, there would be decisive breaks to the future. I have seen one or two of these men actually crying, from some interfused depth of social and personal sadness, and knowing why and knowing the arguments to be set against such a feeling and still in some physical sense absolutely subject to it. I have known this, as a matter of fact, in two of the finest militant intellectuals in Europe; for obvious reasons I'm not going to name them, but they've shown it to me, of their own generation, where they've often publicly overridden it. My writing of Matthew Price, who of course in *Border Country* was quite close to me, was an attempt to understand this in someone who in *The Fight for Manod* has become very unlike me; indeed I feel a coarse hard bastard beside him, but more able, I think or hope, to work and push through.

The Fight for Manod *is your most strongly and directly Welsh piece of writing to date. Your feelings about Wales, including your own sense of identity, have obviously undergone important changes since you first left Pandy. Could you tell us what has been the history of your relationship to Wales?*

Yes, a big change started to happen from the late sixties. There was a continuity in a quite overwhelming feeling about the land of Wales; as feeling and writing that stays through. But then I began having many more contacts with Welsh writers and intellectuals, all highly political in the best tradition of the culture, and I found this curious effect. Suddenly England, bourgeois England, wasn't my point of reference any more. I was a Welsh European, and both levels felt different. There's still a lot to work through from that, but I can hardly describe the difference of talking and relating now in Wales, with writers and political comrades who are all hard up against it – what's seen from outside is a remarkable vitality, and so it objectively is, but there it's a hard, fierce, internally contending yet bitterly communal feeling, which is also where I happen to be and now in the truest sense to be from. Through the intricacies of the politics, and they are very intricate indeed, I want the Welsh people – still a radical and cultured people – to defeat, override or bypass bourgeois England; the alternatives follow from the intricacies. That connects, for me, with the sense in my work that I am now necessarily European; that the people to the left and on the left of the French and Italian communist parties, the German and Scandinavian comrades, the communist dissidents from the East like Bahro, are my kind of people; the people I come from and belong to, and my more conscious Welshness is, as I feel it, my way of learning those connections. I mean that over a whole range, from when Welsh-speaking nationalists tell me, as if I needed to be assured, how thoroughly Welsh *Border Country* and the social thinking are – which I used not to realize – to when highly cosmopolitan Welsh intellectuals offer recognition of the whole range of my work, which literally none of my English official colleagues has seen a chance of making sense of, then I am in a culture where I can breathe. Or at least take breaths to go back and contend with capitalist Europe, capitalist England and – blast it, but it was there and had to be shown in *Manod*– capitalist Wales.

How did you come to write The Volunteers *– a very different sort of novel from the Welsh trilogy?*

I wanted to write a political novel set in the 1980s. My original idea was to centre it on the obscure connections between a Labour Minister or ex-Minister and an underground organization involved in subversive actions against the State, against the background of army repression of a strike. There then occurred a ludicrous complication. The Labour politician in the initial version disappears one day, leaving his clothes on a beach, and is later tracked down by a journalist to a hide-out in Switzerland. Shortly after this part of the novel was written Stonehouse more or less acted it out. From that point on I knew that, while my friends would believe me, nobody else would – everyone would regard me as simply cashing in on the Stonehouse affair after the event. So I had to recast the book. I then had in mind a three-part novel in which there would be different narrative positions that would successively intervene. One of these would be the reporter. But to my surprise I found that as I proceeded, it seemed to be just possible to write the whole action in one viable and economical form from his perspective. This decision meant leaving out a lot, which was what most worried me. But at the same time I got taken up with the formal possibilities of this solution and then wrote the novel very quickly.

To what extent were you deliberating taking the popular form of the thriller and using it for political purposes – much as Costa-Gavras' films like Z *or* State of Siege *have done? Such a strategy transforms the genre in the process, of course. Were you aiming at a wider reading public with* The Volunteers?

No. It was always much more an option for a convention that would allow me to write my material than a decision to use a convention to get a different kind of reader. When I got sent the jacket of the book and saw it described as a political thriller, I was surprised. But when I said so to the publisher, he replied: 'Years ago, you remarked to me that it would be perfectly possible to take a popular format like the thriller and put it to good use.' So who knows? All I'm saying is that during the actual process of writing I was looking for a formal solution. Of course, what appear to be local decisions can often have a structural effect. But at the time I regretted every bit of the quite different novel that I had dropped to get within the reportorial convention. For example, in the first version the man who is killed in the military attack on the power depot was given a pre-history of the sort we were talking about earlier. In the final version, he just appears as a representative victim of class confrontation, not as the man I had wanted to describe, who entirely regarded his job as a source of income for his family and for his scrambling, and suddenly found himself in an industrial conflict playing a role he had never foreseen.

The novel in its completed form still contains heterogeneous materials which defy what is generally prized as fictional unity. There is even a typographical shift to mark the insertion of the Gwent Writers' Group account of the assault on the power depot. You have been criticized for this mixture of tonalities in The Volunteers. *How far was it intended?*

I wanted it to be that way. In fact, if I had been more conscious of writing a political thriller, there would have been more heterogeneity of voices. I meant the novel to be bumpy. The very first page is a signal of that. The reporter makes a sharp take-off after his story, after the news of an assassination attempt has been received. There then immediately follows the transliteration of the brief electronic message into the rounded phrases of news-writing. That was meant to pose the question of language with a jolt straight away. Some people have complained about the insertion of the Gwent Writers' pamphlet, although I reduced it greatly for reasons of overall length. But the bumpiness as you move from one convention to another was a deliberate way of stressing the disjuncture of consciousness between an old idea of industrial conflict and the experience of the workers involved. The character of the journalist himself, Lewis Redfern, is designed to be a plausible centre of different kinds of perception and consciousness. He is a person who because of his left-wing past could have critical reflections on a Folk Museum, for example, although these are entirely incompatible with the way he talks to his professional colleagues – partly too because he has a reputation for deviousness.

The account of the attack on the power depot by the Writers' Group, and the excursus on folk museums, seem in different ways successful changes of gear within the novel. The first is one of the most powerful stretches in it. However, there are other elements of heterogeneity in The Volunteers *which look less controlled, and more liable to an objection of incoherence. The first sentence of virtually every chapter is a laconic utterance, about six or seven words long. An invariable pattern is laid down, in keeping with the reportorial convention. But at crucial points in the narrative, the whole syntactical rhythm of Redfern's account changes without warning, becoming much more complex, meditative and delicate. An example is the long passage reconstructing the scene of the shooting of the government minister, in reprisal for the seizure of the power depot. The break from it back to the clipped diction of the investigator in a formula-thriller seems unintentionally jarring. One might dismiss discrepancies of this sort as relatively unimportant on the grounds that the narrator is a formal device for presenting a variety of experiences and actions, to which he is himself extrinsic. But at the end of the novel, he becomes the narrative pivot of the whole action itself. So in a sense the cogency of the novel is at stake in his credibility as a character. In the final scenes, the journalist who has been pursuing the underground group responsible for the armed retaliation is converted to a provisional solidarity with them, and himself leaves for an uncertain political destination. The possibility of that change really depends on the prior establishment of a capacity in him to respond to events with a subjective depth and nuance which is radically eliminated from the reportorial style. The problem is that by the end of the book the reader may feel Redfern's conversion is not fully motivated, because it rests on the narrator's movement to a different kind of feeling or perception which the bulk of the diction doesn't give one an adequate reason to credit.*

I was aware of this difficulty, and I can't judge the extent to which his change can be felt to be motivated. There is an exchange towards the end which is intended to give an indication of what the narrator thinks of his own flip idiom, when he turns on another character and says 'I know someone who talks like that' – suggesting that the hard-boiled getting-through-the-world style had always involved at least a public control of certain other possibilities of expression. The narrative convention is more his report to someone else than an internal reflection. But it's also relevant, and I thought a lot about this, that the conclusion is not really a conversion. The sentence is meant to have some weight at the end, when it's said, you don't have any identity outside the process. Objective relations are sharply *administered to him* by the end of the novel. Now sure, he could have gone the other way at any point in these last episodes, because he's got a story which would make him successful in his own world, and he could sell out all the people involved in it – he's obviously got the potential for that, which is why it was necessary to indicate at various points earlier on that he is also capable of other kinds of feelings. But I still don't regard him as having in the ordinary sense chosen his way at the end. Hence the play on the notion of volunteers – he doesn't really volunteer to throw up his job and give evidence to serve other people but not himself. He is administered into a situation, where he finds – and it is often so – that commitment is not always as voluntary as tends to be thought. In a more integrated person, the change could have been internal and voluntary. With him, some potential for it is there, and some blocks. Hence the scene which I wrote and rewrote in which the underground group comes to exert pressure on him – he is in a certain amount of danger, he would incur risks if he didn't make the choice, which can also be taken simply as a reversion to a previous political loyalty. I didn't want to make a hero of him but to look at his action in this other way, which is not on the whole the usual way I've tended to present this sort of situation. Whereas the actions of the others really are socially delivered in an important sense, never separated from their individuality, to an important extent he is a product of these actions, rather than being a voluntary agent who decides to leave one side and join another. His final movement is the term of a whole series of adjustments which come from these divisions and unresolved earlier loyalties and opportunisms.

It may be that what look like contradictions in the narrative stance of the book are partly due to the elements of compression in it. One wonders if certain themes or developments had to be left out for reasons of space. For instance, the very important figure of Mark Evans, the former MP, remains somewhat shadowy, because it never becomes clear whether his entire career was a deliverate construction of a cover, or whether at some stage his political views changed dramatically, if silently. The fact that his half-brother is a unionist active in the struggle over the power depot is presented, but not much is made of it. Were cuts imposed on you? For obviously modulation of different ranges of diction is easier if you have more room, whereas in a confined space shifts of stance will be more abruptly evident.

The final version was 100,000 words. But I was still asked to cut out 20,000 words. Perhaps I should have held out for the extra room for manoeuvre, I don't know. It's interesting that you mention the cases of Mark Evans and of his half-brother. One scene I had to omit was a meeting between the two which explained the relationship. Another is the visit of the narrator to Evans's mother, and a longer exchange with his first wife. I also cut quite heavily the final conversations between Evans and the narrator, where Evans talks about himself. But if I'd included these and other scenes, I would have been driven back to more conventional or received forms, with their greater amplitude.

Can 20,000 words really be a decisive publishing consideration – it can't add more than 50p. to the price of a book, surely?

The publishers are now in a different world, they have standard formats for novels. The price of £4.95 is now a fixed ceiling for a lot of fiction.

In the political future depicted by The Volunteers, *the Labour Party has disappeared altogether: a National Government presides over a Britain where there is no organized working-class resistance to capitalism on a major scale. Local strikes and occupations persist, but the premise of the whole action of the novel is that there is no longer any mass politics on the left. The operative choices are thus fined down, in the arguments between Redfern and David Evans, the leader of the main underground group, to different modalities of clandestine or subversive action inside or outside the State machine. How realistic did you intend this projection to be? Even granted a political resignation of the working class, couldn't the range of options presented in the novel be taxed with an exaggerated, even adventurist, narrowness?*

The future imagined in the novel is not a desirable one, but it is a perfectly possible one. Projected forward to about 1987–8, the working class remains capable of militant actions, but its militancy is regional in scope and particularist in aims. Where it functions as a political movement, it is betrayed in the usual ways. In such a situation you would inevitably get these other adventures. The novel tries to understand that kind of initiative, but it also suggests an internal critique of it as a charade. There was a much longer argument between Redfern and the group about it, which I had to omit: a few sentences are left, but there was originally a lengthy passage in which he accuses them of adventurism and substitutionism. *The Volunteers* plays out one set of consequences, if the British working class were contained into a local militancy, managed and by-passed and pretty thoroughly defeated by a repressive right-wing government. Then I think you would probably get violent clandestine actions. I wouldn't want them. But I have endless arguments with Italian friends who are in a situation where these options are being taken by increasingly significant if very small sections of the young. I didn't want to underwrite that model – call it terrorist, if you will. But neither did I simply want to oppose it with the old pieties, because I don't think we can rely on them. The prospects, of course, could change.

Are you projecting further novels?

Yes, I want to write two more. One is called *The Brothers*: somewhere between *Border Country* and *Second Generation*. The other would be more ambitious – an attempt to write a historical novel of a different kind. Most or even all such novels are really about one period, rather than about history as such, in a more active sense. From a socialist philosophical standpoint, writing a novel about history ought to be a possible form. But I don't know yet whether it can in practice be done. The great problem is obviously to find the necessary unity. I thought of trying to achieve it through continuity of place rather than of people – taking the same place as it is inhabited in different periods (I would be very selective about these) by different kinds of people, manifesting different social relations, and exercising different ways of using the land. It happens that the district I know best in Wales would be suitable for this kind of continuity, because of its very long agricultural and industrial tradition, going back to communities of neolithic shepherds. I could begin there and end in the 20th century, or a bit ahead. One of the interesting problems of such a novel would be that the people themselves would usually not be aware of these connections. In one of the episodes I've planned, for example, a wartime American aircraft crashes and the local people go up and get the crew out, one of whom has a Welsh family name. To them this is simply a dead airman, but the reader would know from earlier parts of the novel that this was a descendant of a family which had emigrated to the USA in the 19th century. People can be very blank about their own history; the physical stones, ruins, landmarks, names which represent the continuity of it are quite often incomprehensible to them. The point of the novel would be to show that these connections had been broken, but hopefully one would be showing that in this process of disconnection certain things can be reconnected.

4. The Country and the City

The Country and the City *raises a large number of very complex questions, about literature, politics, history. The first perhaps concerns your conception of the status and role of a literary text in society, which seems to have undergone a slow and uneven change since the war. In* Reading and Criticism, *literature is defined as a 'record of human experience'.*[24] *In* Culture and Society, *you refer to it at once as 'a record' and 'a response',*[25] *yet your discussion of the industrial novels of the 19th century indicates an active process at work in the text which the idea of 'record' does not cover. In* The English Novel *you describe literature as a 'dramatization of values' that is 'an action'.*[26] *These successive definitions seem to mark out the tension between two essentially different conceptions. The first, which relates to the tradition to which Leavis belongs, views literature precisely as record-response-expression. The second, emerging through it and sometimes using its vocabulary, is a very different notion of literature in some sense as production. Now one might say that* The Country and the City *brings the tension between these two conceptions to crisis, because in this book for the first time literature is distanced and contrasted against a history that is systematically and separately analysed. Literature is presented as a distinct mode of production of meaning; it is no longer to be described usefully or fruitfully as a record. Some contemporary currents might draw the conclusion that the next step on the agenda would be a general theory of the means of production – in other words of forms. But you have always strongly rejected formalism as such. What would be your reaction to this construction of your work?*

The Country and the City had a very precise starting point: the much discussed problem of how to read the English country-house poems. Its aim was a transvaluation of the literary critical questions that were put to

[24] RC, p. 107.
[25] CS, pp. 99–100.
[26] ENDL, pp.

them. Now the irony was that those literary questions carried with them unusually explicit socio-political assumptions. That is why country-house poetry was so attractive to me as a point of entry. This was a very antagonistic book, that was conceived like *Modern Tragedy* – as a pointed response to a particular literary orthodoxy. For the poems were customarily presented as records of the country houses, and so of the organic rural society England had once been, and so of the pattern of real civilization, later destroyed by capitalism. But as you moved to criticize that, the same people were always prepared to shift their ground and say: 'After all it was only a convention.' I decided that this had to be challenged on two grounds. First, it was necessary to show, very concretely, that country houses like Saxham and Penshurst were not at all like the poems Jonson or Carew wrote about them; but secondly, it was also necessary to understand that their particular way of seeing them, or not seeing them, lay deep in the very forms and conventions of the poetry itself. Now at that point it is possible simply to go on to say, since all literature is a mode of production employing certain conventions, what we must now do is systematize our perceptions of this fact into an overall literary theory. But it would not be my conclusion. To take the kind of formal analysis I develop as just one more entry in a general repertory of means of production would be a totally inadequate response to the poems. Such a formalism would make any attempt at an accurate account of Saxham or Penshurst, about which we happen to have documents as well as poems, vulgar or irrelevant. My project, a very difficult one in which I am not sure I always succeeded, was quite different: it was to try to show simultaneously the literary conventions and the historical relations to which they were a response – to see together the means of the production and the conditions of the means of production. For the conditions of the means of production are quite crucial to any substantial understanding of the means of production themselves. The tendency in some recent criticism on the left has been to exclude these conditions, dismissing any concern with them as historicism or sociologism. Against that, my intention was to dramatize the tension between the houses and the poems, to pose the contrast between the two. The emphasis of the book is certainly not on literary texts as records, but as representations of history – including what I am still realist enough to call misrepresentations. These are not just one neutral convention or another, some of them are interested lies, some of them are ways of seeing which are related not to mendacity but to privilege, some of them are much deeper and less conscious limitations of the vision of an inherited or class position, some of them are partial breakthroughs, others are relatively complete insights. Unless there is a constant awareness of this substantive range as well as of the technical repertory, then a second-hand formalism is in real danger of taking over what begins as a necessary theoretical acknowledgement that literature is a process of production. Any Marxism which fails to remember those means of production, which involve not just techniques but whole social relationships, is bound to be lost when it confronts a poem by Jonson or a novel by Jefferies. I would rather have risked the danger of which I was very aware in the book of simply saying this rural literature is not like the rural history – the naïve realism for which several people have attacked me – then the opposite course of merely writing Some Versions of Pastoral. But I have no doubt that mine was a very particular and fraught procedure. That was why, after writing four chapters, I did no work on it for years. I was frightened of the project when I had to extend it. I have never written a book where I was more surprised by the directions in which it led.

That is a very lucid reply. There is, however, one major problem that remains unresolved in The Country and the City. *You state at the outset: 'The witnesses we have summoned raise questions of historical fact and perspective. The things they are saying are not all in the same mode. They range, as facts, from a speech in a play and a passage in a novel to an argument in an essay and a note in a journal. When the facts are poems, they are also, and perhaps crucially, poems of different kinds. We can only analyse these important structures of feeling if we make, from the beginning, these critical discriminations.'*[27] *In the case of the country-house poems, you in effect call the poems to the bar of historical evidence and convict them of false witness. Thereafter, the same procedure of confrontation between literary form and historical experience is pursued through a large number of writers. In general, there seems to be a progression towards a greater social verity. Particularly perhaps in the prose fiction of the 19th century, real historical conditions transpire rather more clearly through successive texts, although never in a pure state – they are always liable to some significant correction or modification. But what isn't so clear is this: how does your demonstration of the gap between social reality and*

[27] CC, p. 12.

literary figuration affect a strictly aesthetic judgment of the texts? You seem to go alongside of the question in the book, never directly tackling it. But it is posed very acutely by, say, your spectacular demonstration of the destiny of the estate lauded by Marvell in Upon Appleton House. *What it amounts to asking is how great a discrepancy can there be between the vision of a certain rural or urban reality in a poem or novel, and the actual historical facts, for the literary artefact still to be of real aesthetic value? If the distance is very wide, as in the case of Marvell's poem, wherein does this value reside?*

I think there are two stages in the argument, which both seem to me foolproof. The first is that the very process of restoring produced literature to its conditions of production reveals that conventions have social roots, that they are not simply formal devices of writing. The second is that historical identification of a convention is not a mere neutral registration, which is incompatible with judging it. Indeed, so far as literary evaluation proper is concerned, I would say that while there is a not unhelpful mode – I wouldn't put it stronger than that – of distinguishing between good or bad examples within a convention, the crucial evaluative function is the judgment of conventions themselves, from a deliberate and declared position of interest. Now the most sympathetic response to this book I've had from within ordinary English studies is that it was very rash of us critics to take these forms as if they were historically true observations; you have shown that they were not, they were only conventions. The result is a sort of perverse praise which I push off – as if we can say no more than that these conventions existed, they were historically based, to know literary history as part of a wider history is to know them. For there is also a necessary evaluation to be made *of* them. You have to be able to go beyond an understanding that the poems are not records of country-house experience, to the realization that these conventions produced actions and relationships, as well as poems, and as such they stand to be judged. It is not difficult to distinguish between poems by Jonson and by Carew – the former are better written in a perfectly normal sense than the latter. But what is much more important than that distinction is the distinction of the convention: the capacity to see what the form was produced from and was producing. Certain conventions do less than others. If there is still place for evaluation in literature, then that is what has to be valued. This is not the same as saying, although one also says, that the poems are not like history. For a convention could resemble no actual history at all, yet be positively productive by its representation of possible situations. The soundest conventions are not always realist, although this is more often the case than not. Each convention must be assessed by what it is rooted in and what it does: an assessment that is related to a much more general historical judgment that is also an affiliation – not history as all that has happened, but as where oneself is in it.

But by the criterion of productivity, you would surely have to concede that the larger governing convention discussed in the first part of The Country and the City, *in effect pastoral poetry, is a very productive form? Its achievements are undeniably considerable, even confining ourselves just to the poems which you discuss, from Virgil to Crabbe. You couldn't say this is an unproductive convention.*

Well, maybe I used the wrong word when I said productive. I think that one has to distinguish two kinds of judgment, which, however, it is never possible finally to separate. There is the one level at which we can say that a specific form was historically productive and therefore historically valuable – in that sense it was a major contribution to human culture. But we must also be able to say, in a distinct but connected way, that it was a disastrously powerful contribution. In the same way one can acknowledge the productive capacity of bourgeois society, or its political institutions, and yet distance oneself from them as creations which not only later become, but in an important sense in the very mode of their constitution always were, blocks on human freedom or even human progress. The power of an achievement is not a self-sufficient value. If you cannot make the first judgment, then all history becomes a current morality, and there ceases to be any history. If you cannot make the second, I do not know what an affiliation to the working class would be for me. Jonson had to find a patron and in order to find a patron had to pay that kind of compliment in that kind of house: such was the nature of the convention. But if I cannot be seriously offended that in his poem he wrote out the labourer, what affiliation can I now make to labourers? Of course, if you get to the second judgment without the first, the result becomes naïveté: you will not understand enough history to be able to locate yourself in it or be morally offended by any part of it. On the other hand, if you don't feel offence at this profoundly conventional mystification, in the strictest sense, then what is the meaning of solidarity?

Every socialist should share that position. But one wonders whether, as you put it, you've altogether maintained the balance in The Country and the City. *Let us take a directly relevant example – your memorable account of the genesis and character of feudalism in England, from the Dark Ages through the mediaeval period. You write: 'From inside and outside there was this remorseless moving-in of the armed gangs, with their titles of importance, their kingships and their baronies, to feed from other men's harvests. The armed gangs became social and natural orders, blessed by their gods and their churches, with at the bottom of the pyramid, over a tale of centuries, the working cultivator, the human and natural man – sometimes finding a living space, a settled working area; as often deprived of it – but in any case breaking the land and himself to support this rising social estate, which can be seen to culminate in the mediaeval "order" of the Norman and then the English kings: a more complete because more organized and more extended exploitation. . . . There is only one real question. Where do we stand, with whom do we identify, as we read the complaints of disturbance, as this order in its turn broke up? Is it with the serfs, the bordars and cotters, the villeins; or with the abstracted order to which, through successive generations, many hundreds of thousands of men were never more than instrumental?'[28] That passage, like so many in the book, is a very moving one. Yet, although it commands an immediate assent, on reflection it also arouses a real disquiet. For you say there is only one question. But surely your answer just now is a reminder that there are usually more than one? In this case, it is obvious that there is another question. What your account omits is the increase of population, the improvement of rural productivity, the growth of towns, the whole cultural development of European feudal civilization. You speak of mediaeval churches just as burdens on the poor on whose labour they rested; yet they also clearly represent architectural monuments we can admire to this day. In passages like these, history seen as a conflict of sides, in which the central question is where one stands, appears not just to balance but to eclipse history seen as a cumulative development of forces of production and division of labour, which in and through the very forms of social stratification and exploitation has been responsible for the growth of real human gains. The same problem does seem to arise with the country houses.*

It's a long-standing problem. Actually the phrase 'the only real question is where do we stand' is referred to a specific context: 'when we read

[28] CC, p. 38.

complaints about the break-up of the feudal order'. For most literary accounts of English history induce a curious foreshortening, in which there is a rather vague invocation of the Middle Ages and then the story starts with what is presented as the deplorable disintegration of a venerable cultural order. The force of my polemic is really aimed against that complacent image, which certainly does raise the question of where you locate yourself. More generally, I agree with the perfectly correct Marxist description of the historical contribution of feudalism to civilization, or of the accomplishments of capitalism. But the classical view that these orders make their contribution to civilization, which we must respect and honour, then simply exhaust themselves and are replaced by higher orders, has always left me extremely uneasy, just because the pull of some of these contributions is still so strong on me. I am very powerfully moved by the early churches, by the great cathedrals, and yet if I don't see the enormous weight of them on man, I don't altogether know how to be a socialist in the area where I work. If I were a manual worker this would not be the same sort of problem. But to me it is a problem: I feel that weight, as I feel the weight of those country houses. Who has not admired the admirable architecture or furniture to be found among them? But if we acknowledge them as a contribution, we must also at the same time acknowledge them as an obstacle. The nature of their power does not necessarily end, in the tidy way that the simplest kind of Marxism suggests, with its epoch. The cathedrals are not just monuments to faith, the country houses are not just buildings of elegance. They are constantly presented to us as 'our heritage', inducing a particular way of seeing and relating to the world, which must be critically registered along with our acknowledgement of their value. I always see them as profoundly ambivalent. But, of course, if we did not acknowledge their contribution, we would be regressing to an identification with the simple cultivator before the advent of any civilization at all, which would be absurd.

We are in total sympathy with that statement. Again, however, the problem is whether you keep to it entirely in the book. You've persuasively defended your passage on feudalism as a polemical riposte to the prevalent sentimentalization of mediaeval society to be found in literary studies, associated with Eliot or Leavis. But on the previous page, you seem to make a direct attack on historical materialism as such. You write: 'It has been commonplace since Marx to speak, in some contexts, of the progressive character of capitalism, and within it of urbanism and of social modernization. The great indictments of capitalism, and of its long record of misery in factories and towns, have co-existed, within a certain historical scheme, with this repeated use of "progressive" as a willing adjective about the same events. We hear again and again this brisk, impatient and as it is said realistic response: to the productive efficiency, the newly liberated forces, of the capitalist breakthrough; a simultaneous damnation and idealisation of capitalism, in its specific forms of urban and industrial development; an unreflecting celebration of mastery – power, yield, production, man's mastery of nature – as if the exploitation of natural resources could be separated off from the accompanying exploitation of men. What they say is damn this, praise this; and the intellectual formula for this emotional confusion is, hopefully, the dialectic.'[29] Why is this a confusion? What formula would you advocate? The rhetorical use of epithets like 'brisk' or 'impatient' surely caricatures what is in effect the only responsible attitude to the past. Marx and Engels never wrote paeans of praise to the early ironmasters of the industrial revolution; what they did refuse to make was a purely moral-political condemnation of them, because such an attitude renders it impossible to understand the whole movement of history. The Marxist tradition does insist that capitalism, feudalism, or slavery in the ancient world, all represented massive structures of class oppression and exploitation, yet that each was also empirically related to forms of greater human emancipation. Were you really rejecting that?

No. Let me give you an example where I have taken precisely that position, and been attacked for it on the left. I have emphasized that the achievement of the bourgeoisie in the creation of the modern press was a major historical break-through. I have no hesitation at all about declaring that. The advent of the bourgeois newspapers was an absolute historical progress, which one must acknowledge even as an absolute opponent of the contemporary bourgeois press. I don't find any difficulty in making that kind of judgment. I wouldn't see it as reasonable to criticize the late 18th- or early 19th-century press in England because it was bourgeois.

Well, to take your criterion for Jonson, it didn't exactly report the life of the working class.

[29] CC, p. 37.

I wouldn't limit the judgment to that. The emergence of this press was progressive. I quote it precisely to show that I am wholly in sympathy with reasonable uses of damn this/praise this. For by the mid-19th century the bourgeois press was consciously attempting to squeeze out, buy out, outsell, outcapitalize the popular radical press. By then, even if it was expanding certain areas of bourgeois liberty, it was a negative force. In other words, I think there is a scientific mode of attention in which damn this/praise this is right, but there is a mode of conventional inattention where it is profoundly wrong. That inattention is often related to a confidence that was very typical of the Communist parties when I was young, that you could damn-and-praise at will because you knew what the next epoch of human history held in store. A contemporary example is the way a few people on the left still welcome the development of multinational companies on the grounds that the further growth of monopoly merely facilitates a take-over by socialism.

This is a very important qualification. It is quite true that in the present we do not know exactly what direction history is going to take, so that we cannot readily label certain phenomena as progressive developments that have to be accepted or otherwise, without presumption. But in the past we do have a yardstick; we do not have to be agnostic about, say, historical processes between the 14th and 17th centuries. We can seek to trace out their complex of effects for the evolution of European society. There is, of course, a very coherent and completely alternative view to this classical Marxist position – first tentatively expressed by Benjamin and then systematically codified by Adorno and Horkheimer in Dialectic of Enlightenment. *It insists that the primary reality which cancels every other is always the actual human suffering of every epoch: the whole of history can be reduced to the constant replication of new forms of exploitation – all progress is regression. Do you feel any affinity with this Frankfurt position?*

No. I entirely accept the practice of distinguishing the positive and negative effects, the achievements and the failures of any social order, and of historically tracing the processes whereby positives become negatives over time, as one order is threatened or succeeded by another – a practice that is best represented by Marxism, more than by any other system of historical analysis. But the practice can degenerate into what I have precisely called a formula. At that point it becomes an obstacle. Take the example of the famous slogan of the mastery of nature. Of course anyone who views history in a materialist way must see the processes of understanding and working within nature as the central founding element of any civilization. But to describe these as *mastery* was to treat nature as if it was just material to dominate: a transposition of bourgeois ideology into Marxism, with which it cannot be reconciled. Marx's innocent use of the phrase, or of the terms 'produce' or 'productive', is comprehensible in his time. But its unthinking repetition today, when we have reason to be aware of the consequences of the formula, is really inexcusable. The anger it arouses in me comes out in the book, both for personal autobiographical reasons and for contemporary cultural reasons. For the values of the rural capitalist order which first imposed the notion of mastery are now being presented as the height of civilization. Now it is true that the bourgeois country houses and furniture have not ceased to be valuable in the sense that some of them are beautifully made. But at the ideological locus where this connects with a reactionary affiliation today, I found it necessary to say in the crudest way that these houses were primarily sites of exploitation and robbery and fraud. If anything, the fact that some of them were well-built and are pleasant to look at makes that worse. But so far as the Frankfurt conception of human history as the recurrence of an unending exploitation is concerned, the whole argument of *The Country and the City* is that successive forms of class society are intrinsically different. The brutal physical subjection of the mediaeval order in the passage you quoted is an altogether dissimilar kind of exploitation from that of the commercial tenant or agricultural labourer under capitalism. I am not at all tempted by the notion of social history as permanent misery or suffering, which is in effect a transposed version of the religious conception of fallen man. My position also differs from Sartre's use of the category of scarcity, at least in one of its versions, for ironically it was during a period of major advance in rural productivity that certain kinds of poverty markedly increased in 18th-century England. I have always thought this was the central Marxist teaching – that a social system can produce a liberation of productive forces, which at the same time involve new and durable forms of exploitation.

These are significant clarifications of your argument in The Country and the City. *For one criticism that can be made of the book is that, by writing in a very general way of Marxism, you create an amalgam between Marx and Engels themselves and those later socialists who really were brisk and impatient – indeed often callow and cynical – in their attitude towards the past. There are passages in the writings of Marx or Engels which are subject to your objections, but their work as a whole cannot responsibly be reduced to these.*

Sure. I readily agree that the ideas I was attacking must be separated from classical Marxism, except for a few incidental phrases which give a certain warrant to them. They should also be separated from an effective Marxism today, because I don't find this way of thinking in contemporary Marxist writing of any consequence. But I do think I was dissociating myself from something that has been a quite real and very damaging tradition in the socialist movement, which gave people reasons for hating capitalism that actually took them into it. For it was possible from this version of capitalism as progress, identified with industry and towns, to see the socialist future as the victory of towns and industry over villages and the land. The result was a complete dilution of the complexity of Marxist thinking on the relations between town and country. Engels' fundamental thesis that the opposition between the two was a form of division of labour which would have to be overcome if there were to be socialism was forgotten. Soviet society was presented as socialist, merely because it was becoming urbanized and industrialized in the thirties. The irony of the situation after '45 was the emergence of a quite alternative movement, in China and then in Indochina – with which I felt in total sympathy.

Here we are moving to the other side of your whole argument in The Country and the City. *The book is a sustained polemic against false attempts to idealize and recuperate the values of a ruling-class agrarian order of the past, whether feudal or capitalist. But at the same time it is also a major plea for the continuity and relevance of real values of rural life and labour, created by the direct producers themselves, for the socialism of an increasingly industrialized world today. It might be argued with greater force that Marx and Engels had too linear a conception of historical development to be able easily to imagine this possibility. They were aware that many achievements of the past could be cancelled for a time, but nevertheless re-emerge as potent values and experiences in a more emancipated future: Greek democracy was in many ways in advance of bourgeois democracy, Roman law in advance of mediaeval law. Their conception of history was never one in which at any given moment of historical time the whole of the saved past was encapsulated in the present. But it is true that their work on the whole lacks the idea of a* continuing *tradition of values from the past that informs the struggles of the present. The values of pre-capitalist classes – whether an aristocracy, an artisanate or a peasantry – are discerned and respected in the past: but they are not usually seen as capable of constant effect in the present. Would it be correct to read your argument as in part a criticism of the assumption that the working class could find entirely within capitalist relations of exploitation themselves the necessary strength to overthrow capitalism, as if the severing of that class from its own rural past was not a very damaging blow to its powers of resistance – its capacity to imagine an alternative social order?*

Yes. But the background to my concern is not a quarrel with classical Marxism, it is a conflict with a tendency in socialism which has found its main institutional embodiment in the Labour Party, and its ideological aim in a successful industrial capitalism without the capitalists. That goal will, of course, never be achieved. But the pressure towards it involves the perpetuation of exploitation and privilege, internationally and nationally. In Wales I have friends and neighbours who are being forced out by a whole alliance of forces, from large-scale capital to the left of the Labour Party, because they are 'antique' – meaning they are food-producers. Even a Keynesian economist could tell me – ironically in a country pub, since it is part of the ideology that the country is where you go on Sunday – that 'the sheep is an uneconomical animal' and that the sooner the sheep farmers of Wales give up or get engrossed the better; leaving those hills, presumably as an empty recreation area, for the discovery of nature. When I hear that kind of final economic universalism, I not only feel anger, because I have neighbours who are raising sheep and who are doing a sight more than most economists to contribute to society, but because within the existing bureaucratic system 'advisers' could have more say in the future of hill sheep farming than any hill sheep farmer. I am not sure that every socialist would come out with me in declaring that this is an appalling situation. There's been an extraordinary acquiescence and drift towards the sort of brisk progressivism that talks of rationalizing archaic production when as a matter of fact there is nothing archaic about it. In *The Country and the City*, I had to attack the version of the mastery of nature, represented by urbanism and industrialism counterposed to rural living, as sheer historical error, not only outdated by the pattern of socialist revolutions, but incompatible with any materialist assessment of the contemporary world economy. Having got used to hearing from everyone that rural values belong to the past because that phase of civilization is superseded today, I suddenly saw that what had really happened was that food production had been displaced within the imperialist system, that there was still an acute crisis in agriculture, however improved by urban or metropolitan science, that this was still a crisis of land and labour. But the counterpoint in the book is, of course, the liberating and enlightening character of the modern city – where the first institutions and directions of socialism were found. Some of my strongest emphasis goes to the values, the positive contribution, of the city.

At this point it seems appropriate to re-gather some of the strands of the discussion up to now, and set out a more general response to your book. The first thing to be stated, which we haven't said because we started by exploring specifically literary problems, is that The Country and the City *is a profoundly original and important book politically, which in a real sense represents a progression beyond the characteristic problematic of classical Marxism. It breaks through to what are in substance wholly new areas of debate: the work addresses itself, in effect, to problems which have never been thought out in a deep way within Marxism, although there are phrases and allusions to it within the classics. Anybody who believes that the last word on any important topic is to be found within either the classical or post-classical tradition of Marxism should be given* The Country and the City *to read, to convince them that it is simply not so. There are many important things that remain to be said against and beyond the heritage of historical materialism to date.*

Yet at the same time did you not do yourself a disservice by down-playing in a curious way the extent to which this book is a very powerful, even polemical, corrective to a main tradition of revolutionary socialism? For Marxism as such really appears only twice in the book: first in the early passage we've quoted, where you speak of metropolitan socialists being infected by the long tradition of exploiter contempt for the rural producer, and second at the very end, when you speak briefly of Soviet experience, agrarian revolutions in the under-developed world and Engels's perspective of the abolition of the division between town and country. Wouldn't it have been much better to have given Marx and Engels, or Trotsky to whom you also refer once, the direct and detailed textual treatment that you accord to even quite minor English poets? Your rectification of classical Marxism is surely sufficiently central to the book to have demanded a properly extended engagement with it. Wouldn't that have avoided too the danger of collapsing separate issues and thinkers together in a few paragraphs?

The peremptory way in which I mention Marx and Engels is very significant of my particular biographical trajectory. It should be clear by now that I had such a curious entry into a Marxist culture, at a very specific time with specific difficulties and limitations, and with very complicated circumstances interfering with its continuation, that it is only quite recently that I have thought, when I sit down to work on a problem, that I must relate what I am writing in a sustained way to what Marx and Engels or certain other classical Marxist thinkers had to say on the problem. If you look at the implied relationships of nearly all the books I have written, I have been arguing with what I take to be official English culture. I have done that in different ways in different phases, but always the people in my sights, whether to agree or disagree with, have been this other tradition. Now I don't altogether apologize for this. For that kind of attention still seems to me an absolute necessity for contemporary Marxists, working in a specific national culture. But it did mean – I notice it so clearly looking back – that when I referred to this or that Marxist position, sometimes fairly and sometimes unfairly, sometimes adequately and sometimes inadequately, I was talking about the people and ideas I first focussed as Marxism when I was a student. That specific kind of Marxist milieu, which among other things did dismiss rural life, no longer exists today. It was a deficiency of my own generation that the amount of classical Marxism it actually knew was relatively small; it was also, as it happened, selected from what to me are now often the least important parts of the tradition. This is no excuse, but it is an explanation. The modifications in the intellectual milieu in England over the last ten years have been of decisive importance to me. For now I wouldn't want to write on any question without tracing the history of it in Marxist thought and then seeing where I stood in relation to that. A very fundamental shift of direction has occurred in the people whom I am thinking about when I write. Critics see it as a change of opinion, and of course there have been changes of opinion, but I see it much more importantly as a change of address. One really can't overestimate the degree of change there has been in this. In the introduction to *Marxism and Literature* I have tried to convey my new sense of what the body of thought of Marxism was when I was able to read it much more extensively; I discovered, of course, that there were areas of formed argument which I hadn't previously encountered, which meant that I found that there were certain positions which I ought to have been directly meeting, but had not met.

However, having said this, it is an amusing footnote to notice the positive relief with which some of my students said – at last he's talking about Marxism directly, he's got over his hang-ups and become a real person. It was known that you had lived once, but now there was a sign you were still alive. But, of course, there is a danger in this. I do see the need for the endeavour, with which NLR is most centrally associated, to get into currency, to expand, to revalue the Marxist tradition. What has been done in this respect is an unalterable achievement. It means that even someone of my generation has now got a whole additional intellectual world to address himself to: it is a condition for much more important work to emerge. The negative side of this development, however, which I notice very much in literary circles at present, is that people on the left tend no longer to intervene with the audience, or against the thinking, that I was intervening with and against. In a sense the very power of the expanded Marxist tradition can supply a reason for renouncing what still seems to me the necessary engagement with the established English culture. Why do I discuss a minor 18th-century poet in more detail than I do Marx? Because this is where a really reactionary social consciousness is being continually reproduced, and to till your own alternative garden to it is not enough. In fact, it would be a trap for me. There would be a good many people in English cultural circles who would be delighted if I spent the rest of my time clearing up some questions of Marxist literary theory. I don't propose to give them the satisfaction.

Right. There is a kind of attachment that is made to a Marxist culture in university circles today, which produces such a concentration of attention within it, that virtually everything within bourgeois culture is dismissed or ignored – mostly not read. Since Marxism represents the superior and scientific way forward, other thought is regarded as by definition derisory or insignificant. Your work has always been produced against this facile triumphalism. In one sense you couldn't have written the books you have written if you had been a one hundred per cent convinced Marxist – if you'd stayed within the tradition.

Starting now, however, the tradition would look different.

Yes, but your criticism of the tendency of Marx and Engels towards an unqualified celebration of the mastery of nature, for example, is much more effective and materialist than anything comparable within post-classical Marxism, where the same theme can be found in the Frankfurt tradition in more spiritualized form. It allows your political demonstration that the problems of agriculture and of the countryside on a world scale remain as important today as they ever have been in the past, and will probably remain in any foreseeable future – while the Frankfurt critique was typically arrested at a philosophical speculation. There is, however, one important reservation we would like to enter about your account, not so much of the relationship of Marx and Engels towards nature, as towards rural society. You quote the famous remark in the Manifesto *on 'the idiocy of rural life', which you describe rather mildly as a 'settling archival phrase'*[30] *– one feels that in some moods you could have mustered much stronger language for it, given the kind of evidence you marshal in* The Country and the City. *To read that phrase, which is not an isolated but a recurrent usage by Marx, in the context of your book is a salutary shock. But on reflection, there is a textual question which your glancing treatment of historical materialism avoids. It is this. What does the phrase actually refer to – what did Marx and Engels really have in mind? It seems probable that they were thinking of traditional peasant communities in Europe, socially and economically backward, characteristically dominated by archaic forms of religion – a peasantry still in the grip of feudal forms of exploitation. Within the village communities, there was often a very stark oppression of women and children, as many anthropological studies testify. Within the wider society, exploited peasantries again and again played an ironically conservative role under the banner of clerical or national reaction. The pattern of counter-revolutionary mobilization of peasant populations would always have been very present to Marx and Engels. The Vendée of 1794 in France, the stifling of the Parthenopean Republic by the Sanfedista crusade of the Neapolitan peasantry in 1799, the Tyrolese jacquerie against Napoleonic rule in 1804 were all recent episodes in European memory. In the revolutions of 1848 themselves, the formative political experience of Marx and Engels, the Galician peasantry was manipulated by Habsburg Absolutism for*

[30] CC, p. 36.

the suppression of the Polish revolt, while the Second Empire was built on the votes of the French peasantry. None of this excuses or justifies the term 'rural idiocy' itself. But it does indicate that when Marx or Engels were writing about the countryside, they were thinking of a rural landscape which in certain important ways was very different from the English scene that is the object of your work. For because of the extraordinarily early implantation of the capitalist mode of production in English agriculture, with its triad system of landlord-farmer-labourer, there really was no peasantry in the continental sense in Britain by the late 18th century. In fact, one of the most salutary effects of The Country and the City *is precisely to do away with the myth of the English peasantry, and to show the very specific complications and changes of the rural social order from at least the 16th century onwards. The kind of social reality which Marx would have had in mind was not familiar in English history. Your study, on the other hand, despite its general title, concerns England, whose countryside was in many ways untypical of European experience. Couldn't that contrast be urged in mitigation of Marx's phraseology?*

I should say that when I read the phrase 'rural idiocy', it stuck in my throat: yet I knew instantly what they were referring to even within this very different British rural experience. I can remember a time when I had felt like using the same phrase myself. The persistence of certain established mystifications, superstitions, deferences or political abdications, the lack of exposure to the liberating community of other kinds of settlement – when I was moving out of the countryside, I knew very strongly what these meant. But it still seems to me that Marx and Engels should not have used that phrase, because what they were pointing to was a process of deprivation – of ignorance and illiteracy. They were also aware of that very important process by which the exploited pass on their exploitation between men and women and children, the way in which a man who has been brutalized by very hard conditions of work, which exhaust him physically, can nervously reproduce that brutality in his family. But they should have described these as what they were: the products of social deprivation and exploitation, whereas they picked up the term idiocy as a conventional form of court dismissal of the country.

So far as the political question is concerned, I also of course considered this. I would have been glad to have made it clearer that not only in the classical cases of the past but even today in our own politics the rural areas are reservoirs of certain kinds of reaction – I've grown up in one and am very well aware of this. Again, however, the phenomenon has nothing to do with idiocy. It is partly related to the very complex politics of urban socialism that rural areas often know they have quite substantial material reasons to be against it, quite apart from the persistence of gentry influence. But of course well before the advent of socialism, one can go through history and match the cases where the peasantry has been a progressive force in revolt against an oppressive system, with cases where it has been mobilized or even sometimes intervened on the side of reaction. All that would prevent any mere reversal of the archival phrase. But one would then also have to include in a historical perspective the process I think Marx and Engels were already in a position to observe, and Engels most notably did observe, by which the specific kinds of phenomena they generalized as idiocy have been bred in a particular type of alternative suffering – what deprivation and exploitation have done to people in the city. If one invokes the classical cases of superstition and mystification among the rural peasantry, one must also remember the characteristic variants of urban and suburban idiocy, which are really quite marked. It is by no means the case that irrationalism in the 20th century has flourished in villages and been cleared by the pure light of reason from the suburbs or the towns. Indeed it might even be said that the most prolific generator of modern irrationalism is now a certain kind of urban agglomeration. No Marxist now has any warrant in historical experience for seeing rural settlement or rural labour as tied in any sense to idiocy, or even some much softer term. This is not the way to look at the problem: the right way is through the Marxist categories of deprivation and exploitation.

Entirely so. However, there remains one point of potential divergence between us. You say that in the 20th century cities have witnessed forms of manipulated irrationality and ignorance perhaps even on a greater scale than the countryside. That is true, but it remains too asocial and general a statement. For while there were many agrarian revolts in the 19th century, but also many counter-revolutionary mobilizations of peasant populations, there have historically never been any major counter-revolutionary mobilizations of an urban working-class population: either in the 19th century or in the 20th century. This fundamental difference can be obscured if we speak just of urban and suburban forms of political dementia. For these have classically been outbreaks of the petty-bourgeoisie, the bourgeoisie or the permanently unemployed. No organized working class has ever been swept into such movements. In Weimar Germany, the major Nazi vote actually came from peasant regions, although the NSDAP itself was essentially recruited from the petty-bourgeoisie and financed by the big bourgeoisie. The German working class voted Communist and Social-Democrat solidly to the end. In Italy the fascist movement originated in the rural areas of Emilia and Romagna, and never acquired any grip on the urban proletariat. This is not to idealize the modern history of the working class. After the Nazi counter-revolution, it did generally rally to the German war effort; many American workers supported the imperialist war in Vietnam. But the urban proletariat has been relatively more exempt than any other social class from mass political irrationalism in this century. That negative fact is linked to its positive historical potential. You have demonstrated, valuably and permanently, that there is an underestimation in Marxism of the future role and importance in human life of the countryside. It nevertheless remains true that the necessary social agency that alone can lead the way to a democratic socialism must be the industrial working class rather than any rural population. This is a separate issue, which does not at all mean that such a socialism will be a kind of pan-industrial order. It means simply that the agency of revolutionary change must be located primarily within the towns. In that sense there is an element of ambiguity or unclarity in your final chapter, where you speak of the socialist revolutions that have been made – Russia forms a very significant exception – in peasant societies, and where the main popular force in the overthrow of the old regime has been the rural populations. For these societies have not produced a democratic socialist order, and their lack of democracy is demonstrably related to the fact that they lack the mature conditions of modern industry: all the cultural and social skills that go to the creation of the collective worker, who is capable of technically dominating advanced means of production and thereby preparing for a free self-administration of society, in which the apparatus of a centralized state withers away. That kind of self-government can never be achieved in one jump from an agrarian economy. Any revolution initially based on a peasantry has to pass through a proletarianization to create the conditions for a democratic socialism thereafter.

It's good to put that so emphatically. I think I do say something like that in the book, where I am writing of the growth of the socialist movement in London: 'Out of the very chaos and misery of the new metropolis, and spreading from it to rejuvenate a national feeling, a civilizing force of a new vision of society had been created in struggle, had gathered up the suffering and the hopes of generations of the oppressed and exploited, and in this unexpected and challenging form was the human reply of the city to the long inhumanity of country and city alike.'[31] Certainly one cannot look realistically anywhere else but to the industrial working class for a socialist transformation of our societies today. But at the same time, it's been too easily assumed, against accumulating evidence, that the relations of the working class with rural producers are unproblematic. In my view, the industrial working class is going to have to rethink, radically and painfully, its relations with the producers of raw materials as well as of food, and thus enlarge the customarily foreshortened vision which passes for a socialist future. It is in danger of becoming at times, because of its position as consumer, objectively hostile to these producers. You can hear ludicrous complaints today, including from organized working-class opinion, that potatoes cost more in a drought year than in a wet year. The habit of disregarding the production of raw materials, as if their existence went without saying, leads to the notion that the only real work and real human activity is the second-order working on these materials and their transformation. The recent disputes over Welsh water and Birmingham supply are characteristic of the extreme impatience with which even a very militant working class receives rural protestations against the implantation of reservoirs that deprive people of their land, while piping water in such a way that those living literally below the dam cannot get the supply which is flowing across the country to Birmingham. Conflicts like these reveal a loss of real relations dangerously similar to that of a petty-bourgeoisie or bourgeoisie which thinks it is the only important and responsible productive force in society, simply forgetting where the means of its life comes from. Once such an opposition of interests springs up, it can be exploited at either end by right-wing politicians. A lot of the mobilization of rural opinion for reactionary policies draws on resentment at what I would call – since the phrase has got around – an urban idiocy: the idea that food grows in shops. The same problem is even more acute in international politics, where one can by no means rule out the industrial working class in a late capitalist country becoming quite objectively reactionary in its position towards a raw material producer country which is not its own, supporting all kinds of imperialist pressures to drive down

[31] CC, p. 231.

the costs of primary products. I think this is going to become a major question in the rest of this century, because to an extent one couldn't have foreseen in the fifties, when the imperialist order still held with more force, food and raw materials are really now at the centre of the world economic crisis. Naturally, I don't want the concern I have developed in the book to tip over into an abandonment of socialism for an unpolitical ecologism or ruralism – that wasn't my intention at all. The perspective I think necessary is a renegotiation of the relations between the labouring class that works on received raw materials and maintains itself on received food, and the labouring class still at a much lower level of political and organizational development which produces the raw materials and the food – nationally and internationally. The recent programme of the Italian Communist Party is one of the few in the West which takes up this issue – criticizing the concentration on industrial investment for the export market at the expense of agricultural development in Italy. All over the Mezzogiorno you can see derelict factory sites, where speculators have collected the rake-off from state-financed construction and then abandoned them: it never occurred to the planners that investment might have been preferable in rural productive labour. Meanwhile Italy has become a net food importer. The opposition of the Italian Communists to this whole direction of development is a welcome sign of rethinking among Marxists of the relations between the country and the city, as the types of transport and communications technology which produced these two kinds of contrasted settlement are already changing.

Well, when all is said and done, one should not forget that Engels was full of praise for the Norwegian peasant farmers. Marx too, after all, thought so highly of the Russian village communes that he argued they were capable of a direct growth into socialism. Modern research on the immediate post-revolutionary years in Russia tends to uphold him. Despite the mistakes we've discussed, there are plenty of positive evaluations of the countryside in the classics of historical materialism.

Marx's very first article on politics was about picking up wood in Rhenish forests. You can't get more basic than that.

5. Marxism and Literature

Marxism and Literature *was published in the form of an introductory text. Yet much of it is quite difficult theoretically, and seems to represent a new direction in your work. How did you conceive the character of the book?*

The conditions of publication in a series imposed a very rigid limit of length – some 60,000 words. I wouldn't have chosen to write it in other than its existing form, but of course certain chapters are very compressed. My aim was not to write a general introduction; it was rather to try to bring out certain of the changes in my own thinking over the past fifteen years or so. I hadn't written anything theoretical, apart from two articles, since the first part of *The Long Revolution*. This was an opportunity to set out my present positions. At times I was consciously arguing against previous ideas I had held. Much of the new emphasis was sharpened up by work on language in the years immediately before writing the book – which came out of discussions with people I'm close to about structuralist theories of language, which at that time were the dominant Marxist current in literary studies and I suppose to an extent still are. The book was originally based on lectures which started in Cambridge about 1970. But it's very significant that in those lectures there was nothing on the theory of language, whereas now it is the longest section of the book, and I would say the most pivotal. I don't think any of the rest can be sustained unless that position is seen as its basis. There particularly I felt the limitations of length, because by then I could have written a whole book on that subject alone.

There is a very striking change of overall stance in the book. We have taxed you with bending over backwards in Culture and Society *to make concessions towards very conservative figures, in a kind of political displacement to the right.* Marxism and Literature, *on the other hand, appears at times to veer towards a radicalism of the ultra-left. For one theme of the work is a frontal assault on the very idea of literature as such. In effect, you denounce it as an elitist elevation of certain forms of writing to a special status – the 'literary', a category which you say possesses the same kind of reactionary spell today as that of the 'divine' in feudal society. Now this line of argument provokes a number of resistances. One is certainly that while you seek to sweep away the concept of literature, you want to preserve the idea of culture. Yet culture, as we pointed out earlier, is genuinely vulnerable to charges of ambiguity and redundancy – what does it connote that 'society' or 'art' do not? – in a much more obvious way. Even so, there are good reasons for retaining it in a materialist vocabulary.* A fortiori *there seem to be many for keeping some notion of literature. Your fundamental argument seems to be that there exists a complete continuum of creative practices of communication. Therefore, since all forms of writing are by definition creative, it is reactionary and exclusivist to privilege some as literary, thereby tacitly or explicitly devaluing others. But why is it necessary to attach such connotations of privilege and repression to the concept of literature as a specialized category of writing? Specialization is not necessarily domination. Why is the traditional criterion of aesthetic function inadequate to delimit the field of the literary? Doesn't your current position, if it were strictly maintained, lead to a complete relativism in which it becomes effectively impossible to discriminate between different forms of writing or types of work at all?*

Well this is difficult. What I would hope will happen is that after the ground has been cleared of the received idea of literature, it will be possible to find certain new concepts which would allow for special emphases. Otherwise there is obviously a danger of relativism or miscellaneity, of which I am very conscious. That will have to be done – it will be a necessary stage. Even with the category of the aesthetic, I say it is wholly necessary to reject the notion of aesthetics as the special province of a certain kind of response, but we cannot rule out the possibility of discovering certain permanent configurations of a theoretical kind which answer to it – as we certainly don't rule out conjunctural configurations of a historical kind in which the category effectively obtained. In the case of literature, it was a movement of insight and surprise to discover the historical shift in the meaning of the term. There would be absolutely no need to reject the concept of literature – at least in this way – if it still meant what it did in the 18th century: a group of written works of a certain level of seriousness, capable of sustaining an attention that others could not. But from the 19th century onwards, the definition of literature has rested on an ever firmer separation between imagination and reality, fiction and fact, writing to create an artistic whole and writing in all its other functions. This increasing specialization had two effects. First, the forms of writing which were described as creative or artistic or imaginative were secluded from the kinds of correlation with social reality which in principle were always there – they were constituted as a reserved area. Secondly, all kinds of writing which didn't possess this label offered themselves as writing the real in ways which prevented any examination of their processes of production and composition, which were actually quite cognate with the processes of composition inside the reserved area which was called literary. In fact, it may be as important to establish the existence of a convention – one might even still like to call it a literary convention – within a scientific paper, as it is to trace a convention in a work which has been singled out as literary. Our own time is a bad one for literature in the traditional sense. There is an extreme confidence in other kinds of writing, as against those forms we have been accustomed to call literary. I am well aware that in attacking the concept of literature, there is a danger of demoralizing the situation even further. The reason my attack was nevertheless so radical was that I had decided, from within the tradition of literary criticism itself, that its categories of literature and of criticism were so deeply compromised that they had to be challenged *in toto*. It was necessary to show that all kinds of writing produce meaning and value – to use that shorthand again – by modes of composition and deep conventions of stance or focus. The mistaken assumptions which lie hidden in the old concepts have to be cleared away for us to be able to begin searching again for a more tenable set of emphases within the range of writing practices – I agree that you could not go on with an undifferentiated range. On the other hand it seems to me that from now on we have to accept it as a true range, without any categorical division between what is done on one side of a line and what is done on the other.

Granting that a polemical clearing of the ground was needed, your argument still seems to yield an unnecessary amount of space to the danger of relativism. Taking your example of a scientific paper, what becomes of the status of the discourses on society and nature which are customarily known as scientific within your continuum of writing? Is it possible, in your radically historicized conception of cultural production, which presumably includes the natural

sciences, any longer to speak of truth – which surely is the minimum basis of any conception of scientificity?

There are vast questions here. The first thing to be said is that it is crucial to remember, as the modes of natural science are extended to social science and to cultural analysis, that scientific writing involves literary conventions. The key convention is the stance of the wholly impersonal observer: it would be worth demonstrating the way in which this character is created by a mode of composition which is so to speak an authentication of the impersonality of the observer. Now I am extremely sympathetic – probably more than most people on the left – to a lot of work being done in the natural sciences, which I try to follow. Talking with scientists about it, I find that they regard the transition from experimental observation, for which they know they are trained, to written report,where they are entering an uncertain field, as very problematic. They are more sceptical of the activities of composition than people who are not professionally involved in the transformation of experimental observations, which could be said to be true, into reports which raise other questions. They are less likely to make the mistake of simply extrapolating via paper reports back to laboratory findings. The distinction becomes absolutely crucial when the mode of impersonal observation is extended to the social sciences or cultural life. Now I certainly have no indulgence for the tendency in semiotics to claim that since it is all written, all you can say is that it is written. The result of this kind of developed structuralism is an idealism in which everything dissolves. There is a discoverable and controllable relationship between a scientific paper and an experimental observation. Indeed a lot of scientific work is a very scrupulous reworking back from a piece of writing to experimental observation, as a condition of the scientific method itself. In that sense a scientific text is extraordinarily open as a piece of writing: the data are not exhausted by the fact of composition, an experimental replication is possible, you are never in a situation where there is no appeal beyond the literary composition. A good example in the social sciences is the re-examination by Bourdieu and his colleagues of the statistical data on which certain educational theories about the equalization of opportunity in France were built. They went back from that right through the data and by identifying modes of interpretation in this case, rather than forms of composition itself, were able to show the ideological transitions from the data to the writing and then to the theory – transitions which could be corrected, to produce a different account from the same data. The process of the creation of significance, the creation of meaning and value, is in effect inherent in the act of composition and communication itself.

Now, while it is essential to break down the dualism between literary and non-literary, imaginative versus factual, modes of writing, there clearly is a difference between modes of composition which report on activities that are prepared elsewhere and are recoverable in recurrent forms, and modes of composition at the other end of the spectrum where these conditions do not hold – for example, poems. But you can in the same way, and this is the emphasis I would now want to put, properly return a poem to the conditions of *its* production. This, while it is a quite different process from enquiries at the other end of the spectrum of writing, is the activity which in my view will replace criticism. Naturally, it will integrate some of its procedures – for example, the practice of close verbal analysis, the study of narrative methods or of types of imagery, should of course be retained. But it would move out from the critical analysis we are used to, through what is properly literary historical analysis of technical devices, rhetorical figures or doctrinal influences, for which there is an enormous amount of material in scholarly English studies – although people usually haven't known what to do with it – to exploration of what is then necessarily a wider social reality. This would be not so much a sociology of literature in the familiar sense, although there is no reason at all to exclude such questions as the working conditions of writers or economic relations affecting literary production; but that isn't the way one would primarily go – one would go to the conventions, in that sense the deeper historical forms. When one has done that, one is often going to find work which is not fully explicable in terms of its recoverable conditions of production. In some cases, when you have taken the analysis through to the deep form, you can go on as most of my younger colleagues are now doing to account for this as ideology, and the job is finished. There are works of which this is true, but by no means is it true for the whole of what we call literature. Where it is not, the attention has to be switched back to something which is a more indissoluble composition – which refuses exhaustive and certainly reductive analysis. I am perfectly prepared to say that we have got to put great emphasis on certain works of this type – it is not an emphasis of value but it is certainly an emphasis of distinction. The result would be to show that the practices of writing form a true range: they cannot be encompassed by the traditional duality or any variant of it. I would expect a good deal more precise categorization of different kinds of work to emerge in the future. The crucial relationship is always between a particular piece of writing and its conditions of production. At one end of the spectrum, it would be a criterion of scientific work that it was fully accountable in terms of its conditions of production. At the other end of the spectrum, there would be major poems where the conditions of production were not a full account of the composition.

Your remarks about science rest on a distinction which your theoretical positions do not easily accommodate – the distinction between scientific observation and the written discourse of the scientific paper. Isn't the idea of a scientific observation prior to the discourse of the scientist a return to the opposition between consciousness and the world which you reject very emphatically?

I think there is a very severe problem here, but we have to face the fact that modes of observation, and indeed of communication and of record, are not limited to language. To a very large extent the data of a scientist will not in the first instance be linguistic at all – something which those of us who have had a primarily linguistic education find difficult to realize. Hence the difficulties of their conversion into language, and in particular everyday language. Not all kinds of composition are linguistic. But non-verbal communication, which is evidently of great importance, can still be accommodated within any materialist account of science. Within scientific work, language is often not the primary means of communication, but it is the central mode of scientific communication outside the work itself. No duality of the sort you mention is being posited here – so I don't see any real difficulty.

In Marxism and Literature *you describe structural linguistics as a form of abstract objectivism. Discussing Saussure, you argue that his distinction between* langue *and* parole *is an instance of the ubiquitous bourgeois opposition between society and the individual. Later, you attack the notion of arbitrariness of the sign, which you say could only arise where a linguistic system was seen completely from the outside, its real social relations being abstracted. Now, so far as the opposition between society and the individual is concerned, these two categories coexist on the same plane – most typically, society provides the constraints in which the individual operates. Couldn't it be argued that the relationship between* langue *and* parole *is very different, because* langue *is never realized – only* parole *is present;* langue *is the absent reservoir which is the means of production of* parole; *in other words it is because there is* langue *that* parole *is communication? If so, Saussure's distinction could not be seen as a specialized instance of the categories of bourgeois ideology. So far as the notion of the arbitrariness – more often 'unmotivatedness' – of the sign goes, doesn't this refer to the fact that there is no* natural *bond between signifier and signified, or between sign and referent, rather than to an absence of social relations in language?*

The notion was introduced in opposition to the idea that the sign was an icon, and it is certainly true that there is in general no necessary relation of an abstract kind between word and thing in language. But to describe the sign as arbitrary or unmotivated prejudges the whole theoretical issue. I say it is not arbitrary but conventional, and that the convention is the result of a social process. If it has a history, then it is not arbitrary – it is the specific product of the people who have developed the language in question. You must remember that the society-individual opposition can be conceptualized in many ways: the social order can be taken as prior to the individuals who are merely examples or specimens of it, or society can be presented as the creation of free individuals, for certain purposes and with certain liberties. The force of the ahistorical distinction between *langue* and *parole* is that human utterance is only possible in terms of the constraints and opportunities of a pre-existent system. Now that is perfectly true in one sense: it is not possible to speak or be understood unless one is drawing on the systematic resources of language. But that systematic organization remains the social creation of real people in real relationships. This is a very difficult point, because people always assume one is simply saying that languages have evolved over time. So they have – there must be no argument about that: the movement away from study of the origins and development of language, which is still a crucial field, is an ideological shift. But the systematic character of language itself is the result, the always changing result, of the activities of real people in social relationships, including individuals not simply as products of the society but in a precise dialectical relation both producing and being produced by it. The failure to see this led to the idea of language as a certain socially available quantum of signification which is never fully realized, of which all individual speech-acts are instances; this especially in the later and harsher theorizations of sixties' structuralism, which was very different from Saussurian linguistics. Linguistic activity was simply performance of a pre-existing system, which is at once true and very far from the whole truth; and that distance is ideologically crucial, because it denies the possibility of a constant process of significant present activity which is capable of altering the system, which observably does alter the system of social language. Among other things, the history of what we call literature is an extraordinary demonstration of the discovery of new possibilities of linguistic use. Human beings made language, and they will remake it, not just setting out to do so – though they do sometimes – but as a normal ongoing process in the course of their full social experience.

Your own attitude to Freudian psycho-analysis has always been extremely reserved. Usually when you refer to Freud it is to the later, metapsychological work, of which you say in The Long Revolution *its basic theoretical foundation is precisely the recurrent bourgeois opposition of individual and society. Do you think Freud's work has no pertinence at all to a materialist theory of literature?*

Let me take up the question in terms of the practice of writing. What we know in Freud is a series of specifically written productions. It is extremely important to remember this, because there is normally an elision between Freud's practical experience as an analyst, which is of a broadly medical kind, and his written productions – which are characteristically taken as simply the communication of that experience to us, without composition having intervened. I was deeply impressed by *The Psychopathology of Everyday Life*, when I first read it. But when I went back over it, because I had been trained to analysis of composition, I could not help registering the distance between the evidence Freud collected (which itself has to be returned to its social and historical period, its class situation, and so on) and the way he presents it: certain of the slips he observed can manifestly be interpreted in other than Freudian ways. In other words, it is always necessary to separate the validity of the processes to which he drew attention from the forms of his composition, both literary (his work is very powerfully written) and theoretical (his forging of concepts for an understanding of these processes). This is what the present uncritical use of the psycho-analytic tradition in literary studies fails to do:

it simply takes the interpretations or theoretical constructs along with the findings, as science. At that point the re-examination of Freud's work which some of our literary analysts are now beginning to do, as a series of texts, can be extremely important – so long as it is not done in an expository and reverential way, but as a study of their process of composition. Semioticians like to remark that Freud was a kind of anti-novelist, because he showed the conditions out of which behaviour came, rather than just showing behaviour. I wouldn't call that the procedure of an anti-novelist, looking at the actual tradition of the novel, but the semioticians want to because they want to convict the novel of naturalization. I would say, on the contrary, that Freud, if anything, seems to be doing what the realist tradition at its strongest did – his presentation is centred on certain characteristic cases of individuals, whose history is interpreted and generalized in a very powerful way. I think that this is in fact the correct emphasis: Freud's writings should be read, not so much as a body of science, as what are called in another category novels – and as such they are extraordinarily interesting, although of course they have an extraordinarily different status. One reads them as one would read the closely connected contemporary writing of Strindberg or Proust, granting no necessary prior validity because they were based on clinical experience, simply because between the clinical experience and the text there is the process of composition. After all, what is the validity of Strindberg or Proust? Their work articulates another kind of experience, an observation of experience, which preceded and continued into the process of composition. In the same way the work of Lacan today should not be taken as a confirmatory authority, the provision of a framework within which other compositions are read, but rather as itself a composition which we all believe to be important.

Now once one reads Freud in that light, the experience can be very involved and precarious. I have said that when I was working on European drama after the war, in a very disturbed condition, I really did feel as I was reading that my life was being put in question. I think most people would have that same sense when reading Freud, especially when he is near to the clinical experience of disorders and tragedies. We owe largely to him our knowledge that we often say something to avoid other things or that our difficulty in saying certain things is related to blocks or repressions of which we are not aware. But the more you are aware of that, the more you cannot concede to anybody at all the prior right to judge these difficulties.

You can exchange on an equal level your experiences of them – you can take from somebody else the proposition that you are saying this or avoiding saying that because it moves into areas of pain or shame or confusion. What you should never take is the terrorist application of these insights by the possessors of the special method, who *know*, who are capable of this kind of interpretation. Intellectual discourse becomes strictly impossible when every response can be interpreted as evidence of repressed resistance to the interpretation. Freud was not responsible for this immense mystification, but it has flourished with the later institutionalization of Freudianism, and where it has done so, it has produced a cultural disaster area.

Was I wrong to have referred to Freud mainly in terms of the later works? Surely it is in these that his more general propositions about human history, about the character of civilization, or about the nature of art are to be found. Freud's account of art, in particular, struck me as extraordinary. It presents the artist as someone who is unable to satisfy his real impulses, which are in Freud's version an absolute catalogue of the philistine conditions of male bourgeois society: a very unfortunate result for women – what does the woman artist do? These impulses are then gratified through the circuitous route of sublimation in works of art. The whole theory is profoundly reductive – if only because, from my position, it already specializes out art too much. This relates to the much wider argument, which I suppose I've never set out fully enough, that the emergence of conscious story-telling, the deliberately wrought articulation of an experience – these are developments out of observable components of everyday discourse. There is a point at which you can legitimately speak of a collective awareness of these activities, the setting up of occasions on which they occur, as conventions which signal art. But these aesthetic situations – we are now going to be told a story, we will listen to a poem – still signal activities not too unlike those which occur in everyday discourse but are not so signalled. The idea that this fundamental human associative activity, which in the course of history has developed into so many remarkable and powerful forms, represents the result of some crude frustration is not very serious thinking. The whole conception of the social order as a merely negative system of constraints and inhibitions belongs to the most classical bourgeois theory, to which I am naturally very hostile. Certainly the opportunities for individualization are drastically limited in Freud's world, but that is precisely the mode in which the individual as a bundle of instincts is counterposed to a blocked fact called society. When the imputed causes of individual aggression are projected onto organized movements of social aggression in history, in the Freudian explanations of war or plunder, they end in a mythology of eternal drives which one can only read as one reads Nietzsche – entirely as visions, sometimes very powerful ones.

Your rejection of the concept of literature is accompanied by an equally drastic repudiation of the notion of criticism. You call, most trenchantly in Keywords, *for a 'significant rejection of the habit (or right or duty) of judgment'. You go on: 'The point would then be, not to find some other term to replace [criticism], while continuing the same kind of activity, but to get rid of the habit, which depends, fundamentally, on the abstraction of response from its real situation and circumstances: the elevation to judgment, and to an apparently general process, when what always needs to be understood is the specificity of the response, which is not a judgment but a practice, in active and complex relations with the situations and conditions of the practice, and, necessarily, with all other practices.'*[32] *The logic of your argument here seems to lead to a complete dissolution of the process of discrimination and evaluation that has traditionally been thought to be the central function of criticism. For if any aesthetic judgment of a work must be deconstructed back into a specifically conditioned response, what barrier is there to historical relativism? How do you save yourself from the fashionable nihilism which voluntarily and ostentatiously abstains from any attempt to establish an evaluative basis for judging literary works, and simply purports to decode discursive structures within them? Your modification would appear to be, at most, a further sociological decoding of the decoder. The blunt question must, however, be put: what's wrong with judging literary works? Isn't that what we have to do in every other realm of life – we have to judge political regimes, economic systems, or social structures? Why should the activity of writing be exempt? No doubt there are contexts in which the term has a censorious or punitive connotation, but these are certainly not prescriptive in ordinary language. Judging is surely an ineluctable part of reading – how can you avoid it?*

I would be very sorry if I had been understood as saying that judgment would not occur. That seems to me an inevitable process – I can't abstain

[32] K, p. 76.

from it and I don't propose to try. My theoretical argument should rather be seen, once again, as a clearing operation. It seems to me unquestionable that what has come to be understood as criticism is a detached process. The very phrases you have cited from my own early work underline that – trained attention, adequate response and so on: it is all over this tradition that the process of judgment is something which occurs above any specific instances or situations. I had this training very hard, and what you were told to do was to forget yourself, to forget your situation, to be in a naked relation – but with your training, of course – to the text; while the text itself was similarly taken out of all its conditions and circumstances. My whole encounter with literary criticism really revolved around this pseudo-impersonal attempt to judge works without any sense of the presence of the individual making judgment – its effort to divest itself of circumstances, to rise above history, to talk of literature rather than the individual or group making a critical judgment. My opposition here was much more to later developments in New Criticism than to Leavis. For with Leavis, one is never in any danger of forgetting that a very marked individual is there all the time making the judgments: indeed the elements the New Criticism thought naïve and moralistic in Leavis seemed to me the best defence of him. He didn't always spell out his assumptions, or follow through his premises. But what was seen as a taint by the later New Criticism that was the immediate predecessor of structuralism, now seems by comparison admirable. Yet at the same time Leavis himself paradoxically went along with all the talk about the educated man, the critic with a literary training, and was then appalled by the fact that other people, with just as much literary training as he, had radically different judgments of the same works. He could then only denigrate them.

Now if, as I advocate, one pushes a judgment about some specific work back to the conditions in which the judgment was made, the result is not relativism, because one also judges those conditions. But when one does that one is necessarily involved in something more than what has been understood as criticism. Let me take a case which was very important in clarifying my attitude to Leavis. I said to people here at Cambridge: in the thirties you were passing severely limiting judgments on Milton and relatively favourable judgments on the metaphysical poets, which in effect redrew the map of 17th-century literature in England. Now you were, of course, making literary judgments – your supporting quotations and analysis prove it, but you were also asking about ways of living through a political and cultural crisis of national dimensions. On the one side, you have a man who totally committed himself to a particular side and cause, who temporarily suspended what you call literature, but in fact not writing, in that conflict. On the other, you have a kind of writing which is highly intelligent and elaborate, that is a way of holding divergent attitudes towards struggle or towards experience together in the mind at the same time. These are two possibilities for any highly conscious person in a period of crisis – a kind of commitment which involves certain difficulties, certain naïvetés, certain styles; and another kind of consciousness, whose complexities are a way of living with the crisis without being openly part of it. I said that when you were making your judgments about these poets, you were not only arguing about their literary practice, you were arguing about your own at that time. The reaction to this was scandalized denial that anything so tainted could have entered into the critical process. But it would be possible to prove it if one looked at all the terms of the discussion which had these contemporary roots. The fact is that the abstraction of criticism, its presumed innocence as an activity solely concerned with judgment of our poets, is hypocrisy. You ask me: how can one retain the notion of what we are still calling judgment if we move through to say that no judgment is sufficient unless we know the conditions in which it has been made, the position from which it's been made? Doesn't that do away with judgment altogether, because then the judgment just dissolves into the conditions? I would agree that this is a danger, but if we also judge the conditions in which the judgment was made, there is a protection against relativism. Our response to writing does then become a much more extended practice than this quite extraordinarily privileged area in which the reader is put in the position of a judge, which I don't think anybody can assume without damage. Criticism leads to the hypostatization of the critic *above* the process: making judgments *inside* the process, in the way people do in everyday contemporary argument, is a very different matter.

Your account of literary criticism as a discipline seems disconcerting to a younger generation. After all, even by the fifties the standard introductory work given to students to get a general map of the discipline was surely Wellek and Warren's Theory of Literature *– a comparative survey of positions, theories and schools in Europe and America, much of which is devoted to precisely the problems you've been raising. For example, the congruence* *between the particular historical preoccupations of critics in one epoch and the work of producers in another epoch, and the successive changes in the synchronization between them, is one of the central issues explored in the book. Far from any unproblematic relationship being assumed between the atemporal judgment of the critic and the text, yielding some fixed evaluation which remains on record ever afterwards, the difficulty was repeatedly emphasized that there have been so many critical revolutions. Your rejection of literary criticism appears to be founded on a very narrow identification of it with one American school in the 20th century – it ignores the whole history of German, French or Italian aesthetics, for example. You seem to be arguing that since New Criticism is so objectionable we must reject criticism* tout court. *It is rather as if someone said – I hear a lot of economic arguments now about monetarism, and the influence of Milton Friedman is clearly in the ascendant, so let's do away with economics. Surely this isn't a rational response?*

Remember that the term 'literary criticism' is very much a creation of the Anglo-American tradition. It was not normally the way that these activities of literary discussion were described in other European languages. I think they were in that respect on much surer ground. In the non-English speaking traditions there has always been a historical and theoretical range of a different kind: it was not until the recent preponderance of American culture gave the notion of criticism a certain intellectual prestige that it was widely adopted elsewhere in Europe. Even if you follow the evolution of the term through in England, the position and nature of criticism in the work of someone like Johnson or Coleridge is very different from the later ideological isolation of criticism as a primary activity. Fekete's recent book *The Critical Twilight* traces the moment at which this practice, at once presented as scientific – this was a crucial part of its claim – and at the same time detached from history, emerged as the effective meaning of criticism within the English-speaking world. It then, of course, went through various phases of increasing abstraction and false rigour – Fekete follows it through the phase in North America in which it was still connected with a specific social position, the reactionary Southern agrarianism to be found in the early work of Ransom, to its domination as a presumptively objective technique which excluded any other kind of analysis or interest in writing as uncritical. Structuralism completes that theoretical development. Its evolution in France has been deeply determined by American New Criticism – which is no compliment to its French practitioners or to those who re-imported it from France to Britain, where it was a long-lost cousin grown up and changed, who had emigrated from the England of the 1920s and now came back in this altered and more deeply alienated form.

Now if you take the encounter of the trained reader with the text through to that kind of abstraction and isolation, in effect it does in the end seem absurd to make any judgment. What can you do but read and deconstruct poems? The ironic end of that procedure which had arrogated to itself the name of criticism was – there was no judgment at all. Indeed, what could the basis of judgment be? What it could find was incoherence, as long as it wasn't too rigid in its notions of what coherence could be, which it often was. But there are genuine forms of incoherence, which can be identified by this kind of analysis. On the other hand the questions that are raised by incoherence of convention or radical incoherence of language, which you often find, immediately take you outside the text. But in general the isolation of the pure act of judgment between critical reader and text tends in the end to prevent even judgment. So that if one is to defend judgment as a normal social practice one has to attack criticism. I can see that I should have made this much clearer.

In that case shouldn't you have been waging a battle on two fronts? For while you denounce the 'habit of judgment' in Marxism and Literature, *you really say nothing about what is in some ways a far more ascendant mode at present – the deliberate abstention from judgment. Actually, of course, judgments are inevitably smuggled into the process, but characteristically by a fiat of focus. This kind of criticism typically takes one or two works for a repetitive decoding, which in effect operates as a de facto selection of value. The control of comparison, which is where judgment really starts to be validated and verifiable, is usually avoided altogether.*

I've been watching this process, which I do attack in one paragraph of *Marxism and Literature*. It has been evolving very rapidly. I don't think it could abstain from judgment for more than a brief period of exaltation with its new technical means – some of which, as a matter of fact, are very important. Today it is already into judgment because in the end – this is the correction of emphasis you wanted me to make and which I very willingly make – judgment is inevitable.

Isn't there a contradiction between what you said earlier and the correction you are now making? You argued very sharply that the hypostatization of the reader as a judge is very damaging. On the other hand you stress that no one can go for five minutes without making a judgment. Presumably these judgments are partisan, rather than judgments which are coming down from the chair of the magistrate. Yet in Keywords *or* Marxism and Literature, *the partisan aspect of what you are saying is largely concealed from the reader. For example, neither Leavis not New Criticism are even named in your chapter on literature, let alone distinguished in the way that you have done now. The stance of the book is on the whole impersonally objectivist rather than explicitly polemical. You remarked that you have always tried to keep the mainstream of bourgeois culture in your sights – a combativity we very much admire. In* Marxism and Literature *you know whom you are aiming at – but do you tell your readers?*

Part of that is certainly right – I ought to have been more precise. I was cramped for space, and I suppose I felt that if I got into a discussion of critical schools – in a way just because I am obliged to know so much about them – it would be a work in itself. I also particularly didn't want that book to be a replay of the unfinished polemic between Marxism and the *Scrutiny* of the thirties. In a sense my thrust was much more against the limits of the newly dominant mode of critical structuralism, because this was what was being taken as Marxist literary theory all over Western Europe and North America. You have got to accept certain gains and certain losses in whichever direction you go. This was – it is said specifically in the introduction – a contribution within a much wider area of discourse than that to which my previous books had related. It gained something in that way, in the sense that Italians working in literary studies immediately know what my arguments are about – we're discussing the same problems and the same concepts, whereas it is very difficult for the specifically English kind of practical criticism to be taken seriously enough outside the very English cultural situation which produced it and made it pretty powerful, to discuss it with anyone from another culture – other Marxists even too hastily dismiss it as negligible. It is not, of course, that I think detailed argument with Richards or Eliot or Leavis about the idea of literature is unimportant. But in a sense I've done that elsewhere. This was intended from the beginning to be a different kind of book. But I suppose there was an unexplained rapidity of transition – what could seem an abrupt abandonment of the contest with those people, because I felt that there was a more urgent danger on the other side, of the eruption of a mode of idealist literary study claiming the authority of Marxism and the prestige of association with powerful intellectual movements in many other fields. So I went much more for that, which meant that I had to argue from the outset within the terms of this current, leaving a lot of the difficulties within the English-speaking argument behind.

Your general theory of writing in Marxism and Literature *is founded on radically historical premises. Our social history, however, which is itself very uneven, has always been articulated with the natural history that brought our species into being, presumably changes it according to rhythms which to social-historical analysis are quite imperceptible, and one day may sweep it away again. That second history raised the possibility of a legitimate materialist conception of the human, which is not ideological in the sense that – to take a local example – the Leavisian conception of life is ideological. Timpanaro is a Marxist who has posed this problem with great force and clarity recently – stressing the implication of the social-historical world in a natural world, which certainly does not rule it in any sense that social Darwinism would have understood, but which nevertheless does encompass it and which the domain of relatively short-term social change cannot escape. Do you accept such a perspective? If so, what is its bearing on the themes of your book?*

When I read Timpanaro, I had the sense of an extraordinary recovery of a sane centre of the Marxist tradition, which it seemed to me had been largely forgotten or had persisted only among the dwindling number of natural scientists who were still Marxists. I was acutely aware of the potential importance and relevance of this problem for what has traditionally been called aesthetics, in particular. That is why I had more difficulty with the conclusion of the chapter entitled 'Aesthetic and Other Situations' than with anything else in the book. I was trying to point in the direction of this area by speaking of the quite physical effects of writing, which have certainly been overlooked in a sociologically oriented tradition. For there is a very deep material bond between language and the body, which communication theories that concentrate on the passing of messages and information typically miss: many poems, many kinds of writing, indeed a lot of everyday speech communicate what is in effect a life rhythm and the interaction of these life rhythms is probably a very important part of the material process of writing and reading. From a materialist point of view, this is at least the direction in which we should look for the foundation of categories that we could if we wish call aesthetic. I very consciously reserved the possibility that there may be permanent configurations that would account for the responses to which, for example, the concept of beauty points. It would be a mistake to rule that out.

But only scientific investigations could arrive at such a finding: it cannot be adumbrated speculatively beforehand. If you start with the idea of a biological universal, then you will end where Chomsky ended, which was very sad in that the Chomskian emphasis on generative processes was initially such an important corrective to previous notions of systematic predetermined utterance. Indeed if I had one single ambition in literary studies it would be to rejoin them with experimental science, because of work that is now being done which would make it possible to do so. It is curious that this was an identical ambition of Richards in the 1920s, which got written out of the subsequent Cambridge system. In fact one can see looking back that it was gravely limited by the particular scientists who attached themselves to its failure. Years ago I tried to set up some actual experiments of what happened to physical rhythms in certain reading contexts, but such was the atmosphere of specialization that the work was never done. I believe, however, that we have got to move towards active collaboration with the many scientists who are especially interested in the relations between language use and human physical organization. I have great respect for Lacan, but the totally uncritical way in which certain of his concepts of phases in language development have been lifted into a theoretical pediment of literary semiotics is absurd, in a world in which there is current scientific work of a non-philological kind with which all such concepts have to be brought into interplay. There has been such justified suspicion on the left of the dominance of behaviourism in the experimental social sciences that there has been an over-accommodation to the claims of psycho-analysis and its various derived schools, which have seemed much nearer and more radical, often precisely because of their literary qualities. What is needed is not a blending of concepts of literature with concepts from Lacan, but an introduction of literary practice to the quite different practice of experimental observation. That would be the materialist recovery.

You have argued that in lieu of the traditional practices of criticism, literary studies today should take the form of a dual movement – tracing back any given writing to its material and historical conditions of production, on the one hand, and then tracing back our own social and historical conditions of response to it, on the other hand. You are presumably suggesting that if we effect that double process we will arrive at new evaluations of writers and works. Could you give a concrete example? You have spoken of the case of Milton, in its way a cause célèbre, *but it lacks sufficient force: for it is something of a myth that Milton was ever completely dismissed before the war – Eliot himself backtracked very quickly, while after the war the revaluation of Milton came from so many diverse ideological horizons – from Christopher Hill to Christopher Ricks. A much more powerful case is your own analysis of the country-house poems in* The Country and the City. *There you delve back into the precise connections between poet and patron, the actual history of the houses that were the object of the poems, the conventions that governed their writing – in general the whole relationship of the poetic constructs to the real conditions of their own production. At the same time, not on the same pages but in the same book, you set out to the reader very clearly your own personal and social position as an interpreter or reader of these texts, as the grandson of an agricultural labourer, as a committed socialist. The only final element which is absent from the book is any actual evaluation of the texts themselves, from which you seem in a certain sense to abstain. Yet would not the total act of a post-criticism, if one could put it like that, also involve some kind of evaluation at the end of this dual process?*

I think it would, although I am not sure whether evaluation is quite the right word for it. You could say that while the first process is intrinsically common, subject to intellectual checks by others if correctly done, the second is necessarily personal, a declaration of interest, and therefore completely variable since everyone is initially in a different situation, although we should not forget the true common modes, beyond that, of class affiliation. That is a difficulty, but the movement towards declaration of situation is nevertheless crucial, given the successive mystifications of the trained reader or the informed critic or the cultivated gentleman. It does not have to lead to relativism, because the active valuations to emerge from the whole process would not be connected with those elements of one's own situation which are really just biographical idiosyncrasies that issue into personal preferences – my reaction to Herrick's poem, which I dislike so much for reasons I mention in *The Country and the City*, would be an example; they would instead be related to those which associated one with others in certain more general acts of valuation. In other words, one should be able to distinguish kinds of valuation which are crucial to communicate to others, and preferences of style which one expresses all the time but are not of real importance to anyone else, however significant they may be to oneself. The latter do not command interest at the centre of a major area of discourse, although one kind of criticism has tried to promote them as such – something the best criticism has always attempted to overcome, but sometimes by elevating personal preference via certain suppressions to what is apparently an impersonal judgment. Serious acts of valuation, by contrast, are those which have a wider continuity of effect as an active process. They are modes of standing towards a particular form, which show it in a different light that affects not just some way in which we react to it, but some way in which we live. So many past cultural forms exert an active pressure on the way people judge and act, as they derive formulations from very powerful art which they value as great works, that this process of common and communicable valuation is crucial.

Your reader gets the definite impression that of the first three poems you discuss at length in The Country and the City, *respectively by Jonson, Carew and Marvell, you have a marked preference for Marvell's, although in some respects it represents a more astonishing social mystification than either of the other two, as you show from the career of the family to whom it was addressed – the subsequent marriage of Fairfax's daughter to Buckingham. Is that the sort of evaluation you want to withdraw importance from?*

That's the type of case. There judgment can never go beyond terms of relative power or range within a form. Often a work is clearly very powerful in this sense, but precisely that evaluation may then necessarily involve a more severe general consideration. What I am rejecting is the notion of valuation without the development of either of the two situating processes – that which has come to be encapsulated as criticism. Today it has become divorced even from the historical models to which it used to be attached. A renaissance epitaph will be condemned by a student simply because its language is unfamiliar, 'stilted'. Criticism of that sort is a licence for trivial ignorance and complacency. In fairness to practical criticism, this is the sort of reaction it would have hated when it was still a live force. But if you erect 'my first-hand response' into a criterion of judgment, it is very difficult to exclude such responses on grounds of principle – all that can be said is you've got a very clumsy first hand. . . .

This is now the typical emphasis of a consumer society – the idea that the whole purpose of human production in all its range over history is to bring successive objects before someone who has the sovereign rights of the consumer to pick them over to see whether he likes them or not. That now masquerades as an intellectual activity. Of course this is not the whole history of criticism, but within the tendency in the English-speaking world that I isolated earlier there was a certain inevitability in the descent towards a trivialism of preference, or towards a technicism which ends in no judgments of any kind – a simple technical recomposition of the text.

In their theses on formalism, Jakobson and Tynyanov argued that the category of the contemporary properly includes any work that is active in a given period – so that while one might say, for example, that Naomi Mitchison is not a contemporary novelist, there is a sense in which the works of Shakespeare are contemporary since they continue to play a vital role, if of a complex kind, in the culture of late 20th-century Britain. If that were so, it would seem to raise a problem for any approach to literature which concentrates on its conditions of production. For works can outlive the moment of their production; they not only come into being in history, they acquire a history of their own over time, although not necessarily a continuous one. In that respect it could be said that John Donne scarcely existed in the 19th century, but had a very powerful existence in literary culture in the early 20th century. The emergence of powerfully organized literary studies in this century has compounded the problem, increasing – to use your terms – the volume of the archaic as distinct from the residual within contemporary culture and often assisting the residual and other forms in complex ways to survive. How would you accommodate this phenomenon in your theory of written productions?

Certainly the process of returning a work to its conditions of production could be understood in too narrow a sense. This is very important to clarify. We do not now read Shakespeare, we read editions of Shakespeare and this not just in the technical sense of when the pages were printed, but in a very much more substantial sense of the reproduction of the text in a quite different culture. I would certainly regard the conditions of production of a classic author who is continually re-introduced and widely read in every period as including that process of re-introduction. The case of Shakespeare is a particularly strong one, because of the highly variable ways he has been read and in which his plays have been staged. There is a history of production in Shakespeare which is distinct from that of the original innovating individual writer. Another example would be Horace's famous ode, *Beatus Ille*, which was reproduced in different forms in various successive phases of the revival of classical culture, characteristically often omitting the last line and therefore the social situation in which it was written, and therefore the whole meaning of the ode. Translations, of course, pose this problem especially acutely, as I discovered in working through different editions of Ibsen. The conditions of production thus always include the conditions of making a text contemporary: to forget this would be to fall into a mere sociologism of the originating condition. All the forces which keep the text current are among its conditions of production.

There still seems to be an important dilemma posed by the possibility of contraditions between what you call a socially communicable valuation of the art of the past and other potential sorts of valuation. We could perhaps focus this most clearly by taking not literature but architecture. For architecture is peculiar among the arts in that, unlike painting or writing, its production typically involves large amounts of wealth, and exploitation of labour on a large scale. This is true of the bulk of what is regarded as fine architecture today, which is of course not exhaustive of other forms of building. Successive dominant styles of architecture have been connected much more closely and directly with the material privileges of the ruling order than literature or painting. It is therefore appropriate that one of the most powerful single paragraphs in The Country and the City *should be devoted, not to the country-house poems, but to the country houses themselves. You write: 'It is fashionable to admire these extraordinarily numerous houses: the extended manors, the neo-classical mansions, that lie so close in rural Britain. People still pass from village to village, guidebook in hand, to see the next and yet the next example, to look at the stones and the furniture. But stand at any point and look at that land. Think it through as labour and see how long and systematic the exploitation and seizure must have been, to rear that many houses, on that scale. See by contrast what any ancient isolated farm, in uncounted generations of labour, has managed to become, by the efforts of any single real family, however prolonged. Then turn and look at what these other "families", these systematic owners, have accumulated and arrogantly declared. It isn't only that you know, looking at the land and then at the house, how much robbery and fraud there must have been, for so long, to produce that degree of disparity, that barbarous disproportion of scale. The working farms and cottages are so small beside them: what men really raise, by their own efforts or by such portion as is left to them, in the ordinary scale of human achievement. What these "great" houses do is to break that scale, by an act of will corresponding to their real and systematic exploitation of others.'*[33] *This is an extraordinarily moving passage. Here the summons to the reader to look at actual conditions of production, in a much more gross and tangible sense than anything we have discussed up to now, is brought home with tremendous force. These conditions of production, you rightly point out, include not only the economic expropriation of land and exploitation of labour, but also the cultural will to inscribe domination, command and distance in the very scale and shape of the buildings themselves.*

Now there is a striking contrast to this passage in another paragraph of the book, which forms a kind of pendant to it. You quote the lines from The Prelude *in which Wordsworth looks out from Westminster Bridge and admires the 'ships, towers, domes, theatres and temples', 'all bright and glittering in the smokeless air'. You then say, 'I have felt [the same pulse of recognition] again and again: the great buildings of civilization; the meeting-places; the libraries and theatres; the towers and domes; and often more moving than these, the houses, the streets. . . . I find I do not say, "There is your city, your great bourgeois monument, your towering structure of this still precarious civilization", or I do not say only that; I say also, "This is what men have built, so often magnificently, and is not everything then possible?"'*[34] *Here is the completely opposite response. But in fact historically the architects and patrons of the towers and domes in the city were very often the same people who designed and constructed the mansions in the country. Wren, Gibbs, Hawksmoor, Kent built country-seats as well as churches, magnate villas as well as libraries or law-courts or universitity colleges. The wealth that financed all these edifices was equally extracted from the direct producers. The towers and domes, they too raised on a higher than human scale, were also designed to impress and overawe. You compare the size of the larger country houses with what any one real family could do on its own, and the point is absolutely telling and truthful; but the great buildings of a large city are also moving just because so many people worked to erect them, amidst duress and exploitation, sometimes across many generations. You would not think of calling St Paul's*

[33] CC, pp. 105–6.
[34] CC, pp. 5–6.

or King's College barbarous. However difficult it may be to reconcile the two, the direct intention of superordination and command appears to have been inseparably linked to the capacity to create proportions and order of beauty. The conflict in your responses illustrates the contradiction perfectly. Shouldn't a materialist aesthetic theory be able to address itself to this problem?

It is best, I think, to admit the contradiction. I was writing from strongly felt responses in both cases and the result does raise a theoretical problem. I can go some of the way to resolving it by a distinction between public buildings and private ones. But I know there are complications with that, since there are private buildings which have been converted to public purposes and certain public buildings have reverted to private use. But the more serious question is: how far would the perfectly legitimate criterion of public power and public access on the one hand and private power by command on the other – how far would that take one? Could one work it through to actual differences in message of a quite physical kind? I think one could go some of the way. I wish I could say that one could go all the way. I have very complex feelings in cathedrals, for example, which really do induce awe and reverence in me, which are at once disturbed by some battle honour or flag or the terms of some tablet which make me very aware of what kind of awed reverence the setting is intended to induce. If I've felt both ways about cathedrals, I've on the whole always felt only one way about castles. But even there, I did once find myself admiring a pre-Norman Welsh castle, thinking that it was strong as the rocks out of which it came, and then suddenly realizing – My God, what am I saying? When I look at implanted English castles like Harlech or Caernarfon I hate every fine stone. The fact is that it is very different when you think of a building as somewhere we can go, or as somewhere where our enemies go and from which they control us. I suppose a Norman might have a reverse judgment on these castles. But that would still be consonant with my general position, to seek the maximum disclosure of the circumstances of judgment, which would allow someone else to dissociate himself from it; but then openly and not by a presumptive category.

So far as country houses are concerned, one would have to be quite sure that one is able, in a way that Richards showed to be very difficult with sounds in poetry, to isolate purely physical features of the building – qualities of proportion, character of the stone, geographical position – from not just its own original intention and function, but also what your eyes are quite aware of when you're looking at it: the social impulses which people bring to saying that this is a beautiful building. I really do feel confident in replying, most of them are not beautiful *houses* – you're looking at them as beautiful houses as a way of being deferential to them as mansions. But then I have a difficulty about other buildings on eminences, like the Parthenon. For there are certain qualities in the Parthenon which are quite clearly drawing on the same sensory pull. I find it even more difficult when I take the problem across to very strong aesthetic feelings which I have about land, actually stronger about land than about buildings. I don't fully understand them, partly because I've never had any training in this kind of visual discrimination. In the case of literary works, where I would be able to go further in precise analysis, I think I could generally show that in the end the whole form – for example, panegyric heroic poetry, a particularly powerful mode that arouses strongly conflicting responses in me – has these aesthetic qualities because it has those purposes.

Couldn't the logic of what you are saying be summarized in a proposition that perhaps you initially wanted to deny: that the category of the aesthetic has to be retained as something separate from what otherwise would be a moral, social or political response to a work, and that there may even be a tension between them – which is where the real rub occurs?

The tension is certainly where the difficulty occurs. I don't at all want to deny the experiences you call aesthetic. It is a major human gain to attend with complete precision, often without any other consideration, to the way someone has shaped a stone or uttered a musical note. To deny that would be to cancel so much of human culture that it would be comical. But I think we need a much more specific analysis of the situations, the occasions, the signals which release that response, that kind of attention. I am absolutely unwilling to concede to any predetermined class of objects an unworked priority or to take all the signals as equally valid. We need a very complex typology of occasions and cues, which I think is quite practicable, although it will inevitably be partial. One would then have to look at the situations and occasions in which those signals and cues conflict with other systems which it is really very important not to cede. It is crucial that we resist the categorical predetermination of them as a reserved area, and the extreme training against taking these experiences back out and putting them in relation to other value systems. No doubt in various judgments one will be caught out saying – I really do find this working on me, although I hate the fact that it does so. By really exploring that contradiction, I may find out something about myself and others. That's probably as far as I can tell.

Your commitment to a resumption of the realist project raises the question of the relation of your work to that of Lukács – with whom you have been compared, most recently by Terry Eagleton. There are obvious similarities between your literary positions and the critical realism advocated by Lukács, including your respective critiques of naturalism or even of metaphysical modernism. At the same time, your judgments of writers of this century have often differed quite sharply – most evidently in the theatre, where you have praised Brecht or Beckett in ways quite foreign to Lukács. What is your own view of these affinities and divergencies?

I feel very close in approach to Lukács over the realist novel, although our accounts are not the same when you come right down to it. Lukács's characterization of the essential movement of the realist novel in the 19th century as the discovery by the dramatic hero of the limits of an unjust society, although a very important version, is based much more largely on French and some Russian fiction than on the European novel as a whole. I feel that if I had put this to him he would not have said: you are thinking in quite different theoretical terms, but: well, what are the other models? We would have argued in the same terms, but I think arrived at different conclusions. When, however, we come to the 20th century, there is a radical divergence. For Lukács, although it is difficult to talk about him in a unitary way because his positions varied so much over the decades, did have – much more strongly than I have ever had; for this was the main reason for my distance from Marxist literary criticism for so long – the notion of a pre-existent social reality with which the literary model can be compared. In however sophisticated a form, this remained a constant premise of his thinking, which was a major barrier when he came to consider the modernists. For a novel by Joyce or Kafka is not self-evidently interpretable in terms of a novel by Stendhal or Maupassant. I think that this was where for a generation a certain mainstream of Marxism stuck. All it could assume as the social reality to which that kind of fiction corresponded was a certain state of alienation which it described as decadence. Even now when these works are being recovered in the socialist countries, it is on the basis that there was a condition of class fragmentation and indifference in the actual society which demanded new forms. You cannot usefully follow that road. It is too negative, but more crucially it idealizes 19th century capitalist society, by assumption.

So my accounts and those of Lukács could be very similar for a type of literature in which the question – how does this fiction compare with otherwise observable (a phrase one can settle upon rather than pre-existent) social reality? – seems unproblematic. The realist novel of the 19th century does not make it *essential* to clarify the differences between the otherwise observable and the pre-existent. They can appear virtually identical. But once you move to 20th-century fiction, the substantial theoretical divergence between them becomes critical. I have never been concerned to defend realism in the historically reactionary sense that Lukács gave it or that those who are now attacking realism limit it to. My argument for realism has always been that it is a certain perception of reality and a certain awareness of interrelationships, not that it carries a certain mode of composition with it, nor that it has a second-order relation to a pre-existing reality. There is, in the end, that major theoretical difference, which happened not to be so important in the case of 19th-century realism, but which became very important in the 20th-century novel.

You define your present theoretical position in Marxism and Literature *as a cultural materialism. You argue, in effect, that Marxism has traditionally suffered not so much from an excess but from a deficit of materialism, because in practice its distinction between base and superstructure has tended to etherealize the activities of the superstructure, depriving them of their effective materiality by comparison with those of the base. Throughout your own work, you have always brought out the technical, physical, material conditions of any communicative practice that you have discussed.* Marxism and Literature, *however, contains the first full statement of this emphasis, which is now eloquently foregrounded. You write, for example: 'What is most often suppressed [by the conventional Marxist notion of economic production] is the direct material production of "politics". Yet any ruling class devotes a significant part of material production to establishing a political order. The social and political order which maintains a capitalist market, like the social and political struggles which created it, is necessarily material production.*

From castles and palaces and churches to prisons and work-houses and schools; from weapons of war to a controlled press: any ruling class, in variable ways though always materially, produces a social and political order. These are never superstructural activities. . . . The complexity of this process is especially remarkable in advanced capitalist societies, where it is wholly beside the point to isolate "production" and "industry" from the comparably material production of "defence", "law and order", "welfare", "entertainment" and "public opinion". In failing to grasp the material character of the production of a social and political order, this specialized (and bourgeois) materialism failed also, but even more conspicuously, to understand the material character of the production of a cultural order. The concept of the "superstructure" was then not a reduction but an evasion.'[35] *Rejecting the whole distinction between base and superstructure, you speak throughout the book of 'a single and indissoluble real process' simultaneously integrating economic, social, political and cultural activities.*

Now you are certainly right to emphasize the dangers of an idealist account of culture as a sphere of intangible notions and values, and to point out that any culture is composed of real, physical processes of communication and reproduction. But can we really say that it is therefore 'wholly beside the point to isolate production and industry from welfare, entertainment and public opinion'? We earlier criticized your tendency to miss the importance of causal hierarchies in historical analysis, in which far from being beside the point, it is absolutely essential to be able to isolate the forces which have a superior capacity to induce large-scale social change; and argued that in your previous writings you were inclined to overlook the fact that economic production permits cultural production in a way which is not symmetrically true of the relation of cultural production to economic production. Your latest emphasis now seems to produce a new circularity in which all elements of the social order are equal because they are all material. But actually that is not the case: if you like, some forms of matter are more materially effective than others. In your example, you say that a political order is necessarily a material production – of palaces, churches, prisons and schools. But of course it is not the buildings which themselves constitute a political system; it is the uniformed or civil agents of the ruling order who operate them that define their function. Law-courts or prisons are dispensable sites of a capitalist legal system – in emergencies, tribunals have been held in the open air, prisoners incarcerated in

[35] ML, p. 93.

ships or hotels. The same is obviously not true of the great factories and machine-complexes of an industrial economy. After a revolution, prisons have been converted without difficulty into schools, as happened in Cuba: could steel mills become law-courts? To put it another way, you speak of weapons of war and a controlled press, but you forget that these depend on primary industrial processes, of which they are later products. You should have no difficulty in registering that point, but it seems to get lost in the keenness of your polemic against analytic over-separation of the range of processes within any social totality to the point where there is a deleterious abstraction and reification of them. But after all, there must be few people who believe that the real world is divided up in such a way that all the objects which belong to the economy are in one space, all those involved in politics in another space, and those in culture in yet another space.

By contrast with your emphasis in Marxism and Literature, *there are two significant passages in earlier works whose import seems much more right. One of them is interestingly in* Culture and Society, *generally a much less materialist work than* Marxism and Literature. *You criticize Richards's idea of literature as a training ground for life, which you say is servile. Then you write: 'Great literature is indeed enriching, liberating and refining, but man is always and everywhere more than a reader, has indeed to be a great deal else before he can even become an adequate reader.'*[36] *There is an idea of primacy here which you normally reject. Elsewhere, in a memorable passage of your discussion of* The Return of the Native, *you comment in* The English Novel: *'It is the process also in which culture and affluence come to be recognized as alternative aims, at whatever cost to both, and the wry recognition that the latter will always be the first choice, in any real history.'*[37] *Here again, you acknowledge an order of material priority which you seem otherwise reluctant to concede. Would you be willing to accept these sentences as corrections of your argument in* Marxism and Literature?

This is very interesting. There is certainly a need for clarification because I haven't found myself disagreeing with your critique, which means that I must have been wrong in my formulations, or I must have been misunderstood. I was trying to say something very much against the grain of two traditions, one which has totally spiritualized cultural production,

[36] CS, p. 245.
[37] ENDL, p. 104.

the other which has relegated it to secondary status. My aim was to emphasize that cultural practices are forms of material production, and that until this is understood it is impossible to think about them in their real social relations – there can only ever be a second order of correlation. But, of course, it is true that there are forms of material production which always and everywhere precede all other forms. I am very glad to make that clarification – it doesn't seem to me like a concession. What one then has to say is that these forms of production are really very basic indeed; they are the production of food, the production of shelter, and the production of the means of producing food and shelter – an extended range which is still related to the absolutely necessary conditions of sustaining life. The enormous theoretical shift introduced by classical Marxism – in saying *these* are the primary productive activities – was of the most fundamental importance. Very often today, however, there is a slide from this pattern of activities to the structure of a late capitalist economy, as if everything which occurred in contemporary industry or agriculture were forms of production self-evidently related to primary need, as opposed for example to writing novels or painting pictures. I think in moments of polemic I've tended simply to reverse the emphasis, which is wrong. But what I was reacting against was the characteristic use of phrases like 'the linchpin of the British economy is the car industry'. There is no sense in which the car industry is primary production for the maintenance of human life in the same sense as the production of food or shelter or building materials. It is not even the primary answer to the need for mobility, since there are other forms of transport that are less socially differentiated. At the same time, within strictly industrial output itself, a great deal is now produced that has to do with relative social position or indeed with entertainment or leisure. Now this is where it would have been very much better to have argued my case historically. The economy Marx described was much more directly related to satisfying, or rather failing to satisfy, basic human needs than the economy of advanced capitalism. By the time you have got to the point when an EMI factory producing discs is industrial production, whereas somebody elsewhere writing music or making an instrument is at most on the outskirts of production, the whole question of the classification of activities has become very difficult. Even taking a received classification, the distribution of employment between primary, secondary and tertiary sectors is now without precedent. Precisely because of great advances in the productivity of labour, the necessities that are essential for the sustenance of human life at all – naturally in variable forms: different kinds of food, different kinds of shelter and so on – are today a much smaller part of even industrial production than ever before; once you move outside it, you are into an area which is to my mind indisputably political and cultural in a broader sense, in that the pattern of investment and output is so clearly determined by the nature of the whole social order. The proportion of primary production in the traditional sense is now so small that we could seriously mislead ourselves about the contemporary economy and even about causal relations, where I think you made the strongest point, if we simply retained the classical definition. This involves a correction both to the way in which I put the problem and the way in which you put it, because you were saying that I should have looked at it historically and you were right, but I am saying that if you looked at it historically you would not come out with the formulation quite as you put it.

This certainly meets the general objection. But perhaps you still have a tendency to look at the contemporary capitalist economy too quantitatively – although even there, while it is undeniable that in a country like England the number of people working in primary production in a traditional sense is much more limited than in the past, you should not forget the invisible producers overseas assuring the import needs of the society. Much more important, however, is the qualitative weight and role of respective forms of production within any given economy. It is very difficult, of course, to demonstrate the relative causal efficacy of different sectors of activity, since no society affords us the experimental conditions of a laboratory. But an approximate index of causal hierarchy is provided if we compare the effects of a suspension of each activity. Even a bourgeois liberal will admit, on reflection, that if all novelists stopped writing for a year in England, the results would scarcely be of the same order as if all car workers halted their labour. To take a more relevant example for your argument, a complete cessation of the main communications industries – telvision, radio and press – would serious effect the life of any modern capitalist society: but its effects would not be comparable to major strikes in the docks, mines or power stations. The workers in these industries have the capacity to disrupt the whole fabric of social life, so decisive is the importance of their productive activity. It is at moments like the miners' strike of 1974 that we can see the reality of the hidden causal relations Marx called the determination in the last instance by the economy.

Let me more or less agree with that, and then bring in another consideration. I see no difficulty at all in setting and where necessary revising (because I think historically there would be need for revisions) a relative hierarchy of different kinds of production as suppliers of social needs and therefore as available historical causes. Indeed one of the main distortions of capitalism is precisely its confusion of that hierarchy even in changing human historical terms – it never gets that right for long. I am very willing to concede these questions of hierarchical cause and effect. But I would not be willing to say that at the top of the hierarchy is productive industry, then come political institutions or means of mass communication, and then below them the cultural activities of philosophers or novelists. Not that there wouldn't always be a certain scale of that kind, but it is increasingly in the nature of the modern capitalist economy that there is a slide in the first bracket from indispensable needs to the dispensable conditions of reproduction of this order or of the ability to maintain life within it, for we can imagine certain breakdowns to which human beings could make adaptations of a very difficult kind by living in different ways. The hierarchies, while in general following a line from activities which answer to basic physical needs down through to those of which you at least can state negatively that if they were not performed, human life would not be immediately threatened, are not immutable. After all, stoppages of electrical power or oil would now make life impossible in the very short term, yet it is obvious enough historically that our society didn't possess them until recently, yet life could be sustained by other methods. To take another example: there have been some estimates that over half the employed population of the United States, the most advanced capitalist country, is now involved in various kinds of information handling and parcelling. If that were so, an information strike would call the maintenance of human life *in that social order* very quickly into question. Modern industrial communities are in that sense much more at risk in terms of their primary needs than much less productive societies of the past; they could theoretically and after long dislocation get out of such crises, but the amount of suffering involved would be comparable to the suffering of the famine or the cyclone.

In this sense, the hierarchy of productions is itself determined within a cultural order which is by no means separable as an independent sphere in which people wonder about the ultimate concerns of life. It is qualitatively different to live in an economy in which there is major industrial production of opinion and entertainment from a society in which beliefs were taught by priests or scribes. At every point where determinations of need are being fought out, the cultural order is crucially involved. A typical day-to-day example of social-democratic argument from the 1950s, which we now hear in every government campaign, across the whole spread of bourgeois politics, is that we must first invest in essential production, and then we can have all these other things you want, like schools and hospitals. What are isolated as priorities are in no sense as a sum more essential than schools or hospitals – indeed hospitals (one needs to be reminded of the fact) should be bracketed in any developed society in the primary category of activities maintaining human life, not all that far behind food. What is still described in capitalist terms as essential production actually means profitable commodity production in the narrow sense: everything else is then superstructural to it in a kind of caricature of an oversimplified Marxism. What I would like to see is the vocabulary of the dominant, emergent and subordinate applied to the historically, although never absolutely, changing character of the whole range of processes, and once we start by agreeing that they are all social-material, I think we are in a position to do this. I'm not saying I have done it: I certainly have not. But if I could help to provoke its doing, that would be a contribution.

Discussing the problem of determination, you criticize the notion that determination is only limitation – you argue that this is effectively the bourgeois idea of society as a system of constraints on a putatively pre-social individual. You insist that determination is not only limitation, 'it is also pressure', and then you write: 'It is always also a constitutive process with very powerful pressures which are both expressed in political, economic and cultural formations and, to take the full weight of "constitutive", are internalized and become "individual wills".'[38] *Is the term 'constitutive' really given its whole conceptual weight here? For the individual/society opposition is not superseded by adding pressure to limitation, since pressure as much as limitation is a process externally imposed on someone. So even in the modified*

[38] ML, p. 87.

formulation which is glossed by the very strong and correct term 'constitutive', the actual promise of 'constitutive' is not attained in the notion of pressure and limitation. Isn't there a residual element of the individual/society opposition left here?

That may be fair. I think it is important to distinguish two levels in this matter. There is the fundamental level where limitations and pressures arise long before the individual could be adequately conscious of them. This level forms the true social constitution of those individuals; internalization would not be a conscious process – it would be something that was never separable from the realization of the individual person – it would already have happened. But we also have to consider the question of limitation and pressure as these go on through adult life, at a level which is other than constitutive. There are formations which direct, or in their disintegration block, certain developments, and these are typically felt as limitations or as pressures. It is probably an improvement to stipulate that quantitatively the larger part of determination is always at the level of constitution, where to talk of internalization is misleading because there is no sense there in which you can separate the social from the individual, it is simply a whole process. But by the time someone is a conscious individual, even capable of consciously reviewing elements of his own constitution, doors can be opened or closed; pressures be exerted or resisted; limitations encountered or overcome. I would very much want to keep that active continuing process at a level that is not constitutive, because the danger of current theories which tend to inflect the notion of determination towards that of reproduction is that they underestimate the amount of adult choice that exists – which should not be thought of simply in individual, voluntarist terms, but much more in terms of the availability and persistence of alternative formations.

The intellectual difficulty of any concept of determination is that, on the one hand, it has got to have a certain unity and stability and rigour – it should not be allowed to slide towards a rule of thumb which has constantly to be qualified in the way that, say, all vulgar Marxist notions have to be in practice. On the other hand it must be able to account for the objective fact of alternatives in individual lives, in natural histories, in the whole of world history in fact. In your reply, you seem to be describing in a generalizing way an individual experience as a matter of empirical record, rather than seeking a theoretical definition that would account for that experience of choice, alternatives, or missed turnings. Against the way you've put it, one might make the schematic suggestion, which may begin to meet the two divergent strands of the intellectual problem, that determination can indeed be construed in the strongest possible sense, which is of not only reproduction but production, production and reproduction, but because of the nature of the mode of production, it is always a production of contradiction.

Yes, in general I agree. It is the point I was trying to make about the real nature of 'the base'.

V
Politics

1. Britain 1956–1978

In 1956, the two crises of the Suez invasion and the Hungarian Revolt shook the political configuration of the English Left. Within a year, the Communist Party lost a third of its members, and the Campaign for Nuclear Disarmament was launched with the first march to Aldermaston. In the wake of these events, two new socialist journals were founded – The New Reasoner *and* Universities and Left Review. *What was your relation to these developments?*

After *Culture and Society* was finished but before it was published, I was invited through mutual friends in Oxford to speak to the Universities and Left Review Club in London. At that stage I had no significant political contacts – there had been a gap in my relations with the Communist Party and the informal opposition inside the Party, except for incidental visits to the Historians' Group which had met in Hastings when I was living there. So my encounter with the ULR Club in London was a very important experience for me, because I hadn't been in that sort of group for a long time. These were well attended, lively meetings which opened up quite new areas of discussion. There was a difference of a whole generation between the group which had started publishing *Universities and Left Review* from Oxford, and the group which had separately created *The New Reasoner*, who had come out of the Communist Party over Hungary. But CND soon provided a common movement. I met so many people on those early Aldermaston marches I hadn't seen in years, especially from a Communist background. It was like people who had been separated for a decade meeting up, in all sorts of ways. CND provided that kind of focus, people were now suddenly much more in touch, including the young generation which was then emerging.

Now my paradoxical position in relation to these two generations was that I belonged by age to the group that had just left the Communist Party, but I was really rather nearer in preoccupation to the group which had started *Universities and Left Review*. *The New Reasoner* seemed to me a much more solid journal, worked through by dissidents inside a movement with an international range of debate. It contained discussions of the contemporary status of Marxism, serious historical and philosophical essays. *Universities and Left Review* was often thought to be lively but more lightweight, yet its interest for me was that it addressed itself to issues which had not been very prominent within Marxist debate, including dissident Marxist debate – problems of popular culture, questions of life-style and so on. The ULR people tended to treat the conflicts of the Cold War epoch as a past phase. They were much more oriented to what was happening now in the rapidly changing society of contemporary Britain – while the people coming from *The New Reasoner* were more aware of the whole international Marxist tradition, but with a sense of being less close to some of the extraordinary transformations of scene in England. This was the period of the emergence of the dominant cultural styles appropriate to consumer capitalism, with qualitatively new kinds of magazines, advertisements, television programmes, political campaigning. The 'New Left' cultural intervention, incomplete as it then was, outlined a necessary new kind of analysis of a new phase of capitalism. At its best it was not 'culturalism'; it was an emphasis towards new forms of struggle, indeed what is now widely called 'cultural revolution' (as in Rudolf Bahro for example). *Culture and Society* occupied a particular position in the growing together of these interests, because it was somewhere between the two sets of preoccupations. At the same time, I myself often felt I would rather see energy devoted to exploring current changes in cultural experience than going through the pain of reworking more traditional Marxist arguments. Now I put it that way. At the time I would probably have said that this is new work relevant to what's happening now – which will enter contemporary politics, while the other is just reliving the past. But I now think, with the advantage of hindsight, that the pain of reworking that past was necessary: and that the extent to which it was not carried through and this other style for a time took over was a weakness which was heavily paid for later. But at the time I was very attracted to this other direction, which was very close to the topics I was in any case writing about. This is not to say that I found it easy to relate across generations when it was the younger generation that on the whole had my interests, and yet the older generation had really much more my experience and style.

What was your view of the prospects created by the fusion of the two?

I was not involved in the negotiations which led to the merging of *The New Reasoner* and *Universities and Left Review* into *New Left Review*, which were handled by the editors of the two journals. But I was fairly early brought into the planning stage of the new review, once the merger had been agreed. The two groups, when they fused, went for a whole lot of Left figures over a wide range, who were very diverse in their politics and their experiences. The result was a rather large editorial board, which from the beginning looked better in public than it could be as a working group for a review. But there was a general sense of trying to gather together a whole generation which the experience of the Cold War decade had disrupted. Still I got the sense of an assembled generation rather than one which had truly come together. This was apparent in everything. At the founding meeting of the new review, I remember that I made a very short speech saying that two traditions of the left had irretrievably broken down – Stalinism and Fabianism. A different tradition was now needed, which would have a much wider conception of politics – a 'New Left', although this phrase hadn't started within the group, and several of us were uneasy about it. Edward Thompson, in an earlier speech at the same meeting, had spoken in the perspective of a new popular movement that would completely transform or replace the existing Labour Party. I said that, well one hoped for this, but I would be very satisfied if in ten years' time we had twenty or thirty good socialist books about contemporary Britain, not about the past, and a hundred issues of the review (I thought of that recently when the hundredth number of NLR came out). In other words, what I knew we could do was to get a lot of new work published and set up a new kind of socialist discussion, and what I thought we should try to do was look all the time for the opportunity of a broader political movement as well. I think I got one thing right, but another thing wrong. The editorial board of the review, when it came into being, was also loosely responsible for co-ordinating the activities of a whole number of clubs which were seen not only as forums for discussion but as the germs of a new kind of political movement. This dual role led to a lot of arguments within the board. My position was always that it would require most of our energies and resources to keep the publishing and discussion programme going, and that this was the first priority. I argued that if we went for the big goal – the rapid materialization of a political movement – we might fail to achieve this modest aim. I think I was right about that. What I was wrong about was to assume that a cultural and educational programme alone could revitalize the left or alter areas of popular opinion sufficiently to change the traditional institutions of the labour movement. On its own, it didn't really mesh with the much tougher political problems that the attempt at the clubs implied. But mind you, these were never adequately confronted in what you could abstract as the other side in the argument. I remember particularly discussions with Edward Thompson, who was quite correctly very excited by the prospects of the new movement in 1959–61. Although he had much greater ambitions for the clubs, there was never any clear sense that they were to be the preliminary organizations of a party. So these were only variations on a theme, even if the differences of emphasis at the time were quite sharp.

How do you assess the experience of the New Left in 1960 to 1962?

The magazine did well initially, and attracted a lot of writers. At a time when the Labour Right under Gaitskell seemed to be capitulating completely to consumer capitalism, and the Labour Left, whose bearings were predicated on the existence of general poverty and the old kind of class structure, seemed to be unable to talk about the new society at all, the only people who appeared to be making a socialist case in the contemporary world, as distinct from an earlier one, were the New Left – especially the younger generation, which was particularly conscious of changing cultural patterns in Britain. The price that was paid for that consciousness was an underestimate of everything that had not changed in contemporary capitalism. It was widely felt that some of the classical Marxist problems belonged to a past phase, and you could move on through them. The result was a radical underestimate of the political power of the capitalist state. By our very closeness to the ways in which the society was changing culturally, we overestimated the possibilities of action by cultural change on the left. The group which had left the Communist Party was not, I think, really much nearer to grasping these issues, but to the extent that it kept some of the traditional Marxist arguments alive it was making more of a contribution than was often seen at the time. Both tendencies, however, saw the new kind of popular politics, the marches and clubs, as the way through to a socialist mobilization of an unproblematic kind. When you look at the issues raised on the New Left, it was nuclear disarmament and then a range of cultural and social service questions: there was a whole area of politics in the middle which was not much discussed. Our attitude towards the Labour Party was particularly mistaken. It was never taken seriously enough. There was a general sense that given its integration into the world of NATO capitalism, it was a negligible organization: while the marches were so big, and left clubs were springing up all over the country, this outdated institution could be left to expire. For a year or two CND seemed to be carrying all before it. People were already guessing the dates for the disappearance of the Labour Party – like the end of the Second World War. So the reversal of the vote on nuclear disarmament in 1961 came as an astonishing blow. There was no idea of the strengths of the Labour machine, or of the political skill with which the right was able to organize for victory within it. The marches started to decline, and as the original optimistic perspective dissolved, the journal created by the New Left inevitably underwent strain.

Meanwhile, there had been other problems within the review. When it was launched, Stuart Hall had been appointed editor, and he produced a style of journal closer to the original ULR, in contact with new cultural styles, new modes of visual presentation, in a language that differed from the typical left magazine. Many people on the board were critical of this. I felt very aligned with him because I thought the kind of magazine he was trying to bring out had a real function, even if I didn't necessarily like every issue myself. The pressure on him was enormous, with constant circulation of internal memoranda about the policy of the magazine. I think the editor never got either proper backing for what in the event he was more or less left to do on his own, or clear directives for which the editorial board took collective responsibility. Working under great difficulties, he was often just blamed for whatever came out – a fairly typical situation on the left. There were endless arguments within the board over whether it was running a political movement or a magazine. There were also mundane problems of the usual sort about the temporary debts of the journal. Eventually Stuart accepted a job with Hoggart at the new Centre for Cultural Studies at Birmingham, so the review had to change anyway. A transitional group of four editors took over, and there were soon conflicts between them and the old board. I then found myself in the position of a mediator between the contending groups. A new style of journal started to emerge, dropping the campaign perspective now that there wasn't a movement to sustain it, and concentrating on basic intellectual work. I was the more likely to accept this direction since I had argued for the priority of an educational programme from the start. But I was also a member of the old board, where there was a lot of resistance to the new definition of the journal. At one point there was even a move to exercise legal copyright to prevent the revised journal calling itself *New Left Review*. I sought above all to try and avoid any such action or pronouncement by the old board, because it became apparent that if it stood on its rights there would be no magazine, that it would simply go. For the new editors could only launch with the goodwill of the old title, which still had its subscriptions and some assets. I wrote to people I knew best on the old board and said, 'You may not like what they are doing, but I think it is a condition for sustaining the magazine that we should let them do it.' By then it wasn't a choice of one style or another, it was a question of whether there would go on being any left magazine or not. The experience of *Politics and Letters* had made me feel that I would rather anything had happened to it, even my own exclusion from the journal, if it could have gone on through those years, rather than what actually occurred – that under much the same sort of pressures it simply disappeared, so that there ceased to be any organ for that kind of work. If *New Left Review* had folded in 1962–3, which could easily have happened, doubtless something else would have started later – certainly in '68, but there would have been some years of loss and silence. It was a survival strategy that I mainly argued.

The victory of the right in the Labour Party in 1961 was soon followed by the death of Gaitskell and the succession of Wilson, conventionally identified with the left of the Party in 1963. A year later, a Labour government was elected. What were your attitudes to these rapid changes in the political situation?

After the reversal of the vote on nuclear disarmament, and the missile crisis, CND was much weakened. When Wilson became leader of the Labour Party in 1963, and brought with him a quite new style of rhetoric, there was a very rapid transit of most CND people I knew back into the CLPs – into the 'new model' Labour Party as they spoke of it, curiously, even after the strength of the Labour machine had been demonstrated by the reversal of nuclear policy. In my view the biggest mistake made was not the overestimate of the possibilities of an alternative movement from '58 to '61, but the resigned re-acceptance of conventional politics which followed from '62 to '64 – with the illusions about the Labour Party which went along with it. Of course, I shared the hope that the next Labour government would put through certain measures in the social field with which we all broadly agreed. I didn't expect it to understand the new cultural issues, but at least I thought a dialogue about them would be possible. People like Benn or Jennie Lee seemed interested in these problems, and open to them. But what was generally forgotten was the lesson, not only of the CND experience but also of the left-right controversy in the Labour Party in the early fifties: that there was a necessary interlock between the Anglo-American military-political alliance in NATO and the pattern of possible social-economic priorities at home. Now when many socialists went back into the Labour Party in 1963 they started talking very persuasively about all the reforms the Labour government was going to accomplish in the social sphere and even the chance that they might tackle some of the new cultural issues, but there was an absolutely fatal evasion about foreign policy in a broader sense. The one thing that I'm glad I got on record at the time, writing about the coming election for *The Nation* in the USA, was my conviction that the foreign policy of the Labour Party was so dangerous and so obscure. The consequences became very clear once the Labour government was in office. The real problems of political organization on the left were never confronted or solved in this period, either when it was thought the Labour Party could be left alone since the marches and the clubs would supersede it, or when it was thought possible just to go back into it as an active force and keep it on the correct path. Each was an error.

Your position implies a judgment of the balance of forces within the Labour Party from the fifties onwards. What was your view of Bevanism and of the traditional Labour Left, out of which Wilson himself had emerged?

The Labour Left represented certain very good received demands and positions in the fifties. It had put up a prolonged fight against the whole reconstruction of the Western military alliance, above all over German rearmament, even if with some chauvinist overtones which made one uneasy. They said certain necessary things about the Soviet Union which were right for socialists to say. They always played a key role in industrial struggles – several involving the railways, so I was very close to them on that. They gave a high priority to the social services. They attacked the ideas of the mixed economy. But at the same time it seemed to me that they did not understand at all the changes of post-war Britain. The capitalism they were describing was the capitalism of the thirties which led inevitably to depression and dire poverty. The stress of their socialism was a politics of redistribution, whereas what was now needed was a socialism of production that could resolve the problems of work itself. Nationalization of mines or railways hadn't altered the working relationships or position of the workers inside the nationalized industries; they simply accumulated new institutions around a quite unchanged and deeply undemocratic state machine. Miners or railwaymen quickly discovered that they were no more 'our mines' or 'our railways' than before. The long route of political control went round through a Labour government, but by the time they had gone round that way, conditions had altered very little – in fact in certain ways they worsened, as the mines were run down, the railways were run down. But this was not an argument you could pursue in the Labour Left at the time. Later I used to get annoyed when people started calling them merely the Old Left, with a rhetoric of youth which defeats itself after ten or fifteen years as people themselves get older anyway. But they were an old left in the real sense, I think, that they could be outflanked in so many ways by the changes and innovations of contemporary capitalism. If they hadn't been like that, the new socialist movements after 1958 would not have seemed so important. I broadly identified with Bevanism in its campaigns in the early fifties, but I could never establish real collaborative work with the Labour Left. Typically they could not understand even small initiatives of a newer sort. I remember being greeted with absolute incredulity in a CLP when I gave a talk urging the self-administration of council estates by tenants; or by complete incomprehension when I wrote to *Tribune* suggesting that I write a series of popular articles on vocabulary – what later became *Keywords*.

How did you see the figure of Bevan himself?

I never trusted Aneurin Bevan, for the cynical reason that it takes one Welshman to know another. He came from only twenty miles away and I'd heard so much of that style of Welsh speaking since about the age of two that I was never as impressed by it as other socialists were. It is a marvellous form of public address which always assumes a faith in common. I think it comes out of the chapels where you didn't have to argue whether you should believe in God, everybody did that, so you could just be very witty about the ways of the world, or very indignant about its injustices. But it is not a style for serious argument, because your beliefs are presupposed from the start. So it was very difficult to know what Bevan at the centre believed. If you look at his book, he can give an excellent description of the artificially antique atmosphere of the House of Commons, but his political philosophy is much more uncertain. You can take it as a set of strongly held emotional convictions which come out of a peculiarly Welsh experience – that of a people who have been united for so long in wanting change, yet in relative isolation, that they think that they have really only to sound the trumpet and the walls will fall down. After all, if it could have been done by talking, Wales could have been a socialist republic in the twenties. The Welsh, you might say, were so far aggrieved that there was no need to argue through fundamental questions. This was very characteristic of Bevan's style. So you get the fine social democrat of the Health Service, but also the Labourist metropolitan parliamentarian – a stifling figure – and of course the final equivocator on the H-bomb. So I never thought Bevan was defining the problems of contemporary British society, even when he was leading radical campaigns with some public impact. Of course, Wilson was another matter again. He showed himself very clearly when Bevan was expelled from the Shadow Cabinet: Wilson, who was supposed to be on the left, just took over his position.

The first Wilson administration was formed in October 1964. You've said that you hoped for some degree of sympathetic response from the Labour government to the cultural questions that had been raised by the New Left. Your own book Communications, *which set out a comprehensive programme of reforms for the major media, would presumably have been a test case of its actual reactions. What was the reception of that book?*

Communications originated from a talk about the contemporary press for a NUT Conference entitled, typically for the time, 'Popular Culture and Personal Responsibility'. Penguin commissioned me to write a general book on communications from that. I took the opportunity to combine the aims of producing a teaching book, using methods of analysis I had developed for classes in Adult Education, and a programmatic work for institutional changes, designed to serve the more general political movement on the left. At the time there were on the whole no party policies in the communications area at all. So the chance of putting forward concrete proposals seemed a good one. The result was that I worked out very detailed schemes for changes in three stages: immediate, transitional and long-term, partly thinking there was some possibility that at least the first might be taken up by the Labour Party but also partly to develop a new kind of left politics – constructive as well as critical – in the communications area. The traditional answer of the left to everything was public ownership. But no one had ever worked out what public ownership should mean in a field as sensitive as this. The prospect of bureaucratic monopoly was rightly feared, given the examples of state-controlled media, as just jumping out of the frying pan into the fire. The result was to induce resigned acceptance among people working in the media of the existing capitalist arrangements. The essence of my proposals was that public ownership of the basic means of production should be combined with leasing of their use to self-managing groups, to secure maximum variety of style and political opinion and to ensure against any bureaucratic control. This principle is perfectly practicable in every field from the newsprint industry through to broadcasting facilities and cinema. It represented a clearly new political line. The reaction of the reviewers was consequently very hostile. *Communications* was widely and angrily attacked as a plan for the nationalization of culture, however disguised – all the more dangerous because it called for more freedom and more responsibility, rather than more controls. The book had a very sharp political reception from the right.

In many ways Communications, *which has gone through three new versions since you first wrote it, represents an exemplary model for socialist politics – both in its comprehensive articulation of short-term, transitional and long-term objectives, something very rare in programmatic texts of the revolutionary left, and in its pioneering entry into the specific field of cultural organization, where it raises problems that have perhaps so far only once ever been historically wrestled with, in Czechoslovakia in 1968. Its ideas would have been directly relevant to the Prague Spring. The reaction of the right in England which you have described was quite comprehensible. But what was the response within the Labour Party?*

Ironically, one of the reasons for the alarm and hostility of the right was the assumption that if a Labour government got into office, which seemed imminent in 1963, it would be guided by ideas like these. When Labour won the election, there was in fact a comic episode: *The Sunday Times* published a special spread entitled 'The New Establishment', with a row of faces across the top of the page, including those of Townsend, Hoggart, Abel-Smith and others – and myself. These were supposed to be the people who would be giving the intellectual orders to the Labour Ministers. In reality, throughout the entire six years of Labour government in the sixties, I never had one enquiry, formal or informal, private or public, one invitation to a committee or a conference, from anybody in the Labour government or Labour machine. Not one line. On the other hand, following a private leak from a man in the Civil Service, Hoggart and I and the Musicians' Union had to fight a plan by Benn to set up a reported chain of commercial radio stations. In the case of the Open University, which combined my interests in communications and in Adult Education, there was no consultation whatever. I supported the idea of the Open University very strongly, but I also thought it could be combined with a reshaping of adult education, which, as I said before, had run into new kinds of difficulty. There could be a connection between education by television, radio and correspondence courses, and the kind of tutorial class education which had been so well developed by the WEA. It would not have been easy, and I am sure there were political reasons for wanting to push a prepared idea of the Open University through, against its many enemies on the right. But Jennie Lee later told me, at a *Guardian* dinner, the only time I ever met her, that as the Minister responsible she had decided to steer clear of the old types of adult education and set up what looked as much as possible like a conventional university, including the 'trimmings'. So that was it, that kind of assimilated even where radical initiative, and the Open University still has no properly based tutorial organization, and little of our old educational democracy.

You had few hopes and many fears of what the foreign policy of a Labour government would be like. Soon after the Wilson administration took office, in 1965, the USA decisively escalated its war in Vietnam – with the collusion of the Labour government. How did you view its conduct?

When I moved to Cambridge in 1961, I was soon more involved in immediate politics than I had been in Hastings, a provincial town with nothing like the range of political activity of a centre like Oxford or Cambridge. For the first two or three years while I was there, up to and overlapping the election of the first Labour government, there was a very active local left in Cambridge. So I initially became engaged over Vietnam through the group here. We sent a delegation to the House of Commons to protest about the issue very early in 1965. The atmosphere there was very revealing. Shirley Williams, whom I had met when I gave a lecture to the Fabian Society, just wouldn't talk about the question. Stan Newens started to lecture us about Dien Bien Phu and Ngo Dinh Diem, at a level incredibly below that of the people who had come, as if we knew nothing about Vietnam. The notion generated in Parliament that people come to see you not to discuss where you go from there, but to be told, seemed to have taken hold even of a very good left MP, whom I much respect. I got up and made a scene, saying he shouldn't waste our time – we wanted to discuss what the hell to do to stop the Labour government supporting the American war in Indochina. This was during the period of the minority government and the left MPs could, if they had wanted to, have put tremendous pressure on the Cabinet on Vietnam because the Labour government completely depended on their votes. To them it was unthinkable to risk bringing the government down over an issue like Vietnam. They were much more concerned about getting this or that bill through the Commons; they couldn't see that the alliance with the US over Vietnam was deciding the basic political character of the Labour government.

So later I joined the Vietnam Solidarity Campaign. There were conflicts for some time in the anti-war movement between the call to end the American intervention, and the simple and correct line of solidarity and victory to the NLF. But this was a different world from the days of CND, when one was fighting hypotheses rather than a massive military expedition. Support for the Vietnamese Revolution produced a much harder, more militant movement on the left. Although I had always felt friendly towards American society, for nearly a decade I refused to accept invitations to the USA because of the war in Vietnam.

How did your attitude towards the Labour government evolve, after the revelation of the reactionary character of its foreign policy, and the nullity of its cultural policy?

From 1964 to 1966, most people on the left whom I knew at Cambridge complained about the first Wilson government, but said that it was being prevented from doing what it wanted by its tiny majority in Parliament.

The elections in March 1966 then gave the Labour Party a majority of one hundred. What happened? Within three months, Wilson was on television doing everything he could to break the seamen's strike, denouncing their leaders as a small group of politically motivated men. Nobody resigned from the Cabinet – it was a very complete revelation of what the Labour Party had become. A month later there was the July sterling crisis, when Wilson's rhetoric could certainly have identified small groups of politically motivated men if this had been even a shadow of a left government – but no, there was deflation and cuts in the social services to defend the exchange rate. Watching these two connected performances, I concluded that this was the end of the road. I decided to leave the Labour Party and write some sort of a manifesto, stating very clearly that the Labour Party was no longer just an inadequate agency for socialism, it was now an active collaborator in the process of reproducing capitalist society.

That was in July. By accident, in August, a meeting was called in London of socialists who had lost touch with one another after the breakdown of the original New Left. I went to it and proposed the idea of a manifesto. There was a lot of talk about who would edit it and some of the younger people made a very conscious reconciliation between me and Edward Thompson, because we'd had our differences in the period of the change-over in NLR. In the end, Stuart Hall, Edward Thompson and I were appointed joint editors. That was the origin of the *May-Day Manifesto*.

How was the Manifesto *actually written?*

I wrote nearly all of the '67 issue myself, but there were very good sustained discussions in the final stages of that draft, at a number of well attended meetings, which were like a regrouping again of the early New Left board. Then after the '67 *Manifesto* came out, which we printed ourselves, Penguin suggested publishing a paperback version of it. This time I was made editor, but actually Edward and Stuart contributed more to the second *Manifesto*, although they weren't formally editors, than to the first. Several new people came in to write certain parts of it: a group used to meet here for working week-ends drafting different chapters. Eventually I then edited al' these into a single text, as a rewriting job. The final chapters were done by three of us in my house at the very last minute, to get the *Manifesto* out by May 1968.

The Manifesto *was designed to be a political intervention at national level. What was the organizational conception that ensued from it?*

Our hope was that the *Manifesto* would be widely discussed in the Labour movement, stimulating the creation of forums or left clubs in which people could start forming effective centres for common political debate and action, without giving up their own membership of existing political organizations. In that sense, the perspective was not so dissimilar to that of 1959–61. Initially a fair number of these forums were established. Of course, compared with the late fifties when a lot of people were looking for a home on the left, by this time there were now a whole range of quite substantially organized socialist groups in Britain. The principle of the *Manifesto* was that people should be able to join in the forums without having to break with any other group. This was a very contentious notion, because any formation which offers to be common to a number of other groups is readily perceived as really wanting to substitute itself for the others. So it was decided to call a National Convention: we invited every socialist organization we knew of to a preparatory commission to organize this convention, whose aim was to give the movement more national presence and to launch a wider and more vigorous resistance to the increasingly rightward trend of the Labour government – which had just issued its own 'Mid-term Manifesto' as what seemed to be a counter to ours. We got a very large take-up from different organizations, as well as individual delegates, for the preparatory commission. The Convention itself was a difficult occasion, because the in-fighting between various groups was very fierce; the only people who observed all the rules that had been set up at the beginning were the representatives of the Communist Party. But it was also very argumentative and lively. The disputes were typically over issues of the quite remote past – usually the mid-twenties. On contemporary social issues in Britain and on major international issues like Vietnam, there were common lines. Despite the conflicts, a substantial document did emerge from the Convention – a series of positions more politically pointed than the *Manifesto* itself, and a call to members of all the organizations represented to set up left groups in their own areas, which would be co-ordinated by the preparatory commission in London sitting with national representatives from all the groups.

Now, how did this continue? Most of the main socialist organizations sent representatives to the co-ordinating commission, although not regularly, and a number of new local groups were set up. There was real unity against the Labour government's trade union legislation, against the emergence of Powellism, against the Vietnamese war. But as soon as the 1970 election supervened, it brought to light deep-rooted and persistent differences of political perspective and strategy. Once the commission had to discuss policy towards the forthcoming election, you got a range from, 'We must rally behind the Labour Party come what may, because we must keep out a Tory government', through a much more conditional support of Labour, to the position that we should actually oppose the Labour Party – which I shared. The tendency to which I belonged argued that we should attempt to run Left Alliance candidates in the 1970 elections. Immediately there was talk of this, the Left Labour people who had previously co-operated withdrew double-quick, the socialist groups which denounced the Labour government but insisted on the need to vote for its return also abandoned the commission, and so, critically, did the Communist Party, which as so often had been contributing rather more than its share to the donkey work on it – even though it was committed to putting up candidates itself. All three moved right off when they saw this other line emerging, and so the commission split four ways. It never reassembled. A movement which had managed to sustain a significant amount of left unity disintegrated over the electoral process – over whether it was permissible to make electoral interventions to the left of the Labour Party. A strategy of common activity could survive anything except an election.

The May Revolt occurred in France in 1968, in the very month the Manifesto *was launched in Britain. What was its impact on you?*

I found the May events in France very exciting and felt totally solid with them. The people who were working on the *Manifesto* were to and fro all the time between here and Paris. I felt this was a different manifestation of the same kind of movement. The combination of workers and students was similar to the perspective within which we were working. The Labour government was then pushing through its anti-union legislation; there seemed to be a good chance that there would be a point of junction between a working class which could now perceive the Labour government as an enemy and a student and intellectual movement which had been building up from the late fifties. The French explosion was on a much grander scale than anything we had foreseen happening in England, yet it was in the same dimension. Even in Britain, of course, there were very large demonstrations over Vietnam in October of that year. So the May Revolt was both a surprise and not a surprise – as when something happens which one has foreseen as the only effective socialist answer to the modes of capitalist politics: it wasn't as if no one had talked of a revolution. People must have felt the same way about 1917. What impressed me most at the time was that the movement lasted as long as it did. But also, when it was all over afterwards, I thought the way capitalist society got out of the crisis was also very significant, through the resort to elections – revealing the ease with which the left was displaced to the party of disorder, and the electoral process re-established not only as order but as democracy. There were lessons both ways from that critical event.

The 1970 elections in England were won by the Conservative Party, ushering in four turbulent years under the Heath government. What was your reaction to the new political conjuncture of the early seventies?

The whole series of battles up to the climax of the miners' strike of 1973/4 was a return to real class politics. The re-emergence of genuine socialist militancy on a mass scale under a Conservative government seemed to me to confirm precisely my assessment of the Labour Party: once its manipulation of class forces to avoid any actual class battles no longer held, the situation became much more dynamic and explosive. But that in turn allowed the Labour Party to repeat the scenario of the sixties again. I wrote an article for *The Nation* in 1971, predicting that in opposition the Labour Party would readopt a leftish posture with a mild radical manifesto for the next election, would be re-elected again in the guise of a regrouping of the left as in '64, and would then implement right-wing policies once more, paving the way for a further Conservative government – so that we would simply have gone through the decade again with no significant difference in outcome. The failure of the effort at a real regroupment of the left in the *Manifesto* affected me a lot politically: after that, the one thing I was determined not to take part in was a re-play of the sixties.

When the March '74 election was called, after two years of the most open class struggle British society had seen since the war, it was a calculated attempt to repeat the same sort of operation that had occurred in France. A Tory MP made the very significant remark after the miners' ballot: 'They've had their vote, now we'll have ours.' That was how it was programmed – to use the election to defeat the strike. In that situation, for the Tory government to have got back by triumphing over the assembled working class would have been disastrous. It was necessary to do anything to prevent that. By now there wasn't even the minimal base for an independent intervention that there had been in '70. So I voted Labour, and spoke at some of their meetings. The theme on which I spoke, however, was 'Elect them on Thursday, fight them on Friday' – that was the only position I was prepared to take, and literally Friday, not in a year's time. When Labour won the election, my whole political analysis of its role was very rapidly confirmed. For what was most striking was the completeness of the return to order within the labour movement. The very considerable crisis to which British society had been brought by the conflicts of Conservative rule was speedily contained and defused by renewed Labour rule. It has become ever clearer since then that what I would call a post-social-democratic party is absolutely essential to the working of modern capitalism in Britain, in periods when the general movement of the economy and the society demand a major neutralization of the working class. I think it has been wrong since about 1966 to speak of the Labour Party as a social-democratic party.

What do you mean by a post-social-democratic party?

The British Labour Party was a social-democratic party until 1948–9, in the sense that it was not trying to achieve socialism – that is to say, the transformation of capitalist relations of production by a decisive shift in class forces and class rule; but it was trying to establish certain social priorities over the operation of the capitalist system: for example, the health service, which was not seen as a system for supplying a healthy labour force to industry or as an allocation from the gross national product, but as the assertion of a social purpose over the capitalist market. The classical social-democratic position, as distinct from a major Marxist tradition, is expressed in Tawney's saying that no society is too poor to have a right order of life, and no society too rich to be able to dispense with it – in other words a claim of social need and social justice, rather than only a concern with the distribution of the marginal product. That tradition has virtually disappeared from the Labour Party today. Since about '66, it would be impossible to defend the party's programme in these social-democratic terms. Significantly Labour leaders have even stopped talking about reforms in that way. The reforms they now propose are simply designed to rationalize and perhaps humanize the capitalist economy, accepting the priorities of its investment and consumption, if adjusting the distribution of the residual product. The argument for *overriding* social use and social need is never seriously made today. That is the dividing line between what was once a social-democratic party and what is now a post- or non-social-democratic party.

Isn't your historical account of the Labour Party questionable? After all, the elements of capitalist modernization and rationalization were very evident in the Labour programme and performance of 1945, substantially inherited from Beveridge and the technocratic circles which won so much influence in the state apparatus during the war. Equally, even in the sorry Labour Party of 1978 there are still elements of what you describe as a properly social-democratic project; the party has always envisaged its social reforms financed out of capitalist growth. Isn't Callaghan arguing even today that economic recovery through a huge bonus of North Sea oil will provide a base for the renewal of an upward curve of living standards and an expansion of the social services again? What is missing from your account of the degeneration of the Labour Party through the sixties and seventies is the very drastic change in the economic environment in which it has operated. Wouldn't it be more accurate to say that the Labour Party, like other social-democratic parties, remains a contradictory formation, in which a residual project of social reform has become historically inseparable from capitalist rationalization, and that what determines the shifts in the distribution of those two purposes is in the last analysis the condition of the national and international capitalist economy?

I think this is the reason for the degeneration, certainly. The Labour Party discovered that you can't have social democracy in one country, particularly not in a second-rank, weakened capitalism. Nearly all its ideological shifts can be dated around successive crises when it has been demonstrated to ruling political circles in Britain that they are operating within forces which are much too large for them to control. Within the Labour Party, there has each time been a further reservation of objectives which are desirable but which cannot be achieved now because of international constraints. The sum of those shifts in ideology has by now transformed the balance of forces inside the Labour Party. The programme of the left itself is now largely confined to greater public intervention or participation in the capitalist economy.

Yet the Labour Party preserves the structural features of a social-democratic organization, in which organized labour retains tremendous power at the base of the party and at a national level. It seems to remain a more supple political formation, with correspondingly greater ongoing credibility for the working class, than your remarks suggest. If the Labour Party had degenerated as far as you claim, would that not be tantamount to saying that very large sections of the working class were on the point of a political break with it?

But a break in which direction? A minority of the working class has been moving left, away from the Labour Party, for ten to fifteen years now. On the other hand, there also seems to have been a decline in the political consciousness of significant sections of the working class, together with the increase of industrial actions in the past decade. Today there are patterns of struggle to which the experience of US trade unionism may be as relevant as the past of the British Labour movement. There is a kind of militant particularism, much of it resembling in form the struggles of an organized working class in the classical sense, which is yet part of a capitalist market system – a process of bargaining which lacks any wider political dimension. A comparative example would be the recent consultants' strike in the hospitals, similar in all its features except its class ascription to a traditional wage struggle, yet fundamentally different in its relation to the current political system and social order. Within the industrial working class itself, there can now be a very militant sit-in or strike to prevent a particular factory from being closed, which is resolved by an agreement for the take-over of the plant by an American capitalist. Tool-makers can strike for wage differentials, arguing in much the same manifest terms as consultants. In cases like these, workers are no longer acting out or meaning to act out what Marxists see as the historical mission of their class, exerting such deep pressure on the economic relations and contradictions of this society as to change them. Of course, these actions can still disrupt a capitalist economy, because of the deeper contradictions of the system, which offers these kinds of ambitions and incentives – but when people take them up they may throw the system into crisis. But a qualitatively different sort of consciousness is involved, and that crucially affects what can happen when such a crisis occurs.

Now the movement at present is not all in one direction. The recent miners' ballot on a productivity agreement was a significant example of the contrary principle – it was a rejection of the notion that if you're in a prosperous area you should vote for the benefits, and bad luck to those who find themselves in a poorer area. Welsh miners argued very forcefully that to give such a priority to the wage over all other considerations was anyway to drive people to work beyond themselves to get their bonus, with more risk of accidents not only to themselves but to others, and as such was a socially irresponsible proposal. That is the very opposite reaction. I think there is a genuine problem if one brackets all these different sorts of action together as economic militancy. After all, there is nobody more militant than a stockbroker in pursuit of his killing. The militant action is not necessarily the socialist action, as the whole employment situation becomes more complex, and as the traditional political instrument of the working class has ceased being even social-democratic. There is a decisive difference between militant particularism and militant socialism, which necessarily involves a political movement at the centre, a broad strategic aim to transform society. There are of course all the processes in the middle, where as has often been the case in history, a strike starts against intolerable conditions or for more pay with no more thought in the world than that, but objectively becomes an action which puts the whole class system in question – the next question which has to be asked. With true militant particularism there are no other questions; the only question is your percentage.

Would you say this form of particularism is becoming predominant in the British labour movement?

No, I think it's all still in play. After all the working-class support for the miners in '73–4 was a remarkable example of the strength of resources and the invention of means that are indispensable to socialism. There is no question of writing off the potential for that kind of collective action. You are less likely to get it under a Labour government, when the collective purpose has precisely been displaced. But this can change according to what is happening at the centre. The further growth of a depoliticized particularism, however, will depend on whether the whole framework of the British political order remains essentially unchanged or not. For its development is closely linked to the uniquely stifling mechanism of the two-party system in Britain. The classic way out of every crisis of English capitalism is to alternate the major parties; so long as those parties maintain their cohesion, in the absence of any other electorally significant formations, this process of replacement can fuse and defuse successive crises for years on end. Political coalitions are not built in this country, they arrive ready-made through the voting system, so that the two large parties do not really even have to negotiate their policies – they write one for elections, but once in power they do what they please. This is a very specific peculiarity of British politics which distinguishes it from the other major capitalist societies which confront the same problem of controlling fundamental social conflict through the electoral process.

It is also my main reason for supporting the two movements which seem to me to be putting pressure on that system from opposite ends: the national movements in Wales and Scotland, and the international movement towards an integrated Europe. In Wales, for example, it is very important that there should be a nationalist party introducing another political tendency into the equation, to the left of anything the Labour Party has been since the war. At the same time, to the extent that Britain as a member of EEC is integrated into a European electoral process, alternative alliances will have to be made: at the very least negotiations which are completely blocked in this country, between social-democrats, socialists and communists, open up as a perspective – once we are beyond the confines of this very particular British state with its curious electoral straitjacket. I am sure Tom Nairn is right to maintain, although I don't agree with all his arguments, that the nationalist movements pose a quite significant threat to the British capitalist state, and could precipitate a crisis in the Labour Party itself if they took away its two traditional strongholds in Scotland and Wales. I think he is also right about the positive effects of moving British politics out on to the wider European stage. Neither change will be sufficient in itself, of course – we will still need a proper left movement in the heartland of England. But as you approach the hardest kind of condemnation of the Labour Party, which is a deeply discouraging conclusion to get near, it is some compensation to see the emergence of other movements, other kinds of intervention, which may put this particular managed system at risk and perhaps even start to break it.

How would you sum up the general perspectives for the left in British politics in the eighties?

The whole discussion of its strategy would be significantly altered if, largely as the accidental outcome of the proceedings of others, there was a change in the voting system. For proportional representation would make it far more plausible to build a socialist party or alliance capable of intervening seriously in elections. The degree of opposition in the political establishment to reforming the electoral system, which is indefensible in any other terms, is indicative of how much they fear the rules of the game would be changed if the two-party monopoly were ended. It is very important that the left should be aware of the clear socialist advantages of such a change, never mind any liberal demands for it. In the past the British left has traditionally taken the opposite view – that there must be no fragmentation of the working-class vote, which must be unified to get a Labour government. That perspective is now an anachronism. Proportional representation is not merely abstractly preferable as a voting system, but strategically desirable as the road to a significant political presence to the left of the Labour Party at the national level, capable of exercising pressure back on the Labour Party itself. In Italy, even though the corresponding parties are small, nevertheless their presence is crucial within the political system because they are to the left of the Communist Party within the same spectrum and not in another spectrum. The course of the PCI itself is affected so long as there is an appreciable force to the left of it, not only in an extra-parliamentary or intellectual opposition, but right on its own electoral terrain.

More generally, the stability of British society is now disappearing: in fact the rate of destabilization now seems to me very fast. From one point of view this should be immensely encouraging, because only radical destabilization offers the possibility for new forces to come through. Some of the developments that now look like loosening the British deadlock are welcome: whatever happens in Scotland and Wales, or in the EEC, will probably be a positive change. But there are other destabilizing processes which will involve suffering of a very considerable kind. The whole phenomenon of racism will continue to disrupt the life of English cities, spreading violence and confusion, as attitudes harden, lines are more clearly drawn, certain shabby compromises break down. Then the main destabilizing force of all is, of course, going to be the continuance of major unemployment, once it is realized that this is not a temporary phenomenon. The impossibility of a return to anything like full employment within any feasible capitalist perspective, even at quite rapid growth –

indeed the realization that even socialists will have to stop thinking in the capitalist category of full *employment*, trying to move beyond it to the very difficult alternative concept of adequate and equitable means of livelihood – will inevitably cause growing disorientation and suffering. This prospect will, I think, be a great test of nerves for socialists. For there must be something in every socialist, from the very values involved in wanting socialism at all, wanting a revolution to bring about socialism rather than just wanting a revolution, that continually pulls towards precisely the compromises, the settlements, the getting through without too much trouble and suffering, that is the great resource of longing on which the capitalist parties draw. Perhaps I feel this especially strongly. For until one has realized what has actually happened to people who have suffered as the objects of history, one cannot understand the depth of this desire, which is more than the ideological effect of those parties and institutions which seek to defuse intolerable contradictions in order to preserve the system. It is only when people get to the point of seeing that the price of the contradictions is yet more intolerable than the price of ending them that they acquire the nerve to go all the way through to a consistent socialist politics, understanding that the destabilization and the suffering are not caused by those who organize to end the system that produces them. The objective conditions are now increasing for the left to break out of its marginal situation in England. But I think that it is above all this feeling which is holding a significant part of the British labour movement back – the hesitation of good people shrinking from the consequences of change. At the age of seventeen you can feel glee that the social system which you hate so much is breaking up, but then there is a diminishing scale of elation to the crucial and dreadful point when, realizing what the human weight of revolutionary change would be, the majority of a generation deserts and simply moves to the right, settling for anything under the pretext of a quiet life and a wise resignation to the difficulties of altering the world. But I think that the battle is for those kind of people, because unless you can take out a very significant proportion of them from the Labour Party, there isn't a future for socialism in Britain.

2. Orwell

Your political writings since 1956 have taken a number of different forms. Before discussing the general evolution of your positions on the major issues of socialist politics within Western capitalism, we would like to start by asking you some questions about those texts which confront problems of the Cold War, and of the revolutions in the East. Firstly, can we take up your study of Orwell, written in the early seventies? This is a very attractive and powerful piece of writing, which unites 'politics' and 'letters' perhaps more closely than anything else you have written. It also represents a significant extension of the range of your political writing, in that it is the first book where you reintegrate the facts of empire and imperialism absolutely centrally into your vision of English society as a whole. They appear elsewhere in your work only in asides, but in the Orwell book they move right to the centre of the picture in a very compelling way. What was the background to its composition?

In the Britain of the fifties, along every road that you moved, the figure of Orwell seemed to be waiting. If you tried to develop a new kind of popular cultural analysis, there was Orwell; if you wanted to report on work or ordinary life, there was Orwell; if you engaged in any kind of socialist argument, there was an enormously inflated statue of Orwell warning you to go back. Down to the late sixties political editorials in newspapers would regularly admonish younger socialists to read their Orwell and see where all that led to. This seemed to me false. The Orwell history seemed to me more complex and contradictory. Here was a man who said that every word he had written was for democratic socialism, and who fought for it in Catalonia as a revolutionary, yet so much of whose writing is clearly anti-socialist in a general way and not just on particular questions, and indeed has had an enormous anti-socialist effect. I had been wanting to write a short general book on Orwell from the early sixties. The opportunity for that precise form came only at the end of the decade. The part of the book I am most satisfied with is the attempt to define the peculiar question of the plain style of Orwell's prose, which has been extraordinarily influential as a convention well beyond literature. It has become a reportorial format and a television style. I share with my friends the modernists a profound suspicion of anything that appears so natural. The chapter that I would not have missed writing was the one where I discuss the creation of a character called Orwell who is very different from the writer called Orwell – the successful impersonation of the plain man who bumps into experience in an unmediated way and is simply telling the truth about it.

Many bourgeois readers will have found your study scandalously, even impiously, sceptical of George Orwell. It must stand as perhaps the only principled critique of Orwell from the left. Nevertheless in the last resort you seem to let Orwell off rather lightly, granting him an indulgence which your own evidence does not appear to warrant. The general argument of the book is to suggest that while the sum effect of Orwell's work has been on the whole very reactionary, both in the ferocious anti-communism he helped to unleash in the Cold War period and – possibly yet more so – in the regressive social patriotism he stoked up in war-time and post-war England, nonetheless Orwell was a man who became a revolutionary socialist for a significant period of his life, and then tragically but perhaps inevitably went wrong, but even so left certain writings which have an enduring force and relevance to us today. Now the crux of this case for Orwell is the sudden change in his political outlook at the outbreak of the Second World War. In your account he came back from Spain a revolutionary socialist, and then became a solid patriot virtually overnight. Quoting his regret that he had not participated in the imperialist war of 1914–18, feeling less of a man because he had missed it, you remark: 'On this explanation, Orwell's abrupt change is simply a reversion to type. And in a sense this is true. But under the simple readjustment, which was traditionally available, a more profound process of discouragement had been occurring.'[1] *What, then, was this deeper process? Your answer is as follows: 'He had exposed himself to so much hardship and then fought so hard; had got a bullet in Spain; had been severely ill with a tubercular lesion; and had given so much of his energy to what seemed a desert of political illusions, lies and bad faith. Between the myth of "England" and this profound European disillusion he had to make what settlements he could find.'*[2] *This is really your only*

[1] O, p. 64.
[2] O, p. 65.

substantive judgment on Orwell's volte-face. In fact what you are saying is that Orwell got very tired and his energy ran out. But your language – 'He had exposed himself to so much hardship and then fought so hard' – strikes a note of pathos which seems designed to exculpate him. Now it is of course true that Orwell had fought creditably in Spain, but it is not the case that there weren't other contemporaries who had fought longer and harder for socialism than Orwell, who did not switch sides so easily. Think of someone like Isaac Deutscher, who had worked in the revolutionary underground in Poland, who had much more direct experience of the devastations of Stalinism in the Ukraine, and was a refugee in England at the time. He didn't break under the pressure of Stalinism, become a social patriot, let alone a violent anti-communist. He knew Orwell well after the war, and wrote one of the most penetrating assessments of him to date. One scarcely need speak of Trotsky himself, who was still alive, in conditions of incomparably greater adversity, when Orwell was celebrating the myths of British social unity and characteristically opining that he was 'as much responsible for the Russian dictatorship as any man now living'.[3] Why should Orwell's collapse be excused merely on the grounds that he was tired? Surely that is the wrong way to approach the problem?

I think it probably is wrong. Once you put Orwell in a fully internationalist context, then of course it is true that there were people who sustained more. I suppose there is something sentimental in simply saying that he was tired and wounded. But what is interesting is that he had available to him a way of being tired, so to speak, which was unthinkable for a Deutscher or Trotsky. That was the notion, which was extraordinarily widespread in England, that British society could be transformed through the conduct of the war. There was then a crucial slippage from that position to social patriotism, in the sense which connects with a later labourism and chauvinism. Many people in my generation underwent that slippage. The question is then whether you try to understand that process as it were sympathetically, and so pulling the punches, or whether you draw right back from the process and simply say what it was, in a much harder way. We had the same discussion about my treatment of some of the figures in *Culture and Society*. Between the late forties and the early seventies I usually tended towards the former procedure. I'm not

[3] Cit. O, p. 63.

defending it, I'm just saying that this is what I then came to do.

Beyond the question of Orwell's political turn, of course, lies the problem of an overall assessment of his value as a writer. Disregarding his posthumous reputation, in the final analysis we have to ask ourselves three questions. Did he produce new theoretical knowledge about society or history? Fairly obviously not; few even of his admirers, apart from apologists on the far right, would claim that he did. 1984 *will be a curio in 1984. Did he then produce first-rank works of creative imagination – novels of major literary value? Again, the answer is evidently no: his novels range from the mediocre to the weak. The thinness of works like* Keep the Aspidistra Flying *is generally acknowledged. Did he provide faithful accounts of what he witnessed or experienced – documentation of an outstanding accuracy? The most frequent claim for Orwell's accomplishment as a writer today is that this was his forte. The case can certainly be made for* Homage to Catalonia, *a very fine reportage, whatever its limitations as a general view of the Spanish Civil War. But it cannot be made in any simple way for* The Road to Wigan Pier, *on which his fame primarily rests, because of the elements of suppression and manipulation you show in your book. Orwell's recurrent resort to bully and bluff to impose his prejudices on the reader as if they were plain if disagreeable facts, a technique not dissimilar to that of ordinary Fleet Street journalism, often renders his actual reports untrustworthy. But if Orwell had few or no original ideas, a limited creative imagination, and an unreliable capacity to recount information, what remains of his achievement? The answer seems to be the invention of the character of 'Orwell', a process of creation which you describe very well in the book. But what you abstain from is any judgment of this figure, and the element of masquerade in it – not in the sense that the real writer was a different person, but in the sense that under the guise of frankness and directness the writing posture is more than usually dominative. In the short run, the main charges against Orwell are political – his decline into his own versions of social chauvinism and anti-communism. But in the long run, the cultural damage done by his lack of literary scruple has probably been more lasting.*

I was reminded, as you were putting that, of Cobbett – a case I often reflect on in this way. There is no doubt that in the matter of language Cobbett is very often doing the same thing to the reader. But equally there is the distinction that there is a constant, almost lifelong flow of personal reporting in Cobbett which is not there in Orwell – Cobbett doesn't always fully disclose how he came to be in the position of observer, but he does so far more and is much franker about his prejudices than Orwell. For the key point about the convention of the plain observer with no axes to grind, who simply tells the truth, is that it cancels the social situation of the writer and cancels his stance towards the social situation he is observing. In that sense it is simply the popular journalistic expression of the whole mode of objectivist social study. Orwell's strategy is always to try to write as if any decent person standing where he was would be bound to see things in this way. So you're left with the case of *Homage to Catalonia*, where I get the impression that because Spain was not England or Burma he was much more capable of writing what was happening as something of which he himself was a part, rather than 'our man on the spot' reporting on it, and that he felt the change in himself. There is briefly something of this in the trip down the mine in *The Road to Wigan Pier*, but it is preceded by his suppression of how he got to go down the mine, and how he stayed in the homes of working-class socialists, who he then denied ever existed. I would want to widen the discussion now, because this is the way my own thinking has gone, to the dominant form of which his work is one famous example: in other words, not Orwell writing, but what wrote Orwell. I think if you put it in that way you can reach, not so much an estimate of him as a novelist, a critic or a political journalist, but a more genuinely historical estimate of a collective form.

The comparison with Cobbett is slightly amiss in that Cobbett's language has an exuberance, a generosity which is a long way from the bleakness of Orwell – he had a greater range as a writer. The other point is surely that Cobbett had a relationship through his own background with the rural society which he was describing, and with the popular movement of the time, which makes him a very different figure from Orwell.

But that would begin to answer the question, what was writing Orwell, what was writing Cobbett? That does not mean that a particular generational form comes *en bloc* – there is a general form, and there are variations of instance within it. I mean to write an essay called 'Writing in the Thirties: Blair, Mitchell, Sprigge', discussing Orwell, Grassic Gibbon and Caudwell, which would be a sketch towards this. But it would also be important to study that whole generation, specifically including the people largely lost from sight who didn't make Orwell's move – who were not crushed by the experience of the thirties. This is a very significant phenomenon which is only now coming into view. But the British people of that generation who did not change direction were also, I feel, to some extent silenced by the contradictions they experienced. Edward Upward's trilogy is an attempt to work through that experience. Although it is not a successful one, because in a way it is an even more complete regression than Orwell's, to the aesthetic self-preoccupations of the twenties, it does otherwise represent a more honourable political course. The key question, however, is what deep structures of consciousness and pressure were producing the shifts during the thirties and forties which in Orwell's case resulted not in an isolated major individual, but what was to be a widely imitated style. The next generation received that form as wisdom, achievement and maturity, although it was false to the core. So far as Orwell himself is concerned, once the plain style goes, the centrality goes and this is the question about what was writing him.

If that is the question to be posed, then one answer to it at least seems fairly clear. During the Cold War, the international bourgeoisie had an objective need for extremely potent and, above all, popular works of a blatantly anti-communist direction. Of all the countries in Europe, England was a particularly strong candidate for producing them, because it had no experience of a mass revolutionary movement in the 20th century, the local ruling class was less affected by internal upheavals than any of its continental counterparts, and the social order was the most traditional and stable. It is unlikely to be an accident that it generated the two best-sellers of anti-communist literature on an international scale – Orwell and Koestler. The case of the latter is particularly suggestive since he was of course himself not English. It is always necessary to remember the enormous international resonance of the later Orwell. To this day, for example, tens of thousands of copies of Animal Farm *and* 1984 *are sold every year in West Germany, as obligatory texts in the school system. That is not to mention the broadcasting of his catchwords over the various émigré radio networks to Eastern Europe.*

On the other hand, if you ask what was it in Orwell that allowed him to fulfil the smmons of the conjuncture, so to speak, you refer to a quite separate order of determinants. Here the sort of analysis which Sartre has sought to make of Flaubert would be a relevant model: he first tries to reconstruct the constitution of Flaubert's personality within his early family experience, and then to explore the reasons why the society of the Second Empire should have conferred such a signal if paradoxical success on Madame Bovary. *In the case of Orwell, what his writing seems to suggest is an active predisposition from the start to see – not specifically about socialism in the first instance – the dark side of his subject. That was to bring him a certain kind of truth, when he was later writing about the English left or about Soviet Russia. But what is striking is that Orwell seems to have been temperamentally in his element when he was vituperating causes which in another part of himself he hoped to advance. His very tense and ambiguous relationship to socialism is the most obvious, but not the only example of this strain. It pre-existed the political demand, to which Orwell himself never voluntarily accommodated, for parables of the Cold War.*

I think the other condition of Orwell's later works was they had to be written by an ex-socialist. It also had to be someone who shared the general discouragement of the generation: an ex-socialist who had become an enthusiast for capitalism could not have had the same effect. The qualification one must make is that the composition of these writings predates the outset of the Cold War – he wrote *Animal Farm* during the period of maximum popularity of the Soviet Union in this country. There was an oppositional element in him which made him the first in the field.

The recruitment of very private feelings against socialism becomes intolerable by *1984*. It is profoundly offensive to state as a general truth, as Orwell does, that people will always betray each other. If human beings are like that, what could be the meaning of a democratic socialism? But this dimension of Orwell's writing is also a part of a very large form which has even deeper roots than the neutral observer. For the mode of an extreme distaste for humanity of every kind, especially concentrated in figures of the working class, goes back after all to the early Eliot – it was a mode of probably two successive generations and it has not yet exhausted itself. You can see it in Orwell's choice of the sort of working-class areas he went to, the deliberate neglect of the families who were coping – although he acknowledged their existence in the abstract – in favour of the characteristic imagery of squalor: people poking at drains with sticks. His imagination always and submissively goes to that. There is a powerful sense, which I think is theoretically very interesting, but difficult to understand, in which certain literary conventions really dictate modes of observation, not just of writing, although it's in the writing that the effective dictation comes and that what is taken as vivid and convincing and truthful is actually prescribed. In Orwell's Lancashire it is always raining, not because it often does or doesn't, but because it has to do so as a condition of convincing local detail of the North.

That convention could move, in certain cases, in the opposite direction. For example, the same themes of pervasive disgust can be found in the early Graham Greene. There is a remarkable comparative analysis of Greene and Orwell as novelists, in point of fact, in Terry Eagleton's Exiles and Emigrés. *Yet if the initial sensibility was not dissimilar, the ideological conclusions were widely divergent – interestingly, on precisely the two questions of British patriotism and international communism. The mediation of a kind of Jansenism has something to do with Greene's development, of course.*

It is also that there was more to write Greene than to write Orwell. Because if you take Greene's writing after 1950, you are talking about a different kind of work. Who knows what kind of novel Orwell would have written if he'd turned up in Saigon or in Haiti, where Greene brings that convention to bear on an imperialist situation? We just don't know, and there isn't any point in speculating. A pathetic aspect of the literary world of the fifties and early sixties, in fact, was the imaginary competition to be the heirs of Orwell in the next generation.

Your book is very controlled and sympathetic in tone towards Orwell, through all its criticisms. Some of your comments now seem sharper. Have you altered your views on his work?

I must say that I cannot bear much of it now. If I had to say which writings have done the most damage, it would be what you call the social patriotism – the dreadful stuff from the beginning of the war about England as a family with the wrong members in charge, the shuffling old aunts and uncles whom we could fairly painlessly get rid of. Many of the political arguments of the kind of labourism that is usually associated with the tradition of Durbin or Gaitskell can be traced to these essays, which are much more serious facts than *Animal Farm*. For all its weaknesses that still makes a point about how power can be lost and how people can be misled: it is defeatist, but it makes certain pointed observations on the procedures of deception. As for *1984*, its projections of ugliness and hatred, often quite arbitrarily and inconsequentially, onto the difficulties of revolution or political change, seem to introduce a period of really decadent bourgeois writing in which the whole status of human beings is reduced.

I would not write about Orwell in the same way now, partly because I have had more and more doubts about the character he invented. For example, there was no objective reason at all for the disgraceful attacks he made on pacifists or revolutionary opponents of the war in American periodicals, denouncing people here who were simply in his own position of three or four years before. The impression of consistent decency and honesty that Orwell gave went along with the invention of a character who comes up new in each situation, who is able to lose his whole past, and again be looking as the frank, disinterested observer who is simply telling the truth. When he does that to fellow socialists whose position he so recently shared, I can see the basis for a very much harder assessment of this kind of man and this kind of writing. The book was the last stage of working through a sense of questioning respect. I am bound to say, I cannot read him now: at every point it is these bad moves he made that stick in my mind.

3. The Russian Revolution

Your study of Orwell alludes indirectly to the problems of the Russian Revolution. But you have also written directly on socialism in the East, mainly in Modern Tragedy. *There you develop a cogent argument against any ahistorical universalization of a single concept of tragedy, contending that there are epochal differences in the character of tragedy, new types of which tend to emerge in periods of historical transition. At the same time, there is a powerful and important political theme running through the book, which essentially turns on the fate of the October Revolution. So although in one sense* Modern Tragedy *appears to be the most specialist of your critical volumes, in another sense it is both the most general and the most political. It concludes, in fact, with a play about Stalin. Towards the end of the text, one of the characters declares: 'We kill all these things in ourselves, commit the suicide of the heart, so that it will not betray us, not involve us. And then the process runs faster and we are all become Koba.'[4] This statement seems to summarize one of the themes of the book, explored elsewhere in a number of major passages: the sense in which there is a general necessity of terror within the process of social liberation. In effect, you make a direct association of the terror of Stalin, of the trials and the camps, which in reality destroyed the Bolshevik Party and so many of the achievements of the October Revolution, with the agents and ideals of the Revolution itself. Stalinism is not presented as a consequence of the historical conjuncture in the USSR in the twenties, at a time when other possibilities for Soviet development existed, which could have produced a quite different political order. Instead your account really forces an identification of the original impulse of the Russian Revolution with its conclusion in Stalin's tyranny. Do you still feel that assimilation is valid?*

No, I do not. One of the difficulties about the relation of the play to the rest of the book is that it was written much earlier, in '58–9. I eventually

[4] MT, p. 273.

included it in *Modern Tragedy* because it was on the same themes, but it was written in a different period. But that doesn't dispense with the main question. I would accept that because of the scale of the civil war and international intervention in an incredibly weakened country, the Bolshevik Party found itself very early in a relatively isolated situation in which the original social base of the revolution had disappeared amidst the suffering and fighting, and it then had to maintain the ideas of the revolution against contemporary reality. The identification I made is wrong because the Bolshevik exercise of power in these circumstances during the revolution and the civil war, including military power and the oppression that went with it, has got to be qualitatively distinguished from the regime of the camps in the thirties, which destroyed the Bolshevik Party itself. That was obviously a very different process. I still think that there is a dimension of tragedy which is unleashed by any passage into revolution, but I would certainly want to reject the notion of inevitabilism in the statement you have quoted: it is one of the positions expressed in the play, but the actual ending is very different – something like a recovery of the original impulse of the revolution after it has taken the weight of the disaster and learnt from it. Of course this is distanced from the actual events in the Soviet Union, where a dénouement is still to be awaited.

There are quite other sorts of tragedy that can overtake a revolutionary process. Chile is an example.

Exactly. That is a completely different kind of tragedy, where a good man held back from a confrontation for a range of reasons, from tactical calculation, to reluctance towards that kind of struggle, to the belief that it was against the traditions of Chilean society. His choice was then tragically falsified by a counter-revolutionary intervention, followed by so brutal a regime that the level of violence involved in trying to make a revolution was in the event dwarfed by the results of not preparing to resist the violent overthrow of a working-class government. But that is the sort of case which the left generally understands much better – it was similar to the crisis, with all its complications, of the Spanish Republic when it was invaded by Franco's legions. The left between the wars was faced with a whole series of situations in which a democratic process was assaulted with military force and it had to answer with force, or prepare to do so. That, of course, is one of the rivers to cross in the development of a socialist movement. But it is an easier one than the next, when the extreme difficulty and exposure of a revolutionary movement arriving in power leads to the harshest measures which are not initiated by the right but by the left itself. The hardest contemporary example of all is Cambodia, where if we accept the Cambodians' own account, to feed the population without American grain they had to reverse the movement into the cities and push people back into the country, doubtless with great suffering, but under the imperative of either producing enough food to be able to maintain independence or falling again into a kind of colonial subservience. Many people draw back at the spectacle of forceful repatriation to the countryside and the very brutal discipline employed to enforce it, although it could be argued that these were a consequence imposed by a revolutionary seizure of power in a situation made so exposed by the previous history. The tragedy of a revolution is not at all insurrection or the use of force against its enemies – although it can be a tragic experience in another sense to be confronted with a bitter and cruel enemy aided by outside intervention, like the Chilean junta. The real tragedy occurs at those dreadful moments when the revolutionary impetus is so nearly lost, or so heavily threatened, that the revolutionary movement has to impose the harshest discipline on itself and over relatively innocent people in order not to be broken down and defeated. That kind of hardness, although it shifted around in the complicated politics of the USSR in the twenties, was in different ways taken up by everybody in the Soviet Party. Those who withdrew from the notion of a hard line – hard yet flexible – did stop believing in the revolution. That has been the main block in the minds of most people thinking about the Russian Revolution in another sort of society ever since.

One of the difficulties of the essay on 'Tragedy and Revolution' in the book derives from the ambiguity in your usage of the term 'terror' in it. For example, you write: 'This idea of "the total redemption of humanity" has the ultimate cast of resolution and order, but in the real world its perspective is inescapably tragic. It is born in pity and terror: in the perception of a radical disorder in which the humanity of some men is denied and by that fact the idea of humanity itself is denied. It is born in the actual suffering of real men thus exposed.'[5] *You go on: 'All our experience tells us that this immensely complicated action*

[5] MT, p. 77.

between real men will continue as far ahead as we can foresee, and that the suffering in this continuing struggle will go on being terrible.'[6] *When you speak of pity and terror here, recalling Aristotle rather than Stalin, it is the suffering involved for those who make the revolution and the denial of ordinary humanity to the class enemy in a civil war that are terrible. Later, however, an elision occurs with the meanings associated with Stalin. For you conclude: 'We have still to attend to the whole action, and to see actual liberation as part of the same process as the terror which appals us. I do not mean that the liberation cancels the terror; I mean only that they are connected, and that this connection is tragic.'*[7] *Here the term seems to refer to the institutionalized system of political repression created in the thirties – the Great Terror of the Yezhovschina. That had absolutely no connection with liberation: it was its pitiless negation. A socialist reader must surely protest against this fusion?*

I can see that there are two levels. There is the level of suffering which is involved in any sudden overthrow of an old society and the initial struggle to create a new one. There is another level of terror, brought about by the enforcement of revolutionary discipline not just against the enemies of the revolution, but over people who are involved or were involved in it or who represent a different tendency inside it. Under extreme exposure, a terror can occur which is inextricable from the liberating process: something quite different from the familiar repression of an armed gang exercising a dictatorship to preserve the old order. Through all the complications, I would say that this was basically the case in the Soviet Union during the early twenties. It is a very hard thing to accept, but I think you have got to accept it and see it as tragic. If you do not see it as tragic, you are not taking its full weight; if you regard it as a logical consequence, you reject the revolution. But that does not mean that there is bound to be systematic terror.

To use your image, there is one river that should never be crossed – not the imposition of a very hard revolutionary discipline, but the suppression of political debate and the installation of official untruth within the revolutionary process. You cited the recent case of forcible repatriation in Cambodia. It is clear that the war-time population of Phnom Penh, over three million people,

[6] MT, p 78.
[7] MT, p. 82.

could not be fed in the city once American supplies stopped. An evacuation may have been necessary. But no attempt seems to have been made to explain it to the population, which was driven out of the city at gun-point, in a denial of any conscious political process. However dire the conditions of international or domestic siege, the elimination of free political discussion and communication within the camp of the revolution should never be excused. It strikes directly at the possibility of long-term liberation ahead, beyond the immediate circumstances of emergency. Didn't you tend to overlook this distinction in your account of the Russian Revolution?

Yes, I wouldn't dispute that. All these distinctions have to be made within a historical process as complex as the Russian Revolution. I did not want to say that the hardening to the point of cancellation of the liberating impulse is inevitable in any revolution, because it seems to me it never happened in the Cuban Revolution, and I don't think it will happen in the Chinese or Vietnamese Revolutions, for all the extreme suffering and hard policies involved in them. These experiences are all much more within a normal perspective. The tragedies in them are of a different order – the passing through of a considerable period of siege, in which to hold to the revolutionary project, the enemy may be reduced to a less than human status, but nevertheless there is no question of the priority of the impulse of liberation. On the other hand, that impulse can fail and be forgotten, not only by men who are adventurers and have never known it, but by people who have possessed it and then under extreme pressure have forgotten it and radically reduced themselves. Yet even these people can sustain a broadly liberating movement which would otherwise be defeated by circumstances or confusion or by intervention or recovery by the enemy. If the Cambodian evacuation was as you suggest, and the city population was driven to do something that the revolutionary forces knew to be necessary, yet without the elementary ratification of discipline that would have been an explanation of the reasons why it was necessary, then that would be such a case: where the stress on the revolutionaries takes them to a point where they cancel the impulse of liberation in themselves and become simply an abstract revolutionary will, detached from any recognition of what the will is directed towards. When the pressure is so great that revolutionaries suppress different tendencies within their own movement, or even parts of themselves, as the enemies within, they become a blank agency operating under the name of revolution but now arbitrarily driving people in a predetermined direction. This is the movement of which Büchner wrote in *Danton's Death*, where you become the mask of the revolution, and behind the mask the revolution itself disappears. That is the extreme case. But there are all the equally important and more common cases where there is still a very problematic relation between a liberating humane movement and the necessity of attacking repression, of defending the revolution against counter-revolution and external intervention, of sustaining discipline when differences inside the revolutionary movement appear, while keeping a balance between discipline and democracy inside the revolution. That whole range happens.

There still remains one essential dimension that is completely missing from your account. Stalinism as it grew up, already in the twenties and emphatically by the thirties, was not just a kind of ultra-fortification of the Russian Revolution, against external or internal enemies, a system of inhuman discipline and of institutionalized suspicion. All this of course existed and can be interpreted within the terms that you have been employing till now, which are predominantly moral categories. These are certainly indispensable, but there is a danger if we dissociate them from a more prosaic sociological analysis of the historical forces at work in the Soviet Union. In this respect you seem to have been curiously insensitive to the real power of the critique that Trotsky made of the Soviet state that had been consolidated by the thirties. What Trotsky sought to show were two simultaneous processes: a ruthless logic – the pressures of imperialist encirclement and blockade, the economic isolation and social weakening of the country – that was forcing the revolution in the direction of an ultra-centralized authoritarian system within Russia, and at the same time an internal crystallization, through a very complicated set of social struggles, of a materially privileged stratum which partly grew out of but much more largely replaced the old Bolshevik Party. By the late 1930s and early 1940s the CPSU had very little connection with the movement of Lenin's day: it was a formation of a historically new type. Trotsky always defined its social function as dual and contradictory. It was a ruling stratum which defended fundamental gains of the revolution against the imperialist enemy abroad – it was in no sense a new capitalist class; but on the other hand it also vigilantly defended its own privileges against the working class and the mass of the population. That second function is what is absent from your analysis: the construction of the Stalinist political order as a castellation of material privilege. The functionaries who exercised its terror were not just deadened to ordinary impulses of humanity; they were also living in large villas, disposing of extraordinary amenities, protected from all the economic hardships of the time. Stalin's own tenor of life speaks for itself. Today, without these being equivalent to the scale of exploitation in capitalist societies, there subsist – not only in the USSR but also in China, which is a more egalitarian society – major social inequalities, well beyond those inevitable in any underdeveloped society, which are defended institutionally with a cloak of secrecy and if necessary violence by each regime. A grasp of this social process through which a new political order comes into existence was the deep insight, the great legacy of Trotsky's thought. It was not just that he had an alternative policy for industrialization and certainly a more democratic programme for Soviet development in the 1920s, at the time when he was defeated. After the defeat he attempted to think through and understand what social processes were at work in the USSR.

I would accept this. Discussion of the Russian Revolution cast within the notion of tragedy could not reach this kind of explanation. But the development of a social group which identifies the revolution with its own interests bears back, of course, on the nature of the moral terms themselves, since the revolutionary impulse has then clearly ceased. That is why in our very different societies the maximum generalization of popular self-management would be crucial in any revolutionary process. For it is always probable that in a situation of emergency there will be a tendency to claim that the exercise of command demands special conditions – the rationalizations are infinite and at the very first stage might be willingly conceded. People would clear a room for Lenin, although typically he never asked for one. It is easy to say: the Comrade has so much to do, he oversees such a large range of affairs that he must be granted different conditions from the sentry on the gate. But from these immediate practical necessities of maintaining direction and control there can imperceptibly grow a hierarchy of power and privilege. If Western socialists today take the Bolshevik experience as a model, they have not learnt its tragic lesson. For nobody ever supposes that he will become that person at the end of the line who has forgotten what the revolution was for or who identifies it with his own position, his own sense of power. Even the darkest views in the twenties could not have conceived the end of the process in the thirties. So the one lesson that has to be learnt is not just a moral reservation, it is a perfectly practical conclusion which can be given a precise social definition: the condition for avoiding the final tragedy when the leaders of the revolution lose the revolutionary impulse, as distinct from the early stages when the impulse continues amidst suffering and disorder, is that new forms of popular power and revolutionary self-management should be constantly thrown up. It is quite possible that other kinds of tragic process cannot be avoided, but they are of a different order.

Entirely agreed. We shall have to come back to this fundamental issue of the new forms of popular power. Meanwhile, can we ask a specific question about your image of Trotsky? At the end of The Country and the City *you draw up a powerful indictment of orthodox Marxist thinking about town and country. One of your key arguments in the final pages is an interpretation of the later course of the Russian Revolution which blocks together Trotsky and Stalin without further ado. You write: 'Trotsky said that the history of capitalism was the history of the victory of town over country. He then proceeded, in the critical first years of the Russian Revolution, to outline a programme for just such a victory, on a massive scale, as a way of defeating capitalism and preserving socialism. Stalin carried through very much that programme, on a scale and with a brutality which made that "victory" over the peasants one of the most terrible phases in the whole history of rural society.'[8] This paragraph seems to encapsulate your general feeling about the figure of Trotsky. Now there are a number of comments to be made about it. The first is that it is empirically inaccurate. Trotsky did, of course, say that the history of capitalism is that of the victory of town over country – but he also made it clear in many writings that communism betokened the abolition of the antagonism and division between town and country. It is simply untrue that he advocated a massive capitalist-style attack on the countryside or the peasantry in Russia. What Trotsky argued for in the twenties was an increase in the pace of industrialization to enable the towns to supply the country with the mechanized equipment that would render possible an increase in rural productivity which would then allow town and country to be fed better. No programme of forced collectivization or of a war on the kulaks can be found in the documents of the Left Opposition. These were Stalin's policies. What you are involuntarily repeating here is a version of those latter-day apologies for*

[8] CC, pp. 302–3.

Stalin which seek to relativize his crimes by distributing co-responsibility for them among those who most unrelentingly fought him. In fact, the agrarian programmes of Trotsky and Stalin were antithetical, and Trotsky never ceased to denounce the brutality and folly of Stalin's war on the peasantry, which has crippled Russian agriculture to this day.

The reason why this is an important question and not just a marginal quarrel about one historical personage is that a generational block can be sensed in very many socialists of your age over the question of Trotsky: not so much an attitude of hostility as a kind of repression, a brushing aside. What it seems to indicate is an unwillingness to engage with the legacy of Trotsky as in any sense a living tradition. Whereas for a younger generation today – this is something you will surely have noticed since the sixties – what Trotsky represents at a fundamental level is a non-archivization of the Russian Revolution. That is to say, Trotsky's work provides us with a linkage to October which does not merely relegate it to the far past, because actually of course Trotsky lived up to the Second World War, and went on producing a great many relevant ideas about Western as well as Eastern societies until his death. A serious appreciation of it is a way of keeping the whole question of the Russian Revolution open – the future of it, as well as what is happening in the USSR today – and of not separating it solipsistically from the problems of revolution in the West. This seems to be something that many people of your generation, particularly those who were once in the Communist Party, feel they have settled their accounts with – they above all do not want to go back to it. Is this a correct reading of your response?

I would agree that this is a block, because I find exactly the experience you have just been postulating. I have to make a positive effort to confront this problem. It isn't a crude reaction, as if we were introduced to Trotsky as the enemy of the revolution and therefore found it difficult to readjust afterwards. It is rather a certain reluctance to go back into intricacies which were not present for the succeeding generation. For example, I don't have the knowledge to argue adequately about the difference between the two campaigns proposed for the Russian countryside by the Left Opposition and by Stalin. There seemed to be certain similarities of language. These are a constant difficulty in the whole revolutionary tradition, which for historical reasons has been dominated in modern times by urban middle-class intellectuals who have often had very ambiguous attitudes towards the peasantry. Although Trotsky himself came from a rural environment, which he evokes in his autobiography, his relationship to the peasants was of a kind which would tend to produce the same sort of attitudes. At any rate certain of his phrases appear reminiscent of them. I concede that one has to go beyond these and see what his specific programme was. In general, however, I would say that for various personal reasons I have always noticed a radical underestimation of rural producers amongst urban intellectuals, who typically lump together under the term 'peasantry' what are in fact very different social classes. This is particularly relevant to our own history, given the whole experience of the exodus of the rural labourers from the countryside in England. But the mistake of equating industry with progress, involving an objectively exploitative relation to food producers, has exercised an extraordinary influence on the whole international socialist movement.

Still, your sheering away from the memory of Trotsky cannot have just been due to doubts about his views on the agrarian question. One curious index of this is the fact that your chapter on 'Marxism and Art' in Culture and Society *omits any reference to one of the most famous texts on the subject –* Literature and Revolution. *In the thirties* Scrutiny *had to deal with it very seriously; but by the time that you were writing in the fifties, you could just skip over it. That cannot be an accident.*

No, I accept your description of a generational block.

Do you think that the division between Stalin and Trotsky, which should not be considered as only involving the policy struggles in the Soviet Union in the twenties, is irrelevant to debate over socialist strategy in Western Europe today?

The experience of the Soviet Union under Stalin is a major obstacle to the development of a revolutionary socialist movement in the West. It is impossible for us to get clear directions about our future until that historical past is understood and learned from. You have maintained that, rather than being the complicated but relatively unified experience that my generation saw, the fate of the Russian Revolution involved radical differences of theory and principle which can still be argued and brought up to date, relating to the organization and programme of revolutionary socialist parties in the West and to the interpretation of what has happened in the East. The generation succeeding my own has made these connections better than we did.

There is, however, another aspect of the conflict between Stalin and Trotsky, which was symbolized for me by two men physically fighting for the microphone at the National Convention of the Left, to denounce each other for their positions on the twenties. There is a certain contrast between the banality and frustration of contemporary British politics and the enormous élan of the Russian Revolution and its successors, which can lead to a kind of perpetual miming of these past historical situations. This is something quite different from a real continuation of the major division inside the revolutionary socialist tradition, which relives that essential debate. I know the difference between the one and the other when I see it, although it might be categorically difficult to separate them. A particular kind of political alienation can occur when people opt for revolutionary processes which have happened elsewhere, coming alive more when they are relating to those than when they are engaging with the drabness of their own situation. Now without the international dimension, and without a sense of history, nothing can be solved. But on the other hand problems cannot be solved either by the sort of sloganizing and abuse in which the Russian experience becomes a diversion from urgent political matters closer at hand. At the Convention some people reacted very strongly against these disputes at the microphone, to the point of saying that the whole left had become clients of various foreign movements. This is not true, and is a misrepresentation of the serious discussion which our generation did not have about those two alternative traditions. But I would distinguish discussion of the past from mimicry of it. The crucial values of the historical experience are the operative theory and the concretely specified practice that come out of it; what are not important are the loyalist identifications one way or the other, which in the very form of their making foreclose that which is the really significant inheritance.

Turning to the other great socialist transformation of the 20th century, during the later sixties you showed a considerable sympathy with the process of the Cultural Revolution in China.[9] *What attracted you particularly about it?*

There are a number of ways in which it is necessary to look at the Cultural

[9] *From Culture to Revolution*, p. 298.

Revolution. At one level it is necessary to see the real complications behind the official rhetoric. None the less, it seems to me that the principle which was behind the rhetoric and some of the practice, and which no doubt got tangled up with much else, was a vital one: namely that even in the early stages of a post-revolutionary society it is an indispensable condition of socialist democracy that the division of labour should be challenged by regular participation of everyone in ordinary labour. The fact that the Chinese did not fully put it into practice or that certain people were exempted from it doesn't change the fundamental principle at all. That principle has never been so clearly and powerfully enunciated as in the Cultural Revolution. I do not think that anybody should manage or administer any form of labour without the knowledge that they themselves will perform it, as well as, preferably, having come from it. When I heard pathetic stories about professors being taken from their libraries and laboratories and sent to help bring in the harvest I felt totally on the side of the revolutionaries. If people are genuinely ill it is a different matter, but I do not see why an ordinary healthy man or woman should not participate in manual labour. A socialist movement will have nothing to offer to the working class unless it stands by that. For it is this principle alone which can make it clear to working people that socialism is something other than a new way of managing them, given their deep suspicion of solutions like nationalization. It is the only way of winning the crucial fight inside working-class consciousness against the conviction that the man with the shovel will always be the man with the shovel – that someone else will be directing an incredibly responsible and liberating programme, but will not take a shovel to it.

The spirit of what you say is absolutely right. But the letter of the Cultural Revolution was rather different, for what it typically involved was an extremely voluntaristic attempt to foreclose the division of labour at a very low level of productivity. At the same time it was also a way of attempting to overcome it without instituting real forms of popular sovereignty. For the most important means of limiting and reducing the division of labour is precisely a genuine popular sovereignty, not simply a technical rotation of places, whether freely accepted or coerced. Thus it is far more important in China today that everybody should have equal access to political information than that professors should bring in the harvest, even if in a long-term epochal sense the division between manual and mental labour is the most fundamental social division of all. But full popular sovereignty already represents a decisive mitigation of that division, because thereby every citizen is given access to the general labour involved in the direction of society.

Of course I agree that, apart from the problem of the difference between the principle and the practice, there is also the problem of the available transitional forms. I also entirely concur with the importance of equality of information. As a matter of fact, during the Cultural Revolution I took up this precise point with the enthusiasts for it. I pressed to the point of ruthlessness the questions: what books were in what shops? where could one read the views of the opposition which was denounced as counter-revolutionary? These are the first things that an intellectual thinks of, and they were very irritated that I kept on raising them.

Actually they are more what a political militant thinks of. There are too many intellectuals who don't think about them.

Anyway, I don't want to confine this emphasis to China. It is also visible in Cuba. Instead of thinking – how can we get the workers to work harder? how can we introduce productivity schemes and Stakhanovite emulation? – the Cuban revolutionaries have acted on the principle that when you have a common need you meet it by common labour. Even if such a policy gets nowhere near abolishing the roots of the division of labour, it nonetheless gives a crucial indication of the direction in which the revolution should be going.

4. Two Roads to Change

The charge is sometimes made that Culture and Society, *whatever its intellectual merits, was politically a 'labourist' book – in the loose sense, not of loyalism to the current Labour Party or its leadership, but of allegiance to certain received notions of the British labour movement. There are some remarks in the book which seem to lend themselves to such an interpretation. For example, in your very interesting discussion of Matthew Arnold's reactions to the demonstrations in Hyde Park over the Second Reform Bill in 1866, you write: 'Certainly he feared a general breakdown, into violence and anarchy, but the most remarkable facts about the British working class movement, since its origin in the Industrial Revolution, are its conscious and deliberate abstention from general violence, and its firm faith in other methods of advance. These characteristics of the British working class have not always been welcome to its more romantic advocates, but they are a real human strength, and a precious inheritance. For it has been, always, a positive attitude: the product not of cowardice and not of apathy, but of moral conviction. I think it had more to offer to the pursuit of perfection than Matthew Arnold, seeing only his magnified image of the Rough, was able to realize.'[10] Is not the phrasing here – 'the most remarkable facts about the British working class movement . . . conscious and deliberate abstention from general violence . . . firm faith in other methods of advance' – very similar to the kind of trope that has traditionally been heard from Labour Party platforms? Apart from other difficulties, doesn't your formulation involve a very great simplification, in that the abstention from civil violence at home which you describe as a strong positive attitude has typically gone together with a negative indifference to or acceptance of imperialist violence abroad?*

The comment on Arnold still seems to me well taken in context. The minor disorders at Hyde Park in 1866 were provoked entirely by the action

[10] CS, pp. 133–4.

of the state – Arnold's ascription of violence to the populace is a classic transference which had to be opposed. However, I think that in general I was over-influenced by the period of the English labour movement I knew best, which was the epoch from the 1840s to the 1940s, and under-influenced by the period from 1790 to 1830, which I then knew much less well and found very difficult to bring into focus. One has to discriminate historically between those periods. But I concede that the extension of my comment into a 20th-century argument might be taken as suggesting submission to the conventions of electoralism and the particular machinery of Labour government. I don't think that I would have gone so far, but I can see how such a construction could be put on it. The problem is that within our kind of political world, disorder and violence have been typically projected by the Arnold technique onto the working-class movement, and in resisting that ideological transference one can fall into the opposite danger of stressing a kind of constitutionalism which is not its true character either.

You write, however: 'Can it honestly be said that the working people asked for anything other' than 'a revolution by due course of law', in 'the terms of their own experience?'[11] *Even keeping to the 1840s, which you have just evoked, there was after all the Physical Force wing of Chartism, which was precisely defined by its refusal to accept that due course of law could be the final word on the extension of the suffrage, if the ruling class persisted in denying it. Isn't the accurate answer to your question – yes?*

Historically the Physical Force wing was the heir to the tradition of 1790 to 1830, while the Moral Force wing were ushering in the new period. The Moral Force tendency was, of course, very mixed, but it included people who had a strong commitment of a positive kind to controlled collective action, not confined to a constitutionalism which anyway excluded them. That commitment and the feelings involved in it then got taken up and compromised by a pure conformism, which could eventually lead to a co-operation with the state that was actually utilizing force all along. Modern Labour ideology converts that complex history into something else again. The autonomous popular action of a controlled, non-violent kind which has been a traditional tactic not only of the British working class but of

[11] CS, p. 133.

many popular movements, is turned into the conventional constitutionalism of 'leave it to your representatives in parliament', where the Moral Force wing was very far from wanting to leave matters to their members of parliament.

The phrase 'moral force' still leaves a dangerous ambiguity. A later paragraph in Culture and Society *is an illustration. You cite a statement by Sidney Webb, who was actually the author of the Labour Party's Constitution, in which he characteristically talks of 'the main stream which has borne European society towards socialism during the past hundred years is the irresistible progress of Democracy'. You then note William Morris's objection to it, which was that: 'The Fabians very much underrate the strength of the tremendous organization under which we live. Nothing but a tremendous force can deal with this force.' But you can still refer to Webb's 'calm, admirable assumption of steady progress'.*[12] *Surely what is striking about it is its evolutionist complacency? Why should we admire it?*

I'm sure I was not clear in my mind then, although I think that the issue remains a difficulty for contemporary politics. In a sense it would have been much easier to believe – and there was some not negligible evidence for it, as Marx noticed – that there was an organic connection between the extension of democracy and the movement towards socialism. But I think Morris's intervention against this idea was decisive – he was clearly right.

What you said at the time was significantly different. You wrote: 'The argument between Morris and Webb, between communism and social democracy, still rages; neither has yet been proved finally right.'

Yes – this would have been my position then. I wasn't sure what kind of state could emerge from the development of electoral democracy. I was saying that I didn't know. Classical social democracy believed that the capitalist state could be progressively dismantled, the capitalist economy converted by degrees into a socialist order. Classical communism held the opposite position, that socialism will always be resisted by the capitalist state which will have to be overthrown by whatever force is necessary to do so. In *Culture and Society* I was really saying that I saw the strengths of

[12] CS, p. 184.

both positions and that I did not know, at that time, which one was finally true. You must remember I had a very strong pacifist background from the thirties: both from Wales, where there was a very close connection between socialism and a brave, constructive pacifism, and from that ethos so common in working-class families – the very strong sense that the way to conduct a strike was to be extremely orderly, on the good working-class grounds that if you give the enemy the slightest excuse to act violently against you, you're weakening your own position, so that discipline must be exercised to avoid any disorder which distracts from the main purpose of the action. But my position was still far from being what would now be called labourism, which after all takes an absolute standpoint on the question at issue – ruling out even contemplation of the alternative. I was well aware of that alternative – of the long evidence that the lion was not to be persuaded to lie down with the traveller, to use the image from Tawney, whose moral optimism I criticize elsewhere in the book:[13] that in the end the lion has to be confronted and defeated. But within the British political tradition or indeed within any comparable political tradition, I did not know which of the arguments was finally right.

How long did your general uncertainty about the two roads to change last? From your texts, it would seem to have persisted till as late as 1966, about the time when you've said that your final rupture with the Labour Party occurred. For in the preface to the second edition of Communications, *published in 1966, you argue quite strongly against the conception of social change 'against others', which you term 'pre-democratic'. You suggest that your own perspective is 'change with others', and the word in which you encapsulate this kind of change is 'growth'.*[14] *That seems a more emphatic commitment to a consensualist evolutionism than anything you had written before – as if you now concurred completely with Tawney. Yet in the same year you also published your essay on 'Tragedy and Revolution' which takes the diametrically opposite point of view. There you state: 'Our interpretation of revolution as a slow and peaceful growth of consensus is at best a local experience and hope, at worst a sustained false consciousness',*[15] *and you conclude unequivocally that the perspective of revolution is 'inescapably tragic', and this is so*

[13] CS, p. 219.
[14] C, p. 13.
[15] MT, p. 79.
[16] MT, p. 77.

because it is made 'against other men' – to suppress this fact is 'utopianism or revolutionary romanticism'.[16] *It is impossible to reconcile those two positions.* Modern Tragedy *was actually written before the second edition of* Communications? *What accounts for the oscillation?*

The preface to *Communications* should be seen in a particular context. At the time I wrote it, there were all sorts of movements starting inside the big communications institutions, seeking to explore workers' representation, to establish producers' control, to transform the structure of these industries. Change appeared to be a very much more close-up proposition than in other fields. At the same time, I had noticed the occasional comment on the first edition of *Communications* from the left to the effect that 'the only thing to do about communications is to smash capitalism: then we'll build a socialist culture'. Indeed I remember when I wrote the phrase about change with others I had a particular sample of that argument in front of me, to which I was so to speak replying. I should say that in general the very energies which make up the militancy of an authentic revolutionary left tend to make it much worse at working with others, to its own detriment, than reformists who have adopted the perspective of getting as much as you can within the system, developing skills of co-operation and compromise that any socialism needs. What I was trying to say in the preface was that I believed there were a lot of people to work with in the field of communications, because the crisis in major media had been very widely experienced, and that it was therefore a diversion to postpone action to change them until after capitalism had been smashed. There was thus a special reason why I retained in *Communications* longer than anywhere else the Tawneyan conception. But of course, it was wrong – you could not in the end work peaceably with people in organisational structures like IPC or even the BBC. That preface went out of the third edition of *Communications* and it did not just silently disappear: I wrote a postscript explaining what had happened to the illusions of the sixties.

So far as the shift from a reformist to a revolutionary perspective is concerned, I think that still if I saw an area in which the first kind of course seemed possible, I would always follow it until I was finally convinced that it was not just difficult, or interminable, or intractable, but that it was actually delaying the prospect of a solution. That is the real case for revolutionary politics. If the argument were only that we must have revolutionary action because it is quicker or because it will clear matters up within our own lifetime, it would not impress me so much. It is only when I believe that anything but this perspective in fact erects more barriers to substantive change that I would say the other perspective was false – not inferior because slower, but not possible at all. I think that is a very hard thing to realize and it doesn't surprise me that I kept grasping at every position which would prevent me from facing it. For in one sense at the very beginning of my work I had raced to the end of that position, accepting it unproblematically. In fact, it is still easy to go through to that position without counting it all along the way; I think if you do count it all along the way it is a very heavy weight indeed. It does mean, however, that your commitment is much more serious: when events happen, as they inevitably do in revolutionary processes, which are locally contradictory or even humanly appalling, you are less likely to have the recoil of a romantic revolutionary from the actuality of historical change. That was the general position I was reaching towards when I wrote *Modern Tragedy*. Once you have decided for revolutionary socialism, not because it is quicker or more exciting, but because no other way is possible, then you can even experience defeat, temporary defeat, such as a socialist of my generation has known, without any loss of commitment.

The notion of revolution is, of course, already present in your earlier work – it provides the very title of The Long Revolution. *But you had clearly not arrived at the position which you have just defined when you wrote that work. Could we ask how you would now characterize the overall strategic conception of* The Long Revolution *– what you think were its faults and its gains? In particular, what is your view of the criticism that it suffers from an underlying culturalism, still conceiving social change more in terms of common processes of creative growth, in the vocabulary of the book, rather than conflictual oppositions of class struggle?*

The book was an attempt to think through the idea of revolution in a society with substantial levels of cultural development and of democratic practice – in other words, a capitalist democracy as distinct from an absolutist state, or from societies marked by more absolute forms of material deprivation and poverty. The received images of revolution related to social orders where the majority of the oppressed were largely shut out from the cultural or political spheres. To stress the processes of cultural development, with all their contradictions – in the popular press, in the educational system, in the newer means of communication – and the political complications that follow from them, seemed to me a precondition for rethinking the notion of revolution in a society like Britain. I see now very clearly that in doing so I moved into a perhaps unavoidable specialism – writing more about the new than about the older but still true. However, I still felt at the time that what I took to be the ordinary Marxist explanations of the nature of the political and economic order, and how they should be changed, were valid. It was partly because I gave too much credit to them that I concentrated so much on cultural education.

So far as the question of class struggle is concerned, there is a distinction to which I have alluded earlier, that I now wish I had made in the book. Class conflict is inherent in a capitalist society – that is to say, an absolute and insuperable conflict of interests, primarily of an economic kind yet issuing out into the whole social order. But such conflict must be distinguished from class struggle, which involves conscious and sustained attempts to alter the social relations which are the basis of the class conflict. There are perfectly satisfactory reformist theories which include the fact of class conflict, but precisely stop at the prospect of class struggle. On the other hand, revolutionary theories often unduly assimilate the two: for there are historical periods in which class conflict is mediated through kinds of social, cultural or educational change in a way that does not typically result in class struggle. These periods, when the aspirations of the oppressed are at once given some acknowledgement and at the same time limited and thwarted, I would now define much more clearly by speaking of processes of incorporation. The best tendency in the book is an effort to see what class struggle would mean in areas of cultural and educational development which were normally excluded from socialist politics at the time. I think that tendency has become clearer with subsequent work. But the connections between new forms of cultural practice and political or economic practices, in any general process of revolutionary change in a capitalist democracy, were not worked out in the book.

Political changes are not actually neglected in The Long Revolution. *But what is striking is the modesty of their extent in your programmatic conclusion. The central part of its political section is devoted to parliament. There you write: 'It is very difficult for any of us to feel even the smallest direct share in the government of our affairs.'*[17] *This appears to be a very drastic and sweeping critique of the existing political system in Britain, albeit couched in somewhat subjectivist terms. But to remedy the situation, you propose no more than two-yearly partial elections to parliament, fixed dates for general elections and a more accurate electoral system. Yet there are plenty of capitalist democracies which have fixed general elections and proportional representation – which you don't even specify as an objective, as if it were too iconoclastic a demand in Britain. Are they in any sense qualitatively different from the status quo in England? Finally, you make a general plea for an improvement in what you call 'the present atmosphere of British democracy, which seems increasingly formal and impersonal'*[18] *– a theme taken up again in the* May-Day Manifesto *some years later: 'The criticism of parliament is in the interest of democracy as something other than a ritual . . . meanwhile, in Lords and Commons alike, the process goes on in an atmosphere heavy with rituals, and these are more than picturesque survivals . . . this is the theatrical show in which a precise power is mediated; the mellow dusk in which actual power is blurred.'*[19] *Now no doubt it is necessary to criticize the mystifying role of parliamentary rituals, but the implication here seems to be that a more robust and real atmosphere would somehow produce a satisfactory form of democracy. After the fundamental criticisms you make of the whole capitalist social order, which extend right across the entire range of its work relations, its property relations, its learning relations, its cultural relations, one comes down with a bump to proposals for an amended parliament with an ameliorated atmosphere. The* Manifesto *even conjures up the prospect that 'If the House of Commons were the ultimate focus of this democratic practice on the great national issues, it would quite quickly regain its importance. But while it prefers to remain with a different system and to accept its quite different rules and styles, it will go on emptying itself of democratic reality.'*[20] *Elsewhere the* Manifesto *declares: 'We can conceive, and would like to see, the House of Commons embattled against organized private power or established interests; fighting a popular cause against arbitrary authority and secret decision.'*[21] *The conventional parliamentarism of this perspective, with its flourish evoking a heroic past in the 19th or even 17th century, is surely very surprising by the*

[17] LR, pp. 336–7.
[18] LR, p. 338.
[19] MDM, p. 147.
[20] MDM, p. 149.
[21] MDM, p. 148.

late sixties. At no point is the question even raised whether it is historically likely that an institution of bourgeois democracy can be so simply or readily converted into an instrument of socialist democracy. Throughout all the discussions of democracy in The Long Revolution *and in the* May-Day Manifesto *there is, in effect, an absence of any real class referent. Democracy is treated as something which can be extended or contracted in a quantitative way: the idea that its content undergoes qualitative changes from one social order to another, and therewith fundamental institutional revolutions – from ancient assemblies to mediaeval estates, from bourgeois parliaments to proletarian soviets – never occurs. What accounts for this?*

Your observation on the extreme modesty of the political proposals in *The Long Revolution* is just. They would seem even more improbable as remedies now than they did then. I think there were two factors responsible for them. One was a certain euphoria in the early sixties, which induced the notion that political changes could be put through very quickly in England – a lot of which were either residual Chartist demands or simply processes of adjusting British idiosyncrasies to other advanced capitalist societies. The other was the fact that, like most people working within a British perspective, I was so close up against the peculiarities of the British political system that I was a long time realizing the common features it shared with capitalist democracy everywhere – which really demanded much more attention. In a more general move towards thinking about European politics in the later sixties, I saw that much more clearly. The sense that parliament could somehow be regained for the democratic process by modernization was still there in the *Manifesto*, but it came from the group rather than myself. In fact that sentence you quoted, if I remember correctly, was written by Edward. That perspective was almost totally lost to me after 1966. You must remember that I had grown up in the belief, which was in practice assumed by most of the left in Britain, that a Labour government with a strong majority would be able to overcome the limitations of social-democratic parliamentarianism which had been so evident before. The administration of 1945 could be discounted, because of the abnormal situation of reconstruction immediately after the war. But in 1966, the moment arrived when a Labour government came to office with a large majority in normal peace-time conditions, and for me what then happened was a final experience; it was the end of the notion of parliament as the principal, central agency for social change. The record of that government was nothing to do with the way the Labour Party conducted its business, or with the periodicity of elections, or anything like that. It was to do with the whole character of the party machine and the nature of the capitalist state. Within a couple of days, the long period of trying to live with two latencies or traditions, or at least to suspend judgment as to which would turn out to be the more relevant and active, was concluded. You could say that I was too hasty, but after all this was the climactic moment which had always capped the theory – it was therefore a true test of it. When you have been pondering a decision for fifteen years, you can finally take it in two days without haste.

In *The Long Revolution*, I did start to develop the distinction between representative and what I called participatory democracy – a phrase which has sometimes had an unfortunate subsequent history, because of some of the people who took it up, though its significance for socialist politics is still decisive. I gave the examples, not only of democracy in the work place, but also in housing estates, as forms of self-management which are in the opposite political tradition from the notion of representation. However, I certainly had not at that time developed a full critique of the notion of representation, which now seems to me in its common ideological form fundamentally hostile to democracy. I think the distinction between representation and popular power has to be now very sharply put. I have tried to do that recently in *Keywords*. But I still find that when I criticize representative democracy, even to quite radical audiences, they react with surprise.

So far we have discussed only the limitations of the representative structure of the capitalist state. There is, however, a complementary but more drastic absence in The Long Revolution, *which is any sense of the coercive machinery of the bourgeois state. In the* Manifesto, *there are a few pages about bureaucracy, but these are largely confined to criticisms of a rigid administrative system, authoritarian procedures, distance from ordinary people – in other words rather traditional themes of a kind that can be found right across the political spectrum. There are also one or two passages which speak of the social affinities of senior civil servants with other bourgeois groups, and of their role in frustrating and blunting projects for social change – 'the close connections of family and the association in school, college and club of the leading persons in government, civil service, judiciary, finance and business'.*[22] *The* Manifesto *raises the question 'whether the judges, the chiefs of police, the higher civil servants, the ambassadors, the heads of academies and other public institutions may be said in one way or another to be closely associated with the interests of private capital'.*[23] *There is one glaring absence from this list: the officer corps. Now an unhealthy tradition exists on the far left of feverish over-concentration on the military apparatus of the capitalist state – the jejune apocalypticism of 'there's only one real enemy in the society and that is the army'. On the other hand, it cannot be an accident that what is undoubtedly the main repressive body of the state, far more important than the civil police, one that had repeatedly been mobilized for strike-breaking purposes in the past and was to play an increasingly prominent role in British political life in the seventies in Northern Ireland, is simply never mentioned in any of these texts. What explains their silence on the central coercive machinery of capital?*

You are quite right to say that this was a crucial omission. In fact, I think that from the end of the war until the late sixties it was a general phenomenon: there was a simple blindness to the coercive power of the state. You've got to call it blindness because although the army has been more spot-lit in the seventies in Ulster, it was perfectly visible in the docks in the forties. There is no question but that it was always there in English society. Indeed, not only was there an extraordinary blindness to the coercive powers of the state, but there was even a kind of complicity with it, in that no clear distinction was ever made on the left between the notion of public power and the organization of the capitalist state, or in fact of any possible state. Thus the major transfer of further kinds of power to an increasingly centralized state after the war was partly a function of the needs of the capitalist system itself, but it was partly also the realization of the programme of the British left. This is a dreadful truth. Of course the National Coal Board is not the army, British Rail is not the Special Branch. But to the extent that a generation believed that you could transfer the responsibility of popular power to that state, with those organs, it would be fair for any subsequent period to conclude that it must have been mad – literally blinded in this respect. This is quite apart from the separate question of whether the whole state has to be smashed, or parts of it, or

[22] MDM, p. 118.
[23] MDM, p. 118.

how that is to be done. Of course, there were people who saw the state as it really was, but the dominant currents on the left were guilty of a general failure of perception. Today this has changed. The British police, for example, has always had a different first-stage response from its counterparts elsewhere, but it is very noticeable how much its image altered during the decade of demonstrations, how many more people realized the ultimate character of the force as distinct from its community character. The preoccupying question now is where one goes on to, when one does perceive the coercive power of the capitalist state.

At the end of Culture and Society, *you wrote that the working-class alternative to the bourgeois idea of service is essentially that of solidarity, yet at the same time you demurred at the conflictual and combative connotations of solidarity on the grounds that it implies an aggressive social division which is not fully compatible with the idea of community. One mark of the more militant stance of* The Long Revolution *is that there for the first time you state that a revolution is necessary because the privileged are going to resist any alteration of the present social arrangements. However, at that period you still seem to have lacked any clear concept of the focal points of condensation and organization of this resistance. For there is not just a diffuse obduracy towards social change in capitalist societies: certain institutions are in their internal mechanisms governed by precisely the function of defending the existing order and resisting any qualitative transformation of it. Marxists have traditionally seen the state as being the key revolution-resisting institution, and central terrain of bourgeois power. Today do you accept that as a proposition, or do you think it is too simple?*

I accept the proposition, although acceptance of it raises as many questions as my previous position – for the great difficulty is to think in practical terms of the ways in which the capitalist state can be destroyed. Of course, I also think that alongside the classical institutions of focussed coercion, there is a very widespread reproduction and dissemination of repression inside even the most gentle-looking institutions outside the state, often mediated in surprising ways. I doubt if we will ever mobilize sufficient resources to attack the central institutions unless people have had long experience in tackling those which are very close up to them. But I certainly accept the theoretical perspective you have outlined: increasingly clearly in the last ten years, as my own position has changed and as there has developed a much more overt presence of this kind of coercion and respectable right-wing talk of recourse to it.

That raises the question of the important passage in the May-Day Manifesto *which condemns any choice between revolution and evolution as a false dilemma, an unthinking repetition of received categories. It reads: 'These are not, and have not for some time been, available socialist strategies in societies of this kind. Western Communist parties, defining the road to socialism as they see it, no longer think of the violent capture of state power. . . . Western social democratic parties no longer think about an inevitable, gradual change towards socialist forms; on the contrary they offer themselves as governing parties within the existing social system, which they will at once improve and modify, but in no serious sense replace.'[24] It then goes on: 'Under the cover of a traditional and repetitive contrast between "violent" and "parliamentary" means, the necessary argument about a socialist strategy has been severely displaced. . . . It is not in the obsolete perspective of the choice between "revolution" and "evolution", but in the actual perspective of choice between a political movement and an electoral machine, that we have to look, in Britain, at the situation and condition of the Labour Party.'[25] The opposition between revolution and evolution is scouted here on purely pragmatic and immediatist grounds, which are not really arguments at all. Revolution is caricatured as simply the 'violent capture of state power' – a definition which would fit any military putsch – and is then rejected on the grounds that the Western Communist parties no longer talk about it anyway. The question of whether they are right to do so is not even raised. After dismissing the choice between revolution and evolution as 'obsolete' – the kind of language the Labour right reserved for Clause Four – the real alternative is presented as the Labour Party or a new socialist movement. But of course if the immediate choice for you in Britain at the time was between a democratic socialist party and the Labour machine, that in no way rendered more ultimate questions of political strategy obsolete. Within such a framework it would have been completely impossible to foresee or even to discuss what happened in Chile a few years later. There was neither an 'inevitable and gradual change towards socialist forms' nor any attempt at a 'violent capture of state power', as spontaneous class struggle escalated, against the will of the left coalition in power, to a point*

[24] MDM, p. 152.
[25] MDM, pp. 152, 155.

where the real nature of the Chilean capitalist state was suddenly and brutally unleashed. In Chile the classical strategic choice proved to be in no sense obsolete – the reaction of the right was the demonstration of its necessity. Would you assent to that now?

I think this is correct. There was intense argument in the group during the writing of the *Manifesto* about just this point – where, at the end of the theoretical analysis, you located all the political strategies that go with the Labour Party, not in its degenerated but in a regenerated condition. One could look at the revolution-evolution contrast in another way, however, as an argument aimed at the right rather than at the left. For in England the distinction was most often made on the right of the Labour Party, and it was important to register the fact that the traditional evolutionary perspective has in reality disappeared today. Evolutionary socialism, in the sense of the inevitability of gradualism, is still on occasion evoked rhetorically to counter the idea of revolution, but it has ceased to have any positive existence in British politics. In my mind I always criticized the way the right used the distinction – I think this probably meant I didn't deal adequately with the necessary distinction which has to be made on the left.

There are surely two notions which must be analytically distinguished. One is the idea of the inevitability of socialism, that borrowed its suggestive force from the theory of evolution, as a natural process: in Britain the whole complex of ideas and rhetoric associated with this evolutionary socialism has largely disappeared from the Labour Party. The other is the idea of gradualism as a political principle. That has certainly not disappeared in Britain – far from it. Indeed it seems to represent a fundamental crux in your own political writing: it is there right in the title of The Long Revolution. *Now your term 'the long revolution' remains a deeply ambiguous one in the book. For on the one hand it denotes the transformation of all the practices of a given society on the most wide-ranging scale imaginable, extending all the way from its mechanisms of decision-making to its processes of work, from its cultural production to its patterns of family and personal relations. It is quite clear that the socialist project of accomplishing that transformation has to be viewed as a multi-secular one; it is not going to be completed in anyone's lifetime, nor even in a few generations. It will take a very long period of time, as a historical change comparable to the transition from feudalism to capitalism itself. In that sense, as a warning against facile illusions that the working class just acquires power, nationalizes the means of production, and thereupon achieves socialism, your emphasis on the length of the revolution has a powerful and salutary charge. On the other hand, it also contains a very great danger, which can be indicated by the single word 'gradualism'. For the transition to socialism may be a long-term process, but in no sense whatever can it be described as a gradual process. Why? Because the long duration of this overall transformation can itself be periodized into quite distinct sorts of time-schedules, with different tempos of speed and slowness. One of these times is relatively short, and decisive: that which Marxists have traditionally described as the revolutionary conquest of state power. This is not, of course, necessarily a matter of a few days. The October Revolution was a very quick process; later revolutions were more protracted. The key point lies elsewhere. The transition to socialism can only be inaugurated by an absolutely non-gradual process, because the pre-condition for it is a disintegration of the capitalist state as a structural unity and the emergence of rival institutions of popular sovereignty on the other side of the class divide, which after a period of acute conflict and dual power, crystallize into a new and more democratic type of state that sweeps the old away altogether. By its nature that substitution of one political unity by another is an abrupt and serried process. Revolutionary socialism is really defined by its insistence that only a violent crisis in this sense, which convulses the whole society very sharply in a way that was not true before and will not be true in the same way afterwards, can permit a genuine passage to socialism. That is a perspective which is completely opposed to gradualism in any shape or form. What is your attitude towards it today?*

You have put the distinction between the two processes very clearly – rather as an East European said to me after reading *The Long Revolution:* 'We've had our short revolution, now we begin our long revolution.' When I wrote the book I was mainly conscious of the immense length of the full social transformation, which has usually been under-played, yet which should be intrinsic to all strategic socialist thinking. I have no doubt now that the short revolution, to use that phrase, has also to occur. I wouldn't at all dissent from the traditional notions of the violent capture of state power, but I would put this revolution in a more specific way: it is accomplished when the central political organs of capitalist society lose their power of *predominant* social reproduction – which does not have to mean that some reproduction will not continue afterwards. So to make the theoretical position clear – I now believe, though I have not always believed, that the condition for the success of the long revolution in any real terms is decisively a short revolution, which I would define not so much in terms of duration as of the loss by the state of its capacity for predominant reproduction of the existing social relations. That after all puts the right stress on what is happening all through the society and not just on what is happening at the centre: it is possible that the orders might still be coming in and be refused, as much as that you could stop the orders from coming, making a very complex, scattered process.

Now the only sense in which the notion of the long revolution bears on the short revolution is that to mobilize the resources, and to learn the ways of reaching that point in the classical tradition when the ruling class divides against itself or confronts problems which it can no longer solve in any of the accepted or familiar ways, requires a considerable process of preparation which must not itself be limited to the immediate actions necessary to assure the transfer of power in a revolutionary situation. Talking about the run-up to that situation is not a form of gradualism. It is a reminder that more is needed than a few hastily improvised procedures when the state is disintegrating in some of the more obvious ways. I would not in any way renounce my emphasis on the extraordinary importance of learning the methods and procedures of popular power, which might have been dismissed at the time as reformism or gradualism. The extreme complexity of an advanced capitalist society, with its ever greater dependence on an integrated division of labour and a sophisticated technology, means that much more has to be learnt than has commonly been thought in the revolutionary tradition. It was very remarkable in the General Strike how over the days people learned new systems of popular control in a very complicated technical engineering operation, in deciding what was emergency traffic, what supplies to let through, what supplies to stop, what procedures of authority to develop among themselves, at a time when the essence of the situation was that traditional hierarchies had disappeared.

Similar kinds of organizational skill are needed to occupy or picket a factory today. But that discipline is not always naturally there. Recently, for example, it was very striking at Grunwick that there were often more demonstrators in the street than police. The most significant difference between the two was that the one had deeply learned the procedures of collective organization and action; the others, often because they had started out as peaceful pickets and were not expecting pitched battles, usually acted like a crowd of individuals or small groups. In other societies, of course, certain groups on the left have responded to violent repression from the police by learning the techniques of street-fighting. In general I accept the truth which has been attested in every recorded revolution of the sudden release of popular energies, resources and skills. But I also note, because this is the less pleasant part of the reading, the degree to which failure to think out or practise certain procedures in advance has greatly weakened people who already had enough on their hands. One crucial pattern since the classical theory was formulated, after all, has been that form of crisis of the ordinary capitalist state which leads not to the emergence of a new popular power, but to the hardening of the state itself into an even more repressive form – into fascism. So I am always uneasy about talk of the short revolution when the problems of the run-up to it have not really been appreciated. I have found that most of the images of the inherited tradition do not bear very much on this complicated process of preparation and learning. At least half the features of a revolutionary situation would still, after all that, take you by surprise – that would be in the nature of such a crisis. But I think that the learning of the skills of popular organization and control, over a wide range, would make the prospect of preventing the effective reproduction of the existing social relations a much more realistic possibility in Western capitalist societies.

At the same time, in a revolutionary crisis itself the simple notion of assaulting the citadel of the state against the arrayed force of the modern army is the wrong kind of military thinking. Any strategy which underestimates the armoured power of a contemporary army, once it is manoeuvred into a few set-piece confrontations, is wholly unconvincing to me. I know what a modern army can do from my own experience: even in the most brutal acts of civil repression that we have seen in Britain, the army has been fighting with one finger and not both hands. Even in Vietnam certain ultimate weapons were held back. On the other hand, I also know, with the advantage of having fought in tanks going into a city, that once an army is dispersed against an enemy that is not concentrated in a single target, it is nothing like as formidable. Indeed when a military apparatus has to take over a variety of civil functions it can find itself very weak, whereas it is extremely strong when defending a point of its choice or replacing civil resources in one selected area but not in all. Now in any struggle against it, I share the view that one must not put too much weight, although one must put some, on the goal of winning some of the soldiers to the revolutionary side – there will always be troops which cannot be won. If you have experienced army discipline and the extraordinary sense it instils that the rest of the world outside your unit ceases to exist, you can be in no doubt about that. Moreover, the armed forces would be joined in any revolutionary situation by a large number of volunteers in a combined class operation, not an abstract state operation. The history of the General Strike is not only that of a magnificent popular mobilization but also of a very significant recruitment of OMS to counter it. It is necessary to think very seriously about the areas and the classes they came from. But it is also true that a revolutionary crisis is characterized by a whole series of crucial moments in which the question of whether violence is unleashed by the state or not is in the balance, as a matter in part of the conscience of actual soldiers, in part of their training, in part of the political judgment of the existing ruling class. The popular forces then have to think and act in a very precise way, to put the option for force at a disadvantage. The indoctrination which is given to troops sent in to put out a blaze when there is a firemen's strike is easy enough. When soldiers go into the docks to unload cargo, it is already more problematic because they are now interfering in a much more obvious way, not to save life but to take other men's jobs. The strain on discipline would become even greater if the army were sent in against the occupation of a factory, for example, or still more any central popular resistance. The visibility of the nature of any civil operation, and the possibility of independent perception by the soldiers of the character of the forces which have been assigned as their enemy, are crucial to the ability of a military command to enforce its orders. There are situations where the recourse to brutality and oppression can be challenged, with a real chance of winning.

Such actions are part of what it means to make impossible the reproduction of the existing social relations. Of course, the communications systems are often critical to their success or failure. During the General Strike, the TUC did take some limited measures on printing, which was a crucial resource in the struggle. These were very quickly bypassed by the government, which issued an official gazette in the emergency, while local strike bulletins were being produced on the other side. But it is striking that the trade union movement did not talk about the radio – yet radio was strategically a more decisive factor in the political fate of the strike. Today I think the increased complexity of capitalist society works to socialist advantage: the number of technicians involved in the dissemination of any kind of order and information has increased, while the whole operation of the economic system has come to depend on certain strategic groups of workers. The right realizes this much better than the left. In other words, while the received terms in which a forceful confrontation with state power is conceived are in general absolutely correct, their detail is now so transformed that I get uneasy when I hear the mere repetition of the traditional formulations and notice that the preparations for that kind of confrontation have not seriously been thought through. If one has in the end, and to me it was in the end after fifteen to twenty years of hesitation between the two possibilities, decided that the revolutionary path is the only way, then one really does have to think in a quite new fashion about how to prepare for it. I think also that much of the preparation can and should be combined with forms of learning which are necessary anyway in apparently short-term situations, and which can be shared by people who may not, in the process of sharing them, yet foresee that the struggle for socialism will have to come to that.

How would you envisage the pattern of popular power after any revolution? Socialism by definition involves centralized collective planning, nationally and internationally, of economic and social life. Yet soviets or workers' councils represent a decentralization of political power, whose ultimate term will be the withering away of the central state altogether. What is your view of the articulation between these two principles?

I think the success of a revolution in an advanced capitalist society will come from the spreading out of popular power from a number of strategic localities, where it first emerges, into a nationally co-ordinated process. During the General Strike, the spontaneous resourcefulness and inventiveness of the local committees and popular organizations was extraordinary, compared with the weakness of the central leadership the TUC was supposed to be giving. Such committees or councils can be a very effective form of power in an emergency situation, when the ruling class is faltering. The great problem is the co-ordination or co-operation of these centres, which is after all necessary if a new society is to be maintained at any advanced level. It is at that moment that people still usually project old-style political leadership. It is precisely on the relation of that hypothetical leadership to the centres of popular self-management that most work needs to be done. Soviets, strike committees, self-management councils, workers' co-operatives all present many difficulties of organization at the local level. But when you have established them, the real problem is to move into the dimension of wider organization which will be decisive for the success of local efforts. It is quite conceivable that, saturated by the procedures of capitalist democracy, people would reproduce the conference of representatives or delegates, and soon a very different kind of power would be re-created. This is a very difficult area where there is no simple solution, given the absolute need for co-ordination. The theoretical answer is familiar: the procedures of mandate and recall, together with the flows of information which are possible within this kind of society – where somebody doesn't have to travel back three hundred miles to report what has happened at a meeting, because the technology exists to permit far more people to hear the meeting and participate in it themselves. But the political problems of weaving together the new institutions of popular power, central and local, all still remain to be solved.

At the time of The Long Revolution *you seem to have conceived democracy as a continuous process without any specific class qualifications. Parliamentary democracy would be extended, rather than transformed, as capitalism gave way to socialism. Since* Keywords, *you have made a sharp distinction between the principles of representation and popular power.*[26] *Your reference just now to bourgeois democracy in effect acknowledges that certain types of democratic organization, such as representative structures, belong to the capitalist mode of production. In other words, it is not the case – as is sometimes maintained today – that all democracy under capitalism is an achievement of the working-class movement. Parliamentary democracy is also a mode of the bourgeoisie's own self-organization and organization of society. The advent of socialism would transform the structures of the democratic process, producing a form of sovereignty different in kind from the representative institutions of capitalism. How would you now describe the nature of that change, in so far as we can foresee it?*

The radical difference between socialist democracy and capitalist democracy comes out very clearly in the history of the two terms. Bourgeois

[26] K, pp. 83–6.

democracy has come to mean the internal processes of the capitalist state – developing through different historical periods and electoral systems – and the civic freedoms of expression and association which are a crucial means to any form of democracy. Right-wing writers now counterpose these processes as the essence of democracy to factory occupations which are said to be undemocratic. Now socialist democracy must be the direct exercise of popular power. It can have no other meaning. In the sense that this is also historically the oldest meaning of democracy, it is reasonable to speak of it in very early periods of socialist or even pre-socialist struggle, as well as in the perspective of an emerging socialist system of the future. The key emphasis must fall on the direct exercise of popular power, rather than the internal management of a particular class-ruled state or those generalized means which are not democracy but simply its accompanying procedures. The conventional opposition between democracy and socialism, democracy and Marxism, is now extremely damaging to the left. It is precisely in showing, against it, that socialist democracy is not only qualitatively different from capitalist democracy, but is quite clearly more democratic, that the whole future of the left will lie. This is the one battle that has got to be won, compromised as it has been by two experiences, curiously reinforcing each other: the experience of Fabian-style bureaucracy near home and the experience of Stalinism in the more general movement, which support in millions of minds the otherwise quite false opposition between democracy and socialism. I think we shall have to show in very great detail why a socialist society would be more democratic, and this will involve being implacably clear about the failure of other kinds of democratic processes within socialist revolutions or labour movements.

It is interesting that, despite your flair for discussing political and social changes in the kind of institutional detail from which most people tend to shy away, your unusual willingness to broach what the concrete forms of an alternative social order would be like, you have never really tackled the question of socialist democracy as such, by contrast with existing forms of capitalist democracy. Now there are three essential respects, of which you have so far dwelt mainly on one, in which the forms of socialist democracy would be structurally distinct from those of bourgeois democracy. Each of them involves an abolition of a barrier which exists under capitalism. The first barrier is that between representatives and represented, the focus of your critique, in The Long Revolution *and the* Manifesto, *of what you call the election of a court by single, occasional votes every five years.*[27] *Marxists have classically insisted, from the Commune onwards, that it is only by a system of mandate rather than representation, with the revocation of the mandate always available to the electors, that any genuine non-separation of the will of the masses from the central legislative institutions of society could be assured. Given the perpetual danger of a division between them, the device of the revocable mandate is really critical to the tradition of socialist democracy. The second barrier is that between economy and polity – the division, in your terms, between the system of maintenance and the system of decision. By expropriating the expropriators, and establishing real collective sovereignty over the means of production, socialism inaugurates democracy in the work place. That enormous enlargement of democracy, transforming the day to day lives of the producers, is one of the goals you set out at the end of* The Long Revolution *too. Factory councils have been the normal form of this collective government of the associated producers over the process of production. But there is a third barrier, which you have tended to overlook. That is the division between legislative and executive functions within the capitalist state. The dualism of an elected parliament which enacts laws, and of a professional bureaucracy which administers them, is one of the major landmarks of existing bourgeois rule. It characteristically everywhere creates a separate body of full-time administrators, specialized functionaries of the state divorced from the civil population. A socialist democracy, by contrast, would tend constantly towards the unification of the legislative and executive functions that are separated under capitalism, so that those who take policy decisions themselves increasingly administer them. The ultimate goal of this process is the suppression of the state as a separate rule-making and rule-enforcing institution altogether, as the division between state and society progressively decreases. This third structural criterion of socialist democracy is not present anywhere near so clearly in your work, which seems to be related to the way in which the executive and repressive structures of the capitalist state tend to slip out of your vision.*

Now the Russian experience of soviets, very brief and imperfect though it was – compromised by the defensive class demarcations of its electoral system (bourgeois were excluded, peasants were given far fewer votes than workers), the lack of a secret ballot and other limitations – nevertheless represents the only historical experiment in which we can see all three of these principles in a

[27] LR, p. 336.

very primitive way starting to be at work. The treatment of the Russian Revolution in your work usually tends to suggest that while we should understand and respect it, in the final analysis it remains very remote from us in the advanced West. But that suggestion is only a half truth. It is quite true that it is very far from us in the sense that we can hope to make a socialist revolution in Western Europe without all the crippling consequences that ensued in Russia. But in another sense, in our much more advanced societies we have no model of socialist democracy that is more advanced, we have an absence of any such experience at all – whereas in that backward society sixty years ago certain kinds of institutions were adumbrated which even today remain imaginatively and practically beyond our ordinary range of political discussion in the West.

One question I think you're asking is whether I sufficiently respect the sort of imaginative leap which 1917 represented. The only answer to this is that I have been through all the experiences of attraction and revulsion towards the October Revolution and as they settle down, and I look past them and the orthodox celebrations, I still think that it was one of the two or three great moments in human history. It is as simple as that. Thus I wouldn't dissent from the general principles you have set out. I think that, hard as the new definitions are, the notions of overcoming representative democracy and replacing it with direct democracy, and of extending democracy to work by the abolition of private capital, are easier than the third idea you have advanced – which I would certainly agree is a theme that has not appeared sufficiently in my own work. The unification of legislation and administration is an extraordinarily imaginative model. It will clearly be crucial to any socialist society to prevent the formation of a separate administrative class. In fact, one version of this, the notion of administration by a public meeting, was often tested on a small scale in the student movement of the late sixties, which often abolished the structure of officers and executive committees and did everything through open meetings. That soon raised many practical problems. The separation of administrative and managerial functions can be abolished, but not the administrative or managerial functions themselves. The solution probably lies in the direction of the rotation of offices, with the rule that no one can administer any process without not only having been *but going to be again* directly involved in working in it at a quite different level. At their best, the Chinese have validly emphasized some of these principles. Even so the problems of order and of allocation are going to be very difficult in a democratic socialist society. For example, the regulation of resources will have to include decisions not to do and make certain things, because you need to do and make certain others. It is then very likely that the people who are doing and making those things, and feel their own livelihood bound up with them, will react with the characteristic responses of social democracy in a local sense, posing a severe problem for socialist democracy in a wider sense. In one form or another, the whole question of the necessary administration of a complex society is going to come up against that tension again and again. All I can now say is that while the central problem is political, we shall in fact have the benefit of a qualitatively new communications technology, which makes possible a virtually continuous process of open and responsible decision and administration.

Problems of political strategy are in the forefront of debate among socialists today. But the question of what an achieved socialist society would actually be like remains largely unexplored. Your own work has always been something of an exception in this respect – in Communications, *for example, you set out in some detail a socialist policy for the organization of cultural production, above all in broadcasting. Now, in* Marxism and Literature *you refer to the 'complex societies' of our own time and then to the 'still more complex societies which real socialism envisages'.*[28] *The phrasing of this formulation suggests a very deliberate – and critical – emphasis. What did you have in mind when you stressed the 'complexity' of 'real socialism', and what are the implications for socialist theory and politics in the eighties?*

Yes, I want this to be a distinct change of emphasis in our thinking about socialism. I believe that we are now seriously limited – at times politically disabled – by the inheritance of models of socialism which either simplify or merely rationalise a social order. Of course many socialists have seen the *transition* to socialism as a complex process: difficult and shifting struggles against its enemies; intricate problems of socialist construction under pressure from surviving imperialist and capitalist forces; or the very long struggle – which Mao insisted on – for a new and general socialist consciousness, against many kinds of contradiction or residue. I agree about these problems of transition. If we didn't already believe it

[28] ML, p. 211.

theoretically, the twentieth century has taught us it, very practically.

But what I'm concerned about now is the *nature* of the social order towards which these transitions are directed, and I don't think this is a merely abstract question. Significant thinking about it seems to me absolutely necessary, especially perhaps in the advanced capitalist countries and in the countries of what Bahro calls 'actually existing socialism'. I think we can understand why the models we have inherited are relatively simple and even sketchy. For any historical materialist is bound to be cautious about one kind of futurist specification. But the most important reasons lie deeper. The misery and poverty and disorder of the capitalist world within which the idea of socialism was originally generated made the prescription of an alternative almost too simple. We have seen the same process again in the struggles against colonialism. But now in the last quarter of the twentieth century we are in a majority of cases already in a new situation. In the advanced capitalist countries we have clearly got to generate (I would say regenerate, but that is only structurally accurate) positive ideas of a socialist order towards which the struggles against capitalism can be directed – with some depth and consistency. There is a similar if differently circumstanced need in the Eastern European countries, where there is grave danger of struggles against a repressive system moving away from or actually against socialism, while the *idea* of socialism has been confiscated by the ruling hierarchies – Bahro has emphasized this. The need is differently circumstanced again at advanced stages of national liberation struggles.

Now of course we might all quickly acknowledge this need, and then get no further. Though even that seems at times too much to hope for; the power of the received models, even the deeply learned *names*, seems in some minds to stop thought. So you can have convinced militants insisting that 'socialism' will solve this and that and every other problem, and at the same time rather substantial majorities of people whom you would expect to be with them, or at least listening to them, turned right off by what they identify – sometimes quite accurately – as no more or not much more than slogans. The literal result of this is a quite terrible loss of the future: the loss of a socialist future which people can begin to be physically imagining, and with it, of course, the loss of other futures. It's very striking that even people who are sceptical of socialist slogans – not the existing ruling class and its supporters but all those who belong, potentially, to a socialist direction – have no confidence in the future of the industrial capitalist order either. It is thus a matter of great political urgency, and not just of abstract speculation to start to define a new socialist order. I see my own work for some years as an attempt at this, and I hope very many others will join in.

Could you give us some idea of what kind of considerations this attempt will involve? What are the main defects of 'the received models' to which you refer and how do you think they should now be revised?

Let me begin with what seem like merely negative points. The positive bearings follow from them. First, I think there's no doubt that the rationalizing and controlling elements in the received socialist idea have become, in their received terms, residual. They were basically formed, after all, in a period of chaotic capitalist accumulation and competition. They pre-date both monopoly capitalism and international monopoly capitalism, supported as these now are by the intervention of capitalist states and imperialist alliances of states. Regulation, management, state support and intervention, are all now features of the rationalized capitalist order, which is in fact perpetually pushing for new controls and new instruments of control. It is enough to make you weep to hear several of these developments described as socialist advances, or as the socialist elements in a mixed economy. The regulating, organizing, standardizing pressures of existing international monopoly capitalism, with its huge public and private bureaucracies, are even identified by many people as the horrors of socialism. In a way who can blame them, when half the socialists they hear are talking about more of the same thing, and the actually existing socialist states display just these features in an extreme and even pathological form?

At the same time there is the other received socialist model: simplification. It's very striking how many of the socialist utopias portray small and simple and essentially unorganized societies: a kind of relaxed happiness in plenty, governed by controlling general moral impulses. And who hasn't had that dream? It is often explicitly seen as a kind of rest after struggle: a happy and friendly evening after the noise and stress of the capitalist day. Or again, changing the metaphor (this tendency is very fertile in them) it is the delightful air of early morning, the dawn of socialism: fresh and invigorating, before a day's work that may not even have to be done. All right, without some such idea the strain might be too heavy to bear. But I'm pretty sure I know who will hunt in the morning, fish in the afternoon and do critical criticism in the evening, and it won't be the working people of any socialist society. In the mornings and evenings, in any case, there are much better things to try to do.

Now the current importance of the simplifying idea is that at some points it touches realistic assessments of our material economy. Not only the lunacies of industrial-capitalist growth, but the much more serious crimes of imperialist plunder which underlie them – the literal looting of land and resources which is now going on – have brought many people to demand simplification. Of course there is some playing at it, but there is also some serious thinking. However, much of this thinking rests on too facile a conjunction between ideas of community and ideas of self-sufficiency. The connexion between them is now only occasionally socialist, in any real sense, but it tends to rest on the memories of socialist and anarchist utopianism. At the same time, it also catches up ideas of self-government, self-management, care and balance in our use of the material environment, creative work, community living and so on, that are genuinely necessary elements of any new socialist order that is to be at once realistic and attractive. The task of socialists now is to think through the complexities of what is otherwise, at its present level, much too simple an idea; to think them through essentially as historical materialists.

The first thing to say is that any idea of a future social order has to be very precisely located; the usual general ideas will not do. This is the materialist part of the socialist emphasis, that in any particular country or particular region we have to start from what is physically there or available. This is so positively in the sense that we have to learn to look at resources in a socially useful rather than a capitalist way. It is also so negatively, in that in only a very few cases will it be possible, when we have looked, to retain any of the usual ideas of self-sufficiency. The international division of labour has its imperialist and capitalist forms, but some version of it is in effect inscribed in the earth: where the coal is or where the fish are; where the sun can be depended on or where the land is arable; where the iron-ore is, or the bauxite or the uranium. The most simplifying ideas cancel as many of these factors as they can. Now, part of this impulse is right. It is probably better, for example, as Phil Williams of Plaid Cymru has argued in Wales, to invest in energy from the Severn Bore and the waves of Cardigan Bay, which would mean self-sufficiency in power, than to be permanently dependent on nuclear energy systems stretching back to distant uranium supplies and the forms of international and centralized control which inevitably go with them. Wherever that kind of material choice is possible at an acceptably high level of provision, it should of course be made, for its physical and political advantages. But it is in the very significant range of material problems beyond such solutions that the complexities enter. We are all faced, as socialists, with a hard datum of physical and material unevenness. Capitalism has spawned its own forms of uneven development, with great damage, but socialism has to start from the true data of unevenness, and the institutions and modes to negotiate these, towards equitable relations, will be very complex indeed. Both the imperialist mode and the centralized socialist mode, appropriating and governing and disposing of these unevenly distributed yet interdependent physical resources, have at least grappled with these problems. A higher socialist form will not only have to meet as complex difficulties as these; it will have to be more complex, since it will by definition not avail itself of the crude appropriations and dominating mechanisms on which those other modes now depend.

The point can be made in another way if we think of the very important tendency in contemporary socialist thinking towards increasing self-management of our enterprises. It is clearly a central element of socialist democracy that we should develop this tendency. There is a tremendous reservoir of social energy, now locked in resentment of bureaucratic and hierarchical organisations, which can be drawn on for this effort. But it is already apparent from practice and from studies that the forms of self-management are necessarily both complex and diverse. There is no realistic short-cut via the permanent open meeting, as some people thought in the sixties. The internal procedures of preparation, record, accountability, continuity are nowhere simple. But then self-management can anyway never be only an internal or local procedure. For there are the necessary economic interrelations with other groups, subject to all the problems of unevenness that I've already mentioned, and to the great variations of efficient scale which real processes indicate. There is also a necessary range of political relations at many different levels. We've all noticed, I suppose, the general vagueness of the social location of socialism: at one stage it was the world, or perhaps a continent; or it can now be half a continent, or one of the old nation-states, or a new federation of them, or some nation or region breaking away. Any democratic and realistic socialism must start by acknowledging not only the great diversity of the solutions to this problem of location, extent and area which people will themselves decide to take; it will also have to recognize the problem of the interaction of those different solutions, the facts of unevenness and of tension – and surely often of dispute and conflict – which the very principle of autonomy not only does not dispose of, but may even accentuate. The complexity of adequate institutions and modes to resolve the interrelations of autonomous groups hardly needs emphasis. Whether you are a hotel collective on a charmed coast in direct or indirect negotiation with a mining collective in a bleak region – and there will be thousands of such cases, all different – or an attractive autonomous region faced with problems of mobility – some of it desperate, some exploitative – from other regions, you will know soon enough that you need complex procedures of negotiation and resolution at any of these external levels as well as the necessary complexities of internal procedures.

Now we should accept and indeed welcome this kind of complexity, because we can show that it is our best guarantee of the kind of socialist, democratic, non-exploitative order we are proposing to construct. I don't mean just as reassurance to doubters, though this is important. I mean as a way, now and in the future, of liberating our real energies as the simplifying or central-regulating models don't. The complexity is an energizing challenge – and its means are becoming increasingly available, if we can find the political forms in which to use them.

Thus it is clear that while we can conduct many of our internal affairs on an immediately participatory basis, using the time we can save with new productive techniques to do so, for many other purposes we shall still need what we can for the moment continue to call representatives. The political idea which we perhaps most need to grasp is the principle, not just that any socialist representative is a delegate, subject to mandate, accountability and recall, but that a representative or delegate in a properly socialist society is not, so to say, all-purpose. Such a person will not be, as almost everywhere now, our representative or delegate for a whole body of compacted purposes. Rather he, she, we, they – not the same people, but necessarily different people – will be making this specific contact, that particular inquiry, this outline of a negotiation or a settlement. Some of us will be better at some of it than others, but the principle of closeness to the issue in question must prevail: speaking for ourselves, in all real senses, rather than for 'my people' or even 'our lads'. A socialist representative or delegate system, that is to say, would be very much more diverse and therefore more complex then any existing parliamentary or assembly models, condemned as these are to some singular all-purpose role. I look very hopefully to the new communications systems to make such a new diversity practicable. First, almost all the different debates, votes, negotiations could be seen and heard while they are happening. Consequently there could be not only intervention in them, while they are going on (subject obviously to problems of scale, but as a principle applicable everywhere), but quick and efficient reference back before decisions are taken or for the decisions actually to be taken. The new electronic communications technologies have quite extraordinary capacity for this kind of self-government and self-management and, crucially, for full available information and record and recall of information. Thus the kinds of democracy previously imagined only for very small communities, and thus driving towards the simplifying idea, can become quite normally available for larger communities. More important still, they can be implemented by communities which, because of the facts of material unevenness and necessarily diverse political interrelations, *will be effectively of different sizes and composition at different times, according to the nature of the issue being discussed and decided.* Some socialists have got so used to the idea of machines and media as manipulative, and have thought so little of modern communications as means to new kinds of social organization, that they have to fall back on models of the enlightened vanguard or the simplified local community. Just as commonly, they are stuck in the idea of fixed, all-purpose nations, states and regions, to which in some primitive sense we are held to 'belong', in delimited social relations. They should go and look at some of the new technical possibilities, which we cannot afford to allow to be confiscated, and realise how marvellously active, complex and mobile a socialist democracy could now quite realistically become.

You've concentrated mainly on the 'base' of a socialist society, so to speak – its primary resources and their pre-existent distribution – and on its 'summit', the systems of decision-making. But what about the whole intermediate range of social activities, such as the organization of work and consumption? Presumably these are equally subject to the general rule of complexity, as you see it?

I've raised only a few of the issues. There will be quite new complexities of work and of working lives with much more possibility of variety, and quite different kinds of relation between periods of education and training and periods of production. Partly because of this, there will be greater variety in our relations with and care of each other, and so there will be very few simple or uniform solutions, if any. Rather there will be a need for complex resources to meet so many diverse situations and problems. These resources must include democratic systems of law, which are often absent from socialist utopias, and also democratic systems of deciding problems of entitlement and responsibility, for if these are not assured and seen to be fair any community can be disrupted. One example I'd give relates to the existing but thoroughly alienated complication of the social welfare and transfer-payment regulations, which are in actuality insufficiently complex and sensitive to deal equitably with the real diversity of cases and circumstances. A socialist mode would have to include general principles of entitlement and responsibility, but the complexity would begin from the other end, within actual social relations, and while it would by definition be generous it would also have to be systematic. There is no point in trying to evade the *social* character of socialism, in favour of some hopefully liberal dissolution of obligations. Our case is after all the sociality of general freedom.

Self-management provides another example. This is not just a procedural variation of management within existing or slightly modified forms of ownership. When it is only that it is nowhere near socialism, in which the whole question of what constitutes ownership has to be transformed. Working individuals in some cases, working groups and collectives in the great majority of cases, will not, by some alchemy or more practical residue of capitalist and other earlier forms, inherit, acquire or take over that share of the general resources and means of production with which they are working. Procedures of proposal and verification, of accountability, and of regular reconsideration of proposals and allocations, are the indispensable means of general socialist self-management. For in such a system there would be no settled displacement of property but a steady, responsible and open assessment and negotiation and distribution of resources and means of production.

This is a challenge, but it is one deliberately pitched at a level that engages with the intricacies of our diverse experiences of real production and actual and possible organizations. For while we still have to fight capitalism and imperialism in so many immediate ways, often on ground more of their choosing than of ours, we can find in some of our current working and social experience definitions of problems and modes of solution which can indicate shapes of specific practicable futures. From the details of these the energy of a socialist future can again begin to flow. Many thousands of people will be involved even in the outlining of what is necessary. Many millions will be involved in putting different solutions into the beginnings of practice, and a whole host of details are inevitably and understandably beyond our most vivid projections. But now if ever is the moment to turn our energies in that direction. Left to itself, the present crisis of capitalism – and specifically of industrial capitalism – can only destroy us. We want more, much more, in its place than a chaotic breakdown or an imposed order or the mere name of an alternative. The challenge is therefore to a necessary complexity. I have been pulled all my life, for reasons we've discussed, between simplicity and complexity, and I can still feel the pull both ways. But every argument of experience and of history now makes my decision – and what I hope will be a general decision – clear. It is only in very complex ways that we can truly understand where we are. It is also only in very complex ways, and by moving confidently towards very complex societies, that we can defeat imperialism and capitalism and begin that construction of many socialisms which will liberate and draw upon our real and now threatened energies.

Index

Adam Bede (Eliot), 245
Adorno, Theodor, 311
Althusser, Louis, 168
Animal Farm (Orwell), 70, 389, 390, 391
Anti-Dühring (Engels), 40
Arena, 112
Aristotle, 217, 396
Arnold, Matthew, 97, 109, 114, 124, 130, 406
Arts Council, 224
Attlee, Clement, 70, 101
Auden, W.H., 73, 196
Austen, Jane, 51, 102, 244–5, 248–50, 256, 267

Baal (Brecht), 216
Bahro, Rudolf, 296, 362, 430
Balzac, Honoré de, 222, 228, 257, 270, 276
Barnett, Anthony, 9
Bateson, F.W., 84
Beckett, Samuel, 349
Bell, Clive, 97
Benjamin, Walter, 311
Benn, Anthony Wedgwood, 367, 371
Bergman, Ingmar, 230, 231
Berlin Crisis, 86
Berliner Ensemble, 231
Between the Lines (Thompson), 92
Bevan, Aneurin, 368
Blake, William, 101, 115, 256
Bloomsbury Group, 44
Bolshevik Party, 394
Booth, Charles, 171
Bourdieu, Pierre, 327
Brecht, Bertolt, 160, 166, 209, 214, 216, 217, 218, 220, 229, 232, 269, 349
Brontë, Emily, 245, 254
Büchner, Georg, 210, 398
Bukharin, Nikolai, 49
Burke, Edmund, 100, 103, 107, 117, 120, 123
Byron, George Gordon, Lord, 101, 111, 165

Caleb Williams (Godwin), 123
Cambodia, 395, 397
Cambridge, 39, 47, 49
Cambridge Socialist Club, 40–41
Campaign for Nuclear Disarmament, 361, 366
Camus, Albert, 260
Capital (Marx), 40
Carew, Thomas, 304, 306, 343
Carlyle, Thomas, 99, 103, 105, 107, 115, 116, 117, 120, 252
Caucasian Chalk Circle, The (Brecht), 216
Caudwell, Christopher, 44, 127, 144, 183, 388
Chapman, Frank, 246
Chartism, 407, 414
Chekhov, Anton, 205, 215, 230
Cherry Orchard, The (Chekhov), 205
Cheviot, the Stag and the Black, Black Oil, The (McGrath), 224
Chile, 394, 419
China, 86, 397, 403
Chomsky, Noam, 341
Churchill, Winston, 59
Claudel, Paul, 207
Cobbett, William, 104, 115, 268, 387, 388
Cocktail Party, The (Eliot), 190, 202
Cold War, 58, 86, 385, 390
Cole, G.D.H., 78
Coleridge, Samuel Taylor, 99, 101, 111, 114, 120, 337
Collins, Clifford, 64
Collins, Henry, 70
Communist Manifesto, The (Marx), 38

Communist Party, 33, 35, 42, 43, 53, 65, 92, 93, 112, 375
Comte, Auguste, 113, 130
Condition of the English Working Class, The (Engels), 116
Connolly, James, 72
Conrad, Joseph, 257
Conservative Party, 34, 47, 48, 59
Constitution of Church and State, The (Coleridge), 99
Costa-Gavras, 297
Coward, Noel, 73
Criticism and Ideology (Eagleton), 8
Crossman, Richard, 134
Cuba, 397, 405
Culture and Anarchy (Arnold), 109, 130
Czechoslovakia, 86

Daily Worker, 48, 90, 93
Daniel Deronda (Eliot), 245
Darwinism, 340
Days of Hope (Loach and Garnett), 217
Defence of Poetry (Shelley), 103
Deutscher, Isaac, 90, 386
Dialectic of Enlightenment (Adorno and Horkheimer), 311
Dickens, Charles, 51, 171, 222, 243, 245, 247, 251, 252, 253, 254, 256, 257, 262, 264, 268, 269, 276
Disraeli, Benjamin, 118, 268, 290
Doctor Caligari (Wiene), 232
Doll's House, The (Ibsen), 197
Dombey and Son (Dickens), 171, 253
Donaldson, Lord Chief Justice, 48
Donne, John, 344
Dostoyevsky, Fyodor, 270
Drama and Society in the Age of Jonson (Knights), 92
Dream of John Bull, The (Morris), 129
Durbin, Evan, 391
Driberg, Tom, 65

Eagleton, Terry, 8, 110, 244, 349, 391
East German Rising, 88
L'Education Sentimentale (Flaubert), 220
Eighteenth Brumaire of Louis Bonaparte, The (Marx), 41
Eisenstein, Sergei, 46, 232
Eliot, George, 62, 84, 108, 112, 117, 122, 156, 166, 190, 222, 228, 244, 245, 249, 256, 263, 277, 342
Eliot, Thomas Stearns, 67, 97, 101, 190, 201, 202, 207, 208, 239, 268, 283, 309, 390
Elvin, Lionel, 50
Emma (Austen), 248
Empson, William, 190
Encounter, 73
Enemy of the People, An (Ibsen), 197
Engels, Friedrich, 40, 116, 312, 315, 318, 319
Essays in Criticism, 84
Europeans, The (James), 256
Exiles and Emigrés (Eagleton), 391

Fabianism, 118, 363, 408
Fears and Miseries of the Third Reich, The (Brecht), 218
Fekete, John, 337
Finnegan's Wake (Joyce), 45, 278
Flaubert, Gustave, 220, 222, 257, 389, 396
Foot, Michael, 31
Forster, E.M., 263
Four Quartets (Eliot), 67
Fox, Ralph, 44
Frankfurt School, 260
Freud, Sigmund, 99, 181, 182, 331, 332, 333
Friedman, Milton, 337
From Culture to Revolution (Eagleton and Wicker, ed.), 110
Further Studies in a Dying Culture (Caudwell), 127

Gaitskell, Hugh, 134, 364, 366, 391
Galileo (Brecht), 214, 217
Garnett, Tony, 217
Gaskell, Elizabeth, 116, 165
General Strike, 27, 423, 424
Gibbon, Lewis Grassic, 267, 388
Gibbs, James, 346
Gissing, George Robert, 70, 222
Godwin, William, 99, 123, 243, 245
Gogol, Nikolai, 294
Golden Bowl, The (James), 256
Goldmann, Lucien, 139, 222, 249

Good Woman of Szechuan, The (Brecht), 216
Great Tradition, The (Leavis), 244, 245, 246, 264
Green, T.H., 98
Greene, Graham, 391
Grundrisse (Marx), 116
Guardian, The, 132

Hall, Stuart, 365, 373
Hard Times (Dickens), 251
Hardy, Thomas, 51, 222, 223, 245, 246, 247, 256, 262, 264, 268, 283, 352
Hartley, Anthony, 132
Hawksmoor, Nicholas, 346
Hazlitt, William, 98, 100, 109
Heart of Darkness, The (Conrad), 237
Herrick, Robert, 243, 342
Highway, 81
Hill, Christopher, 130, 342
History of the CPSU(B) – Short Course, 41, 48
Hobbes, Thomas, 131, 161
Hobsbawm, Eric, 42, 54, 61, 65, 152
Hodgkin, Thomas, 67, 80, 87
Hoggart, Simon, 84, 371
Holt, Felix, 222
Homage to Catalonia (Orwell), 387, 388
Horace, 345
Horizon, 72
Horkheimer, Max, 311
Humphreys, Emyr, 295
Hungary, 88

Ibsen, Henrik, 62, 125, 160, 166, 189, 193, 197, 200, 208, 210, 215, 221, 222, 223, 228, 345
Illich, Ivan, 184
Illusion and Reality (Caudwell), 127
Industry and Empire (Hobsbawm), 152
Ireland, Northern, 416
Isherwood, Christopher, 196

Jakobson, Roman, 344
James, Henry, 245, 246, 256, 257, 258, 261, 262, 264
Jefferies, Richard, 305
Johnson, Samuel, 160, 241
Jones, Gwyn, 273
Jones, Jack, 273
Jonson, Ben, 304, 305, 306, 307, 337, 343
Joyce, James, 45, 69, 200, 239, 256, 278, 349
Jude the Obscure (Hardy), 222, 223, 246

Kafka, Franz, 270, 349
Kamenev, Lev, 49
Keats, John, 101
Keep the Aspidistra Flying (Orwell), 387
Kent, William, 346
Kiernan, Victor, 8, 110, 111
King, Cecil, 290, 291
Knights, L.C., 67, 92
Koestler, Arthur, 389
Korean War, 87
Kraus, Karl, 179

Labour Party, 11, 15, 24, 27, 33, 35, 73, 314, 366, 367, 378, 379
Lacan, Jacques, 332, 341
Lady Chatterley's Lover (Lawrence), 127, 245, 249, 259, 264
Lang, Fritz, 232
Laski, Harold, 101
Lawrence, David Herbert, 45, 62, 106, 110, 124, 126, 127, 202, 237, 245, 246, 249, 256, 258, 259, 264, 268, 273
Leavis, F.R., 44, 61, 65, 66, 68, 92, 97, 101, 109, 112, 164, 167, 176, 190, 191, 192, 194, 195, 240, 242, 244, 245, 246, 251, 256, 258, 265, 303, 309, 385
Lee, Jennie, 367, 371
Left Book Club, 11, 28, 31
Left Review, 215
Lehmann, John, 46
Lenin, Vladimir Ilyich, 41, 172
Leviathan (Hobbes), 161
Lewis, Cecil Day, 285
Lewis, John, 73
Liberal Party, 24
Literature and Revolution (Trotsky), 402
Little Dorrit (Dickens), 251, 253
Loach, Ken, 217
Locke, John, 168
Lukács, Georg, 141, 201, 220, 221, 222, 349, 350

McGrath, John, 224
Madame Bovary (Flaubert), 390
Making of the English Working Class, The (Thompson), 108, 152
Mallock, William Hurrell, 99, 128
Mankowitz, Wolf, 64, 76
Mann, Thomas, 114, 270
Mansfield Park (Austen), 248
Mao Tse-tung, 429
Marlowe, Christopher, 216
Marvell, Andrew, 306, 343
Marx, Karl, 38, 40, 41, 115, 116, 154, 309, 312, 315, 318–19, 350, 353, 355, 408
Mason, H.A., 69
Maupassant, Guy de, 220, 349
May Day Manifesto, 373, 374, 413, 414, 415, 416, 418
Mayhew, Christopher, 171
Meaning of Treason, The (West), 73
Mencken, H.L., 179
Metropolis (Lang), 232
Middlemarch (Eliot), 244–5, 264, 265, 267
Mill, John Stuart, 108, 109, 114, 118, 121, 124, 126
Milton, John, 130, 342
Minority Culture (Leavis), 246
Mitchison, Naomi, 344
Molière (Jean-Baptiste Poquelin), 208
Morris, William, 102, 104, 116, 125, 128, 129, 408
Mother Courage (Brecht), 214, 216, 217
Murder in the Cathedral (Eliot), 201
Murry, John Middleton, 190

Nairn, Tom, 381
Nazism, 43, 321
New Criticism, 239, 266, 335
New Left, 74, 364
New Left Review, 14, 80, 134, 363, 366
New Reasoner, 110, 362
New Statesman, 47, 91
Newens, Stan, 372
News Chronicle, 91
News from Nowhere (Morris), 129
Nietzsche, Friedrich, 334
Nineteen Eighty-Four (Orwell), 387, 389, 390, 391
Notes towards the Definition of Culture (Eliot), 97, 101

O'Casey, Sean, 194, 199, 200
Open University, 371
Orrom, Michael, 39, 64, 229, 233
Orwell, George, 70, 84, 105, 385, 387, 388, 389, 390, 391
Outlook, 12, 47

Parrinder, Pat, 244
Parthenon, 348
Peer Gynt (Ibsen), 228
Persuasion (Austen), 248
Pickard-Cambridge, A., 88
Politics and Letters, 65, 68, 69, 74, 76, 77, 82
Pope, Alexander, 50
Portrait of a Lady (James), 258
Prelude (Wordsworth), 346
Priestley, J.B., 240
Proust, Marcel, 270, 332
Psychopathology of Everyday Life (Freud), 331
Pudovkin, Vyacheslav, 46

Racine, Jean, 249, 250
Rainbow, The (Lawrence), 127
Ransom, John Crowe, 337
Raybould, S.G., 81
Read, Herbert, 99
Reed, John, 48
Reflections of an Unpolitical Man (Mann), 114
Return of the Native (Hardy), 352
Ricardo, David, 116
Richards, I.A., 122, 190, 191, 192, 193, 242, 347, 352
Road to Wigan Pier, The (Orwell), 387, 388
Ricks, Christopher, 342
Robertson, T.W., 230
Rosmersholm (Ibsen), 201
Rotha, Paul, 64, 71
Ruskin, John, 117, 128, 129
Rutherford, Mark, 130

Saint Joan of the Stockyard (Brecht), 216
Saint-Simon, Claude-Henri, 113
Sapir, Edward, 182

Sartre, Jean-Paul, 70, 168, 226, 260, 261, 312, 381
Saussure, Ferdinand de, 329
Saville, John, 88
Scott, Walter, 256
Scrutiny, 44, 66, 82, 92, 110, 112, 163, 167, 192, 237, 246
Sergeant Musgrave's Dance (Arden), 209
Shakespeare, William, 50, 67, 193, 209, 216, 344
Shaw, George Bernard, 45, 197
Shelley, Percy Bysshe, 101, 103, 111, 165
Shooting Niagara (Carlyle), 105
Signs of the Times (Carlyle), 99, 105
Singing in the Rain (Donen and Kelly), 233
Snow, Edgar, 31
Socialism Utopian and Scientific (Engels), 40
Socialist Register, 127
Solzhenitsyn, Alexander, 290
Sons and Lovers (Lawrence), 245
Southey, Robert, 111, 114, 115
Spanish Civil War, 387
Spinoza, Baruch, 168
Spiral Ascent, The (Upward), 73
Spoils of Poynton, The (James), 258
Stalin, Joseph, 41, 48, 88, 363, 393, 396, 398, 400
Stanislavsky, Konstantin, 230
State and Revolution (Lenin), 41
State of Siege (Costa-Gavras), 297
Stendhal (Henri Beyle), 223, 258, 349
Stonehouse, John, 296, 297
Strindberg, August, 193, 195, 201, 215, 221, 228, 332
Studies in a Dying Culture (Caudwell), 127
Synge, John Millington, 194

Taplin, Frank, 69
Tawney, Richard Henry, 79, 377, 409
Ten Days that Shook the World (Reed), 48
Theory of the Novel (Lukács), 222
Therborn, Göran, 113
Thomas, Dylan, 279
Thompson, E.P., 8, 54, 65, 74, 77, 88, 91, 108, 127, 128, 129, 139, 363, 373, 414
Thomson, Roy, 291
Thompson, Denys, 92
Threepenny Opera, The (Brecht), 216
Tillyard, E.M.W., 50
Times, The, 91, 179
Times Literary Supplement, The, 91, 133
Timpanaro, Sebastiano, 167, 260, 340
Tolstoy, Leo, 57, 228, 269, 270
Tönnies, Ferdinand, 114, 119
Tourneur, Cyril, 161
Tribune, 91, 179
Trollope, Anthony, 264
Trotsky, Leon, 48, 49, 315, 386, 398, 400, 402
Tynyanov, Iuri, 344

Ulysses (Joyce), 45, 246
Universities and Left Review, 362
Upward, Edward, 73, 389
USSR, 41, 43, 49, 53, 59, 232, 393, 397, 398, 428

Varsity, 46
Vietnam, 372, 397
Vigo, Jean, 46
Voice of Civilization (Thompson), 92
Vološinov, V.N., 181

Wagner, Richard, 229
Wales, 23, 221, 225, 226, 228, 229, 295
Way of the World, The (Congreve), 249
Webb, Beatrice, 171
Webb, Sidney, 408
Weber, Max, 114
Webster, John, 161
Wells, Herbert George, 45, 128, 246, 261
West, Alick, 44
West, Rebecca, 73
When the Boat Comes In (TV series; James Mitchell), 217, 227
White Devil, The (Webster), 161
Wild Strawberries (Bergman), 230
Willey, Basil, 130
Williams, Phil, 432
Williams, Raymond, *passim*:
——, *Adamson*, 277
——, *Border Country*, 27, 271, 278, 280–4
——, *The Brothers*, 301
——, *Communications*, 137, 148, 369, 370, 409, 410
——, *The Country and the City*, 85, 115, 125, 171, 244, 260, 303, 309, 315, 342, 343, 400

——, *Culture and Society*, 84, 97, 99, 100, 104, 111, 112, 113, 114, 116, 117, 120, 122, 123, 124, 126–31, 134, 143, 175, 179, 243, 251, 262, 324, 352, 406, 408, 417
——, *Culture is Ordinary*, 36
——, *A Dialogue on Actors*, 189
——, *A Dialogue on Tragedy*, 211
——, *Drama and Performance*, 88, 192
——, *Drama from Ibsen to Brecht*, 62, 113, 132, 184, 197, 199, 202, 214, 230
——, *The English Novel from Dickens to Lawrence*, 244, 245, 251, 254, 256, 258, 263, 265, 266, 270, 352
——, Introduction to *English Prose*, 104
——, *The Fight for Manod*, 271, 291, 294
——, *Grasshoppers*, 277
——, *The Idea of Culture*, 84, 97
——, *Keywords*, 109, 137, 167, 175, 239, 334, 415, 425
——, *Literature and the Cult of Sensibility*, 44
——, *The Long Revolution*, 98, 111, 127, 131, 133, 134, 137, 140, 143, 145, 147, 148, 150, 151, 152, 153, 154, 156, 161, 165, 172, 173, 243, 252, 266, 331, 411, 412, 414, 415, 417, 419, 425, 427
——, *Marxism and Literature*, 8, 127, 137, 145, 156, 160, 239, 252, 324, 325, 352, 424
——, *Modern Tragedy*, 63, 196, 200, 210, 211, 243, 258, 259, 260, 393, 409
——, *Mother Chapel*, 31, 37
——, *Mountain Sunset*, 30
——, *My Cambridge*, 62
——, *Orwell*, 384, 386, 393
——, *Preface to Film*, 39, 158, 191, 229
——, *Reading and Criticism*, 62, 74, 190, 237, 238, 239, 242, 263
——, *Red Earth*, 47
——, *Ridyear*, 277
——, *Second Generation*, 284, 285, 287–9
——, *Television: Technology and Cultural Form*, 233
——, *The Volunteers*, 271, 296, 297, 298, 300
Williams, Shirley, 372
Wilson, Harold, 71, 291, 366, 373
Women in Love (Lawrence), 126, 245, 258, 259, 264
Woolf, Virginia, 246
Wordsworth, William, 100, 101, 111, 115, 346
Workers' Educational Association, 67, 78
Wren, Christopher, 346
Writer and Leviathan (Orwell), 70
Wuthering Heights (Brontë), 254, 255

Yeats, William Butler, 195, 200, 203, 206
Yugoslavia, 58

Z-Cars (TV series; various authors/directors), 208
Zhdanov, Andrei, 73
Zilliacus, Konni, 32
Zinoviev, Grigori, 33, 49
Zola, Emile, 220, 222, 283